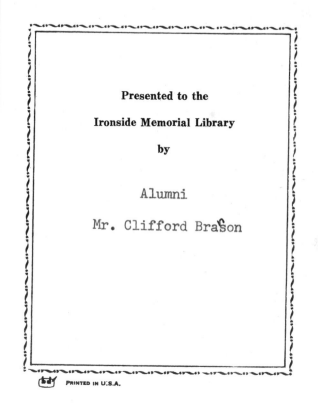

✄✄✄

TRUJILLO

Little Caesar of the Caribbean

✄✄✄

By Germán E. Ornes

TRUJILLO: *Little Caesar of the Caribbean*

CARIBBEAN STORM CENTER (*in preparation*)

TRUJILLO

Little Caesar of the Caribbean

GERMÁN E. ORNES

THOMAS NELSON & SONS

EDINBURGH   NEW YORK   TORONTO

Library of Congress Catalog Card No.: 58-9038

MANUFACTURED IN THE UNITED STATES OF AMERICA
AMERICAN BOOK-STRATFORD PRESS, INC., NEW YORK

26474

TO DIANE

Whose drive, perseverance,
courage and loyalty
made this book possible

PREFACE

THIS IS NOT A FINAL WORK—NOR FOR THAT MATTER EVEN A COM-
plete one—on the oldest, harshest and most fiendish personal dictatorship in
today's Latin America. Yet it is a long book, longer than I anticipated when
more than two years ago I began to do intensive research on the dean of the
"strong men" of the Western World—the Dominican Republic's Generalissimo and Benefactor Rafael Leonidas Trujillo Molina.

At the end of the process I found that I had written two full volumes instead of one and there was still much to be included. This is the first of these
two volumes. The second covers the external aspects and ramifications of
the Trujillo regime—its intrigues, crimes and shameless lobbying in foreign
lands, including the United States; its high-pressure methods of publicity
and advertisement; its friends and foes all over the world.

The process of selecting—and above all of abridging—the material for
these volumes was further complicated by the fact that Trujillo is not typical,
either as a man or as a dictator. He does not seem to have a definite, rounded
personality nor does he adhere to any political philosophy. As a man, he is
totally unpredictable and as a politician his motivating impulses are self-
deification, expediency and opportunism at the service of a single clear
purpose: the search for and safekeeping of power for power's sake.

Trujillo's great accomplishments and most celebrated feats, all well advertised as the embodiment of patriotism and selfless dedication to the welfare
of the Fatherland, are difficult to appraise accurately since they are always
surrounded by an almost impenetrable fog of lies and deceit. It may truthfully be said that although Trujillo and his propagandists speak with much
fire and conviction of patriotism and other lofty principles, the Generalissimo's long sustained sway over the Dominican people adds up to one of
the most brazen swindles ever perpetrated against a nation.

Moreover, these are only part of the difficulties one confronts when writing a book on Trujillo. Others are the scarcity of reliable documentation on the man and his background; the cloud of censorship which hangs over all his actions and motivations and, last but not least, the all-pervading fright that shakes the hearts and paralyzes the tongues of those who know about the all-powerful, revengeful despot.

All in all, this document is not a treatise of political philosophy or a sociological anatomy of the most durable of Latin American satrapies, nor do I venture to advance solutions of the tragic Dominican ordeal. It is not the definite analysis of dictatorship I would like it to be. It is plain, unadulterated journalism. It reflects, however, a sincere effort to give an accurate picture of life and death in the Dominican Republic under the iron grip of the dean of the "Free World's" dictators.

In writing this book I have tried to detach myself as much as possible from my personal problems. When I cite my own experiences it is only because I consider them relevant to the narration or because being easier to document—and always typical of what happens to Dominicans during the "Era of Trujillo"—it is convenient for me to use them to illustrate a point.

Yet behind every book there is a reason.

During my adult life I have traveled the entire road open to a Dominican, especially one of those who can be properly called children of the dictatorship—I was only eleven when Trujillo assumed power in that faraway period when Herbert Hoover was still President of the United States.

I underwent the full treatment. Reacting against the evils of dictatorship in my student days, I rebelled and tried to fight. I suffered imprisonment and social and economic ostracism. Due to my own weakness or the strength of the adversary I eventually succumbed, as do most Dominicans living within the country and many who live outside. I was "broken in" and became an active collaborator of the regime.

Freedom, in the long run, is a pretty indestructible instinct. Finally, there was enough reserve energy in me to reassert the dormant passion for emancipation, and new desires of liberty were awakened. This did not happen overnight, of course. It was the end-product of quite a long process in which several factors and influences were instrumental in shaping the decisive course. To my own principles were added the principles of my courageous and highly idealistic wife, Diane, as well as the guidance of the Inter American Press Association with which I maintained uninterrupted contact during the years preceding my breakaway from the poisonous Dominican environment.

When I left the Dominican Republic in 1955 Trujillo was at the summit of his power. He was stronger and more influential than ever before. The dictator did not kick me out. I chose to leave wealth and social and political prestige for the uncertain world of exile under one compulsion: that of my own inner conscience and my longings for freedom and dignity. After finally disentangling myself from Trujillo's web, and being thoroughly familiar with the prevailing Dominican system by personal experience, I felt it was time to undertake the task of writing this book.

To thank the collaborators in this case could be dangerous, not for the author but for the recipients of his gratitude. Therefore, I content myself with a general expression of gratitude to all who helped me. However, there are a few persons who, quite courageously, have never hidden their direct or indirect help in this project. Their names should be mentioned.

First and foremost, I want to thank my wife. When we finally found a courageous publishing house willing to meet Trujillo's challenge, she provided me with the needed incentives to almost meet the deadline. To her loyalty and her devotion to the cause of the Dominican people I owe much of the peace of mind that I now enjoy.

Second, I must mention my editor. It is said that no writer is ever complete without a good editor. Mr. Gorham Munson—without discarding my own words or betraying a single one of my thoughts—made readable copy out of my imperfect English.

Finally, I want to convey my gratitude to Mr. Angel Ramos, publisher of *El Mundo,* of San Juan, Puerto Rico. He not only offered me a position on the staff of his newspaper when I was already tainted as "controversial" by the persistent *trujillista* propaganda, but later, when he heard that I had found a publisher for a book I was writing, gave me what was tantamount to a paid leave of absence without even asking me about the contents of the book. To this day he does not know what I say here.

GERMÁN E. ORNES

Santurce, Puerto Rico
February 25, 1958

CONTENTS

CONTENTS

TRUJILLO

Little Caesar of the Caribbean

THE DICTATORSHIP

1.

DOMINICANS ARE A SICK PEOPLE, VERY SICK. BUT, AFTER twenty-seven years of a totalitarian dictatorship this is not easily discernible. For the most part, rank-and-file Dominicans are content to keep their eyes on their jobs and off political affairs. They look healthy, well-fed, well-clad and fairly competent. However, they do not have, nor do they expect to have, a voice in the conduct of the national affairs, which are run by Rafael L. Trujillo and his hand-picked lieutenants as they please. In politics, Dominicans are either uninformed, indifferent or scared.

Under a misleading surface of seeming peace and quiet, terror runs its red threads through the fabric of Dominican society. The cancer of fear gnaws at the vitals of the people and affects with paralyzing force every human activity. High tension, despair and a sense of impending danger are dominant aspects of the social situation.

Dominicans fear one another and are in mortal dread of foreigners. They suspect their servants, doubt their friends. They fear denunciation; they have the spooky feeling of being constantly watched; they dread the shattering, harsh decrees and the mesh of regulations that, in totalitarian style, prescribe their course from cradle to grave.

Last but not least, Dominicans fear the ever-present, far-reaching, vindictive and implacable hands of "the Big One"—"The Chief"—Generalissimo Doctor Rafael Leonidas Trujillo Molina, Benefactor of the Fatherland and Father of the New Fatherland. "One thing that impresses the visitor to the Dominican Republic," wrote Robert M. Hallett, Latin American Editor of the *Christian Science Monitor,* "is the fact that whenever anyone mentions the Generalissimo in critical terms—even if the speaker is a foreigner—the tone of voice immediately drops, and a conspiratorial air is given the whole conversation." Another American reporter, Milton Bracker of the *New York Times,* stated that "diplomats are reluctant to discuss the regime while in rooms at the luxurious *Jaragua* or *El Embajador* hotels. Sound-recording systems are feared even where they cannot be proved to be in operation."

A whole generation of Dominicans has been brought up without knowing the meaning of permanence and inner security. The only thing permanent seems to be the dictatorship, all else being mutable and provisional, in accordance with the Benefactor's whims. For Dominicans only two words have definite meaning: uncertainty and terror.

A monopoly of force is in the hands of the dictator and everyone is aware of his readiness to employ it. Force has been used so effectively in the past, that to keep his subjects submissive Trujillo no longer needs to turn loose in the streets the storm troopers of *La 42* or the "Veterans" (the dreaded gangs of thugs employed to murder the Generalissimo's opponents in earlier days of the regime), nor is it likely that there are jails or concentration camps teeming with political inmates.

Nevertheless, terror, one of the main weapons of the regime, has been applied so successfully that Dominicans feel they cannot escape "the Big One." They feel as though living on the flanks of a live volcano.

Under the circumstances the characteristic signs of the Dominicans are the scared look, the mask-like face, the hush-hush voice. People are careful not to utter an unguarded word against the regime. They are on watch against the indiscreet gesture, the tell-tale smile. A man entering a nightclub at a moment when the orchestra is not playing feels that he is crossing the threshold into a big, neatly ordered temple dedicated to the cult of silence. As *Time* once pointed out: "After a quarter-century of ruthless policing, the Dominican Republic is the land of the poker face."

No one stands before the Dominican tyrant in full human stature. Abasement is so thoroughly practiced that when Trujillo appears in public each citizen must remove his hat, place it over his heart and bow his head. Probably that is the reason why so many Dominicans go out bareheaded.

The lowering of moral standards is evident in all phases of Dominican life. The foremost outward sign of Dominican "morality" is at present a love of gain—an inordinate fondness for profitable business or government careers. The desire to get rich as fast as possible or to become one of the members of the small circle of favorites of the Dictator seemingly rules the conduct of the majority of educated Dominicans. Money appears to be the sole criterion of a man's social status. Therefore, even knowing that everything may be lost at the slightest whim of the Benefactor, everyone tries, regardless of the means, to acquire riches.

Besides Trujillo's own large fortune (estimated at over $500,000,000), there are among the relatives and cronies of the Dictator a handful of people who can brag of an accumulation of several million dollars. With unconscious irony the American magazine *International Markets,* edited by Dun & Bradstreet, had this to say about the situation, in a Government-sponsored issue dedicated to the Dominican Republic: "The Generalissimo is a big businessman in his own right. Members of two other families, the Martínez's and the Alba's, are active in scores of island enterprises. Probably the country's top private industrialist is Francisco Martínez Alba." What the magazine failed to say is that Martínez Alba, the head of the alleged two other families, is the brother of Trujillo's third wife.

The newly rich (a class formed by high officials and military men) have found it obligatory to display their wealth. As a result, the country has entered upon a period of what Thorstein Veblen called conspicuous consumption. Trujillo's aides and relatives have built ostentatious homes that are too large for their own families. Their children are sent to the best boarding schools abroad, particularly in the United States. Their houses are staffed with more servants than they need, and several luxury cars make splendid each garage. The cars, clothes, art collections, and social gatherings proclaim that the new elite are the ones with the money.

However, in spite of the glittering cars and luxurious suburban homes, the new aristocracy has not polished itself enough. Proofs of crudeness may be found in the constant public reminders to the members of the official elite on how to behave in society. The letters-to-the-editor section of the daily *El Caribe* is full of stories on how improperly dressed high officials frequently attend formal functions. Trujillo himself got so incensed on one occasion that he wrote an anonymous letter to *El Caribe,* chiding his cabinet ministers for appearing at a formal gathering wearing white tie and tails minus the proper shoes. When Queen Angelita Trujillo, the Benefactor's eighteen-year-old daughter, was crowned in December, 1955, the same newspaper complained there were people who attended the ball improperly dressed. They forgot to wear the vests of their *fracs.*

But, if they are not as well bred as they should be, Dominicans are a civic-minded lot. They salute the flag and listen with devotion to the national anthem. This was not always the case. In fact, Trujillo, a great patriot himself, could hardly wait to take power before he started teaching his own noble feelings to the Dominicans. When he heard that many were paying no attention as the bands played the national anthem, he sent out a company of his well-disciplined soldiers with instructions to teach patriotism to disrespectful Dominicans. One of his American biographers proudly describes the excellent results of the measure, but wisely omits to say what happened to those caught in inattention. A further step was to pass a law to make certain that national holidays will be properly observed. Every window must now prominently display the Dominican flag on Trujillo's birthday and other patriotic occasions.

But the *trujillista* way of life is not confined to wealthy upstarts. Under constant pressure from the new high society, the few remaining members of the old landed aristocracy try desperately to keep their fortunes and social standing intact. This requires constant adjustment as well as compromise of principles, which some aristocrats have already regretted.

For old and new classes alike, success depends on the extent to which they show subservience to Trujillo. Any Dominican who wishes to climb the political ladder must pay constant homage to Trujillo; adulation has been elevated to the status of a science. The deification of the Benefactor, under the slogan "God and Trujillo," has become a major industry.

Under relentless press indoctrination, Dominicans have learned that praising the Generalissimo at every opportunity is a "must," and there is a permanent scramble going on not only to say more about Trujillo, but to say it faster than the other man. For ambitious Dominicans the indispensable art of paying Trujillo extravagant compliments has become an ingrained habit, and more than one promising young man has made a career out of proposing new sorts of homage. But Trujillo does not seem to care about repetition as long as the people are kept busy making genuflexions.

The twenty-fifth year of the Era of Trujillo (in Santo Domingo time is officially measured by Act of Congress from the date "the Big One" came to power) afforded an opportunity for the staging of a prodigiously successful festival of adulation. Trujillo's twenty-fifth wedding anniversary with the "Fatherland," "the glory" and "destiny" was a burst of triumphal pageantry. The years of 1955 and 1956 (officially proclaimed "The Year of the Benefactor") were a national orgy of government-directed abjectness. No publication dared suggest the thought that the Generalissimo might be anything less than a divinely inspired genius. Said the newspaper *La Nación:* "Men are not indispensable. But Trujillo is irreplaceable. For Trujillo is not a man. He is a political force. An economic force. A social force . . . A cosmic force . . . Those who try to compare him to his ordinary contemporaries are mistaken. He belongs to . . . the category of those born to a special destiny."

This self-deification drive hit a high point at the "International Fair of Peace and Brotherhood of the Free World," which Trujillo with unconscious irony arranged as a device to inform mankind of his anniversary. He spent some $40,000,000 on the Fair, which occupied a 125-acre tract on the outskirts of Ciudad Trujillo, the capital city, known in pre-Benefactor days as Santo Domingo. The Fair consisted of seventy-nine imposing buildings—including a Temple of Peace, a vast Coney Island imported from the United States, a $1,000,000 Fountain of Music and Light, and enough effigies of the Benefactor to fill a museum.

Angelita Trujillo, the handsome buxom brunette who is the young apple of the old man's eye, was groomed for her role as Queen of the Fair; and from the day of her proclamation and for a long time after (until criticisms in the foreign press caught up with the Generalissimo) she was addressed only as Her Majesty. She was crowned with a diamond-studded gold crown that many real sovereigns might envy. At official ceremonies she wore an $80,000 Italian gown and carried a heavily bejeweled scepter. This outfit was stunning in more ways than one; in a country whose per capita national income is $226, its cost represented the annual income of approximately 800 people.

For all the fortune that was squandered on it, the Fair did not produce much in the way of increased tourist trade. In its first seven months of operation it attracted only 24,000 tourists, though 500,000 were expected. Although great sums of money were spent in publicizing the event in foreign countries, it excited a good deal less attention than some other aspects of the Trujillo regime. Of course, not everything was a failure at the Fair. There were some happy results. According to the Foreign Agriculture Service of the United States: "Undoubtedly stimulated by the Dominican International Fair . . . baby chicks for broiler production are being imported from the United States in unprecedented numbers."

"The Year of the Benefactor" was finally over, but every day is still loyalty day for some sector of Dominican society. One day the chiefs of the armed forces or the labor leaders gather before the cameras; the next day, it is the dentists; then the rice growers or the foreign colony or the university students. At parades, rallies, masses, all sorts of new honors— scrolls, medals, collars (of which he is inordinately fond), honorary degrees, titles—are presented to "The Chief." These seemingly voluntary affairs come in waves, either to celebrate a new glorious feat of the illustrious and peerless statesman or to endorse a new policy or attack against the enemies of the regime.

It is not enough to pay homage to Trujillo personally. Every function must include something in honor of Trujillo's parents. Either a floral tribute for the late father's tomb or a visit to his living mother. Practically every day Dominican newspapers print touching photographs of one delegation of citizens or another surrounding the old lady. In addition to the kind face of the *Excelsa Matrona* (the Most High lady), a feature common to all the photographs is a big flower basket in the center.

Slogans such as "God and Trujillo," "Trujillo Forever," "Trujillo Is My Protector," "All I Have I Owe to Trujillo," "Long Live Trujillo," "We Will Always Follow Trujillo," adorn public and private buildings, fortresses, pushcarts, and even shoeshine boxes. Every public building, every store, practically every home, must hang pictures of the Generalissimo and his little brother Héctor—the present President of the Dominican Republic. (Some far-seeing people display as well the photograph of Trujillo's elder son, Lieutenant General Rafael Leonidas "Ramfis" Trujillo Martínez.)

The pictures are carefully exhibited in the most public places. A familiar sight is the bronze plaque, with Trujillo's picture in colors, which can be found in every hotel lobby, restaurant and in most private homes. The plaque reads on one side: "In this place Trujillo is the chief"; and on the other: "National Symbols: Rectitude, Liberty, Work and Morality." The existence of such a plaque is odd enough in itself, but what few visitors to the country know is that this "national symbol" is another of Trujillo's businesses—they sell for $30 and bring in a nice bit of revenue to *Ferretería Read C. por A.,* the hardware concern owned by Mrs. Rafael L. Trujillo, which issues them on an *or else* basis. However, recent rumor is that when it became common knowledge that the wholesale cost of the plaque, manufactured in Mexico, was less than $2, the *Ferretería* gave way to public opinion and lowered the price. Merchants must pay in cash, but other people may acquire the plaque on credit: "hang it now, pay later."

During 1955 and 1956 the automobile license plates reminded people of the act of Congress christening the period "The Year of the Benefactor." Some willing drivers added a smaller plate with *Viva Trujillo.*

The missing Basque scholar Dr. Jesús de Galíndez—a personal witness to this process of moral disintegration—pointed out in his perceptive analysis of the regime entitled *The Era of Trujillo* that "at times this adulation becomes, unwittingly, a form of cruel irony, as in the case of the sign which I saw hanging over the door of the lunatic asylum in Nigua: 'We owe everything to Trujillo!' "

As chief vehicles for this massive brainwashing operation, the three Dominican dailies vie with one another in singing Trujillo's praises. Reading their daily offerings people get the impression that the only reason for their existence is to print flowery tributes to the Genius of Peace, Hero of Labor and Paladin of Democracy. "The only thing worse than Trujillo's former contempt for democracy is his latest pose as its champion," wrote the American journalist and historian, Theodore Draper, in *The Reporter.* And he added: "Not merely any ordinary variety of democracy, to be sure, but one specially adapted to his people's needs, a Trujillista 'neo-democracy.' He has his editorial writers compose absurdly pompous little essays on the superiority of his unique and inimitable political system."

The pagan character of the adulatory pageant is further emphasized by a string of quasi-religious oaths daily proffered, not to God but to the Benefactor, by the armed forces, labor unions, government employees, student associations and other groups. In the face of these blasphemous activities in open violation of Pope Pius XI's encyclic "Non Abbiamo Bisognio" condemning the oath given to Mussolini by Italian fascists, the Church has remained mute. In fact, at every propitious opportunity the Pope cables cordial greetings to Trujillo. The Vatican contributed with a religious exposition as well as its blessings to Trujillo's jubilee. To the 1956 Congress of Catholic Culture, held in Ciudad Trujillo under the Benefactor's sponsorship, Francis Cardinal Spellman brought, as the

Pope's special representative, a warm-hearted message. Cardinal Spellman traveled down from New York to be triumphantly received by the Generalissimo himself. Their cordial embraces were displayed in all Dominican front pages the next day, and to cap it all a Dominican priest formally proposed, without receiving any public rebuke, that Trujillo be named "Benefactor of the Church."

This account may sound like a piece of fiction lifted from a Broadway musical comedy on a mythical oriental kingdom, but it is no joke. These are the props of Dominicans' ordeal at the hands of Trujillo. They account for the singular order and regularity, or perhaps it should be called monotony, marking Dominican life. It also accounts for Dominicans' behavior in public—their seriousness, quietness, and an apprehensiveness bordering on somberness.

Observers usually misinterpret the existing situation as a true mirror of the national character. However, those who are old enough to remember life before the Benefactor know the average Dominican to be hospitable, warm, gay and fun-loving. Even now, despite Trujillo and his police system, humor occasionally manages to break through. Those who have heard them know the jokes are good.

The last one in hush-hush circulation, shortly before I left the country in 1955, was about a bus passenger, who suddenly put aside the newspaper he was reading and exclaimed out loud: "Damn Government!"

The secret policeman on duty in the bus jumped up to arrest him. Somehow the passenger was able to explain that he had been reading about Argentina's dictator Juan D. Perón's persecution of Catholic priests. Since he was such a religious man he could not help making the objectionable remark.

The spy, seemingly convinced, left his man alone. However, as the bus was passing in front of a police station, the informer stopped it and asked the newspaper reader to accompany him. The man argued he had already given a reasonable and quite satisfactory explanation, to which the spy replied:

"Yes, but I am not convinced. I have been thinking it over all this time, and I'll tell you something: in this world the only one that can be called 'Damn Government!' is ours."

There is also the story of how Josef Stalin, Adolf Hitler and Rafael Trujillo each died and went to face the God who forgives all sinners.

First to be taken to the Divine Presence was Stalin. He confessed that he had been a harsh man and too often a cruel one, but that he had served his notion of human welfare as best he could. And the Lord, so the story goes, arose and shook Stalin's hand and said: "Go, Josef, there is a place here even for you." Next came Hitler with a similar story, and the Lord rose and shook his hand and tendered him the same mercy.

Rafael Trujillo came last. He said that he had owned a small country, one perhaps beneath his talents; but he had done what he could with it. The Lord sat in His chair and forgave Trujillo and waved him on.

As the Benefactor departed, Saint Peter turned to the throne and remarked: "Lord, there is one thing I do not quite understand. You forgave all three knaves; but you rose and shook hand only with Stalin and Hitler. You sat and waved Trujillo past. Why, oh Lord, did you not rise?"

The Lord answered: "My son, if I had risen only a split second to shake that rascal's hand, he would have taken my throne from me."

In addition to the secret humorists, there are secret cynics who, though placed high in government positions, speak with tongue in cheek, but most of the Dominicans behave with a disturbing sense of duty and acceptance. People seem to take their permanent humiliation for granted and the great majority sing in the chorus with shocking alacrity. Some, it is true, privately condemn the tyranny, terror and corruption of the regime, but when asked what they propose to do about it they simply shrug their shoulders.

2.

RARE IS THE OUTSTANDING CITIZEN OF THE DOMINICAN Republic who, in one way or the other, has not collaborated with the Trujillo regime; but subservience, whatever its advantages, is not per se a fully satisfactory solution.

Woe betide anyone who indulges in the slightest criticism of the regime, but even to be left alone it is not enough for a person to demonstrate on all occasions that he is a proven follower of the dictator. A man's fortune is absolutely dependent on the Generalissimo's caprices, and the history of the past twenty-seven years is full of examples of government, business and professional careers ruined overnight for no apparent reason—other than a gust of the Benefactor's wrath. When this happens, the wreckage is total.

Since adulation must be the paramount concern of all Dominicans, no gathering is permitted—not even a birthday party—without the participants showing appreciation for Trujillo. In August 1955 a group of lawyers from Santiago, second largest city of the country, gave at the local Matum Hotel a testimonial dinner to a distinguished colleague, Dr. Federico C. Alvarez, who had completed forty years in the profession. The gathering had no political significance, but in accordance with the rules its organizers cleared the matter with the local authorities and even invited a large group of high government officials. There were in all about 110 guests, including legislators and jurists.

Two of the after dinner speakers, the toastmaster, Dr. Eduardo Sánchez Cabral, and the guest of honor himself, committed the grave mistake of not mentioning the Benefactor's name nor his glorious achievements during their orations. Worst of all, no one shot them on the spot. The omission was not overlooked, however, by an attending high priest of the regime, Senator Nicolas Sosa, who on the same night wrote a lengthy report informing the Generalissimo of the scandalous oversight.

Sosa's report found its way to *El Caribe* where, except for its heading and signature, it was fully printed in the letters to the editor section. Within a few hours all the attending government employees—about two score—had lost their jobs. The resignations of two senators and several deputies were accepted by Congress.

This proved to be only the warm-up. Within the next few days the whole matter grew in noise and turbulence, becoming an immense public issue. Under Trujillo's personal direction, newspaper editorials, employing most pungent words, assailed the guests of the fateful dinner.

Perhaps the most bitter attack was leveled, in two front-page editorials of *El Caribe,* against Trujillo's old crony and sometime adviser, Senator Rafael Vidal, reportedly the mastermind of "The Chief's" successful bid for power in 1930. What seemingly enraged Trujillo in Vidal's case was that his former favorite neither spoke up for him nor reported, as Sosa did, the intolerable outrage of silencing his august name.

Trujillo had no qualms about letting people know what had enraged him. "Unjustifiable Omission" was the headline he himself chose to run over a series of letters written by hand-picked aides. The literary output on the subject was enhanced by a number of abject letters of recantation by the people under fire. They all admitted guilt and begged for mercy.

Both the accusatory letters and their answers were not lacking in comical overtones. Sánchez Cabral was called a "drunk." Vidal was reminded of his "Negro blood" in a country where in social relations there is no color line. But the best ones were reserved for Federico Nina, one of the resigning members of Congress, who had particularly displeased "the Big One." Nina had tried to lessen his guilt by asserting he had arrived late at the dinner and therefore had not heard the outrageous speeches. Had he been there, he stated, he would have undertaken the defense of the Benefactor. (By this time a man reading a Dominican newspaper without any background knowledge might have gathered the impression that someone had actually proffered insulting words against the beloved Generalissimo.) Nina complained as well that he had heard of his resignation from Congress when a friend told him that at a party in his home town of San Pedro de Macoris the local Governor had celebrated the "election" of his successor. It did not take long for Nina to be publicly rebuked. He was called a "liar" and a "prematurely born baby" (*sietemecino*) on account of his short height and frail constitution.

Then newspapers reported a cheering crowd of 50,000 at a rally held in Santiago to right the wrong committed against "The Chief." The group of speakers, headed by the current Vice President, Dr. Joaquin Balaguer, spared no words to chide the offenders.

For weeks the big huff went on. Next on the schedule was a stage-managed, Moscow-style, public purge. A "Tribunal of Honor" of the *Partido Dominicano* (the sole Dominican political party to which all present at the memorable banquet belonged) was called to pass judgment upon the accused's conduct. The newspapers enjoyed a field day reporting the trial's opening. Pages were filled with pictures of the proceedings and lengthy accounts of the bewildering pattern of self-accusations, recantations and shocking lies that marked the first hearing. The second day a curtain of silence fell upon the press. Not a single line was printed that day, and for that matter any other day, on the "Affair of the Matum." For all practical purposes it had never happened as a news story; and therefore, it was never mentioned again. The general public was left only with the grapevine to feed them the results of the formerly widely-publicized trial.

What happened to warrant such a blackout? It is not quite clear yet, but it seems that when Federico C. Alvarez' wantonly adulatory defense speech at the trial was brought to Trujillo's attention he decided to act with even-handed justice. He gave Alvarez a medal as well as a high government office, disbarred the still only half-heartedly repentant Sánchez Cabral, ordered a severe reprimand for the defendants not on his pay roll, and deprived membership in the *Partido Dominicano* to those who had been high government officials. A large group of prominent Dominicans thus became ineligible to work for the Government and unable to obtain passports, certificates of good conduct, or any other of the many licenses necessary to conduct business of any sort.

Generous as he is, the Generalissimo, after receiving enough letters of recantation, lifted the sanctions imposed on the ousted former collaborators. The last to be pardoned was Vidal, but even he now sits again in Congress—as a member of the lower chamber.

If further proof is needed that even silence may on occasion be subversive, less than two years later, in April 1957, another unjustifiable omission received wide publicity. This time Trujillo's own private secretary, the poet Ramón Emilio Jiménez, wrote a scorching article in *El Caribe* to take exception to the maiden speech of a new member of the Dominican Academy of History, Dr. Guido Despradel Batista, who was charged with the grave sin of ignoring in his essay—which dealt with the actions of the founders of the Dominican Republic—the patriotic deeds of the Benefactor. Consequently, Despradel lost not only his newly earned Academic post but his other paid posts in Government. A resolution passed by the Municipal Council disavowed him as a native son of the town of

La Vega. Today he may or may not be restored to the good graces of "The Chief."

Whatever its outward ridiculous appearance, the real significance of this remarkable incident must be found in its connection with the underlying ramifications of a subtle campaign now under way to whitewash Trujillo's character as a wilful collaborator during the American military occupation between 1916 and 1924. As a result, a thorough rewrite of Dominican history is being performed, primarily by the Academy of History.

As a political weapon alteration of history has been practiced by almost every self-perpetuating modern dictatorship—rewriting is part of the well-known technique of the "big lie." But nowhere, except perhaps in Orwell's *1984,* has this been so boldly done as in the Dominican Republic. An Orwell-like act of Congress, passed in August 1955, makes a criminal offender of anyone whose writings or speeches fall into disagreement with the historical "truth" as set down by the *trujillista* Academy of History.

Hence, when the Academy says that in 1920 patriotic-minded young Lieutenant Trujillo ordered military honors for the Dominican flag in the town of El Seibo, no one may ask why this piece of "historical truth" was not unearthed before 1955. Nor may any one ask "how come?" if the would-be Benefactor was not obeying orders to do so, he was not court-martialed or even reprimanded afterwards for flagrant public breach of military discipline. This sort of thing might explain why people who show so blatant a disregard for the Benefactor as to omit his exalted name in a speech dealing with one-hundred-year-old happenings, as Despradel did, are not welcomed among the guardians of the historical party-line.

The remorseless meat grinder of Dominican politics touches everything in the country, including beauty contests. The election of Carnival queens has always been the occasion for installing in power the newest of Trujillo's favorite girl friends. The custom was somewhat modified, however, after Mrs. Trujillo clamped down on it. Lina Lovatón, a high society girl elected Queen of the Carnival in 1937, came closer than anyone else to wrest the throne from the First Lady. It was only after a long desperate struggle that Mrs. Trujillo retained her place in the Generalissimo's heart and Miss Lovatón left the country. She now lives in Miami with her children—named Trujillo. In the meantime Carnivals were relegated to a second place until Trujillo's own daughter Angelita was ready to hold the scepter. She was chosen as Queen of the Fair in 1955.

Nevertheless, someone of the ruling circle conceived the idea of promoting Dominican participation in the "Miss Universe" contest at Long Beach, California, in 1956. The idea was taken up with enthusiasm and shortly thereafter a host of beautiful candidates for the title of "Miss Dominican Republic" sprang up from all over the country. Questioned by Dominican newspaper reporters about their reasons for wanting to represent the country, almost all the candidates gave a standard answer. They wanted the world to know the progress of the Dominican Republic under the peerless leadership of the Benefactor. Questions about their tastes in literature met also with near unanimity: most of them loved the moral writings of the First Lady.

When the moment to select the winner arrived, so did the problems. The majority of the members of the selecting panel received word from Mrs. Trujillo that they were permitted to vote for any except two of the candidates: the prettiest girl (who happened to be the daughter of Eduardo Sánchez Cabral, of the "Affair of the Matum") and a niece of the still hated Queen of the Carnival of 1937, Genoveva Lovatón Ricart. The judges wisely settled for a distant relative of the Trujillo family, one Olga Fiallo Oliva.

As should have been expected, when the controversial verdict was announced to the crowd gathered at the Jaragua Hotel to witness the final selection, there were a few shouts of protest. The names of the alleged ringleaders of the demonstration were written down by the secret police. Most of them were severely scolded in *El Caribe,* particularly a young Under Secretary of Industry named Eduardo Leon Asensio, who supposedly should have known better. Leon was accused of conduct unbecoming the dignity of a high government official during the enlightened Era of Trujillo. On the other hand, Mrs. Trujillo seemingly knew what she was doing in vetoing the candidacy of the prettiest girl. By sheer coincidence Sánchez Cabral had been pardoned by "The Chief" and reinstated in his good graces in those days.

Under such a system, independent groups and associations cannot exist. Unlike Hitler and other dictators, Trujillo has not banned certain organizations like the Rotary clubs, Boy Scouts, Masons and religious associations. All these formerly respected civic groups have been transformed into Trujillo fronts. Thus, when some *trujillista* manifesto needs the backing of internationally known groups for foreign consumption, there are always the Rotary, Masonic lodge or religious groups to lend a hand.

There is the case, for instance, of a two-page spread addressed to "the members of the American Newspaper Publishers Association" by their self-appointed "friends in the Dominican Republic," that appeared in the May 5, 1956 issue of the American magazine *Editor and Publisher.*

After calling the Benefactor "one of the extraordinary figures of our time" as well as one of "that small handful of men who . . . have changed the course of history," the so-called "message" to ANPA summoned the publishers to provide Trujillo's full story—Dominican style of course—to the American people. "We value," the self-styled "friends" asserted, "the good opinions of the American citizens highly—as a man must value the opinions of his friends. And we are enraged when scurrilous rumormongers tamper with that opinion—as any man must be angered when malicious untruths about him are spread among his friends."

Trujillo's detractors, the ad went on to imply, were only a bunch of Communists; in fact, the same group that had been maligning the United States. But, it was added, Dominicans do not believe such lies about Americans. However, a veiled threat followed: "We are proud to say that unlike some other 'friends' of your country [the U.S.], we give no ear to these venomous slanders, *nor will we so long as you remain our friends.*" (Italics added.)

With the obvious purpose of adding an extra note of respectability to their assertions, the sponsors of the ad pointed out that former American Secretary of State Cordell Hull had considered Trujillo "one of the great statesmen of the Americas."[1]

At the bottom of this patent piece of *trujillista* self-adulation—placed and paid for by the Dominican Information Center, a registered publicity agency of the Trujillo regime in the United States—appeared the names of Monsignor Ricardo Pittini, Archbishop Primate of America; Dr. Pedro Troncoso Sánchez, Rector of the University of Santo Domingo; Dr. Arturo Damirón Ricart, President of the Rotary Club of Ciudad Trujillo; Dr. Amable Lugo S., President of the Dominican Red Cross; Rev. Carlos Amado Ruiz, Pastor of the Consultative Council of Evangelical Churches of the Dominican Republic; Dr. Hipólito Herrera Billini, President of the Supreme Court of Justice; Franklin Mieses Burgos, Director of the Institute of Hispanic Culture; and Dr. Julio Jupiter, President of the Dominican American Cultural Institute (an organization officially supported by the U.S. State Department).

Commenting upon this tour de force, Robert U. Brown, editor of *Editor and Publisher* and one of the leaders of the Inter American Press Association, stressed the fact that the same group of gentlemen had signed a letter printed in the April 28, 1956 issue of the *New York Times*. In their letter to the *Times* they took exception to that newspaper calling Trujillo a dictator and repeated the charge that regardless of nationality the majority of Trujillo's critics were "known or hidden Communists." "That," Brown said, "didn't have to carry the printed endorsement of the 'Information Center' that our ad carried although we assume it was present."

Brown noticed that the "notables'" letter followed a clear pattern. Just a few days before in a statement to the press, the Dominican Consul

---

[1] In all fairness to the memory of Mr. Hull it must be said that a thorough check of his two-volume memoirs failed to produce a single instance of such appraisal. It seems that the much boasted about friendship between Trujillo and Hull is another *trujillista* fable with no other foundation than a few protocol exchanges of official letters, one or two brief personal interviews and a letter Hull wrote to a Dominican diplomat calling Trujillo "a splendid President, who is outstanding among all those in the American nations."

General in New York had accused the Communists of trying to "disrupt the unreserved support of Generalissimo Trujillo toward the United States." After singling out these and other examples of vicious *trujillista* propaganda, Brown concluded: "So it would seem that anyone who attacks Trujillo is a Communist."

Far more significant is the lack of any record concerning an official representation on account of the improper use for partisan politics of the Dominican American Cultural Institute, an organization sponsored and paid for by the American taxpayers. Nor did the Vatican chide the Archbishop, either on that occasion or when in September 1957 it was announced that in response to a query by U.S. Representative Gardner R. Withrow, Monsignor Pittini asserted that the "absolutely anti-Communist" Dominican Republic gave its law-abiding citizens as much freedom as United States citizens have.

3. THE CASUAL VISITORS WHO PUT UP AT THE LUXURIOUS tourist hotels soon learn to recognize the Dominican Republic as seemingly a land of paradoxes. These people, sometimes newspapermen, do not succeed in understanding how, although revolutions have been recently plaguing almost every country south of the Rio Grande, the Dominican people remains passive, showing not the slightest outward sign of dissatisfaction or dissent. Nor can they see why—if it is true that there is such a lack of civil rights in the country as claimed by Trujillo's enemies—Dominicans have been left unmoved even by nearby explosions of popular unrest such as the general strike that in December 1956 unseated the dictatorial regime of President Paul Magloire in Haiti.

Conversely, Dominicans feel at a loss trying to understand why people coming down to their land from supposedly free lands—where human dignity is highly prized and people are allegedly taught never to bow under the pressures of tyranny—do not wait long to express unrestrained approval of the Dominican dictatorship.

Bound to his land by the virtual impossibility of obtaining a passport, the average Dominican is unable to grasp why people who enjoy freedom of movement sink themselves into the poisonous morass of Trujilloland and, worst of all, act as if they enjoyed it.

"We are very happy to have the opportunity to express the affection and the loyalty that we feel toward President Trujillo." These words did not come from the lips of a native courtier. They were uttered by an executive of a large American sugar corporation on an occasion of public homage to the Benefactor. Then Mr. E. I. Kilbourne added: "This loyalty is born not only as a consequence of our friendly personal relations that always have existed between each one of us individually and General Trujillo, but it is also the result of the wisdom and foresight that he has shown in considering the problems of the industry with which we are associated."

Incapable of understanding the reasons for this conduct, Dominicans reach the false conclusion that servility is not the exclusive patrimony of enslaved nations. The local press prints many dispatches showing the favorable international disposition toward the Benefactor's achievements and the regime spares no effort to convince its subjects that they can expect neither encouragement nor sympathy from the outside world should they try to stand up against Trujillo's rule.

It is with profound pessimism, therefore, that Dominicans see the honors paid to Trujillo by distinguished foreigners, including influential statesmen, military brass, clergymen and the diplomatic representatives of the most democratic powers of the world. It is impossible to estimate the demoralizing effect wrought when more than thirty diplomats offered a glittering testimonial dinner to Trujillo on the night of January 9, 1956, to celebrate his so-called silver wedding anniversary with the Fatherland. Upon that occasion, speaking in the name of his colleagues, the Vatican representative, Monsignor Salvatore Siino, praised in no uncertain terms the Christian spirit and humanitarian content of Trujillo's most Catholic statesmanship. Whereupon, as a token of warm affection the Benefactor was given an autographed silver platter.

The diplomatic corps offered somewhat similar homage on the night of May 18, 1957 to President Héctor B. Trujillo, whose name had headed the single-party ticket in the elections held two days before—extending for another five years the dictatorship's sway. Although Héctor was the man supposedly being feted on this occasion, the Generalissimo, true to form, stole the show from little brother. He barely allowed Héctor to receive a scroll signed by twenty-two chiefs of missions.

By the same token no international conference ever set down to business in the Dominican Republic without first electing as honorary presidents the Generalissimo and his little brother the President.

Individually, too, foreign diplomats give the impression that their duty is to make exaggerated curtsies to the Generalissimo. In the last fifteen years a big nation like Brazil has failed to accredit to the country a single ambassador willing to show, if not dignified and open adherence to democratic principles, at least some restraint and discretion in his dealings with the Benefactor. The question which puzzles students of the Dominican situation is: How does Trujillo go about persuading free men to accept this sort of thing in the first place?

As far as the Benefactor is concerned, the answer lies in his practical knowledge of human nature. Diplomats are tempted by flattery and by actions that tend to enhance ther sense of prestige. Thus, in exchange for medals and honorary degrees, in many cases, diplomats turn themselves into shameless propagandists of the *trujillista* gospel.

Paulo Germano Hasslocher, who retired as Brazilian Ambassador to the Dominican Republic full of *trujillista* honors, exemplifies this type of diplomat. He developed a reputation as something of a "shadow" to the Benefactor at receptions and other functions, and his mouth was always full of eulogies for the Dominican regime he would never lavish upon his own government. Upon his return to Brazil, Hasslocher openly engaged in public relations work for Trujillo in the Rio de Janeiro press.

The present Brazilian Ambassador, Decio Martins Coimbra, did not wait long to follow in his predecessor's footsteps. Shortly after his arrival in September 1956, he earned for himself the dubious distinction of receiving a congratulatory communication from all the members of the Dominican cabinet, who were elated by his pro-Trujillo statements in a speech broadcast by the Trujillo-owned radio network, *La Voz Dominicana,* on Brazil's Independence Day.

Another outstanding example of a diplomat turned *trujillista* in detriment to the best interests of his own country, is afforded by Dr. Enrique Loudet, Chargé d'Affaires of the Argentinian regime of General Pedro E. Aramburu. While Trujillo was engaged in actively helping the former Argentinian dictator Juan D. Perón to plot from Venezuela against the Aramburu government—as officially charged later by more alert Argentinian diplomats—Loudet's mouth was filled with laudatory adjectives for the Benefactor. So intense was Loudet's admiration for the Generalissimo that on several occasions he broke all the rules of diplomatic propriety and called his hero in public "Trujillo the Great."

Finally recalled by his Government, Loudet was showered with honors before his departure. Upon Trujillo's orders, the University of Santo Domingo bestowed upon him the honorary degree of Doctor of Philosophy, and he was appointed an honorary professor as well. The diplomat paid back in kind. Prior to his investiture Loudet dedicated his last book, published in Ciudad Trujillo, to the Benefactor "in homage of sincere and deep admiration for his peerless achievements of visionary statesmanship." Then, to crown his performance the outgoing Chargé d'Affaires printed a farewell message in *El Caribe,* stating that he considered himself unable to repay his debt of gratitude to the Dominican people and, particularly, to their illustrious statesmen—meaning no doubt the big and little brothers.

Mexico is another country which lately betrayed its time-honored democratic traditions through the antics of its Ambassador to Trujillo's court. The head of the Mexican diplomatic mission in Ciudad Trujillo, Dr. Francisco del Rio Cañedo, was recalled in the long run but only after his increasingly vocal support of Trujillo had proved a source of embarrassment for the Mexican Foreign Office. He, too, left the country with his hands full of the highest Dominican decorations and with honorary degrees awarded by the University of Santo Domingo and other Government institutions.

Foreign adulation is not limited to diplomats. Ordinary people indulge in the practice with equal gusto, and some cynical natives point out the fact that strangers soon show a remarkable command of the art of toadying to the Benefactor and even a knack for outrunning natives in their adulatory race.

At the beginning of 1956, a group of foreigners, headed by the late John Hagen, American construction tycoon, set up a widely-advertised committee for the purpose of erecting a statue of the Benefactor in the center of Independence Park in Ciudad Trujillo. After Hagen's untimely death, another American millionaire, William B. Pawley, has been closely associated with this project, announced as an expression of gratitude from the "foreign colony" to the Generalissimo.

By the same token, when the hotel operators decided it was high time to show their "gratitude" to the dictator for allowing them to accommodate the few American tourists still coming to the country, it was a well-known American businessman (then associated with Dominican Government hotel properties) who was chosen as president of the organizing and fund-raising committee: Robert K. Christenberry.

Foreign corporations are actively engaged in publicity schemes in the Dominican Republic, which would be unheard of in the countries they come from. Esso Standard Oil, for example, announced to its clients the introduction of a new type of gasoline in January 1956 with a full page ad in *El Caribe*. Instead of explaining the many advantages of the new product, the American corporation let it be known, as its only and most convincing argument, that this progressive step was a result of its earnest desire to keep abreast of the country's achievements in the "highly propitious Year of the Benefactor." A few days later the inauguration of a new Pan American World Airways flight was advertised in similar terms. On national holidays the foreign corporations deem it their duty to join in the chorus of benedictions to "The Chief" and place full-page newspaper ads written in the usual flowery language. It may be, of course, that this attitude is an application of "when in Rome, do as Romans do."

One of the ironies of the situation is that the Johnny-come-latelies from overseas seem to be not only great admirers of Trujillo's domestic accomplishments, but most enthusiastic collaborators with his foreign policy. Their unreserved support of "The Chief" goes so far that it may run counter to the best interest of their own countries. If the Benefactor gets in a quarrel with a neighboring leader—a thing likely to happen over any trifle

—it is a sure bet that the nationals of the "enemy" country residing in Santo Domingo will "spontaneously" rally to Trujillo's defense. Their statements chiding the Government back home for its obnoxious behavior toward the Benefactor are prominently displayed by the press and broadcast by the radio networks. The files of the Dominican newspapers will reveal during the past two years a number of such derogatory letters against the Governor of the Commonwealth of Puerto Rico, Luis Muñoz Marin, who has lately become one of Trujillo's pet hatreds. The Benefactor highly resents the uncompromising democratic stand of the Puerto Rican statesman. Before blackmailing Cuban dictator Fulgencio Batista into the Caribbean axis of tyrannies, the Cuban regime was a favorite target for the most slanderous attacks by the Dominican press and radio. Many Cubans were willing collaborators with "The Chief's" designs.

In deference to truth, it must be said that regardless of nationality all residents of the country are subject to almost the same types of pressure from the dictatorship. Hence, to protect their means of livelihood, peoples of all nationalities react in much the same way. There are, however, an increasing number of visitors for whom this excuse is not applicable—the transient intellectual and political beachcombers. Usually newspapermen, writers, legislators, government officials, lecturers, professors, or labor leaders, these people come down to the country either to further their own political game or to seek an opportunity to exploit Trujillo's unquenchable thirst for publicity.

The modern privateers of the pen who hop from dictatorship to dictatorship throughout Latin America find an exceedingly fertile ground in the Dominican Republic. A mysterious grapevine tells them that a few gold coins may easily be obtained whenever they feed the dictator's ego. To secure economic gains they feel no qualms in joining with alacrity the extragavant pageant of tributes.

Occasional visitors to the country, whose contacts are normally limited to the tourist hotels, government guides, embassies, and perhaps a few business associates, hardly notice the full extent of the situation. With the exception of a handful of well-trained, alert newspapermen (who know that a brief visit to a totalitarian capital cannot give insight into the country's real nature) most of the visitors seem to take the outward signs of Dominican life as a true reflection of national character.

Latins are known to be explosive—to eat politics, breathe politics, sleep politics—but not Dominicans. However, their political disinterest seems so well adjusted to the strange setting in which they live that few people pay any attention to it. Not even their silences, lack of opposition and near somberness, coupled with a remarkable show of unanimous support of the regime, make the passing visitors suspicious. Even the most perceptive among newspapers correspondents—with a few honorable exceptions, of course—leave the country after a brief visit and report: "It is a dictatorship, but there is peace, progress, stability, and the people seem to support it." These reporters fail to grasp the solid fact that what they see are results, not causes.

THE WIDE GULF

1. UNDER THE STEWARDSHIP OF RAFAEL L. TRUJILLO THE Dominican Republic still has a Constitution which, adorned with an elaborate bill of rights, reads like a very democratic document. Yet the techniques of Government are obscure, and there is a wide gulf between the letter of this "Magna Charta" and the actual workings of the regime.

However, this should not be strange. The Generalissimo has revealed himself as a firm believer in tradition and there is not a more ingrained tradition in Latin America than that of giving a legal democratic appearance to strong arm regimes. Observers of the situation, including the missing Professor Jesús de Galíndez, point out that the typical Spanish American dictatorship has a characteristic which identifies it and, at the same time, isolates and differentiates it from other dictatorial regimes: to wit, "it's adoption of the formal structure of western democracy."

Noting that Latin American dictatorships feature a constitution, periodical elections, and a Government—whose structure is sometimes inspired by that of the United States—divided into the three classical branches, Galíndez asserted that "each and every one of these democratic institutions become perverted in practice so that they turn out to be mere instruments at the service of a strong man, who usually is the president of the republic."

By these standards Trujillo qualifies as a prototype of the Latin dictator. He, however, has far exceeded anything the pace-setters might have taught him in this field. Despite his absolute power, he has paid lip-service to the external trappings of democratic rule. Instead of discarding democratic procedures, he has managed to make a mockery of them. Instead of sweeping away the Constitution he found in full force when he came to power, he chose rigorously to observe its precepts and scrupulously to maintain such cumbersome and seemingly unnecessary stage props as a separate executive, legislature and judiciary. If some constitutional provision bothers him or stands in his way, he sometimes overcomes it by stretching the extremely pliable fabric of Dominican political institutions. But if the obstacle appears insurmountable, he promptly brushes it aside with the help of properly passed constitutional amendments. This he has done four times through the twenty-seven years he has been in the saddle: in 1934, 1942, 1947 and 1955.

In some measure, by indulging in this pastime of changing the constitutional canon at will, Trujillo shows a steadfast adherence to another tradition inbedded in the political *mores* of the Dominican nation. The utter disregard for the sanctity of the Constitution, shown by local chieftains through all the years of independence, has always been regarded as one of the chief obstacles to orderly democratic government in the country.

Benjamin Sumner Wells, one of the keenest students of Dominican history, put the matter clearly in his book, *Naboth's Vineyard.*

"Constitutional government, in brief, is to the average Dominican but an empty phrase. The Constitution originally proclaimed has been changed innumerable times merely to satisfy the selfish aspirations of the individual or the party in power. It has never been amended or reformed in the interest of the Dominican people as a whole. Instead of being regarded as the sacred charter of the people's liberties, the Constitution has been considered a legitimate source of advantage to the party or to the person in control, and has consequently been modified at frequent intervals without due reflection, and without proper consideration, solely to satisfy the desires or requirements of those enabled thus to advance them."

Had Welles been writing about the current Dominican situation he could not have chosen better words to assess it. At its best, government in the Dominican Republic today is by Trujillo, of Trujillo, and for Trujillo.

The present constitution was adopted in December 1955, and it is one of the newest in Latin America. In its present form it is a relatively short document. The constitution has no preamble and at once proceeds to a number of general statements concerning the democratic nature of the government and the inalienability of the national territory.

Article Four declares communism incompatible with the fundamental principles recognized by the charter and authorizes Congress to pass laws punishing those who advocate such a doctrine. Another article calls the only political party in the country, the *Partido Dominicano,* an agency of civilization, and still another proclaims that the titles granted to Generalissimo Trujillo are permanent and cannot be revoked.

The Constitution has an imposing list of guarantees of individual liberty. First among the rights is the "inviolability of life." According to the Constitution the death penalty may not be imposed except in cases of treason or espionage during wartime.

Then comes "individual security." According to clause 2 of Article 8, no one may be arrested without a court order save in case of *flagrante delicto*. There are different provisions guaranteeing that anyone arrested must be presented in court within forty-eight hours after his arrest or else released, and that anyone deprived of liberty without cause or without legal formalities must be released immediately upon his or another's request (*Habeas Corpus*). In practice, however, none of these precepts is ever fulfilled. The courts as a rule deny in political trials the right to an accused person to confront his accuser. There are situations where star-chamber procedures are employed in preference to public trials, and there are even persons and groups to whom the right of any trial at all is denied. In many circumstances, individuals are subject to double jeopardy. On one occasion my own father, while a judge of first instance in the court of Santiago, acquitted a young student, Rafael Moore Garrido, charged with "communist activities." Upon acquittal the boy was apprehended at the doors of the court and brought back to trial. My father acquitted him again. Thereupon the Government demoted my father as a judge and later on another judge condemned the unfortunate youngster. As a rule in cases involving political crimes the accused is denied the individual right to a public trial, to due process of the law, or to freedom from excessive bail and fines.

The right to own property is also guaranteed by the Constitution. This right is usually respected as long as a conflict with the private interests of Trujillo or members of his family does not arise. If such a thing happens, the constitutional guarantee is soon forgotten. Anyone can start a new business—provided, of course, that it does not compete with a Trujillo enterprise—but if it prospers the proprietor is likely to find that a member of the Trujillo family has become a silent partner. Enemies of the government are stripped, either without due process of law or through phony law suits and alleged claims for back taxes. Innumerable are the cases of people who have lost their fortunes just because they did not agree with the Benefactor about something. One of the best known examples is that of Juan Rodriguez García, the second richest man in the country, who in 1946 went into exile and soon thereafter headed the abortive revolutionary attempts of Cayo Confites and Luperón. All Rodriguez' properties, worth according to conservative estimates around $8 million, were confiscated by the Administration and later sold for a pittance to members of the Trujillo family and hand-picked associates of the Benefactor.

A reading of the constitutional provisions concerning labor and social security will lead anyone to believe that Dominicans live within the perfect welfare state. They are supposedly assured protection from the day they see light for the first time to the fateful moment in which they depart from this world. A labor code, properly called *Código Trujillo de Trabajo,* was passed by Congress to implement the constitutional provisions. The code is an almost perfect instrument of protection for the toiling man, drafted in accordance with the highest standards set by the International Labor Organization (of which the Dominican Republic is a member), but in practice it is an almost forgotten blessing and the workers are discouraged from making use of its provisions for collective bargaining and the right to strike. Since the promulgation of the code not a single labor pact has been signed to regulate wages and labor conditions and not a strike has been called by any of the government-dominated unions.

These examples show that the value of a bill of rights depends, of course, on its interpretation. It has been pointed out before that a declaration of human rights is no better than the officials who enforce it. Yet, even though the interpretation of the bill of rights is left to his absolute discretion and that of his subservient judiciary, Trujillo does not take chances. According to clauses 7 and 8 of Article 38 of the Constitution it is possible to declare either a state of siege—under which certain individual freedoms are suspended—or a state of national emergency with suspension of all rights except that of inviolability of life.

Following another Latin American custom the constitution provides for a very strong executive. In the scheme of Dominican political life—even under normal conditions—the president is more important than Congress or the courts, or the two combined. He is elected for a five-year term, but there is, unlike most Latin nations, no constitutional restriction to prevent further reelections. The president is authorized to appoint and remove almost the entire personnel of the national administration; only for diplomatic appointments does he need Senate confirmation. He is allowed to call special sessions of Congress and also to extend regular sessions. The executive can impede by decree the entry of foreigners into the country and deport them without appeal. With regard to lawmaking the president's authority is not at all unusual, except that he is specifically permitted to issue decree laws on budgetary matters when Congress is not in session. He may also introduce bills in Congress (in practice he is the only one who does it) and may veto congressional proposals. A two-thirds vote in each chamber is necessary to override the president's veto.

For years Trujillo has been toying with the idea of grooming his elder son, Lieutenant General Rafael L. "Ramfis" Trujillo, Jr., to take his place in the Dominican scheme of things. This has not happened because Trujillo is inimical to sharing any portion of his absolute power with anyone else, even his own beloved son. However, in 1955, when the young Trujillo was already 26 years of age, certain constitutional amendments were passed in order to lower the required age for the presidency to 25 years and to restore the post of Vice-President which had been eliminated in

1942. Somehow the Benefactor's plans for making his son first Vice-President as a step to the next higher position backfired. Ramfis who has strong ambitions of his own resented not being offered the presidency right away and haughtily refused the vice-presidential nomination. The excuse he gave publicly was that he did not want to give up his military career.

Though unquestionably the boss, the Generalissimo no longer bothers about the title of President, a post which has been held since 1952 by his younger brother, General Héctor B. Trujillo Molina. No one, not even the "president" himself, however, has any illusions about where the real power resides. A special law declares that the Benefactor is entitled to the same privileges as the nominal president, but aside from this act dealing with protocol details, there is no other description of "the Chief's" role as "super-president" either in the laws of the country or in the constitution. For all purposes, however, Trujillo is recognized even by foreign governments as the actual head of the state, a fact of which international organizations take cognizance. Cabinet members, and other high officials, when appointed to office address their thanks not to Héctor but to Rafael. In his own speeches the Generalissimo takes credit for all things done since 1930, despite the fact there have been periods when he has been technically out of office.

Thirty-one articles of the constitution elaborate in a detailed manner the rights and duties of the legislative power. There is a two-chambered Congress, elected by popular suffrage for five-year terms. Although an avowed rubber-stamp body, whose members are all picked followers of the Benefactor—elected either in the single-ticket of the only existing party or by the vote of their congressmen on the floor of each chamber—the Dominican Congress has a record number of meetings, not exceeded by any other popular assembly in the globe. It never recesses in the whole year and when a session is about to end it is either prolonged by Congress itself or by a presidential decree it convenes for a special session. As a result, there is probably no other Congress that legislates so profusely as the *trujillista* one. Dominican legislation is casuistic to the greatest possible degree. Trujillo send bills to Congress to accommodate the law of the land to his passing caprices. So, when in 1935 he wanted to divorce wife number two (Mrs. Bienvenida Ricardo) to marry wife number three, Trujillo sent a message to Congress which promptly passed a law providing that a married couple may be divorced, by the unilateral will of one of the partners, after five years of childless marriage. Later when he wanted to disavow and disinherit his daughter Flor de Oro, Congress passed a law making it possible for a father to do such a thing. Other examples of this type of legislation are the law making it a crime to resign a government post while its holder is on foreign soil; the law giving equal rights to children born out of wedlock (which benefits the large Trujillo flock); and a host of tax exemptions and other financial provisions passed to meet *trujillista* needs by simple changes of legal arrangements.

Almost everything can be made legal in the country. Lacking the balance provided by opposition groups, the main function of the legislative power is to give speedy sanctions to the policies laid down by the executive. The chambers display exemplary dispatch in the approval of laws presented by the President and it is not uncommon for a bill declared "urgent" to be given two readings by both houses and passed—all in one day. For two years I was a member of Congress and throughout that period I do not recall a single argument over the passage of a bill. The few occasions in which bills were introduced directly from the floor (and I had to do it twice) were upon direct orders from the Generalissimo, who would pick a legislator for that purpose.

Although members of congress are supposedly elected by direct vote, actually they do not represent their constituents. They are chosen entirely from above in accordance with standards determined by Trujillo himself, which are very fluid and vary with individual cases. An able pimp, a crooked lawyer or a paid thug has as much a right to sit in Congress, in Trujillo's opinion, as an honorable merchant, farmer or professional. All of them, accordingly, mix freely in the chambers of the Senate and the House of Representatives. The head of the political parties—and since there is just one in the Dominican Republic, Trujillo himself—has exclusive power to appoint new congressmen as vacancies occur, a thing bound to occur frequently because every legislator (as well as any other elected official) must sign his resignation before taking the oath of office.

Congress, it must be noted, is the only body empowered by the Constitution to declare war on a foreign power. This has been done only once during the *Era of Trujillo*—in 1941 when the Dominican Republic took the Free World's side in the war against Fascism and Nazism. Credit for doing this has been shamelessly taken away from Congress by Trujillo. He even asked and was granted upon one occasion, in December 1949, the authorization, obviously unconstitutional, to declare war against any nation harboring enemies of the regime.

Several articles of the Constitution deal with the legal system. There are courts in the Dominican Republic and even a Supreme Court. Justice, however, is corrupt. Judges have no independence and are so accustomed to take their cue from government officials, even in cases in no way connected with politics, that the situation became a matter of growing concern even to Trujillo himself. The racket of selling court decisions (a privilege not of the judges themselves but of certain members of the Trujillo family, as well as a handful of their henchmen) grew to such scandalous proportions and the majesty of justice sunk to such low depths that in 1956 Trujillo felt compelled to send a bill to Congress making any attempt by a

Government official to influence the course of legal procedures a punishable offense.

On the whole Trujillo's structure of power is tyrannical and arbitrary; but it is also fluid and adaptable. Its main characteristic—one that is apparent in almost all modern "popular democracies"—is a fake reliance on popular approval; force is disguised by forms of law or justice.

EDUCATION OF A DICTATOR

1. GENERALISSIMO RAFAEL L. TRUJILLO'S STORY HAS BEEN rewritten so many times by his biographers in the Dominican National Palace with such notable changes, bold omissions and emendations that the Dominican Republic now possesses a new, fully slanted history. The technique—popularized in fiction by George Orwell—has proved greatly successful for Trujillo. As a result, in the Dominican Republic the color black is not necessarily black nor is white white—the color depends entirely on how the Generalissimo sees it.

Rafael Leonidas Trujillo Molina, fourth of a family of eleven children (ten are still alive), was born in San Cristobal, Dominican Republic, October 24, 1891. The place where Trujillo saw the light of day for the first time was a poverty-ridden, sleepy, agricultural village on the southern coast. Trujillo's family, like practically every other family in that backward community, was struggling to make ends meet. His father, humble, amiable José Trujillo Valdez, better known as *Pepito,* was a nonentity.

Pepito never rose by himself above the level of a minor postal clerk in his home-town, whose salary, when not in arrears, was substandard. With so many mouths to feed it is not strange that the Trujillo children walked shoeless during their early days. It is not improbable that as a side-line the *pater familias* and his elder children resorted occasionally to cattle rustling.

Rather than seeing advantage in their hero's humble beginnings, rather than exploiting the cruel but nevertheless honorable handicap of poverty, Trujillo's biographers have drawn a screen over these early days. The published facts dealing with this period are sparse indeed. It is officially said that he was taught to read and write by his maternal grandmother, Erciná Chevalier, described by one of the chroniclers as a "woman of great charm and culture." It is also said that Rafael attended grammar school, and that he suffered an attack of diphtheria.

Dr. Jesús de Galíndez, the Basque scholar whose disappearance has been generally attributed to his research into the Trujillo regime, left behind an exhaustive, soundly documented history of the Generalissimo entitled *The Era of Trujillo*. But even a trained historian like Galíndez met with little success in his search for facts about Trujillo's early life. "Published references to his (Trujillo's) childhood and adolescence are vague and at times contradictory," wrote Galíndez. "It seems that his first employment came to him at the age of sixteen when he became a telegraph operator."

Here again we find a curious reluctance for a sympathetic exploitation of Trujillo's underprivileged youth. "The Big One" could have easily been described as a Dominican Thomas Alva Edison. This reluctance is partly explained only by the fact that Trujillo's home was not only poor but unhappy. Lacking proper guidance and care, the children grew up without much respect for law and property. Intent on feeding the increasing family with the meager means at hand neither José Trujillo Valdez nor his benevolent, godfearing wife, Julia Molina, could instill much Christianity as a way of life upon their tattered household.

My research for data concerning Trujillo's boyhood has been as disappointingly unsuccessful as that of Dr. de Galíndez. I am familiar with an account saying that "the Chief's" formal education was acquired at Pablo Barina's grammar school in San Cristobal. I also know that as the principal and only teacher of the village's only school, Señor Barines had his hands full and was barely able to keep a watchful eye on every child put under his custody. Discipline was hard to maintain in the loose establishment and truancy was rampant. No wonder it is impossible to find documentation that Trujillo rose higher than the fourth grade.

But if the children did not learn much at school, the dusty streets which separated in those days the monotonous rows of San Cristobal's shacks provided them with an excellent schooling in lawlessness. To survive the rowdyism of the neighborhood's kids, a boy had to be tougher than the others. Or, at least, as in Trujillo's case he had to belong to a large, clannish family. In frequent street brawls the solid front of the Trujillo boys proved good enough to lick all opposition, a fact they never forgot later in life. From such an environment Rafael emerged as a resourceful, headstrong character. "As a boy Trujillo was always in trouble" recalls one of his neighbors. "Always trying to cheat someone, always bragging about how he would one day make big money without much effort."

Trujillo quickly earned himself a nickname. He was called *Chapita*. For some unknown reason Trujillo never liked his nickname. No one knows for certain how he acquired it, but the fact that he strongly resented it might be the cause for a number of unsavory versions about its origin. In Spanish the word *chapita* means a small metal token or medal, but by a rather slangy extension it also means "bottle cap." People who knew "the Chief" in those days assert that he developed an early passion for hoarding caps of soda pop and beer bottles, as well as other little trinkets. Upon discovering this hobby, it is said, other children began calling him *Chapita*. Trujillo's detractors argue that the passion itself was not responsible for the nickname, but the fact that Rafael was not too particular about the means by which he acquired his trifles. In support of their contention they note that collecting caps was a widespread hobby of children in those days. Somehow the nickname was eventually eliminated as result of one of Trujillo's earliest biographical rewrites. To accomplish this, however, he had to banish the word from the language. Many people who stubbornly disregarded the prohibition paid dearly for their daring. Though successful in suppressing the word, the Generalissimo has failed to abolish its meaning. The natural and probably innocent boyhood passion for collecting meaningless trifles remains with him to this day although considerably changed in scope. In his maturity Trupillo collects medals and decorations, of which he possesses more than fifty.

The diphtheria attack has received a curious interpretation in the official annals. Trujillo's recovery from this illness is explained as a Divine Manifestation. Dominican children are instructed in their class rooms that God reached down and saved the suffering Rafael so that he might one day lead the "Fatherland" forward to its present glorious state.

Apart from these bare facts, a thick blanket is thrown over Trujillo's early years by his apologists. A brief tear is shed for his youth, however. "Both his environment and the times curtailed his early formal education," writes one of the official biographers. He also states that "the same set of circumstances soon set him (Trujillo) to earning his own livelihood, and it was then that, under the guidance of his uncle, Don Plinio Pina Chevalier, he started as a telegraph operator."

There was a time in Trujillo's early life when he did some honest work. The guiding uncles (there were two) who provided him with the means of earning his daily bread at such an early age were Julia Molina's half brothers, Teodulo and Plinio Pina Chevalier. From the outset both men exerted a large influence in shaping their nephew's life and character.

Plinio, a quiet, soft-spoken, short man of no small personal charm and intelligence, was for years one of Rafael's most trusted advisers. After Trujillo became President, Plinio came to live in the United States, accredited as a Counselor to the Dominican Embassy in Washington. However, he spent most of his time in New York City, where during a long period he acted as a sort of personal representative of Trujillo in political and business fields. Shielded by his diplomatic immunity Plinio had his fingers in many international political pies and his New York City apartment was a hotbed of high political intrigue. He died in New York late in 1956 and his body was returned to the Dominican Republic where upon Trujillo's orders an elaborate official funeral was held. One of Ciudad Trujillo's streets has been named after him.

The other uncle, Teodulo, dedicated himself to domestic politics as well as the sensuous pleasures of life. A colorful character with a real zest for life, for food and for alcohol. In his youth he had sported a flair for writing poetry and prose which made him the only "intellectual" in the Family. He finally drank himself out of existence.

A highly voluble extrovert who easily made friends and connections even in stations higher than his own, Teodulo was instrumental in finding Rafael a place in the Dominican scheme of things. For this, when the time came, he was rewarded by his nephew with wealth and high office. Teodulo's antics, however, soon proved to be a liability, and his advice was sought less and less until he stopped playing any active role in Dominican politics. He died in a sort of mild disgrace. Late in life he found, according to one of the unfriendly biographers (an assertion born out by fact), pleasure in the exhibition of pornographic motion pictures and in the erotic chasing of beautiful *señoritas*. "There were those who fled the now rotund, flabby Uncle Teodulo, to refuge in foreign legations," adds the same source.

A further search for the truth concerning the early period of Trujillo's life shows that another of the fact-twisting "rewrite" men on the National Palace staff points out that the need to earn a livelihood led Trujillo into "other avenues." The careless euphemism calls for some elaboration. Distasteful as it is, to do so I have to resort now to facts in the wide literature on Trujillo that is the property of his detractors. To some degree, both the sources and the information need a careful weeding out.

There is available, however, still another piece of friendly evidence bearing on Trujillo's youth. While in his middle twenties he was hired as a policeman by one of the sugar companies then operating in the country. In the interim he had taken as his wife in a Catholic Church ceremony one Aminta Ledesma. Aminta's name would have been erased from *trujillista* history books by now had not she borne Trujillo a fabulous daughter named *Flor de Oro* (Flower of Gold). The image of her sire, Miss Trujillo has earned some measure of international recognition, independent of her father's name, for running the matrimonial scale as if it were an exercise in velocity. Married seven times, Flor de Oro counts among her conquests the international lover Porfirio Rubirosa.

According to official biographer Gilberto Sánchez Lustrino, the "Central Boca Chica" (a sugar mill Trujillo now owns) employed Rafael as *Jefe de Orden* or chief of the company's private police. However, an official memorandum admitting Trujillo to the Constabulary gives as his occupation at the sugar mill that of *guarda campestre* (forester). Anyway, whatever his title, the job was that of an informer or, as another biographer has dressed it up, "in charge of security arrangements." Trujillo's duty was to reveal labor discontent and to help stifle it. The ways and means of discharging his duties were left to his own invention and soon he was congratulated for a job well done. Sanchez Lustrino tells us that the future Generalissimo's "strength of character" as well as other qualities won him a commendation by the mill management. Considering that the rope was the favorite method of settling labor disputes in the sugar properties, it is not risky to assert that in Boca Chica, Trujillo received his elementary education in strongarm tactics.

None of the friendly biographers, however, gives an account of how Trujillo happened to lose a job for which he was so well fitted. Albert C. Hicks, an American journalist and author of a book on Trujillo entitled *Blood in the Streets,* reveals that Rafael's travels along "other avenues" were started around that time and that while controlling others he could not restrain himself, finally running afoul of justice.

Hick's impartiality of judgment has been lately recognized by Trujillo, who hired his biographer for an investigation of the Galíndez' case on the basis, as printed in American newspapers, of his alleged knowledge of the Dominican situation. However, if Trujillo went to jail, as Hicks asserts, it was for something not connected with his job, since in later days there has been produced the photostat of a letter of recommendation, addressed to the American military authorities, in which the manager of the Central Boca Chica, Antonio Trigo, praises his former employee.

Nevertheless, it is necessary to state that in those days jobs were not too plentiful in the Dominican Republic and, where they existed at all, they brought a pittance. So, it is not strange that a gifted man like Trujillo would try to figure out easier ways to make a buck than working sixteen hours a day at a sugar mill. There were seemingly limitless opportunities in the field of forgery, cattle rustling and informing. The oldest profession as well provided almost princely positions to those willing to pimp a little. People who knew our man in those days claim that Trujillo proved to have little moral hesitation to work in any and all of these markets.

Hicks, who interviewed many people regarding Trujillo's background, asserts that once when Rafael "got wind of three newly arrived and highly valued English imported saddles at the San Cristobal Agricultural Experiment Station (where he was a trainee) he stole them and later got caught with the goods." If this is true, there is no proof he was taken to court.

2.

2.   AFTER TRUJILLO BECAME A SOLDIER IN THE SERVICE OF
a foreign military force, we can easily trace his sudden rise to power. It
is an almost incredible story with much that is comic and much that is
tragic, but the tone never drops from the melodramatic.

What, for example, is more theatrical than the thunderous arrival of the
United States Marine Corps? The year is 1916, and we find the leather-
necks not in the Halls of Montezuma but on the beaches of the Dominican
Republic. Their avowed mission is to "maintain domestic tranquillity," to
make the country safe for foreign investors, and supposedly to teach
Dominicans how to handle their own financial matters.

There is not much evidence that they accomplished all these aims. But
there is no doubt that they performed an unforeseen feat: the launching of
Trujillo's successful career. The architect of the Dominican Republic's
future seemingly had a very gloomy future himself up to the moment of
United States intervention in his country. Whatever the juggling of the
historical facts by his Academy of History no one can find reasonable evidence to refute the percipient Galíndez statement: "It was the landing of
the American Marines which brought him (Trujillo) his opportunity to
rise from obscurity." The American columnist Murray Kempton, of the
New York Post, subscribes to the same theory. Says he: "It is odd to think
that the legend of this national hero began with his entreaty to serve a foreign force in his own country." In the Dominican Republic itself it is
common belief that without the American occupation Trujillo would have
sunk into oblivion as a minor underworld figure.

The supporters of the latter contention stress the fact that at the time
when the Marines started to organize the *Policía Nacional Dominicana* or
National Constabulary, Trujillo was suffering from either one of two calamities. If he was not actually in jail, he was out of a job.

Albert Hicks asserts that, with the Marines already in Santo Domingo,
Trujillo tried his hand at forgery, and was sentenced to a short term in
jail. To corroborate this charge I have found nothing but hearsay, although
the American writer Ernest Gruening, a man of experience in Caribbean
affairs, confirmed the story in an article written for the *Nation.* Said he:
"In his early days young Trujillo ran afoul of the law on more than one
occasion. He was tried and convicted of theft, sentenced to and served a
term in jail. He was convicted and served another term for forgery. For
still other offenses his arrest was sought but managed to escape punishment by temporary flight from the country."

The lack of documentary evidence is not strange. Trujillo has had years to clothe his origins in mystery, and as the sole custodian of all the records in the Dominican Republic, he has been able to conceal his early life pretty much as he pleases. People remember the strange fire that in 1927 destroyed the Supreme Court building, where all criminal records were kept at the time.

A few solid facts about this period can be ascertained. Unquestionably one of Trujillo's uncles was once more in a position to help. Teodulo had developed a close friendship with an American customs receivership officer named James J. McLean. Initiated during night-long drinking sessions at an isolated Customs house along the Haitian border, the acquaintance-ship evolved into a full literary partnership, with both men writing in collaboration a leaflet on the Haitian-Dominican frontier entitled *Datos Históricos sobre la Frontera Dominicano-Haitiana*. People who knew them both say that McLean was absolutely charmed by Teodulo's conversation. Thus, when shortly after their arrival the Marines appointed McLean a major in the Dominican Constabulary, the Family tried to take advantage of their contacts with the former customs official. While searching for a suitable job Rafael asked his uncle to put in a good word for him with the major, which Teodulo did.

"It was shortly after being released from jail that he (Trujillo) met Colonel McClean (sic) through his Uncle Teodulo," narrates Hicks. He adds that McLean "when sufficiently sober, found a profound satisfaction in the company of harlots. Rafael, immediately recognizing a job he could fill, played the pimp to the chief of the constabulary."

Whatever its immediate consequences the moment of introduction between Trujillo and McLean, as accomplished by Teodulo, proved to be a turning-point in Dominican history. At first Trujillo was at the service of McLean, but once connected with the occupation forces he made himself equally useful to other American officers. For his willingness to please, the Marines' command considered Rafael good material and soon he was to climb up the military ladder. He was assigned to serve as a guide and informer to the Marines' forces operating in the eastern part of the country, a region he was familiar with since the days when he worked for the Central Boca Chica.

Someone who remembers well that epoch—a person whose name I cannot reveal because he still lives in Santo Domingo—assured me that Trujillo served under Captain Merckle, a man whose name has become infamous in Dominican history, if not in the annals of the U.S. Marines Corps. Trujillo took naturally to his role as informer. It was in his blood since his paternal grandfather, Jose Trujillo Monagas, had discharged much the same duties for the Spanish police in Cuba.

There are several accounts of Captain Merckle's depredations against Dominican nationals written by Americans and also a set of official documents pertaining to a U.S. Senate investigation. Benjamin Sumner Welles, distinguished American diplomat who wrote *Naboth's Vineyard,* has this to say: "While it is therefore difficult to reach any definite conclusion as to the actual extent and number of the more flagrant outrages perpetrated, it is a fact that a policy of repression was carried out by the Forces of Occupation over a protracted period in the eastern Provinces of the Dominican Republic which was inherently unwise, which reacted primarily upon peaceful civilians, and as the result of which many atrocities were undoubtedly committed."

Another competent observer, the historian and economist Melvin M. Knight, says in *Americans in Santo Domingo:* "A number of Dominicans —we may be certain that nobody knows exactly how many—were put to death off-hand by the Marines. And some were tortured without ever having their day in court at all."

In fairness, however, it must be said that Captain Merckle's end was appropriate to his corrupt practice. "The assassinations by Captain Merckle were repudiated by his superiors and he committed suicide while awaiting for trial," asserts Knight. Knight's version is supported by Sumner Welles in his aforementioned book. Nevertheless if Merckle himself paid dearly for his cruelty and sadism, his methods, unfortunately, did not disappear with him. In young Trujillo he left behind a keen, proficient disciple who has carried on the sadistic tradition long after his teacher's name is no longer remembered.

There can be no question that the participation of Trujillo in Merckle's acts of terror was a major contribution to the formation of his character. While serving as a guide and mastering the content of his military manual, the would-be Benefactor was also assimilating his first lessons in dictatorship. He learned that military rule cannot bear criticism and how to deal with offenses against authority. Moreover, the late Captain's forms of torture and arbitrary "justice" have been perfected by "the Chief" and used on a larger, more terrifying scale.

With Merckle's suicide, Trujillo's period of irregular service ended. The Marines were then organizing a permanent Dominican Constabulary force in preparation for the eventual end of the Military Government. Trujillo applied for enrollment and was accepted. In December 1918 Trujillo received word that he was going to be appointed a commissioned officer and on January 11, 1919, according to his official military biographer Lieutenant Ernesto Vega y Pagan, "Colonel C. F. Williams, Commandant of the Constabulary Guard, sent Lieutenant Trujillo his appointment and oath." Once again Trujillo's guardian was Major McLean. He was in charge of processing the application and no objections were recorded.

How much gratitude Trujillo felt for McLean is illustrated by the following. Eventually, drunkeness caught up with the Major and he was dishonorably discharged from the service. Relieved of his military responsibilities, McLean stayed on in the Dominican Republic. He was still around in the sugar mill district long after the withdrawal of the Marines in 1924. This was a slight miscalculation for which the former Major was bound to pay with his own life. "The Colonel [sic] who knew more intimate secrets about the rapidly rising Rafael than probably any one man, was murdered in Barahona province," asserts Albert Hicks.

At this point impartial observers express amazement that a man with supposedly such a besmirched reputation as Trujillo's could so easily join and stay in the National Constabulary. Many feel inclined to give "the Big One" the benefit of the doubt. However, acceptance of Trujillo by the Marines can hardly be interpreted as a clean bill of health. First, past services entitled him to a certain measure of gratitude. Second, due to the fact that the right kind of people were showing no eagerness to enroll, the Marines were facing rather a tough time in the formation of the Constabulary cadres. As a matter of fact, according to people in the know, almost the only question asked of an aspirant was whether he could read and write. Sumner Welles writes that "while no great difficulty was encountered in recruiting the number of privates required, it was found almost impossible, from the outset, to persuade Dominicans of the necessary education and standing in the community to serve as officers in this force under the Military Government." It might be said, therefore, that the blame for letting disreputable people into the Army falls on the Dominicans themselves. Who else but such characters would like to serve in a force known as an instrument of oppression in the service of a foreign government?

From August 15 to December 21, 1921, Trujillo received all his formal military education at an "Academy" established in Haina, near the capital, by the Marines in order to train officers of the future Dominican Army. "On December 22, 1921, Second Lieutenant Trujillo left the Haina Military Academy after a brilliant period of training. His rank of Second Lieutenant was confirmed," writes the official military biographer.

During the time elapsed since his enrollment Trujillo had acquired a new protector to replace McLean whose drinking habits made his future uncertain even in such an outfit as the Constabulary. This time Trujillo's promoter was a professional Marine officer, one Thomas E. Watson, then serving in the constabulary with the rank of Lieutenant Colonel. The friendship, which proved everlasting, was very profitable for Trujillo then and in the years to follow. Watson rose in rank and influence within the American military circles; at the time of his retirement after World War II he was a Lieutenant General.

Prior to "graduation"—on January 12, 1921—Trujillo saw combat service against the *gavilleros* or "bandits"—the name then given to resistant groups of Dominican patriots—in the eastern part of the country.

He participated in a military engagement at *La Noria* and his deportment under fire obviously pleased his commanding officer. "His conduct prior and during the engagement was excellent," reads the Marine report.

Although he had been reprimanded on September 4, 1920, for slowness in reporting escape of a civil prisoner, his service aptitudes were considered "excellent." Also "excellent" was his interest in and vocation for his career. His personal characteristics were described as "calm, even-tempered, forceful, active, bold and painstaking." He was also labeled as a man of "initiative, intelligence and good judgment." This efficiency report bears the signature of T. E. Watson, Major.

Due to the glaring fact that his heroic deed at *La Noria* was committed against Trujillo's own countrymen, this glowing commendation has become the source of sharp official embarrassment in ensuing years. Finally, the citation, like the childhood nickname before, has been removed from the Dominican school texts. *La Noria* is not even recalled in the law which awarded Trujillo in 1955 the made-to-order "Captain General Santana" decoration for bravery. Stripped of the only citation for conduct under fire to his credit, this distinctive military order might as well have been awarded to Trujillo for catching butterflies. To obviate the point, the legislation bestowing the medal clothed as acts of bravery otherwise meaningless and quite innocuous incidents (sometimes of a political nature) of "the Big One's" life. The *La Noria* engagement is today a closely guarded skeleton in Trujillo's closet—surely the most crowded closet in the Hemisphere.

During the remaining years of American military occupation Trujillo acquired, if we are to believe his military biographer, a reputation as a trouble shooter. According to Vega Pagan, when our hero was Commanding Officer of the Sixth Company in San Francisco de Macoris in 1922, "there was a border incident in the northern sector of the country. Part of our armed forces, under the command of Captain Trujillo, was mobilized to that place in order to reestablish peace and order." Then, less than a year later, he was hurried to Barahona. "This was due to the fact," asserts Vega, "that a group of outlaws were disturbing the peace in Enriquillo." As an afterthought the biographer makes a remarkably pointed observation: "The situation was similar to that which had occurred before in the eastern sector of the country."

After the Marines left, Trujillo rapidly rose in rank and reputation within the *Policía Nacional Dominicana*. Between the years 1924 and 1926 he rose from Captain to Lieutenant Colonel. His promotion to Major is marked by a strange story of violence. A certain Major César Lora was a step ahead of Captain Trujillo, both in rank and seniority. This meant that as long as Major Lora was in the Army Trujillo would be forced to trail him. An enormous inconvenience for Trujillo, particularly since Major Lora was young and ambitious as well.

Soon, however, Major Lora's amorous antics provided Trujillo with the awaited opportunity to get his rival out of the way. Hearing that the Major was carrying on an illicit love affair with an Army dentist's wife, Trujillo subtly revealed to the scorned husband—out of pure friendship, of course—not only his wife's infidelity but also the meeting-place of the clandestine lovers. One day, Lieutenant Sanabia, the outraged husband, shot to death both Major Lora and Mrs. Sanabia. That day he unwittingly paved the way for the fulfillment of Trujillo's ambitions. "The Chief's" rivals, thereafter, were only old and bungling bureaucrats whom he could easily calumniate, blackmail and frame-up. Biographer Sánchez Lustrino wrote this appropriate epitaph for the murdered officer: "On February 23 Major Lora was killed and that marks the beginning of Trujillo's brilliant military career . . ."

Promoted to a position of responsibility as military commander of the Northern Department, comprising the northern half of the country, Major Trujillo further distinguished himself as an able administrator and a clever schemer. He soon caught the eye of the aging President, General Horacio Vásquez, and thereafter his career rolled along by itself.

By exposing the shortcomings of his superiors, Trujillo rose to the highest military command. By 1928 he had elbowed his way to the post of Chief of Staff of the newly renamed "National Army." He was now a brigadier general and a feared and trusted aide of President Vásquez. Says Nanita: "Trujillo was already the most powerful man in the country. Holding in his hands control over the armed forces, he also controlled everything else." Moreover, ambition had already set upon the hitherto obscure character, who was now ready to set off for higher worlds to conquer.

As trained by the American Marines the Army was meant to be a non-political force. After becoming its chief, Trujillo turned it into an instrument of personal power. Through adroit manipulation of officers' promotions, the General further stripped its rosters of all unreliable elements, meaning those who showed no willingness to conform.

It is true that Trujillo enforced rigid discipline within the military compounds. Besides he did not tolerate the slightest vacillation in the personal loyalty he expected from his men. As long as they showed unwavering loyalty toward him, Trujillo guaranteed his faithful officers security and protection, even against criminal prosecution. The case of Major Ernesto Pérez illustrates this point. Arraigned on charges of raping and kidnapping a young society girl from the town of Montecristi, the Major found refuge in Trujillo's own headquarters. Disobeying a Presidential decree sacking Pérez, the General kept his ousted subordinate out of the reach of ordinary justice at the Ozama fortress. Eventually, the change of regime saved Major Pérez from facing trial and today he is a retired Brigadier General and wealthy businessman.

Nonetheless Trujillo was making his mark as a rigid disciplinarian who brooked no nonsense. Blind obedience to his commands and an unrestricted cult of his personality were the main props of Trujillo's sway over the Army. The extent to which the cult of Trujillo's personality had already infiltrated the Army is demonstrated by a seemingly minor incident in the small town of San Francisco de Macoris. Lieutenant Rafael Espaillat with his commanding general's approval named a little open space in front of the city's fort "Trujillo Square." Espaillat, a man who certainly got wind early of his boss's developing megalomania, rose to be a Major General. Retired from the armed forces, he now warms a chair in Congress.

With Trujillo's elevation to the post of head of the Army the American dream of creating a "non-partisan" force had all but backfired, but this neither President Vásquez nor his civilian head of the Army the Secretary of National Defense seemed to realize. If they did, they kept their thoughts to themselves. Complacency over Trujillo's antics reached a high point when the Government granted—upon request by a group of Army officers —the public awarding to Trujillo of a special medal of honor on the occasion of completing his first ten years of service. The President made himself available to present the medal at a parade January 17, 1929.

The chicken hatched during the American military occupation days was coming to roost. As Ernest Gruening put it, elaborating in terms of the Dominican national pastime, "the chicken had turned out to be a fighting cock, equipped with the long, sharp spurs that kill."

3.

AS CHIEF OF STAFF OF THE ARMY, BRIGADIER GENERAL Rafael L. Trujillo had climbed in 1928 to the summit of military life in the Dominican Republic.

It was a far cry from the squalid surroundings of his childhood. He had not only become a general, but a rich man too. However, Trujillo was not satisfied with his position in life. The journey from his childhood surroundings was far from completed. President Vásquez, growing ineffectual after more than thirty years in politics, was now little more than a figurehead of a confused, decentralized administration. There were, therefore, higher plateaus to scale, and politics as well as society were bigger games for an ambitious young man. With the sweet smell of recent success in his nostrils, Trujillo's hand at first stealthily reached into the field of society.

As Chief of the Army the General now came frequently in contact with the most elevated spheres of the Dominican social and political world. However, it was implicit from the outset that "the Chief's" presence in these refined areas was simply out of regard to his rank. Dominican society was not willing to give him full recognition—it was the military dress which was accepted, not the man wearing it.

To the more discriminating figures in the capital the General was still *Chapita.* This fact came into the open when Trujillo forced a showdown with his application for membership in the old, exclusive *Club Unión,* then the center of Dominican social life. As would be expected, "the Chief's" application was rejected almost unanimously. However, on that occasion the aristocrats underrated the power of Trujillo's ambition and pride.

If Trujillo was rankled by this social setback he did not brood over it. He conducted a tactical retreat but was more than ever determined to bull his way into the select circle. To force his acceptance he resorted to his military talents. He mapped a campaign to outflank the aristocratic camp. He sought to rally with the help of an effective though time-worn device and his frustrated ambitions were soon focused on the virginal form of a young lady of social standing but no wealth named Bienvenida Ricardo. The good-looking General started courting proud but poor Miss Ricardo. Overwhelmed with costly presents she finally started looking in his direction. The promise of an early marriage won her. Before complete surrender could be accomplished there was, however, one more obstacle to surmount: the prospective groom was himself a married man.

Trujillo's first wife, the humble and colorless Aminta Ledesma, made things simple. She gave the General an uncontested divorce, henceforth suffering absolute banishment.[1]

Once Aminta was out of the way, Trujillo made Miss Ricardo his second wife. A religious wedding had to be ruled out since he had married the first time according to the Catholic rites, but the civil ceremony was performed with the pomp and style becoming people of high station. The aristocrats, however, refrained from attendance.

Notwithstanding the rebuff, Trujillo felt himself in a position to launch a new assault upon the *Club Unión.* Again fortune refused to be at his side and the early skirmishes forecast defeat. However, with Bienvenida's name as a persuader and with the help of dissension within the hostile ranks of the aristocracy, Trujillo's longing for social success was finally crowned with victory. Invaluable was the assistance of the influential lawyer Dr. Jacinto B. Peynado, a newly acquired friend, who used his powers to push the General's name through.

Peynado, though a very prominent practitioner of his profession, had no wealth and a large family to feed. Shortly before his open sponsorship of Trujillo's application became known, people heard that the General had retained him for a considerable fee. Thus started a mutually reward-

---

[1] Though the first Mrs. Trujillo still lives in the Dominican capital in the company of her daughter Flor de Oro, few people in the country are aware of her existence.

ing association, one of the few lasting friendships between Trujillo and a collaborator. Prior to his death in 1940, Peynado held the post of puppet President of the Dominican Republic for two years (1938–1940).

Although eventually admitted into the highest social circle, Trujillo did not forgive the resistance put up by the élite. Despite his marked desire to be acknowledged a born aristocrat, the Benefactor has displayed since that time an almost fanatic bitterness toward the members of the old social families, whom he has humiliated in every conceivable manner. He decided to destroy the *Club Unión* but not without first forcing abasement upon its members. Upon seizing power in 1930 one of Trujillo's first acts was to sponsor membership applications by all his Army officers stationed at the capital. Needless to say, all passed. Then Trujillo had himself elected to the club's presidency. But he did not feel that the old score was yet paid off, so as a further humiliation he forced the dissolution of the highly respected organization. Then the secret police politely advised the proud aristocrats that they should found a new club to take the place of their esteemed institution—its name to be the *Club Presidente Trujillo*.

This was promptly done and the board of directors of the new club was studded with names belonging to the loftiest Dominican families. It was a bitter lesson for the Dominican élite, but its members were to know greater bitterness as the years passed and "the Chief" expanded his powers. "The day we blackballed Trujillo," said one of the men who did it, "we destroyed the *Club Unión* as surely as if we had set fire to its building." We also destroyed our own class, he might have added; they had certainly showed more taste than prudence in their opposition to "the Chief." As a result, there are to this day retaliations carried out against the surviving members of the old aristocracy.

After subduing the Dominican Four Hundred, Trujillo revealed that he was personally more aristocratic than all of them. To give this newly unearthed fact the fullest possible circulation, "the Chief" turned to his writers. They announced that the General had noble blood in his veins. On his paternal side, it was discovered, Trujillo was a descendant of the purest Spanish nobility. His maternal blood was of equal, if not a more imposing, strain. Julia Molina, his mother, was a direct descendant of a Napoleonic courtier—Joseph Chevalier, Marquis of Philborou.

Yet, before accomplishing such a triumphant vindication, "the Chief" had to surmount a few stumbling blocks. Early in 1929 his military career came close to a severe setback. A group of American financial experts, headed by former U.S. Vice President Charles Dawes, while conducting a survey of the Dominican Government's administrative methods, discovered some irregularities in the Army. The true nature of the discovery was never made public, but some people assert that what was found was nothing less than a $500,000 deficit in the Army's expenditures. Other say that because of the exaggerated expenditures and rampant graft under Trujillo's administration the Commission suggested an Army clean-up.

Although no direct charges appeared in the commission's final report, the fact is that the greatest emphasis was put upon urging a reduction of the country's military budget. Faced with the worst crisis of his career General Trujillo decided to take the bull by the horns. He set off a wave of reprisals against those who had cooperated with the Commission in its efforts to dig out the facts. Captain Eduardo Baez and other officers fled the country to avoid the vindictiveness of their commanding general. Trujillo followed through with a bolder maneuver. Within hours of the discovery he was engaged in an astounding piece of political blackmail. With the help of Army spies and informers (of whom there were plenty at Trujillo's command in those days), he spread the rumor that in his possession there was evidence pertaining to grave irregularities in several other Government departments. He also let it be known that he was fully prepared to make them public should charges against him be pressed.

Whether or not Trujillo's maneuver was a desperate bluff is anyone's guess, since no one dared to call it. As Trujillo had calculated, the Administration, then faced with a violent opposition campaign conducted through the free press, could in no way afford a dangerous controversy within its own ranks. All talk of taking action against Trujillo was promptly dropped.

On the other hand, to pacify the opposition—which was in a position to use the story without fear of retaliatory exposes—Trujillo initiated a series of political contacts with its leaders, laying the groundwork for the successful uprising that brought the Vásquez regime down.

Trujillo's "Minitrue" has since conveniently dressed up for posterity the Dawes Commission incident. It was just much ado about nothing. It happened that confronted with conflicting views on how to cut the Army's budget, the General submitted a magnificent plan allowing a fair curtailment of certain expenditures without sacrificing the "system of organization" prevailing in the armed forces. Trujillo's plan brought a telegram from President Vásquez, then vacationing at San José de las Matas, expressing approval "without reservation."

The re-write staff brushed aside, without even a passing reference to refute it, the much-talked-about subject at the time of the rackets unearthed to Trujillo's discomfiture. Among the things then discovered was that Army laundry was being handled in the establishment owned by Trujillo's present wife and then his mistress. The rates charged were exorbitant. Of the $16 paid to the soldiers each month, it was estimated that from $8 to $10 went to laundry bills. Soldiers with courage to protest were sent to the guard-house or simply disappeared. Furthermore, the army rolls contained many straw men who received full pay but never shouldered a rifle.

Defense through blackmail proved almost fatal to Trujillo. Right after his defiant campaign of rumors, the General went through what was probably the most critical period of his career. His aggressive attitude had brought upon him the hatred of powerful men and there was a group within the Administration ready to take advantage of the earliest set of favorable circumstances to trip up the rising General. Confronted with his enemies' desire to stop him, Trujillo knew that time was running short. As a desperate gamble, "the Chief" thought of throwing his hat into the ring of political rough-and-tumble. In a roundabout way, by the honesty of its investigation, the Dawes Commission unwittingly set the General upon a new course of action.

First thing to decide was which way to address his efforts. The choice did not prove difficult. The already antagonized Government élite would have nothing to do with him. They were already in power and there was little he could offer them.

For their part, the opposition leaders though desperately in need of help were not receptive at the outset. Nor were they willing to give recognition to a newcomer without prestige or background, especially at a moment when mounting popular dissatisfaction with President Vásquez aroused great expectations. Government prestige was at a low ebb, since Vásquez had just announced the unpopular decision of accepting nomination for another four-year period starting in 1930.

Notwithstanding that his initial secret overtures to the opposition had convinced Trujillo that his name meant nothing outside the Army circles, his position, though difficult, was not hopeless. In any Latin American country, whenever there is a showdown between the Government and a disarmed opposition, it is the Army which holds the balance of power— and Trujillo was the Army.

To exploit possibilities to the limit and to further his own political ambitions, the General decided to play both ends against the middle. From the beginning, Trujillo's dealings in politics were marked by double-crossing and sharp deals. To begin with, while swearing steadfast loyalty to Vásquez he was dealing with the opposition behind closed doors. Through trusted go-betweens he soon advised the opposition that short of open armed revolt it could count on Trujillo's sympathy. And even armed revolt was open for consideration, provided he was duly taken into account.

At the end of 1929 President Vásquez' health forced the aging statesman to make a trip to the United States for medical treatment. Before leaving, the President was advised by a few of his closest associates to get rid of the Chief of Staff of the Army. However, at a last-minute interview Trujillo managed to convince the President of his unfaltering loyalty.

The General reportedly promised he would look faithfully after the Government's interests in the President's absence.

On the night of Vásquez' departure occurred an incident which throws light upon Trujillo's willingness to fulfill his promises. Receiving a summons from acting President Dr. José Dolores Alfonseca to appear at the Presidential Mansion, Trujillo flatly refused to comply with the order. He cagily gave ill health as an excuse. Upon second thought he decided otherwise and went to the Palace in the company of a group of heavily armed Army officers.

"The Chief's" unnecessary display of force touched off unfavorable publicity. Knowing that he could not yet afford an open clash with the Administration, Trujillo decided to retrace his steps. To avoid losing face either with the Government or the opposition, the General set himself upon a devious course. On one hand, he increased his secret contacts with the opposition, through a young journalist named Rafael Vidal, then serving a short jail term under Trujillo's custody for killing in a duel a hireling of the Vásquez regime. Encouraged by Trujillo the opposition parties gathered strength under the leadership of a forceful orator and lawyer—Rafael Estrella Ureña. For the time being Trujillo considered it prudent to advise Estrella Ureña, through Vidal, that he viewed with sympathy the opposition leader's aspirations to the Presidency.

On the other hand, to erase further doubts from Alfonseca's mind, Trujillo released a public statement that the "Army always acts under orders from the Central Government and all its actions are an echo of the thoughts and actions of the Executive in conformity with the Constitution and the laws."

The statement was issued November 27, 1929. There are good grounds to believe that about the same time took place the first shipments of arms from Santo Domingo to the opposition stronghold of Santiago.

Upon Vásquez' return to the country, January 6, 1930, some of his aides warned him anew on Trujillo's dealing with the opposition. Again Vásquez sent for the General only to hear the same rigmarole from his subordinate's lips. This time there was, however, a slight change in the proceedings. Vásquez asked his informants to repeat their charges in the presence of Trujillo. The men wavered and ultimately failed to substantiate their previous charges. Then Trujillo renewed his loyalty vows to President Vásquez and, tongue in cheek, returned to his headquarters.

He had saved his job for the last time. Shortly afterward, on February 23, a revolution broke out in Santiago.

BIRTH OF AN ERA

1. FOR SOME TIME THE U.S. DEPARTMENT OF STATE HAD been receiving reports from the American Legation in the Dominican Republic that political unrest was rife and revolutionary disturbances should be expected. By February 22, 1930 news from the Cibao region— the rich agricultural valley in the northern section of the country—became more specific. The Legation had been given definite intimation of the imminence of an outbreak.

The next night was one of unaccustomed activity in the usually slumbering city of Santiago. In the early evening groups of armed men, apparently from nowhere, started to gather at several points, while the inhabitants, sensing impending trouble, shut themselves up in their homes. Soldiers and policemen were conspicuously absent from the streets.

At zero hour, different groups began marching in the darkness toward the San Luis fortress, where the army garrison was concentrated. Shouting revolutionary slogans and firing into the air, several bands converged upon the fort's main gate. Strangely enough, the big doors of the sixteenth-century stronghold were thrown wide open from the inside, and the assailants came in without a fight. Frightened neighbors heard a few volleys but these were fired in celebration of the bloodless victory.

The "civilian" revolution (something that later has been made to appear as a tremendous popular upheaval) had thus been launched, under the leadership of Rafael Estrella Ureña, a belligerent, scathing local orator and firebrand politician, head of the oppositionist *Partido Republicano*. Tired of airing his protests, Estrella had decided not to wait for the national elections to be held on May 16, less than three months away. Actual command of the revolutionary forces was given to Estrella's uncle, General José Estrella, an old cutthroat and guerrilla chieftain.

Estrella Ureña knew quite well that as things stood he did not have a chance of being elected President, the thing he wanted most. There was a widespread feeling of dissatisfaction with the current administration; corruption was rampant and economic mismanagement had brought the country to the brink of disaster, but it seemed likely that all this would add up to nothing in the face of the popularity of aging President Horacio Vásquez.

Vásquez' immense prestige, linked with the Government's political machinery plus a very compliant electoral law, made the President a sure bet in his bid for reelection. Thus, the restless political chieftain from Santiago found himself facing the only alternative for further political advancement left open to those Latin American candidates without a chance at the polls: an Army-backed revolution.

To insure the latter course contacts were established with General Trujillo, Chief of Staff of the Army, who showed willingness to cooperate provided the secret would be kept. Though unknown to the opposition, Trujillo's decision to deal with the democratic opposition had nothing to do with ideals or principles, but with his well-founded fear that his days in the Army were numbered. What followed was a natural development— the hopeless politician and the threatened General leagued together to overthrow the legitimate Government.

By accepting the cooperation of the Army chief, Estrella had unwittingly given the General a much needed political foothold. General Trujillo, wisely enough, played no role of leadership in the early stages of the alliance, thus making Estrella believe he would be satisfied to remain head of the Army. Furthermore, in his dealings with the disgruntled opposition Trujillo took care not to show his face openly, making all contacts and arrangements through civilian go-betweens, namely, two of Trujillo's closest friends and advisers—the journalist Rafael Vidal and the lawyer Roberto Despradel. These two, or at least Vidal, were seemingly inspired by idealistic motivation and were doomed to be victims, in the long run, of Trujillo's lack of gratitude.

The tight secrecy over the dealings between Trujillo and Estrella Ureña explains why, though otherwise correct in their appraisal of the situation, the American diplomats stationed in the Dominican Republic failed at the outset of the revolution to recognize the presence of a behind-the-scenes manipulator. Not that they had never suspected the personal longings for power of that young, shrewd upstart named Rafael Trujillo. It was that only last December they had received from the General's own lips assurances of his irrevocable loyalty to President Vásquez. They simply could not believe he was a perfect double-crosser.

Word of Santiago's uprising did not reach the capital until the morning of February 24. The report was that the San Luis fortress had fallen to Estrella's rebels "after a fight." The Government was thrown into confusion and immediately made contact with the American Legation to arrange for the personal security of the President.

In that way the American Minister Charles B. Curtis and his Third Secretary John Moors Cabot (currently American Ambassador to Colombia) were cast in the role of mediators between the Government and the rebel leaders.[1] When advised of the role Curtis and Cabot were playing, Acting Secretary of State J. P. Cotton authorized them to offer in the name of the American Government their good offices. They were further warned to handle the situation with utmost care and without a show of force. "If you can do it," asserted Cotton, "it will materially strengthen our position in the Dominican Republic and in the rest of Latin America."

Nevertheless, it was very reluctantly that on the morning of February 24 the American Minister granted asylum in the Legation to the President and his wife as well as the Vice President, Dr. José Dolores Alfonseca, on the grounds as stated by the Secretary of Foreign Affairs Dr. Francisco J. Peynado that their lives were in danger from revolutionists coming by automobile from Santiago.

Finding it difficult to believe that there was any real danger to the lives of the President and his wife, Curtis told Peynado that he thought it most desirable that General Vásquez should either remain in the Presidential Mansion or take refuge in the Ozama fortress, where Army headquarters were located.

Notwithstanding Curtis's advice, an hour later the President, his wife, the Vice President and a big entourage of high Government officials came to the Legation. In the interim Curtis had telephoned General Trujillo at the fortress, receiving once again the latter's assurances of his full loyalty to the President.

"When, therefore," wrote Curtis in a report to the State Department, "the President spoke to me of my recommendation that he go to the fort, I assured him that he could depend on the loyalty of General Trujillo." Subsequently Curtis cabled to inform Washington that "the National Army and its Commander in Chief are true to the President."

Upon discussing the matter further with his companions, President Vásquez left the Legation, followed by the rest of his party except Mrs. Vásquez. Thereafter the First Lady spent each night and most of each day in the Legation until the morning of February 28.

What happened immediately after Vásquez left the Legation is not clear. To unearth the facts, if this be at all possible, we have to dig deep under the muck of conflicting narrations. However, from the contradictory evidence it appears that Vásquez and his followers went from the Legation

[1] The American diplomats' first-hand accounts of what happened in the Dominican Republic during the revolutionary period are a treasure of contemporary information, upon which I have heavily leaned in recounting the early days of the regime.

straight to the Presidential Mansion. Then the President—not so trustful of his Chief of the Army's loyalty as the American Minister—sent for General Trujillo. The General, feigning illness, sent word back from his headquarters at the Ozama fortress that he was confined to his bed. It was then that Vásquez' close advisers definitely warned him that Trujillo was the man behind Estrella.

The President, who still had some of his celebrated youthful courage left, decided to go and see Trujillo in his own den. Arriving at the fortress, followed by a caravan of automobiles, Vásquez found that the General had commanded that only his car should be allowed within the premises.

Chewing on this humiliation, the old President went into the fort with only a small group of aides. Yet, instead of finding Trujillo in a state of open rebellion as expected, the President found a humble collaborator. Meekly the General reiterated his loyalty to the Executive and agreed to send a party of soldiers to head off the rebels. At Vásquez' request, Colonel José Alfonseca (a distant relative of the Vice President) was called in to take command of the column. According to Curtis, late the following day Trujillo recalled Colonel Alfonseca and placed Colonel Simón Díaz in command of this force.

The *trujillista* version of what happened that fateful morning, as expounded by Lawrence de Besault, is simple enough. "The President," says de Besault, "rushed to the American Legation for refuge. Once there, he changed his mind, and sped to the Ozama fortress. Later he changed his mind once more, and returned to the Presidential Mansion." A confused child this poor President! [2]

At this point, however, we find a solid fact in the reports addressed by the American Minister to the State Department. On February 24, while the President was still at the fortress, Curtis called on him there. The diplomat wanted to ascertain whether the President was prepared to yield to any of the demands being made by Estrella Ureña and other revolutionary leaders from Santiago. During the conference it was agreed that the Vice President would resign, the Government would get Congress to pass a law annulling all the amendments to the Electoral Law of 1924, and the question of the withdrawal of President Vásquez' candidacy for reelection would be taken under consideration. Curtis took advantage of the occasion to have another private talk with Trujillo. Once more the General assured him of his loyalty to the President.

On the same morning, John Moors Cabot left for Santiago to see the

[2] The picture of Vásquez as a petulant old man, unaware until the very end of the imminence of his fall, due to a popular uprising over government corruption and bad financial administration, is one of the main contributions of the *trujillista* propaganda to the literature of the period. Furthermore, Vásquez is depicted as a cowardly elder who finally thought only of flight to save his skin. No one would fight to defend such a corrupt regime.

leaders of the revolution. He succeeded in talking with Estrella Ureña, but could obtain no definite statements beyond a promise that a conference of rebel leaders would be called the following morning.

On the evening of the same day the Secretary of Finance, Martin de Moya, told the Legation that the revolutionists were advancing on the city. De Moya informed Curtis that the President and Mrs. Vásquez desired now to take definite asylum in the Legation. The Minister answered he would gladly receive Mrs. Vásquez, but persuaded the President that "it was to his own best interest to go to the fort rather than to a foreign legation." Whereupon once again Curtis telephoned Trujillo. He was then informed by the General himself that the Government troops had been "outflanked and partly surrounded" by the revolutionary forces advancing upon the capital.

When at six o'clock on the morning of the 25th no indication had been received of the entry of the revolutionists into the capital, Curtis decided to drive out in the direction of their former positions. Nineteen kilometers from the capital he found the Government forces. He had a short conversation with Colonel Alfonseca, who showed him a note signed by the rebel commanders Generals José Estrella and Antonio Jorge, stating that they had agreed with Cabot not to advance or make any attack until the latter's return from Santiago. Alfonseca asserted that they had kept this agreement scrupulously. Trujillo, therefore, had been caught in a lie.

Upon his return to the Legation Curtis received a telephone call from Secretary de Moya. The President was coming to see him at the Legation. Vásquez arrived a few minutes later. "The President was extremely angry concerning the now quite obvious treason of Gen. Trujillo," wrote Curtis. He noted that the President had told him that the night before he had found Trujillo in the company of General Luis Felipe Vidal, described by Curtis as one of the President's "most bitter personal enemies."

At this meeting with Curtis the President pointed out that with the Army unfaithful to him "he could not hope to accomplish anything but was resigning immediately." Curtis argued against what he thought were "precipitate intentions" on the President's part. Later he was informed that Vásquez, impressed by his arguments, had decided not to resign.

By then Curtis had in his possession additional data concerning the attitude of the Army and its higher officers. "General Trujillo," he reported to the State Department, "in spite of all the promises he made to my predecessor, was disloyal to President Vásquez from the first moment after his (Vásquez') return to the country on January 6.[3] Probably in Decem-

---

[3] Trujillo's eulogists always take pains to assert that during the revolt the Chief of the Army, in order to avoid needless bloodshed, remained neutral in his military headquarters. "General Trujillo," says biographer Lawrence de Besault, "remained at his post, waiting to carry out the orders of the government, but these were vacillating and confused. The President appeared to be terror-stricken by the menace of the throngs marching toward the capital."

ber, he stripped the fort in Santo Domingo City (now Ciudad Trujillo) of practically all spare arms and shipped these arms to the fort in Santiago. He most certainly was in league with the revolutionists from the very beginning and never severed his connections with them."

Curtis also heard that Colonel Simón Díaz, the commander of the fortress at Santiago (conveniently absent from his post the night of February 23), had planned to permit the seizure of San Luis fortress on the evening of February 8. The action was postponed owing to the fact that Curtis himself happened to spend that night in Santiago.

On the 26th the main body of the rebel forces—two or three hundred strong—entered the capital. Trujillo's troops, far superior in number and armament, remained within the fortress. In this way the General was keeping to the letter his earlier promises to the American diplomatic representatives. He kept a scrupulous "non-intervention" attitude during the whole revolutionary period, staying at the fort in Santo Domingo, which he nominally held in the name of the Government and to which he did not permit the entry of any revolutionists, or, for that matter, of any all-out Government supporters.

Commenting on Trujillo's dubious conduct, the American Minister said: "It is safe to say that if General Trujillo had been truly loyal to the Government, the revolution could not have succeeded—would probably not have broken out; the quantity of arms in the fort of Santiago would hardly have been worth seizing and certainly the revolutionists would not have had more arms than the Government."

Trujillo's treason upset Curtis to the extent that on February 26 he sent a message to the State Department that "it appears highly desirable that General Trujillo be not named on the list of any party. It is furthermore necessary that General Trujillo and Colonel Díaz, who has likewise been unfaithful, be removed from the Army, but this will hardly be accomplished without the assistance of the Legation."

By February 27 (Dominican Independence Day) the Government's position was untenable. Although only two days before Curtis had expressed fears of a "serious danger of unorganized street fighting and rioting," the people had stayed away from this peculiar "civilian" revolution. The average Dominican remained at home and at no moment did any riots, demonstrations or disorders occur. A strange, self-imposed order prevailed during the whole process, as if the people wanted to show their total divorce from the coup. "Loss of life and damage to property seems to have been very small indeed," reported Curtis. Later he asserted that there had been no bloodshed or property losses.

On the morning of the 27th began a long series of conversations between Vásquez and Estrella Ureña at the American Legation. Two days later an agreement was reached. At the same time the first public meeting between Trujillo and Estrella Ureña was arranged. These two also met at the American Legation. Reportedly the purpose of their conference was to discuss "the military disposition necessary to preserve order in the city, and to prevent a clash." The latter was prevented by authorizing the Chief of the Army to disarm the civilians in the revolutionary forces (the military were already back in uniform). Upon collecting the arms loaned to Estrella Ureña (and a few more as well), Trujillo assured his position as sole arbiter of the situation. Thereafter, his will was to be final.

In order to avoid international problems of recognition of the new Government, Trujillo insisted on a "legal" transfer of power. It was stipulated that the President and the Vice President should resign, but prior to this action a new Secretary of the Interior acceptable to the revolution had to be named to assume power in accordance with the Constitution.

President Vásquez, however, almost upset the apple cart. While discussions were still under way, Vásquez notified the American Minister he was submitting his resignation to Congress and had signed a decree appointing his Minister in Washington, the young and influential diplomat Dr. Angel Morales, to the post of Secretary of the Interior. This maneuver to save the regime backfired when the revolutionary leaders refused to grant permission for Congress to meet.

Now Trujillo's hand began to show. Obviously he was cherishing the idea of becoming Acting President. At the end of one of the meetings at the Legation, Estrella asked Curtis what was the American Government's attitude toward Trujillo. He was informed that the Legation would under no circumstances recommend the recognition of a Government headed by Trujillo.

The conversations finally produced an agreement. Estrella Ureña himself was appointed Secretary of the Interior on February 28. On March 2 Congress accepted the President's and Vice President's resignations.

The following day Estrella Ureña was inaugurated as President of the Dominican Republic. Legality (a form Trujillo loves so long as he can use it) had smoothed the way for the rise to power of an illegal armed movement of rebellion.

As conclusively worked out, the agreement contained nine provisions. There is no point in going into all of them; the gist of two will suffice. One stated that "all arms shall be surrendered to the new Government." This was a provision that suited Trujillo. He had been taught by the American Marines that disarmament of the opposition is the basis of military rule and he is a man who takes this kind of lesson to heart. In a speech years later he flatly ascribed the success of the American Military Government's pacification efforts in the Dominican Republic to "its drastic methods of disarmament." The second important clause established that "there shall be no restrictions as to candidates, except that neither Alfonseca nor Trujillo shall run."

Analysing the revolution and its causes, Curtis found that one of the reasons for its success was that "the country has always opposed the re-election of its chief magistrates" and "saw itself gagged and bound to the acceptance of some years more of the Vásquez regime, to be followed by Alfonseca, on account of a grossly unfair electoral law."

He pointed out that the country's finances were in deplorable state, due to maladministration, and that peculation on the part of Government officials was common. However, he concluded that the revolution had been unjustified. In support, he cited the success attending the Legation's efforts to obtain adequate guarantees of a fair election, "through which the great majority of the abuses cited could have been better rectified. Unfortunately, this success came too late, and only after Estrella Ureña and Trujillo were already in full accord to undertake a revolution."

The triumph (and tragedy it could be added) of what Estrella Ureña had called, rather pompously, a *civico* (civilian) movement, killed for a long time to come the marked progress heretofore made by the Dominican people on the road toward democratic procedures.

The Vásquez regime, to be sure, had not been a model one. But whatever its shortcomings, it had been a democratic one. The press had been free, even if some repressive measures had been undertaken against it, such as the closing of *La Inormación* of Santiago by the military authorities. The citizens had been able to speak frankly and to criticize loudly without fear the most important figures of Government, including the President. There was corruption, but at least the people could kick freely against the crooked practices and could expect correction of them.

As the people watched Trujillo gathering back his "lend-lease" hardware and redistributing it among his storm troopers in preparation for the forthcoming electoral campaign, the "civilian" movement came to be known as the *cínico* (cynical) movement.

2.

RAFAEL ESTRELLA WAS INAUGURATED PRESIDENT OF THE Dominican Republic in strict accordance with the Constitution and laws on March 3, 1930.

"Trujillo was blocked in his plan to become Acting President," reported the American Minister Charles B. Curtis, who, nevertheless, injected a note of caution. "He may, however, attempt to run for President in the elections, in spite of the terms of the agreement."

Curtis knew his man. The recent rebuff to his presidential aspirations, along with the obvious dislike shown for him by the influential American Minister, would have been deterrents to a weaker man, but not to strong-willed Trujillo. He had been slighted many times and his skin had grown thick. Moreover, his political instinct (reportedly helped by the advice of friends in the American Marine Corps) was telling him that United States opposition would melt in the face of a resolute stand on his part. He knew the Americans would not dare to intervene openly lest the wrath of Latin American public opinion fall upon them. He had made up his mind and the antipathy of Curtis was not going to force him to leave the arena.

Under the circumstances the most important thing for Trujillo was to get hold of instruments of political power other than military force. A careful assessment of the political situation showed him a complete lack of unity and leadership among the triumphant revolutionary groups. He adroitly started troubling the disturbed waters of Dominican politics in order to fish better in them.

While Trujillo's rivals were beset by vacillations, the General's actions betrayed no doubts. In contrast to irresolute President Estrella Ureña, who would not dare to take a step without consulting him, Trujillo's attitude was from the outset one of wholehearted, single-minded defiance of all opposition to his will. He held the military power and used it to stamp out possible competitors. He would stop short at nothing, even if in the process he had to shoot down a lot of innocent people.

With ruthlessness unprecedented in local politics, Trujillo set himself to establish his personal rule in all levels of national life. By force or bribery he gained a foothold within each of the several political parties making up the loose coalition that had overthrown Vásquez and by the middle of March he had secured the Presidential nomination of the so-called *Confederación*. He made it clear that in the future he intended to make Dominican politics a one-man show.

Estrella Ureña's aspirations to the Presidency had been shattered, but overtaken and overwhelmed by the new events, he did not dare to protest. He knew who was boss and without a word accepted the Vice Presidency, thrown his way by Trujillo not as a reward but as a means of prostrating him at his feet. Thus, the General did not let a day pass without reminding Estrella that he was only a subordinate. For instance, on the night of March 17, 1930, while the Presidents of the Senate and the Chamber of Deputies were at a conference with President Estrella Ureña at the Presidential Mansion, soldiers sent by Trujillo confiscated the revolvers of their chauffeurs. To no avail they showed permits signed by the President himself.

This petty incident seems to have been a little too much even for puppet President Estrella Ureña. The next morning—during a "very frank and long interview" with the American Minister—the President asserted that General Trujillo was dominating him and preventing the preparation of fair elections. "The President asked me," wrote Curtis to the U.S. State

Department, "to make it public that the Government of the United States would not recognize Trujillo as President in view of the agreement reached through the mediation of the Legation which ended the revolution." Excusing his failure to take a definite stand, Estrella explained that any opposition on his part to Trujillo's candidacy might be ascribed by the latter to self-interest.

The State Department did not authorize Curtis to issue the statement suggested by Estrella Ureña. The Department, however, concurred in Curtis's views that it was most unfortunate that the head of the Army should use that position for his political advancement and as a means of obtaining the Presidency.

Furthermore, the Minister was instructed to talk "personally, confidentially and in the most friendly manner with Trujillo" to urge upon him, but only as Curtis's personal advice, "the damage which he will do to the political development of the Dominican Republic by being a candidate rather than by using his power to guarantee free and fair elections."

It was the feeling of the State Department that a friendly appeal to Trujillo, "on the basis of the good of the Dominican Republic," would succeed in preventing his candidacy. Any duress, through a public statement, was considered self-defeating.

Curtis was advised that, without overlooking the great difficulty of bringing such a thing about, the Department hoped he would be able to persuade Trujillo. But, should he not succeed and Trujillo be elected, the Department thought it most important that "you (Curtis) should not impair in any way your relations with him (Trujillo). Therefore the Department cannot emphasize too strongly the necessity of making your appeal in a most friendly spirit."

Lastly, the State Department revealed confidentially to Curtis that the United States expected to recognize Trujillo and "maintain the most friendly relations with him and his Government." It was suggested that in his talks with Trujillo, Curtis should be assisted by a man the Department understood exercised great personal influence over the Dominican General: Colonel Richard M. Cutts, of the Marine Corps, then stationed in Haiti. "Colonel Cutts," said the U.S. State Department, "was Trujillo's commanding officer and trained him in his present duties, and the Department understands that Trujillo frequently consults him on important matters relating to Trujillo's personal conduct and attitude." However, Cutts's visit to Santo Domingo left things unchanged.

Ignorant of American willingness to appease Trujillo, the Dominican democratic forces were rallying behind a unification drive. The two most powerful political organizations then in existence joined forces in an effort to check Trujillo's drive for power: the *Partido Nacional,* of former President Vásquez, and the *Partido Progresista,* whose chief was a most respected elder statesman, Federico Velásquez y Hernández, with a long past of selfless public service on his record. The *Alianza,* as the fusion of these two political organizations was known, nominated Velásquez as its Presidential candidate. As Velásquez' running mate, the young and promising nationalist leader Dr. Angel Morales was chosen; he had resigned as Minister to Washington and was back in the country. The two opposition candidates tried desperately to rouse the liberal elements and there is no doubt that *under normal conditions* the *Alianza's* appeal would have gained an overwhelming majority on election day.

Yet normalcy was an illusion. With the drawing of battle lines things took a sharp turn for the worst. Knowing that the *Alianza,* supported by thousands of Dominicans from all walks of life, was gathering momentum, Trujillo decided to break the spine of the rising opposition. The spirit of protest was so great, however, that a very popular slogan, chalked on walls and curbstones throughout the country, was *No puede ser . . .* (It cannot be), referring to Trujillo's bid for power. Sometimes to these words would be added: *por ladron de caballos* (for horse thief).

Faced with mounting popular opposition, Trujillo retaliated with the convincing argument of bullets, rope and knives. While the President and the civil authorities assured the American Legation of their real or feigned willingness to take all possible steps to maintain order, Trujillo, with the help of a gang of thugs known as *La 42*—after the Forty-second Company of American marines which left such bitter memories in Santo Domingo— unleashed a wave of terror.

A chilly wind of terror started blowing. The storm troopers of *La 42,* led by an Army captain (now a colonel) named Miguel Angel Paulino, dealt out beatings, broke up meetings of the opposition, kidnapped and murdered alleged enemies of the regime. Several hundred people were killed because they persisted in expressing their opinions.[4] An American observer, Charles A. Thomson, wrote the following in a report for the Foreign Policy Association: "The period succeeding General Trujillo's entry into the Presidential campaign witnessed the death or mysterious disappearance of a great number of his opponents. These included former cabinet ministers, ex-Senators, leading politicians, journalists, ranchers, businessmen, students and labor leaders."

A most dreaded feature of those fateful days, and one about which old Dominicans still talk with trembling voices, was *La 42's* terroristic *Carro de la Muerte* (death car)—the huge red Packard, driven by an ex-convict,

[4] *La 42* formed a special body which had its particular living standard, its special ethics, code of honor and even slang. Drawn from the dregs of Dominican underworld, *La 42* organized itself right after the February coup. Its members were allowed to steal and murder without hindrance and received part of the spoils taken from the victims. Among *La 42's* most prominent graduates is Dominican diplomat Dr. Felix W. Bernardino, former Dominican Consul General in New York.

used to take the regime's earlier enemies for a ride. Each night was one of fright for Trujillo's foes. But the long list of those assassinated comprises more than people openly opposed to the regime. Many citizens were killed to satisfy personal vengeance, and many more were disposed of, especially plantation owners, because they objected to soldiers stealing cattle or resisted confiscation of their estates.

The electoral campaign officially opened on April 1. By the middle of the month, however, it had become apparent that it was no longer possible to expect any kind of pre-electoral guarantees. With terrorism in full sway, campaigning was a most daring enterprise. One day a group of leading members of the *Alianza,* including Vice Presidential nominee Angel Morales, were ambushed but miraculously escaped.

In letters dated April 17 and 18 to the President of the Central Electoral Board, Velásquez accused Trujillo adherents—in many cases army officers —of firing on opposition rallies. The letters also stated that *trujillista* gangs had attacked the *Alianza* leaders and the officers of the opposition groups in various cities as well as its propaganda committees throughout the country. A considerable number of *Alianza* supporters had been killed and wounded; others had been imprisoned.

On May 1 the Central Electoral Board (in charge of supervising the electoral campaign) published in the *Listin Diario* a notice of protest: "The Central Electoral Board requests that the Army remain in its barracks and that house-to-house search cease at once."

The protest was ignored and the President of the Board, Mr. Enrique Estrada, resigned. Some days later the other members of the board likewise resigned. According to Charles A. Thomson, "they had been named as the result of an inter-party agreement and in consequence had merited general confidence." Trujillo's apologists deny things were that way. Biographer Abelardo R. Nanita accuses the opposition leader of causing all the trouble. According to Nanita, the opposition was working in an "underhanded and subtle manner" to obstruct the electoral process and in complicity with the Electoral Board was plotting to flout the Constitution. Nanita also accuses Estrella Ureña of being in cahoots with the *Alianza* and says that upon his return from a "triumphant campaigning trip" through the Cibao region Trujillo was informed of the situation, "whereupon the necessary steps were taken to meet the danger. The members of the Central Electoral Board submitted resignations." What is not explained is why the plotters easily acceded to Trujillo's way of foiling the conspiracy.

Anyway, by decree of May 6, Provisional President Jacinto B. Peynado (Estrella Ureña as a candidate for the Vice Presidency had scrupulously taken a leave of absence beginning April 22) named another Central Electoral Board to be presided over by Roberto Despradel. The *Alianza,* charging that the members of the new Board were partial to the Trujillo candidacy, refused to recognize the appointment. Velásquez at once brought suit in the courts to test the legality of the Executive's action. Judge Heriberto Nuñez, of El Seibo court of first instance, decided in favor of the plaintiffs. The Government appealed the decision.

The case came before the Court of Appeals in the capital on May 15. Two days later, when the judges were ready to pronounce the sentence (supposedly upholding the original findings), the courtroom was invaded by a group of armed members of La 42. With the turbulent mob already within the courthouse, the judges had to run for their lives. The late Dr. Carlos Gatón Richiez, one of them, told me years later (at the Labor Department where we shared an office in its Legal section) that he had been forced to go in hiding for several days afterward. On his way to a friend's home, where he took refuge, Dr. Gatón went through the streets of the capital disguised as a woman.

The decision never became law; notwithstanding all the pressure exerted upon them, the five judges (Francisco A. Hernández, Esteban S. Mesa, Carlos Gatón Richiez, Gregorio Soñé Nolasco and M. E. Cáceres) filed a protest with the Supreme Court on May 22.

Neither terror nor the glowing promises of the *trujillista* platform were enough to quiet the popular ferment. Organized labor would not be wooed by Trujillo's hollow promises. Most vocal in their opposition were the members of the Chauffeurs Union. Feelings ran high and at this point the chauffeurs decided to agitate in the streets. They staged a rally on plazas and street corners of the capital. The demonstration wound up in Independence Park where leaflets calling Trujillo a "cattle thief" were distributed. At that moment a detachment of soldiers, reinforced by the ubiquitous La 42, appeared at the park and turned their guns upon the demonstrators, mowing them down. A score of men, several dead, were left on the ground. That same night the Union headquarters were invaded by La 42. An electoral convention was promptly held, at which Captain Miguel Angel Paulino was "elected" President of the Union, a capacity in which he thereafter served for almost ten years.

In the interim the opposition hopes that Washington would not recognize a government headed by Trujillo had been disappointed. Unknown to them, they received a severe blow on April 23. On that day the new Dominican Minister to the United States, Rafael Brache, called upon the Acting Secretary of State to discuss the Dominican political situation. Cotton let Brache know that the Department agreed with Curtis's opinion, which had been politely expressed to Trujillo, that it would be a pity for a man who was the head of the army to be candidate for President. Brache argued that Trujillo was a "very able man, a good organizer, very clever, intelligent and honest."

The Dominican Envoy must have come from the conference favorably impressed. The next day Trujillo decided to call the Americans' bluff and formally accepted the presidential nomination. In his acceptance—a remarkable document—the General promised freedom for all, improved health measures, improved finances, more jobs and better living conditions. He asserted that, above all things, he was against dictatorship. To cap all, he promised those who followed him they would never regret it.

Trujillo had touched off a blaze of violence that was sweeping the country, but it still took a little longer for the opposition leaders to concede defeat. However, after a meeting on May 14, Velásquez and Morales announced their withdrawal from the race. Inasmuch, they asserted, as electoral campaigning in its most democratic aspects had been suppressed by a policy of terrorism that stopped at nothing, elections could only prove a farce. They asked their followers to abstain from voting.

"Elections" were held two days later and Trujillo and Estrella Ureña were declared elected unopposed. The people, according to Nanita, had chosen whom they should—"gallant" General Trujillo, the man destined "by an inscrutable Providence to change completely the course of history."

"I have the honor to confirm my report that there were no disorders during the day of the elections, but that all is by no means quiet here," wrote Curtis to the State Department. He further noted that "the *Confederación* announces that 223,851 votes were, according to early reports, cast in favor of General Rafael Leonidas Trujillo for President of the Republic, and of Rafael Estrella Ureña for Vice President. As the number given greatly exceeds the total number of voters in the country, further comment on the fairness of the elections is hardly necessary; however, there is every reason to believe that, as anticipated by the Legation, the intimidation of the followers of the Opposition had already been so great prior to the day of the elections that none was needed, and it would seem than none was practiced, on the day of the elections, in order to keep them away from the polls."

The violence rending the country did not end with Trujillo's election. The General made it known that he had no intention of letting bygones be bygones. Now that he had been elected he considered the moment had arrived to deal with the major opposition leaders. Thus far *La 42* had only disposed (with a few exceptions) of the small fry, though casualties could be counted by the thousands. Many victims were secretly buried or thrown into the sea.

No sooner had the electoral returns been announced than Trujillo threw Presidential candidate Federico Velásquez in jail. Similar orders were issued against Morales, but alert followers managed to smuggle him out to Puerto Rico a step ahead of *La 42*. Considering that during his long exile Morales has been the subject of several murderous plots, it is only fair to assume that he wisely left the country.[5] After eight days in prison Velásquez was released, on May 26, and likewise went into exile in Puerto Rico, where he died four years later.

The spree of violence followed a vicious circle. Trujillo turned loose his soldiers and thugs, who now roamed the streets of cities and towns as well as the countryside. First to fall victims to the iron fist of *La 42* were distinguished citizens high on the list of Trujillo's personal hatreds.

On June 1, 1930, Virgilio Martínez Reyna, a poet and sometime cabinet minister under President Vásquez, was shot dead, together with his pregnant wife. According to *Listin Diario,* the gunmen who assaulted his country home at San José de las Matas (led by General José Estrella as was established later) had slashed the poet's body and severed the nose from his face. Since Martínez was chronically ill and practically retired from politics, it seems that the only reason for this dastardly murder was that in the early days of the Vásquez regime he had sought to have Trujillo removed from the Army.

Next on the proscribed list was José Brache, former Secretary of the Treasury. Brache was killed in Moca by a group who fired upon him from the moving *Carro de la Muerte* as he emerged from a movie. The former high official, it was reported, had once refused to lend Trujillo a considerable sum of money.

Terror had its political motivation as well. One night as Moncito Matos, leader of the opposition in Barahona, strolled into his home, a gunman followed and shot him down. Eliseo Esteves, an opposition chieftain in Moca, was removed in like manner. So was Juan Paredes, opposition leader in San Francisco de Macoris, and hundreds of lesser known freedom-loving citizens.

Cornered and hunted down, some opposition leaders tried to put up a desperate armed resistance. But then, as now, arms were almost impossible to get. Without arms and ammunition the overwhelming military might of the Government proved too much. One of the abortive uprisings in the city of La Vega provided the Government with a good excuse to imprison and kill a number of opponents.

On June 10 a group of rebels led by General Alberto Larancuent, leader of the *Partido Progresista,* left the town of La Romana and headed for the woods. After a few skirmishes with the Army the group, including Larancuent, was induced to drop their arms, under promises of guarantees for their lives and personal security.

As result of this short-lived uprising, Dominicans were given the opportunity to appreciate one of the earliest demonstrations of Trujillo's ca-

---

[5] Morales is at present one of the most respected exile leaders, because of his honesty, forthrightness and courage.

pacity for deceit and brutality. He lured Larancuent to his slaughter by inviting the defeated enemy to a peace meeting in the capital, in which both men embraced each other. On the same night trustful Larancuent was taking a breath of fresh air at Colon Square in front of his hotel, when suddenly the lights went out. Several shots were then heard. When the lights snapped on again, the bullet-ridden body of Larancuent was lying on the ground. Again and again Trujillo used in those early days the ruse of inviting opponents to negotiate and then arresting or killing them.

As the time for the presidential inauguration approached, terror increased. This compound of terror, cowardice and treachery finally achieved its avowed end—it broke the proud and democratic spirit of the Dominican people.

The most candid among the Dominican press agents explain the reports of early violence as the inevitable accompaniment of a momentary breakdown of public order. The armed bands are explained as organized by excitable individuals, many of whom sincerely believed they were doing good for their country. The explanation has a Fascist ring—the reign of terror was in essence a patriotic crusade.

Whether the *trujillista* crimes of 1930 and 1931 were justified by conditions or whether they would have never occurred had not Trujillo himself granted immunity to their perpetrators, is rather academic. However, it must be pointed out that long after an era of peace, order, law, progress, and justice, to employ *trujillista* language, has succeeded, people still pay dearly for democratic convictions.

3.

ON SEPTEMBER 3, 1930, EIGHTEEN DAYS AFTER PRESIDENT Rafael L. Trujillo assumed office, a hurricane struck the capital city and played great havoc. When the long hours of nightmare and destruction were over, dazed *capitaleños,* as the inhabitants of the city are named, started combing the rubble for survivors. Disaster's toll was heavy for a city having a population of less than 80,000—2,500 dead, more than 8,000 injured and an untold number unaccounted for.

The aggregate of sorrow, consternation and tragedy was heavy too. For days the nightmare could not be erased from the minds of the survivors. As the dead were counted—many days passed before an accurate tally could be made—care for the living became the most pressing problem. Material losses were estimated at several millions, but fortunately the old colonial quarter of the city had not suffered much. There, hundreds of families from the devastated slums found shelter in churches, schools and public buildings still standing. But the threat of famine and epidemics loomed over the ruins.

To give the devil his due, credit must be given to Trujillo for prompt, sweeping measures intended to alleviate the plight of the inhabitants. In doing so he faced problems which would have discouraged a less energetic man. And he coped with them with energy, determination and sagacity.

But Trujillo is no magician and he could not do the immense task without outside help and the collaboration of the Dominican people. Without minimizing the extent of the crisis, it must be said that the picture of Trujillo as the single-handed rebuilder of the city is a gross exaggeration put forth by his propaganda machine. The people, as well as their President, rose to meet the crisis.

The President declared the city a major disaster area and set himself to work out plans for rebuilding. However, aside from the money spent in repairing damaged public buildings and clearing the streets as well as caring for the wounded in the State hospitals, the relief program hardly cost a penny to the Dominican Government. Most of the property owners performed, without any financial assistance from the Administration or the relief agencies, the reconstruction of their private homes and places of business. Even the portion shared by the Government in the reconstruction work was launched with the help of money, medical equipment, building material, foodstuffs and other supplies rushed from neighboring countries. Airplanes flew supplies in from the United States, Puerto Rico, Cuba and Haiti and all manner of naval craft were engaged in the same task. Hospitals were improvised with Cuban and American personnel brought into the country by the respective branches of the Red Cross. Crews of British, Dutch and American ships were employed in the thankless task of removing debris. An inspiring example of international cooperation!

In many respects the hurricane proved a blessing for Trujillo. To meet the crisis, the National Congress passed a law suspending constitutional guarantees and investing the President with authority to take any steps, economic or otherwise, to raise funds on public credit, to distribute relief supplies and to do whatever was demanded by the circumstances.

The General did not let his newly legalized dictatorial power rust. He personally assumed the direction of the Red Cross and relief operations, whereas the Government "borrowed" idle funds lying in bank accounts or vaults. Tight controls were imposed over the stocks of necessities, medicines and building materials, but instead of diverting them directly to the needy, they were turned over to relatives of Trujillo and Army speculators. An idea of the way in which necessities were handled by speculators and profiteers can be gained from the fact that several known fortunes were made in a matter of weeks. As head of the Red Cross the President was himself the sole administrator of the large sums of relief money sent from abroad. To date no one knows how the money was spent, since Trujillo never deigned to make public an accounting that was due to the foreign contributors.

Since Congress had legalized dictatorship, it was easy for Trujillo to take advantage of the situation to wipe out the already decimated ranks of the opposition. Thus, many of his opponents, done away with by strong-armed squads, were reported victims of the hurricane. The day after the hurricane Trujillo ordered Captain Paulino, the head of *La 42*, to secure large quantities of gasoline and that evening the dead bodies of the victims of the hurricane (as well as a few killed by *La 42*) were drenched with the fluid and burned. This method of corpse disposal was hailed as an ingenious device of the President to save time and prevent epidemics. Trujillo, as a matter of fact, takes great pride in his original health measure. "Without this drastic step," he asserted, "we should have suffered an epidemic that would have destroyed the capital itself."

Terror seemed to be insufficient, however, at least at the outset, to control people who, as in the wake of big calamities, were getting restless. Even the Army rank-and-file could not be trusted. To stave off trouble, and assure himself of a firm seat in the saddle, Trujillo conceived another original idea: he tried to bring foreign soldiers into the country.

Therefore, Trujillo made a most unusual appeal to the American and Haitian Governments. He personally requested of his friend Colonel Cutts at least fifty American Marines and as many more as available. He wanted them to be temporarily assigned to Santo Domingo on any excuse. Cutts was in no position to do such a favor for his friend, but he transmitted the request to Marine headquarters. In the interim Trujillo asked the Navy Department liaison officer in Santo Domingo, Major W. B. Sullivan, to put a similar request to the United States Minister Charles B. Curtis.

Upon receiving Trujillo's petition for foreign military help, Curtis wrote to the State Department backing it. "The Dominican Army and police are almost completely demoralized," he asserted, "and the moral effect of having 50 Marines here would be enormously beneficial."

The acting Secretary of State Cotton ruled out any idea of sending Marines to the Dominican Republic. Such a step, he noted in his answer to Curtis, might create misunderstanding in other countries.

Still determined to secure foreign soldiers, Trujillo turned toward Haiti and made a similar request of President Roy. This time he specifically asked, according to a message from the American Legation in Port-au-Prince to the State Department, for the sending of a detachment of 50 or 100 Haitian guards to Santo Domingo City. President Roy dismissed the request since he thought that the dispatch of guards would probably be ineffective and "might lead to unfortunate friction."

Despite his failure on that occasion, it is well-known fact that Trujillo still subscribes to the theory that in times of crisis the presence of foreign troops contributes to bolster the morale of the incumbent regime and, in case of need, may be used more effectively than the native soldiers. When his long-time ally and personal friend President Anastasio Somoza, of Nicaragua, was felled by the bullets of a young martyr, in 1956, the Benefactor promptly sent off to Managua part of his Presidential Guard. The gesture was repeated right after the murder of the President of Guatemala, Colonel Carlos Castillo Armas, in 1957.

Trujillo, however, had to get along without outside help in 1930. Whatever his own doubts, he was fortunate or capable enough to overcome by his own means the immediate emergency. It is only in the face of his subsequent record as a loud-mouthed "non-interventionist" that the strange requests must be recorded. They contribute another paradox.

Moreover, if Trujillo considered it normal to request foreign aid, military or otherwise, still he strongly objected to similar actions on the part of his subjects. In February 1931 his Congress passed a law making it a punishable offense for any citizen to resort to a foreign government or legation, to request help or to complain against the Dominican Government.

Trujillo's early difficulties were not limited to the political field. Like almost any other contemporary ruler, he was faced by an acute financial crisis. Although in later years the Benefactor has made it a chief feature of his propaganda for external consumption that all Dominican progress has been achieved without the help of outside loans or financial entanglements, it is a matter of record that right after the hurricane the Dominican Government sounded out in vain the State Department on the possibilities of getting financial assistance. Nonetheless the President of the United States, Herbert Hoover, designated Mr. Elliot Wadsworth as his personal representative to the Dominican Republic and directed him to decide on the practicability of authorizing a new bond issue chargeable to the debt-ridden Dominican Government. Wadsworth advised against such a bond issue.

To complicate matters, demands for payment of the external debt now became pressing and as a result $3,000,000 per annum had to be diverted from the national budget for the servicing of foreign bonds. Trujillo now stood in front of an empty treasury, a floating debt of $1,750,000 and a foreign debt of $20,000,000. Revenues that in 1929 had reached the highest peak in the history of the country, totaling $15,385,000, had dropped in 1930 to $9,879,843.75 and in 1931 to $7,350,000.

To meet the challenge, Trujillo attempted various not always orthodox and often erratic economy measures. He reduced personnel in government offices by 15 to 20 per cent, and salaries, if not in arrears, were cut by 15 per cent. He closed many schools in all levels of learning, leaving the country with only two high schools, and an enrollment smaller than in 1920. The only budgetary appropriations he did not slash were those of the Army, which was allotted in 1931 the sum of $1,141,000, or 11.5 per cent of the total budget.

Despite Trujillo's frantic efforts the situation kept its downward trend until the amount of funds going into the treasury was not enough to cover a minimum of the Administration's ordinary expenses and meet as well the heavy payments of the external debt. A commission was sent to the United States in an unsuccessful effort to secure a loan, "At this point we needed help and assistance. I sought them eagerly but did not find them anywhere," recalled the Benefactor years after.

The American creditors, however, could no longer close their eyes to the frightful economic conditions in the Dominican Republic. To prevent complete national bankruptcy, an Emergency Law was passed in October 1931 diverting to governmental expenses $1,500,000 from customs revenues which were pledged to service of the foreign loans; the United States Government contented itself with the statement that it was following developments "with attention and care." In accordance with the new law interest payments were to be maintained, but payments on the sinking-fund were practically suspended.

The Emergency Law was kept in full force until 1934, when a new permanent agreement was made with the Foreign Bondholders Protective Council of the United States, permitting very substantial reductions in debt payments in exchange for more powers for the American General Receiver of Customs.

During the negotiations of this new agreement one of Trujillo's clearcut methods appeared for the first time. The Dominican Government did not employ as negotiators its own diplomats, but American lawyers and lobbyists. Joseph E. Davies, well-known lawyer and Democratic Party politician, acted as Dominican representative in dealings with a Democratic Administration and Democratic Secretary of State Cordell Hull.

Davies was assisted by Oliver P. Newman, a journalist with little previous experience in financial matters or Latin American affairs, who had formerly been associated with the Democratic National Committee as director of publicity, when Mr. Cordell Hull was chairman of that body. Thereafter, Newman, who died in Miami, Florida, in 1956, was associated with Trujillo for almost twenty years in diverse capacities both in the Dominican Republic and the United States.

Convinced at last that he would not be able to solve the economic problems of his regime with the help of foreign loans, Trujillo chose crushing taxation as the best alternative to increase the flow of revenue. A group of so-called emergency taxes were imposed, never to be repealed. Though they markedly increased the cost of living, taxes helped the regime to cover expenditures for its costly machinery. Through an extreme protection of certain articles, taxes encouraged the growth of a series of Trujillo-owned monopolies. Last but not least, they were a fool-proof instrument of terror, adroitly exploited to keep in line the wealthy classes. Fear of additional taxation, coupled with visits by Treasury agents, has been the favorite method of keeping in check businessmen and wealthy farmers.

Resentment over taxation is tantamount to political opposition. To raise prices following a new levy or to close down a business for the same reason is a severely punishable crime. Late in 1934 and early in 1935, following imposition of heavy taxes upon several necessities, some merchants raised prices. The Government retaliated by throwing a few domestic merchants in jail and threatening to deport foreign businessmen if such practices continued. To maintain a cloud of fear over the employers, the Government printed a notice in *Listin Diario* warning businessmen they would be held responsible for any expressions of disloyalty voiced by employees or relatives. When a match factory in Puerto Plata shut down, Trujillo announced to the press that the government would "not permit the stoppage of any industry" and that if the owners could not keep them running, the Administration would take charge and give them an "efficient, honest and economical administration."

Money was still scarce. Although Trujillo has always taken special pride in his public works program, during the first four years of his regime the only activity the government could show along this line was the erection of several permanent steel and concrete bridges, one of which was baptized "Ramfis Bridge" in honor of Trujillo's four-year-old son. The materials for this bridge had been contracted and paid for by the Vásquez administration; it had dealt with the United Steel Products Company of New York since 1928.

Coincidental with stopgap economic measures came Trujillo's search for stable formulas to perpetuate his power. Beyond a determination to capture supreme authority by hook or crook, he had brought no plan to the Presidency. Now he needed a little more than that, and the General proved himself equal to the task. His formula to remain in power was simple enough—diabolically simple: from then on no opposition was to be permitted.

Trujillo's views were enforced by the vigorous arguments of the rope and the bullet. Murder again raised its ugly head and *La 42* scoured the country beating actual or potential opponents. Discontent with the regime, indifference toward the regime, opposition toward the regime, all found a common denominator in persecution by Trujillo.

If the pre-inauguration atrocities had been a horrible example of rule by terror, what happened after "the Chief" was already installed defies efforts at objective description. Just to list those who have died on Trujillo's orders is an impossible task. According to Albert C. Hicks, "during the immediate post-election period, from the summer of 1930 to October

1931, at least one thousand Dominicans who were on the Trujillo black list were killed. Thousands of others were imprisoned and tortured."

Opponents dragged from their homes were dumped into vermin-infested cells at the malaria-ridden *Nigua* prison near the capital. By illegal search, kidnapping or murder, *La 42* terrorized the population. An entire generation of Dominican democratic leaders was wiped out, all opposition rooted out and every spark of political energy smothered.

To be plunged into the blood bath a man did not have to be himself active in politics. It was enough to be a close relative of someone who was. Dr. Gerardo Ellis Cambiaso, an active opponent of the regime, sought refuge abroad to avoid persecution, but left behind in the Dominican Republic his son Gerardo Ellis Guerra, a high school student with no political affiliation. At dusk, on October 7, 1931, young Ellis was walking with his fiancée along the main street of Santiago when shooting broke out. When it was over the student lay dead at the feet of his fiancée who miraculously escaped unhurt.

Whole families (the Perozos, the Bencosmes, the Patiños, the Vallejos) lost nearly all their male members during these early purges or in the years that immediately followed. The Perozo family may be the one that has given most martyrs to the anti-Trujillo cause. In the early Thirties all men carrying the name of Perozo and their in-laws were dispatched by the Trujillo secret police. José Luis Fermín Perozo, however, was only a boy of two when the regime took power, and he was spared. At 17, however, José Luis was already "dangerous." On the afternoon of June 13, 1945, while the boy was strolling along one of his home-town streets he was approached by a lottery ticket peddler who, without warning, stabbed him to death. The police promptly arrested the killer and released a communiqué announcing that he would be indicted for the crime. The following morning, however, the police issued a new statement that the murderer had hanged himself in his cell the night before.

It is a strong tribute to the Dominicans' character that these outrages did not break their spirits outright. There still was some opposition; though weak in numbers, it was high in character. Various were the revolutionary movements that broke out. Even *trujillista* propaganda cannot deny the existence of men of determination and courage, willing to sacrifice their lives in the fight for democratic rule. Lawrence de Besault calls them "obdurate malcontents who desired to ruin the new administration, who plotted in the shadows and headed by a few disturbers attempted to resurrect the past." Trujillo, according to his biographer, answered their active hostility with conciliatory gestures, and only when persuasion and generosity failed did he employ the Army to crush incipient revolts.

One such case was that of Senator Desiderio Arias, a veteran politician and leader of the revolution that put Trujillo in power. As a worthy man,

Arias, after an abortive uprising, took refuge with a handful of followers in the northern mountains of Mao in the summer of 1931. Upon hearing of his former collaborator's uprising, Trujillo accused Arias, along with his other comrades, of a common crime—the murder of an obscure farmer named Vetilio Reyes. Then he ordered General José Estrella at the head of an impressive military force to persecute the Senator. Arias and all his comrades were killed in a bloody skirmish.

Around the killing of Arias there are several unsavory stories which do not rate much credit, but there is a feature of the incident that reveals an interesting aspect of Trujillo's personality. The night of Arias' killing "the Chief" showed up at his widow's home and insisted upon staying with the tormented lady while she mourned over the body. Then Trujillo made the Senate pass a resolution declaring three days of mourning.

Following Latin American tradition, Dominican students stood in the forefront of the fight against Trujillo during several years. The National Association of University Students (ANEU) held a series of anti-Trujillo demonstrations, all dispersed by Trujillo's mounted police and *La 42*. Finally the association was disbanded and several leaders thrown in jail.

In Santiago a group of high school students planted a few bombs throughout the town and planned to assassinate Trujillo during one of his visits. The plot miscarried at the last moment when the would-be murderer lost his nerve. Finally discovered, some forty young men were arrested and held in prison for more than a year.

Having routed all opposition, Trujillo turned on his own collaborators. They, too, surrendered without giving battle. Torn by the conflicting interests of its leaders, the coalition that put Trujillo in power soon disintegrated. Methodically, the General undermined the influence of his principal associates, playing up with skillful shrewdness the rivalries between them, a method he strongly favors in dealing with his own household.

Vice President Estrella Ureña was the first among the collaborators to be shoved aside. The man had too much prestige to be left alone, so Trujillo did not spare pains to humiliate and harass him. On August 16, 1931, in a statement full of praise for Trujillo, Estrella announced he was leaving for Europe to fulfill an official mission. From Puerto Rico, however, he cabled his resignation and boarded a ship for New York, starting a period of exile that ended nine years later with an unexplainable reconciliation with Trujillo.

Estrella's downfall was followed by a far more important one: that of Rafael Vidal, one of the "brain trust" of the February revolution. With much fanfare, Vidal was thrown into jail on trumped-up charges. Later he was pardoned and seemingly restored to the favor of the President.

By 1934 all opposition had been silenced or driven underground, but Trujillo was not satisfied. He craved the all-out support of *all* Dominicans.

People soon learned that they had to be vocally on "the Chief's" side, since to be "indifferent" was as bad as to be "subversive." This end was achieved very successfully through fear, through the hope of personal advancement or through vulgar bribery. The lure of public office, after a brief visit to jail, was usually sufficient to gain converts. The list of the men who went through this cure during the first years of the regime and subsequently is a long one. Those who were really fortunate removed themselves from the local scene and went into exile (a method no longer possible since it is practically impossible to get a passport and the Trujillo regime does not recognize the right of asylum). Those who exiled themselves were promptly declared "traitors" to the Fatherland, sentenced to jail terms, and their properties within the Republic confiscated.

For nearly four years Trujillo pounded the politically hopeless opposition. Now in 1934 his reelection was considered a well deserved reward for selfless devotion to furthering the welfare of the Dominican people. Perhaps unknowingly "the Chief" had scrupulously followed Machiavelli's advice to the tyrants of four hundred years ago—to get their murders over with at the beginning of their reign. Now he was able, at least outwardly, to show restraint and generosity, provided the rest of the Dominicans played the game according to his own rules.

In well-organized "civic reviews" organized throughout the country by the only party any longer in existence—the *Partido Dominicano*—masses of peasants were brought together to voice their support of their self-styled Benefactor, in preparation for the 1934 polls. This was hailed as a sign of democracy on the march; *trujillista* democracy, to be sure.

THE PHENOMENON NAMED TRUJILLO

1. WHEN THE AVERAGE AMERICAN HEARS THE NAME OF Rafael L. Trujillo—especially after the much written-about Galíndez disappearance—he pictures "the Caribbean Little Caesar" as a cruel, sinister image of evil. As a matter of fact, "the Big One," if seen out of uniform, could be mistaken for a prosperous, well-dressed, civic-minded American business executive.

A strongly-built, erect, agile, untiring and well-proportioned graying man, Trujillo seems exceptionally healthy at 66. His good carriage and military bearing, as well as his quick, well-coordinated reflexes help him to keep an athletic, outdoor look. Forced by incipient stoutness to corset himself, he still manages, with the help of built-in elevator heels, to give the impression of being taller than his five feet eight inches. When he marches into a reception room, his face set straight ahead and only his quick brown eyes glancing about, he cuts an imposing figure.

Described a few years back by an American writer as a handsome man with a copper skin and twinkling eyes who "drank a mighty good glass of wine," the Generalissimo's personal tastes used to impress visitors as sybaritic. Although he clings to most of his former tastes, over the last eight years he has gradually modified his living habits to conform to the requirements of advancing years.

Without losing completely his hearty appetite for the good things of life, Trujillo has become frugal. He keeps a watchful eye on his diet, exercises regularly, never smokes (he has never tried) and plans to get seven hours' rest on most nights. A shorter period of rest is likely to make him snappish in the morning.

Although there is no recent indication that "the Big One" is in anything but the best of health, notwithstanding a formal announcement made in September 1957 that he had suffered a "mild" indisposition, a string of foreign doctors have been visiting his household during the last three years. In March 1956 the *New York Times* reported that President Eisenhower's heart specialist, Dr. Paul Dudley White, had made an urgent visit to Ciudad Trujillo. According to a Dominican physician who declined to have his name used, the purpose of Dr. White's visit was to examine the Generalissimo. Later, several European and American physicians have gone to the country for the same purpose.

This should not be taken as a definite sign that Trujillo's health is deteriorating. The fact is that despite his seemingly good health "the Chief" is overcome by an almost pathological fear of illness. He is always testing new types of medicines, mysterious injections and stimulating pills. Special emphasis is put on products whose avowed purpose is either to rejuvenate or strengthen virility.

Trujillo's cronies are always on the watch for strange medications and a great deal of time is devoted, during after-dinner conversation at the Palace to the alleged properties of the latest competitor of "Spanish fly." From all corners of the globe packages containing the newest filters as well as scientific and pseudo-scientific discoveries arrive at the Palace. There was a time when guests at his dinner table were given a glass of molasses as a stimulant to their appetite as well as a digestive agent. "The Chief's" approval of the efficacy of a novel "fountain of youth" is likely to start a rush for the concoction among the members of the inner circle. This, in turn, sets off a chain reaction in the outer circles; the drugstores are deluged with requests for unheard-of remedies.

Whatever the present state of his health, Trujillo is known to have been near death at least twice during his tenure of power. In 1935 a chronic prostate affliction almost carried him off. A French specialist, Dr. George Marion, was rushed into the country to operate on him and thus saved his life. Ever since Dr. Marion has made periodic visits to the island to check on his patient's health. Reportedly he did it for the last time in September 1957.

Then, in 1940, an anthrax in the neck, contracted at his farm, put Trujillo's life in peril. This time it was an old Dominican country doctor, Dr. Darío Contreras, who saved his life with a daring operation, performed against the best advice of cautious colleagues.

The aftermath of this surgical feat throws some light upon the Generalissimo's personality. Upon recovery "the Chief" threw in jail his personal physician and Minister of Public Health, Dr. Francisco Benzo. The former favorite lost his job and his personal fortune was confiscated, when he was accused of having advised Dr. Contreras not to operate because the "corpse's smell" had already started upon their patient. Benzo's place was taken over by Dr. Contreras, but only for a short while. Years later the old, forsaken Contreras committed the unpardonable indiscretion of writing an article in *La Nación,* reminding the Benefactor, with the help of Aesopian language, of his famous life-saving operation. Instead of the expected expression of gratitude, Contreras received a sharp rebuke. The Generalissimo does not owe anything to anyone, he was told. He, Contreras, was showing how ungrateful he was by failing to appreciate the unique privilege bestowed upon him when he was allowed to treat such an illustrious patient.

Always conscious of his good looks as much as of his health, Trujillo affects extreme elegance in his dress and personal appurtenances. Even as a young telegraph operator in his home town he tried to dress above his station. Today he meticulously resorts to the most elaborate uniforms and immaculate clothes.

Such is the Generalissimo's passion for clothes that he keeps complete wardrobes—which according to biographer Nanita "might well be envied by a prince"—in each of his twelve main residences. "The best tailors in New York, London and Paris fashion his clothes," asserts Nanita. Impeccably attired in mufti (he favors single-breasted, white linen suits), the Generalissimo could pass for a man born to wealth and good taste. His shirts are custom made, with initials on the left sleeve. His links, sometimes of extravagant design, are either gold or platinum. A near-feminine token is a bejeweled military identification bracelet. But it is in neckties that he excels. Nanita points out that "his collection of neckties is famous." Trujillo adores hand-painted originals, often costing as much as $100.

Yet, in uniform—his chest bedecked with medals—the Benefactor takes on the gorgeous appearance of a tropical macaw. His favorite dress uniform (worth $10,000) which might come straight from a comic-opera stage, is a symphony of gold. It combines a white-plumed hat thickly crusted with gold braid, gold brocaded swallow-tailed coat with hefty epaulets, tricolored sash and gold-striped blue trousers. The sash is a distinctive feature of all the Generalissimo's uniforms.

It is the plumed hat that Trujillo considers the supreme symbol of his rank. He, and occasionally little Héctor, the President, are the only persons in the country permitted to sport such headgear. When Anselmo A. Paulino, the Benefactor's favorite and right-hand man for seven years, fell into disgrace in August 1954, one of the charges against him, as printed in *El Caribe,* was that he had been photographed in the privacy of his bedroom wearing a plumed hat. For days the entire machinery of government investigated the whereabouts of Señor Paulino's hat and the photo of it.

The Benefactor moves easily with people of wide culture. "The Generalissimo himself is known as a host who combines dignity with a great sense of humor," wrote the American journalist Stanley Walker, author of two eulogistic books on Trujillo printed and distributed at the Dominican taxpayers' cost by the Caribbean Library of the Dominican Information Center of New York City. "He talks well, easily and confidently, on many subjects, whether in ordinary conversation or in set speeches."

It is well known, however, that Trujillo is neither an eloquent nor a forceful speaker. His high-pitched voice has proved an insurmountable stumbling block. His delivery is stiff, and it is rather pathetic to hear him stammering and struggling through the pronunciation of the strange, high-sounding words which Palace ghost-writers insert in his written speeches. Trujillo's style, however, is not cramped by these shortcomings since, unlike other modern dictators, his political success is not based on his ability to move vast masses of men by force of words.

Though sometimes flamboyant and usually pompous in his public behavior, Trujillo is deliberate and even modest in private and direct conversations. A man of few words, his answers—usually preceded by a silence of seconds—are sharp, brief, always to the point. He is an attentive listener, but at times he takes on an absent-minded appearance and then there is no answer forthcoming to the requests put to him. This is the situation most feared by his aides, because no one is supposed to press thereafter any issue thus dealt with by Trujillo. Those few daring enough to break this rule have regretted it.

In his conferences with foreigners these qualities are exceedingly helpful and tend to cover much of Trujillo's ignorance and lack of culture. By listening attentively he manages to give the impression of a readiness to deal with issues on their merits without the usual fog of demagogic ideological jargon expected from most dictators. "He never gets bombastic," a foreign collaborator remarked. "He talks to you as one man to another. He does not try to indoctrinate you," was the reaction of an American newspaperman whom I accompanied on a visit to the Palace.

As a rule, visitors come from a short visit to Trujillo's office convinced that "the Chief" is unfailingly well-informed on international developments. The truth is, however, that beneath his well-groomed appearance and social charm, acquired late in life, the Generalissimo remains at heart the same crude village tough who enlisted in the Constabulary. Under Trujillo's outward self-assurance and seemingly controlled physical reactions lies a flaming and lethal temper, which explodes in fierce outbursts of wrath at the slightest show of opposition to his will whenever things go wrong or subordinates do not carry out orders with the expected celerity. Then Trujillo's voice takes on a shrill quality, almost effeminate.

In my personal relations with Trujillo I never had to suffer one of his outbursts of temper; I tried always to keep our contacts on a businesslike level. In my frequent interviews with him he never used a biting word, although sometimes when I was waiting in the anteroom of his office I would hear him dressing down one of his subordinates: *"Imbéciles, imbéciles,"* he would shout, "I'm surrounded by *imbéciles."*

Few people know, however, when Trujillo is really mad or just acting. He possesses an enormous histrionic talent, which he does not waste. I remember one particular occasion in which after scolding and humiliating in my presence his long-time favorite the present Ambassador to the United States, Manuel de Moya, in the most degrading fashion, I caught the Benefactor making gestures at the back of his departing bowing and worried aide. Then he laughed as if nothing had happened and sat down to business with me in a jovial manner. (De Moya forgave Trujillo but not me. That day I earned a powerful enemy inside the inner circle.)

This talent allows Trujillo, when occasion warrants it, to assume a contrite look. His face can look very sad to a widow whose husband has just been murdered on his orders.

2.

RAFAEL L. TRUJILLO IS AN ENERGETIC MAN WHO HAS gone places all his life because he toils while his competitors and foes rest. The Generalissimo marches on as the dean of all living dictators. Asked once why it so happened, Trujillo snapped: "Because I work at my job."

Trujillo's working day is a grueling routine. It is not unusual for him to spend nine or ten hours a day at his desk, working longer and harder than any of his subordinates. He is an early riser, and sleepy cabinet members are often aroused at four in the morning to be asked by the Benefactor about matters concerning their departments. On one occasion a Secretary of Agriculture was called from bed about a missing mule.

A normal working day begins with appropriate pomp a few minutes before seven on the morning when Trujillo is in the capital. The palace guards stiffen at attention and bugles sound when a black limousine glides through the main gate. A few seconds later the Generalissimo steps out and goes up in a private elevator to his offices in the eastern wing of the enormous building. Contrary to what many people believe, the Benefactor does not live in the four-million-dollar Palace he built in 1947; his offices are there. In the Palace's gilded salons he conducts state business, receives ambassadors and delegations and entertains foreign dignitaries.

As an important part of his early morning routine he sees the group of civilian aides working at the Palace, led by the Secretary of the Presidency, who at present is his nephew Luis Ruiz Trujillo. To them he gives instructions for official decrees, directives and appointments, which once prepared are taken to the opposite wing of the Palace for brother Héctor's signature. Then he receives his military and secret police aides and finally hears complaints against high-handed unauthorized treatment by local Government officials in the interior as well as appeals for personal help. Next, his business manager Tirso Rivera comes into Trujillo's office with reports about the vast ramifications of the *trujillista* business empire, with the exception of sugar, which is handled by "the Big One's" financial wizard, Dr. Jesús María Troncoso.

Then he starts his reading chores. Since he does not like to look over any document longer than one page, a small specialized staff digests the voluminous reports pouring in daily from ministries, provincial governors, police agencies, informers and the *Partido Dominicano*. All this summarized correspondence provides a weathervane to indicate currents in people's feelings as well as the raw material for the slashing letters and news stories planted in the newspapers to terrorize foes and friends.

To keep himself abreast of developments abroad the Generalissimo relies on the secret service reports, which include monitored versions of news agency dispatches, editorials or opinion columns of direct concern to the Dominican Republic or of general interest.

Next come the audiences, which start at about 11 o'clock and take the rest of the morning. Trujillo talks almost daily with each of his senior aides (who are not necessarily cabinet officers) but no one visits him without explicit invitation. Each aide is allowed a few minutes of "the Chief's" time, but hardly anyone is asked to sit down.

At 12 sharp the Benefactor takes his private elevator to the third floor, where lunch is served for him and a handful of his most trusted assistants, including the President. While eating, Trujillo keeps on discussing official business. Luncheon is followed by a half-hour walk and then Trujillo goes home for his siesta.

Around 3:30 in the afternoon the Generalissimo is back at the National Palace for another two or three hours of intense labor. Sometimes he does his afternoon work at home, with the help of only one or two secretaries. Though a professedly devout Catholic, "the Chief" has not missed a single Sunday morning at his office during the past twelve years. However, Sunday afternoons he goes to the race track to see his own horses win.

When in town Trujillo performs a well-publicized piece of filial duty every evening—at 6:30 he visits his mother's home. "A warmly affectionate son," he is called by one of his official biographers.

Trujillo regards walking as the most healthful exercise. After visiting his mother, he takes a two or three mile walk daily. These strolls are a torture for some of his younger, less robust cronies forced to follow him at a very fast pace along the sidewalks of George Washington Avenue, the broad thoroughfare that borders the Caribbean Sea shoreline.

It is on this Avenue that, four times a week, "the Chief" sits at the sea-wall and holds evening court or what a friendly American reporter called "impromptu cabinet meetings." Nothing important, however, is ever decided in these meetings, dedicated almost exclusively to small talk. The newest piece of local gossip and the unprintable stories currently in vogue are welcomed, but serious matters are seldom brought up, and then only if Trujillo himself shows an interest.

"This is a moment of relaxation and the Chief must be amused, not over-burdened with the dead weight of official business," explained one of the habitués. Yet, if the boss always derives fun, the amusement is seldom shared by his subordinates attending these evening sessions. They are usually the butt of practical jokes, not always in the best taste. Sometimes a timely and sharply pointed joke or a particularly pugnacious comment from a rival's mouth has proved to be a high official's undoing.

Foreign observers who have seen the Benefactor setting the pace for his small army of aides often inquire about the methods used by Trujillo when selecting these companions. I do not know of any special invitations being issued, though when a man is not wanted he is told so in a very blunt way by one of Trujillo's bodyguards. High army officers are always welcomed, as long as they keep their mouths closed and participate in the general conversation only when asked a direct question.

In mid-week there is a change of routine. From Wednesday to Friday "the Big One" retires to his estate at his home town of San Cristóbal. While in seclusion, the telephone is Trujillo's most important channel for communicating with subordinates. He talks several times a day with his most important collaborators, but only a few hand-picked aides can visit *Las Caobas,* the luxurious mahogany mansion built by Trujillo in the center of his huge farm, *Hacienda Fundación.*

There, however, not all is rest, nor does "the Big One" retire to plough fields, search the writings of the greatest philosophers or ponder the mission of man. Sometimes—though not with the frequency of bygone days—retirement is a front for the celebration of brilliant, prolonged soirees.

Trujillo's antics at *Las Caobas* have generated his widespread fame as a hard drinking man. Yet, this much talked-about subject is one on which even his official biographers have not reached an agreement. For instance, Nanita says: "Despite his ability to withstand the intoxicating effects of alcohol, (Trujillo) is a light drinker." Stanley Walker says: "He enjoys good liquor in the company of friends, especially fine old Spanish brandy, and he sips it with the aplomb of the true *caballero.*"

The truth is that the Benefactor used to be a real *aficionado* in his youth and middle age. Lately, however, he barely touches the cup outside *Las Caobas* and even there parties are no longer as gay and prolonged as they used to be. At diplomatic and official receptions he slowly sips an occasional glass of champagne or a cup of *Carlos Primero,* the aged Spanish brandy he strongly favors.

Let us not imply that Trujillo is reaching retirement. Nor may anyone call him a saint—his escapades with the opposite sex (not always gentlemanly or discreet) are still too numerous for that. He is still much the same person whose charm has deceived many men and enthralled as many women. As he lives in a Latin country, where manhood still is measured by the number of females a man has been able to subdue, Trujillo's prowess with women commands a great deal of public attention. As Theodore Draper pointed out, "One of the few liberties that his hangers-on take with his private life is to joke boastfully about his exploits with women."

Nanita describes Trujillo's charm, in the fourth edition of his widely circulated biography, in the following terms: "Women delight him. He is unfailingly gallant, attentive and considerate toward them. He enjoys being in their company. *A pretty feminine face is for him the best introduction card.* Handsome and striking in bearing, it hardly need be added that his enormous popularity with the fair sex stems from something other than politics. When he makes his way through enthusiastic crowds, many a look of admiration from feminine eyes and many sighs are sent his way for the man he is, independently of his being a national hero." (Italics added.)

The phrase *"A pretty feminine face is for him the best introduction card"* was dropped from subsequent editions of Nanita's book, now in its tenth. The dropping followed the publication in the American press of sly remarks of the kind to which the Benefactor is allergic.

Being too busy to court beautiful girls himself, Trujillo has special aides charged with that chore. The years pass but the fires of passion are not smothered in Trujillo's heart, so even to this day many Dominicans, including fathers and brothers, make their good fortunes over the virtue of a beautiful and willing female relative or friend. Notwithstanding rumors to the contrary, other men's wives are not in demand, since Trujillo likes to hold exclusive rights upon his women. His favorites and former girl friends are all "marked women" and no man can get close to them without risk. Women, moreover, are invariably one of the main sources of much information as well as useful gossip for the Benefactor.

There are still other things about which Trujillo brags—his horsemanship and his capability to dance a good *merengue,* the Dominican national dance. Moreover, during his stay at his country home he practices the only two sports at which he is proficient: riding and shooting. The *merengue* he dances well, and when he is at a party the orchestra always plays a good many of them, especially those whose words describe his glories.

Unquestionably "the Big One" is a man without hobbies or cultural and artistic interests. Looking for a justification of this, Nanita put it this way: "He is free of fetishes and quirks. He likes animals but not exaggeratedly.

Nor is he exaggeratedly fond of hunting and fishing; neither can he be called a sports fan." Then the biographer adds: "Unlike Franklin Delano Roosevelt he is not a philatelist; nor does he collect coins as did the late King Victor Emmanuel; nor lions and tigers as did Goering and Juan Vicente Gómez of Venezuela. His sole hobby is horses, which he rides masterfully." Lately, indeed, "the Chief" does not miss a horse race or a polo game.

"Although the Generalissimo for years has had several residences, or at least homes which he could call his own, in various parts of the country, his official residence is adjacent to the residence of the American Ambassador in Ciudad Trujillo," wrote biographer Stanley Walker.

This latter place is called *Estancia Rhadamés,* after Trujillo's youngest legitimate son. A huge marble compound, one finds in it a curious jumble of decorative styles: undistinguished Spanish oil paintings on the walls, delicate French furniture and an almost absurd display of mahogany. Trujillo is so obsessed with mahogany, which he considers the hallmark of luxury, that he made Congress pass a law in September 1957 instituting the flower of the mahogany tree as the "national symbol."

Walker's description of Trujillo's residence is almost complete. "This splendid estate is one of the finest in the whole Caribbean area. The mansion has rooms for receptions, study and entertainment. There is a dentist's office, a motion picture theater, lounges, a beauty parlor, a barber shop, sewing rooms, a swimming pool, a gymnasium, an ice-skating rink built especially for young Rhadamés, and several bars. The parlors, dining halls and living quarters are splendid. There are also quarters for the military guard." Walker missed the nine-foot wall that surrounds the estate.

3.   AS WITH OTHER DICTATORS, RAFAEL L. TRUJILLO, HAVING surmounted powerful disadvantages, has fallen under a humorless constraint to prove himself a superior being. Trujillo regards himself an instrument of God, a chosen man with a great mission to perform. He longs for people to fawn upon him and call him the greatest humanitarian ever. He derives immense pleasure when his hired or conscripted apologists write lengthy accounts of his achievements as protector of the needy, as forgiver of his foes and as the open-hearted, benevolent father of his people. Spiritual values, however, have no genuine appeal for Trujillo. Nevertheless, for publicity purposes he will carry to any length his efforts to give an overlay of humanitarianism to actions inspired by the most selfish impulses of his insatiable egotism.

The following incident will serve as illustration. On January 1, 1950, I was called to appear before Trujillo, who explained to me that he was considering the possibility of releasing my brother Horacio, condemned a few months earlier to thirty years in prison for participation in the abortive revolutionary invasion of Luperon. Generously enough, the Benefactor advised me that my brother's health had been impaired as result of prison life and showed a concern lest grave complications would be forthcoming. He suggested that a trip to the exclusive mountain resort of Constanza would do a lot of good.

Ten days later Horacio was released, and even though the Benefactor's reports on his health had proved exaggerated, he was sent for a rest cure to Constanza. In the glow of seeing my brother free I sent a warm letter of gratitude to the Benefactor, written in the only language Dominicans are allowed to address themselves to him.[1]

Without seeking a belated justification for my action, I may say that at the time I was not assailed by any uncomfortable suspicion that what was going on was just another of Trujillo's "humanitarian" plays. I thought that "the Chief" was beginning to feel normal pangs of conscience. Prior to that moment, ever since my brother's capture in the wake of the unfortunate landing he had led, Trujillo had been adroitly exploiting the circumstance that two brothers were so prominently placed on opposite sides of the fence. Since all through the revolutionary attempt—which lasted only one day—and thereafter, I had been allowed to stay at my job as editor-in-chief of *El Caribe,* the *trujillista* propaganda machine found itself with an excellent melody to play in support of their contention that "the Big One" was an understanding, open-minded, good-hearted, democratic leader. To say the least, they were cannily using my brother and me to bolster Trujillo's forlorn prestige before international public opinion. Though the obvious maneuver could hardly escape my attention, there was not much I could do. Fearful of further endangering Horacio's personal security, I did not take refuge in a foreign embassy (a recourse not yet closed to Dominicans) as advised by trusted friends.

But when I was advised of Horacio's freedom, I did not know that the curtain had not been drawn over the sordid play. My first contact with the hard face of truth did not take place until a few days later, upon receiving word that my brother was on his way back from Constanza, and that he would stay at my home. Then I learned that he was scheduled to appear as a witness before a fact-finding group of the Organization of American States, then conducting a sweeping investigation of the troubled Caribbean political situation.

Had I needed any further proof of the motives behind the Benefactor's sudden concern for my brother's health, I would have found it at a forth-

[1] Lately my letter to Trujillo has been widely circulated by Dominican press agents to show my ungratefulness and my former unreserved admiration for the Benefactor.

coming reception held at the Jaragua hotel. To convey the news of his latest act of "generosity" to his distinguished guests, Trujillo played another mean trick. While talking with a group of the visiting diplomats he sent for me. After introducing me to the ambassadors, "the Chief" asked me a few irrelevant questions and then, in a matter of fact tone, inquired about my brother's health. "How was his trip down from Constanza?" was his next question. Expertly prompted by him I was forced to tell the full story of his humanitarian gesture, for the benefit of the foreign ambassadors.

There are brighter sides to Trujillo's touching concern for the health and welfare of his friends and foes. He stakes a claim as a man of wide cultural interests as well as protector of arts and sciences, and for his efforts in favor of the full enlightenment of his fellow citizens there have been bestowed on him such titles as "First Teacher of the Dominican Republic," "First Journalist," etc. The University of Santo Domingo made him a "doctor honoris causa" in all its disciplines, a gesture that found its counterpart in another such honorary degree awarded to the Benefactor by the University of Pittsburgh.

Notwithstanding his array of titles and degrees, it is the truth that Trujillo not only lacks formal education, but has not made any effort to acquire any culture by himself, except the formal social manners which permit him to carry on a conversation and impress casual guests at social functions.

Trujillo's detractors claim that he has never read a book in his life. In rebuttal one of his apologists cites the titles of two books "the Chief" has not only read, but keeps on top of his desk. Nanita asserts that "of the fine arts he prefers music and poetry, although he has not delved deeply into either." The official biographer further claims that Trujillo once wrote a sonnet.

From what I personally know, the Benefactor's reading habits are not very discriminating. He does not read much and when he does, he rarely shows good judgment. He is an avid reader of pulp magazines and according to Hy Gardner, columnist of the *New York Herald Tribune,* the Benefactor is one of the distinguished foreign subscribers to *Confidential* magazine.

As a "doctor honoris causa" and also as a duly appointed professor of economics at the University Law School, the Benefactor can extend, and usually does, his authority into any area of professional conduct. Through his reading of magazines of the kind that carry patent medicine advertisements, Trujillo has acquired such a high medical culture that in the summer of 1956 he felt himself ready to offer his advice to Dominican physicians. He printed an advertisement in *El Caribe's* issue of July 8, 1956, arrogating for himself the right to be called in consultation by Dominican doctors whenever they were faced by a particularly difficult case. This remarkable advertisement suggested that doctors write him, care of the Medical Department, National Palace, any time they wanted the help of his medical knowledge.

The reception given by the medical class to the offer has not been recorded, but a few days later *El Caribe* printed a letter to the Benefactor, signed by one Doctor José G. Sobá, thanking him for his "lofty disposition" to assist the Dominican physicians. Sobá pointed out the enormous benefits the doctors might derive from Trujillo's advice, since the latter had at his disposal the means of acquiring information that were beyond the physicians' reach. Soon thereafter Sobá was appointed Secretary of Public Health. On October 18, 1956, *El Caribe* printed another advertisement stating that as result of a consultation held with the Benefactor a dying patient had recovered his health.

This was not a joke. To be sure, the Generalissimo is a man with a sense of humor, but of quite another sort. Two examples will suffice to show Trujillo's humor at its best. In 1952 Trujillo spread the rumor inside the country that he would soon start training a military unit to be sent to Korea to fight side by side with the United States forces. True enough, the drafting of its members started shortly thereafter. Helped by the stringent provisions of the Conscription Act, the Benefactor ordered the military authorities to recruit 400 men, but only among those classified as "subversives" by the secret police. "Since they love democracy so much, I'll give them an opportunity to die for it," said the Benefactor.

Within a few weeks men from all walks of life as well as all ages were drilling at the naval base across the Ozama river opposite downtown Ciudad Trujillo. Only the beginning of the peace talks at Panmunjon kept these people from giving their lives on foreign soil for the democracy they do not have at home.

In April 1956 the distinguished socialist Norman Thomas, who had expressed some barbed criticism of Trujillo's methods of terror, received a telegram inviting him to visit the Dominican Republic, where he would be given an "apotheosis as welcome." Supposedly sent by the *Partido Socialista Popular* (communist), the telegram carried the alleged signatures of four well-known Dominicans who were at the time serving jail terms on Trujillo's orders, including my own father. None of the signers had ever been a sympathizer of the communist movement.

"Beware of the small things with Trujillo. They cause the biggest outbursts and the worst crises," explained to me a man who had worked close to "the Big One" long enough to know that much. As a journalist I had several opportunities to prove the wisdom of my friend's advice. During my early days of reporting, one of my jobs was to write the social column of the daily *La Nación,* then owned by Trujillo personally. The Benefactor himself made that reporting job one of the most taxing I have ever performed. He was the severest censor of the requirements for a person to appear in the social column and censorship even affected members of his own family. There were no definite criteria to keep a person out other than Trujillo's caprices, so I never knew what to do. Consequently, hardly a day went by without receiving a summons to the publisher's office who, patiently enough, would explain to me the nature of the latest complaints from, as he used to call it, the "heights." The most frequent one was about the appearance in my column, not the name of an enemy of the regime (I was not that stupid), but the name of a relative of a relative of some obscure exile. I finally quit the job.

Before giving up, however, I remember a furious call personally made by the First Lady on me instead of my publisher, objecting to the insertion of the name of a socially prominent person. To my dismay I found out later that by doing this I had reopened in the kind lady's heart an old wound caused by a still remembered social slight received years before.

On another occasion I was fired and rehired within two hours. The trouble began with the publication of a front-page story reporting the arrival in the country of the late poet Osvaldo Bazil, one of Trujillo's earlier collaborators and most consistent drinking companions. He rated a front-page story, but what no one seemed to know at *La Nación* was that Bazil, who had been serving as Trujillo's Ambassador to Brazil, was returning in total disgrace. The Benefactor had sacked him upon receiving word that his friend, while drinking, had exposed himself in his underwear at a Rio de Janeiro hotel.

As I would normally be in charge of covering such a story, Trujillo thought I was guilty of the misdemeanor and ordered my publisher to fire me. Naturally, upon notification of the drastic measure I wanted to know what it was all about. Convinced of my innocence, since someone else had written the story, the publisher called the Palace to explain and Trujillo condescended to reinstate me.

These were my first, but not last, contacts with this aspect of Trujillo's personality. Years later as editor and then publisher of *El Caribe* my experiences along these lines were bound to multiply. In the latter period I became accustomed to hear Trujillo complain about things ranging from the use of an objectionable photograph of himself (he hates to be shown smiling) to the failure to run the cut of Trujillo's late father on the front page. Once I spent a full morning with the peerless leader scanning the collection of His Excellency's pictures then in *El Caribe's* morgue. After a thorough look at each one, Trujillo himself red-penciled those he wanted to be discarded.

This shows how difficult it is to work under the Benefactor's supervision, especially since for him practically everything depends on personal whims.

4.   ONE OF THE UNSETTLED MYSTERIES IN RAFAEL L. Trujillo's life is whether he is courageous. No one can produce facts to support the contentions that he is a gallant knight or a coward.

Twice he has received medals awarded by Congress to honor his supposed bravery. However, none of the acts cited in the whereases of the "heroic laws," borrowing a phrase from de Galíndez, can be properly covered by a comprehensive definition of courage. Furthermore, outside of a few skirmishes against so-called bandits during the American military occupation, there is no record that the Generalissimo has ever been under fire. On the other hand, the recalcitrant enemies who describe the Benefactor as a physical coward have not been able to produce any evidence in support of this charge.

The Generalissimo no doubt is a man who takes good care of his personal security. But this might be because he wants to live longer and better than any other man. Many acts which are interpreted as betraying cowardice are normal precautions which no Chief of State would shun. Whenever necessary, Trujillo confronts peril with resolution. Although avowedly wary of airplanes (he does not allow his Air Force General son, Rafael, Jr., to fly), he has traveled by air several times. Of course, he prefers his yachts of which there are two always ready to sail.

Trujillo is one of the most closely guarded rulers in the world. *Estancia Rhadamés* is surrounded by a nine-foot wall and guarded day and night by hand-picked sharpshooters of the Presidential Guard. As an extra measure of security the residence was built next door to the American Embassy. Its other neighbors are carefully screened by the secret police; those who do not satisfy these exigent watch-dogs are invited to move.

Also guarded by high walls and scores of sentries and secret service men is the National Palace. Within its walls are quartered the seasoned veterans of the Presidential Guard, whose loyalty is constantly checked.

Before entering the Palace enclosure, visitors must check with security officers inside the building. Only after a careful investigation of the purpose of the visit are they allowed to pass the gates. Once inside they are kept within sight of guards and plain-clothes agents of the secret police. Even high officials working at the Palace need a special entrance card.

American journalists who have seen Trujillo during his daily stroll or at work in his Palace office, his back to an open door one hundred feet from the street, have gathered the impression that the Benfactor is a man who does not take much care of his personal security. They wonder why no one has tried such a seemingly easy thing as taking a pot shot at him.

Others, however, have had an opportunity to see better, for instance, the *New York Herald Tribune* reporter who interviewed "the Chief" in September 1957. "Five persons were present during the interview in the large, mahogany paneled, blue-walled reception room adjacent to the Generalissimo's private office in the National Palace—the Generalissimo, Manuel de Moya, Dominican Ambassador to the United States, an interpreter, this reporter, and an armed soldier who remained unobtrusively in the doorway." Anyone who late in the afternoon happens to follow the planned itinerary for Trujillo's evening strolls could hardly miss seeing a police van discharging policemen armed with sub-machine guns. The men are discreetly placed, ten to fifteen paces apart, inside front yards, behind bushes, on the cliffs and other carefully selected points along the route. Two officers always precede Trujillo and his entourage, advising people on the boulevard to move along. Sometimes, though not as a rule, traffic is detoured. When Dominicans see discreetly placed sentries and convoys of police around any public place or residence, they know that "the Big One" is in the neighborhood.

But if Trujillo has been denied opportunity to show courage under fire, in the field of verbal battles he has fought with distinction. He enjoys exchanging blows and he never hits above the belt. His punch is directed where it hurts—the reputation, character and private lives of his opponents. He has become so accustomed to this kind of warfare that, as one of his collaborators said, "He is like a fighting cock. When he does not have an adversary he gets restless and sometimes pecks at his own shadow."

However, he will not fight if there is not a good omen. This he once admitted to one of his biographers. "There is luck in life, of course," Trujillo said. "Chance plays its part. Destiny has its effect. But for me these things don't matter. I believe in them, but I'm not affected by them."

However, it is said that his well-known fear of hurricanes comes from the prophecy of a witch who told him that as he came into power with a hurricane (the one that struck the capital city seventeen days after his first inauguration), he would go out with another one. The strange thing is that since 1930 not one has struck the country. But at the slightest warning of a big blow my office at *El Caribe* used to be deluged by frantic phone calls from the Palace.

Ostensibly Trujillo is now a practicing Catholic. In 1954 he traveled to Rome to sign a Concordat with the Pope, and Catholicism is the official religion of the Dominican Republic. The Vatican representative and the Church hierarchy are his best propagandists, and a Dominican priest, Fray Zenon Castillo, has compared him with Charlemagne and has advanced the opinion that the Generalissimo should be officially appointed "Benefactor of the Church."

Presumably, Trujillo joined the Church actively because his third wife, whom he had wed in a civil ceremony, wanted to sanctify their union. Twice divorced, Trujillo, whose first marriage was in the Church, was not a likely candidate for a Catholic wedding. Yet somehow he won the necessary indulgences and the rites were performed by the Papal Nuncio on the First Lady's birthday, August 9, 1955.

THE PRACTICAL POLITICIAN

1. TRUJILLO'S BASIC MOTIVATIONS REST UPON THE CRUDEST sort of self-interest, concealed now by one, now by another, mask of high-sounding words. It is almost a hopeless task to seek out any political principle to which the Generalissimo has adhered consistently.

Trujillo's lack of a social philosophy or a definite political creed has never hampered his successful bid for absolute power. Everything he does is done with one purpose in mind: to retain absolute power. In his unwavering determination to do so, he has not hesitated at any betrayal of earlier friends or alleged convictions, nor shrunk from any alliances in order to gain his ends. His is pragmatism in its basest form. Thus he has been at one time or another either a friend of the Nazis or an apologist for the Soviet Union and then a few years later a champion of the Church and a valiant knight fighting almost single-handed the Red Dragon.

Whatever his inner beliefs, Trijullo always assimilated without much effort what is good for him even if it means a reversal of previous attitudes or a synthesis of discordant theories.

There is not a shred of evidence (except in matters of anti-Communism) that Trujillo has contributed anything constructive to the contemporary philosophy of Government. His remarkable material accomplishments as well as his astonishing shortcomings puzzle many observers of the Latin American scene. Here they have a man who eludes classification, either as a modern totalitarian dictator or as a classical Latin *caudillo*. But, anyway, the fervor of his followers—among whom are a few sincere believers—the fury of his enemies, along with his own frenetic energy, assure Trujillo a place as a living legend.

His supporters and paid apologists picture Trujillo as a genius if not a demigod. (The most popular *trujillista* slogan has been for years "God and Trujillo.") He is the avowed enemy of Communism, the defender of the faith, the creator of the New Fatherland, the benefactor and paternal leader of a whole nation.

Still to a few others, including a highly influential group of American legislators, high diplomatic and defense officials, Trujillo is a strong political and military ally of the United States and an uncompromising foe of the Soviet Union, whose many faults must be forgiven just for that reason. These torch-carriers for the Benefactor quote him as saying that he would throw Dominican sugar into the sea rather than sell it to the Reds as Cuba has been doing lately. A remark prompted perhaps by the fact that the Soviet Union had never approached "the Chief" with a good proposition.

After visiting the Dominican Republic, Theodore Draper wrote that Trujillo is by no means clearly classified. "He disgusts some people, fascinates others, and can disgust and fascinate simultaneously."

Certainly there is no possible neutrality with respect to Trujillo—either you are for him or against him. He, himself, recognizes only allies or enemies and eliminates neutrals whenever possible.

I knew Trujillo for several years and worked close beside him. I know that any honest attempt to be objective about this man, who almost defies objectivity, is likely to be unsuccessful. Yet I recognize that he is a practical psychologist with the instincts of a pirate—a tough, intelligent and canny character, from whom it is folly to expect either scruples or mercy.

Trujillo's absolutism has many points of contact with modern totalitarian dictatorships. Yet it lacks a significant feature common to all one-party states: an ideology. Most dictators want power in order to carry out some idea which may or may not be essentially an expression of their egos, but Trujillo has not developed a coherent doctrine of his own.

The Generalissimo is not a systematic thinker, nor has he tried to build a comprehensive order of political philosophy in which his rule could find a theoretical basis, in the manner of Juan Perón's *justicialismo* or Colombia's former dictator Gustavo Rojas Pinilla's "third force."

Nowhere can even a speech be found in which Trujillo sets forth ideas that might be evolved into a theory of government. His famous primer *Cartilla Civica,* which is required reading in Dominican schools, is a hodgepodge of platitudes coupled with a few banal pieces of advice on how to apprehend revolutionists attempting to overthrow the regime.

Nor are there any original political ideas in Trujillo's widely distributed speech "Evolution of Democracy in Santo Domingo," which is always handed to foreign visitors (including Vice President Richard Nixon) as a summing-up of the Dictator's wisdom. The picture Trujillo paints in this tract is simple enough: he has done a lot of good for the country. He keeps order and has eliminated the Dominican deep-rooted practice of revolt by following through the policy of disarmament of the population set forth by the U.S. Marines. He paid the country's external debt, setting what the United States State Department called "an example worthy of emulation," and through a policy of "honesty and efficiency" he has improved sanitation and carried on a vast program of public works and economic development. Above all, he is a friend of the United States. "Side by side with the United States we entered the armed conflict in view of the treacherous Pearl Harbor attack." (It must be noted that not a single Dominican soldier ever fired a shot in World War II.)

The importance of the fight against Communism scarcely needs emphasis, and Trujillo's innate political intuition indicated to him from the outset that here was an issue to grab. Thus, when self-preservation and Soviet treachery forced the Western World into the "cold war," the Generalissimo came forward to offer substantial verbal assistance. Without qualms Trujillo dropped his former Communist allies with whom he had made common cause at the end of World War II in an effort to bolster his dictatorship then tottering under the democratic winds sweeping away Latin American dictators.

Again and again Trujillo has demonstrated his complete lack of interest in any positive theory of government. He has already given the Dominican Republic three constitutions, but save for a few provisions inserted in them to adjust the nation's legal structure to his passing whims, they have followed the democratic lines of practically all Latin American constitutions, based upon American and French liberal traditions. This does not mean that the Benefactor adheres to the letter or spirit of these instruments. Except for attaching his name to the brand-new Magna Chartas, Trujillo has never paid any heed to their provisions. For years he has ruled the country without bothering to be elected its President. He governs while nominally holding the rank of Generalissimo of the Armed Forces. Although a big array of honorary titles imbedded in the Constitution, such as "Benefactor of the Fatherland" and "Father of the New Fatherland," gives him the official status of an elder statesman, there is not a single constitutional provision authorizing the existing dual system under which Trujillo rules and the President is a figurehead in charge of receiving foreign ambassadors and rubber stamping executive orders.

To Trujillo politics is not a system—it is a great and contradictory panorama providing an outlet for his acute megalomania, his lust for power, his demagogic talents as well as his sharp ability for maneuver. At its best, Trujillo's is totalitarianism at the service of the absolute and untrammeled personal will of one man. Notwithstanding broadly different opinions on "the Chief's" work and personality, he still must be regarded as an example, though outstanding, of the classical unprincipled, ruthless Latin American dictator. "As a blend of the Emperor Jones and the European authoritarians," pointed out *Time*, "Dictator Trujillo and his ilk always seem bizarre to North Americans. But the southern dictators must be understood if Latin America is to be understood by the big neighbor in the North."

The following reasons were the best the newspaper *La Nación* could find to explain why Trujillo should stay in power:

1. His work must be protected from sacrilegious hands which might sully or destroy it.

2. He guarantees respect for Dominican sovereignty.

3. He is forging a spirit of true nationality.

4. He has put a stop to outrages, restored the principle of territoriality, and cleansed Dominicans of their old sins.

5. His genius for statesmanship is essential to the part the country must play in the new world order.

6. He will make the Dominican Republic the key of the new Americanism in which all the peoples of the New World will cooperate.

"Let the mad dogs bark," the newspaper wound up saying. "His enemies lack the stature to challenge him. While they talk, he works. While they try to destroy, he builds. While they discredit and like to satisfy petty passions, he preaches harmony, imposes order, pays tribute to justice, furthers peace, and fosters work."

All clues for the existence and performance of the regime must be sought in the character and personality of Trujillo himself—in his serious, elusive capacity to reconcile the most flagrant contradictions and to rationalize the grossest inconsistencies. Only by taking into account Trujillo's preoccupation with what is good for Trujillo may we find the key to many of the seemingly contradictory policies of the regime.

Trujillo has always shown a lightning-like perception of the needs of each passing moment. His extraordinary flair for the main chance, for the winning side of any controversy is illustrated by the remarkable changes that have taken place in his political attitudes. He incessantly preaches international peace at any price, but has seldom hesitated to saber-rattle without embarrassment in matters of his own interest, as he did in December 1949 when he forced Congress to pass a law authorizing him to declare war against any nation harboring enemies of his regime.

Trujillo's complete lack of political inhibitions explains as well his baffling turnabouts, timed to keep him on the winner's band wagon in the field of international politics. Right after Pearl Harbor he was one of the first Latin American rulers to take his country into the war on the United Nations side, despite his former well-known Nazi sympathies.

The Benefactor has boldly taken the place of self-appointed leader of the "anti-Communist crusade," and the Dominican press never misses an opportunity to remind its readers that "the Chief" is a "champion of the Church, defender of Christian traditions and crusader against Communism." High-ranking American guests are always told by Trujillo: "If I do not rule the Dominican Republic, the Communists will." He has conveniently forgotten, of course, the occasion when he declared that the Soviet Union "will be forever recognized as one of the great forces for welfare and progress on which the democratic world can count."

Today, in speeches and other public utterances Trujillo shamelessly proclaims his right to the title of "First Anti-Communist of the World." In support of this contention, the Benefactor asserts that "this humble country of the Caribbean (the Dominican Republic) anticipated the bewildering, world-shaking events of today and initiated the great battle that will decide the fate of western civilization."

Since the day he jumped on the anti-Communist band wagon, Trujillo has been discovering Red plots everywhere. Since he outlawed the Communist party he himself had allowed to operate in the country, his propaganda presents him as a gallant knight fighting single-handed the Red dragon. "Communism found us alone," Trujillo also asserted in his "democratic" speech, "but indeed not lacking in courage and strength to thwart its designs and ward off its influence in the Caribbean."

The Benefactor argues that his great anti-Communist feats were accomplished without even "moral succor from an unbiased press." It seems that everybody else was bent on helping the Reds and "American newspapers either held off in a frigid, baffling silence favorable to the Communist scheme, or, to go along with the plotting governments, plunged into a foul campaign to discredit our country and its leaders."

Whether Trujillo believes his own scare stories is not important. What is frightening is the number of gullible ears in which they have been sown. Trujillo has evolved anti-Communism into a flourishing political business.

Moreover, whatever the sincerity of his present vocal support of the struggle against Soviet imperialism, Trujillo has managed to instill into the important issue a dangerous element of confusion, particularly with respect to the identity of the actual communist leaders in Latin America as well as in the United States. There can be no doubt of the presence of Communists within Dominican opposition groups as well as in many other political organizations—both in Latin America and the United States—but Trujillo's habit of branding as a "communist agent" even his mildest journalistic critic and of forging alleged evidence of communist links on the part of his opponents hinders the work of those bona-fide agencies engaged in the all-important task of uprooting genuine Red conspirators.[1]

[1] A personal incident illustrates this aspect of Trujillo's methods. Shortly after my break with the Dominican regime I was confronted by the United States Immigration

However, Trujillo no longer fools as many people as he used to with his far-fetched anti-Red arguments. Recently, the Benefactor pompously announced the uncovering, presumedly by his all-seeing spy system, of a "Caribbean Comintern," with headquarters at the Soviet Embassy in Mexico City and branch offices in New York City, Puerto Rico and Miami. Thereupon the *Miami Herald* took him to task and, without denying the existence of a Communist conspiracy, challenged "the Big One" to substantiate his charges. "We have had a lot of dead cats thrown at us from time to time as we grew in size and international prestige," said the *Herald*. "This is the first time that we have heard it said that Red Russia is doing business here on an organized scale in an established office." The charges remain unsubstantiated.

Asked to comment, Governor Luis Muñoz Marin, of Puerto Rico, brushed aside Trujillo's diatribes with disdain. Said he: "This is one more expression of the well-known tactic of dictators to try to represent themselves as great enemies of Communism."

Sometimes his own red herrings entice the Benefactor to odd positions. While, on one hand, he denies for foreign consumption the existence of Reds in his well-policed "anti-Communist Caribbean bulwark," on the other hand, he charges with "communism" all local opposition. When both assertions are made on the same day, they provide queer reading in the Dominican press. This happened when *El Caribe* reprinted on its front page an assertion made by Trujillo to the *Kansas City Star* that he had destroyed all vestiges of communism in the Dominican Republic. On an inside page the newspaper printed charges of communism leveled against a group of Dominicans living within the country.

However, despite Trujillo's press-agented hatred of "communism," there is an impressive parallelism of institutional features in his system of repression and in the Soviet Union. True, the totalitarianism of the Soviet Union differs from Trujillo's in doctrinal content—a thing completely lacking in the latter—but in their ground-level operations there is real similarity between both tyrannies. The fundamental resemblance reveals itself in many ways, even in their having some common enemies, as the persecution of the Jehovah's Witnesses in the Soviet Union and in the Dominican Republic shows. During the summer months of 1957 the Dominican press printed a string of accusations by high Government offi-

Service with photostat copies of membership cards, allegedly issued to my brother Horacio Ornes and myself by the Dominican *Partido Socialista Popular* (communist) on November 8, 1944. Under oath I charged the Trujillo regime with forging the evidence and pointed out the fact that the PSP did not come into existence until 1946, that is to say, two years after the issuing of the cards. I was faced with the same charge at the American Consulate in Havana, where I have gone to apply for a visa to enter the United States as a permanent resident. The fact that I was granted such a visa shows that the proof of Trujillo's forgery was established to the satisfaction of the American authorities.

cials charging the Jehovah's Witnesses with "seditious and pernicious" activities. The chain reaction was set off the day a Jesuit priest named Mariano Vásquez Sanz denounced the sect over the Trujillo-owned radio network, *La Voz Dominicana,* as servants of Communism and labeled its adherents as "a perverse, astute, criminal, traitorous enemy." Thereupon a pastoral letter signed by Archbishops Ricardo Pittini and Octavio Antonio Beras invited the priesthood to protect their parishioners from this "terrible heresy." The Witnesses were called in the press "Moscow's witnesses" and tools of international Communism.

At the end of July Congress passed a law banning the sect and the following month brought a storm of arrests, beatings and police brutality upon its members. As reported by *Time,* in the town of Salcedo 100 members were penned up in an army post. Elsewhere two missionaries were hauled into a cell, handed whips and ordered to lash each other. When they refused, each one got 21 lashes. One Witness "was beaten in the face until his eyes were nearly shut" and a boy was left "unconscious with blood coming from his ears and nose." It was found out later that his eardrums were broken. Ten American Jehovah's Witnesses preachers were thrown out of the country, on orders from the Secretary of Security, Major General Arturo Espaillat. True to Dominican custom, the wave of terror was followed by a flurry of letters of recantation, whereby members of the sect renounced their faith and denounced their former associates.

Almost simultaneously a similar persecution was being conducted within the Soviet Union. On September 4, 1957, the *New York Herald Tribune* printed an Associated Press dispatch, under a Moscow dateline, reporting that the Soviet newspaper *Kazakhstan Pravda* had charged "American imperialists" with organizing groups of Jehovah's Witnesses in the Central Asian Russian Republic of Kazakhstan. In a full-page article the Soviet organ asserted that publications from Brooklyn were being sent to Soviet citizens to "lure" them into joining with promises "of salvation after death." The tune was the same, but the devil's horns were painted a different color.

Examples of striking similarities between the two regimes could be multiplied. Trujillo, like Stalin and his heirs, claims to run a "democratic" state and, as in many countries behind the Iron Curtain, the majesty of the law has been invoked in the Dominican Republic to defend the purity of youth against the assaults of "rock'n'roll."

These things do not seem to embarrass Trujillo whatsoever. With shrewd insight into the devious paths of practical politics, the Benefactor goes on performing elusive maneuvers, surprising trades, deals and alliances. When trouble looms ahead he shows caution, but when success beckons he becomes bold. Though presently he prefers the smear to the smash, he still employs physical terror to keep enemies in line. He has always been able to surprise and frustrate the timorous and divided forces of his opponents.

Trujillo makes the most fantastic about-faces. He once allowed Hitler to operate in the Dominican coasts an around-the-clock refueling station for German submarines and proudly displayed on his chest Fascist and Nazi decorations, but he was also one of the first to proclaim adherence to the Charter of the United Nations.

Although the Benefactor operates a police-state of his own, people the world over are accustomed to hear about his theatrical gestures in favor of oppressed minorities. Quite recently he offered haven in the Dominican Republic to 20,000 Hungarian "freedom fighters" as well as 5,000 Jewish refugees from Egypt. This strange situation prompted the New York Post to comment that "when political opponents are forced to flee Trujillo's domain to protect their lives, it is small solace to be told that Trujillo is helping some victims of another oppression."

Faced with so many contradictory actions, there is hardly a Dominican who would pay any attention to "the Chief's" public statements. They have become increasingly wary of anything sounding like propaganda. Wittingly or unwittingly, Trujillo has gradually brought to the surface one of the most dangerous and destructive impulses of the collective soul. A seemingly profound cynicism characterizes the Dominican people's attitude toward public affairs. They do not care for formal expressions of political creeds and always expect a great cleavage to develop between the spoken words and the actions of their leaders. Clearly, Trujillo profits by this situation since it tends by popular apathy to maintain the status quo.

Distrust pervades public life in the Dominican Republic. Ever since he succeeded in grabbing all power for himself, Trujillo has been apprehensive that somewhere in his political woodpile there is a latter-day Rafael ready to do to him what he once did to his former protector and friend, General Horacio Vásquez. The Benefactor cannot escape the obsession that the same fate dogs his own footsteps and for that reason he never relaxes in his frantic efforts to entrench himself.

"No hay enemigo pequeño" (no enemy is small) emphatically stated Trujillo in my presence on several occasions. This belief largely accounts for his peculiar manner of fighting even those enemies who after giving up the unequal battle on the home soil join the hosts of exiles. They are usually deprived of their legitimate civil rights; their property is confiscated and their relatives left behind in the country are held in prison or maintained under constant police surveillance.

Trujillo's sheer distrust of fellow human beings is so deeply entrenched, that he does not confide even in his closest associates. "Trujillo has no advisers," writes Abelardo Nanita in an admiring vein. Then he adds: "He is more impenetrable than a Chinese wall." Nanita also reveals that although various subordinates can be informed at the same time of a plan conceived by the Generalissimo "each one knows only the part assigned to him, the rest remaining in ignorance."

According to Nanita, a man who has been close to Trujillo most of the last 27 years, it is "the Chief's" innate suspicion that will always save him from the political error that has ruined other Latin American rulers: "that the President himself supplied the arms and provided the prestige to the one who overthrew him."

Trujillo's gift for snatching victory from seeming debacle was clearly demonstrated in 1937. Then the jury of international public opinion found him guilty as charged of ordering and directing the massacre of more than 15,000 Haitians living in the Dominican Republic. Confronted with the grim evidence of his crime and caught beneath the crushing weight of international disapproval, the arrogant Generalissimo was all humbleness and humility. There was nothing left for the powerful Benefactor to do but retreat and without much further proof he agreed both to pay an indemnity to the Haitian Government and to step out of the Presidency at the end of his term in 1938. With the latter provision he complied only after assuring himself of the safekeeping of his political and financial interests by assuming active command of the army and through the presidential nomination and eventual election of his trusted and absolutely reliable hireling, Dr. Jacinto B. Peynado.

His well cultivated garden in safe hands, the Generalissimo then retired to travel throughout the United States and Europe. As soon as the first fury of the international storm had blown over, the Benefactor emerged stronger and bolder from his apparent retirement, and, strangely enough, he was again enjoying the good graces of the community of nations.

How was this miracle accomplished within a few months? Though the full story should have an entire chapter, we may say here that responsible for the sudden reverse of the tide was one of the boldest masterstrokes of modern press agentry. When no one wanted them, President Trujillo offered haven in Dominican territory, in 1938, to 100,000 suffering German refugees seeking safer homes. By a colossal propaganda stroke Trujillo blurred the international sense of outrage over *his* recent *pogroms*. The massacred Haitians were forgotten in favor of the persecuted Jews and many a liberal who had been declaiming against Trujillo suddenly discovered that, after all, the Benefactor was not such a devil. That the pleasant dream never came true and not even 1,000 of the 100,000 invited refugees ever set foot on Dominican soil was of small consequence. The gesture, the nice words, the accompanying hopes were enough to reverse for many years to come the tide of public criticism against Trujillo outside the limits of his well-policed domain. The transformation of Trujillo the devil into Trujillo the "great humanitarian" had been successfully accomplished.

Judging by the long list of agents, apologists and admirers operating within and without the island republic, it must be admitted that Trujillo's system has been highly successful. That the method is not entirely fool-proof is illustrated, however, by the story of the visit to the Dominican Republic, early in 1953, of Herbert Matthews, of the *New York Times*.

Trujillo knew of Matthews' probity, so upon hearing of the journalist's forthcoming visit to the country, the Benefactor decided to employ the "sweet" approach or red carpet treatment. The most important dignitaries of the regime received word to treat the distinguished visitor with all con-sideration. Anselmo A. Paulino, then Trujillo's "shadow," powerful alter ego and publisher of *El Caribe,* threw a lavish party for Matthews in his private home, which the pick of the *trujillista* retinue attended. Trujillo himself received Matthews for a long, cordial, off-the-record talk. When the journalist inquired about transportation to the refugee colony of Sosua, *El Caribe* put a plane at his disposal.

Matthews' reaction was negative. "There is a measure of surveillance," he wrote, "or at least the impression of being watched, at all times, even though it takes the usually pleasant form of being accompanied everywhere by those who offer to help, and of being given parties and the most gen-erous sort of hospitality." He added that the Very Important Person treatment was so nicely tendered and so openhanded "that it is made to seem the height of ingratitude to be critical afterward." The duty of being frank, he asserted, carried inescapable regrets, but nonetheless he exposed all sides of the Trujillo regime.

For his objective and straightforward rejection of the Generalissimo's trap, Matthews has since been one of the main targets of vitriolic *trujillista* propaganda. Upon Trujillo's personal instructions, Dominican newspapers occasionally print editorials and articles associating the name of the vet-eran correspondent with Communist causes. Lately, the slanderous cam-paign has been extended to foreign publications. A libelous article, signed by the President of the *Partido Dominicano,* Francisco Prats Ramirez, was printed in the Mexican newspapers *El Universal* and *Excelsior,* which lent themselves as sounding boards for Trujillo propaganda. Matthews was subjected to a particularly scurrilous attack, which included trumped-up charges of criminal association with Communist spies.

Due to this ruthless method of dealing with enemies, Trujillo's impact outside the boundaries of his own country has been a strong one. Despite the fact he is lacking in an ideology, so well regarded is Trujillo's success by other Latin American dictators, that the latter have adopted his meth-ods as standard procedure. Rulers of larger countries, such as former

Colombian strong-man Gustavo Rojas Pinilla, Venezuela's Marcos Pérez Jiménez and Cuba's Fulgencio Batista, copy many of Trujillo's formulas of smashing his enemies through libelous propaganda, falsehoods, smear campaigns and the hiring of American public relations counselors. This *trujillista* influence was perceptively noticed in 1956 by the Inter American Press Association, when Colombian newspapers, supporting the then Dictator Rojas Pinilla, launched a drive intended to link certain IAPA officials with the American Communists. The Colombian response to the IAPA stand in defense of freedom of the press, according to the Association's monthly bulletin, "smacked of similar fictitious rot ground out by Dictator Trujillo's propaganda machine." But, more ominous yet, Trujillo's lack of respect for the life of foreign citizens seems to have extended to his counterparts of the Haitian military ruling board, whose police killed an American citizen at the end of September 1957 and blandly reported him dead of a "heart attack."

As an integral part of Trujillo's political "philosophy," the smear has turned out to be double-acting and occasionally it is spattered on collaborators as well. Drunk with power, the Benefactor looks with contempt upon the self-respect of his fellowmen. He expects loyalty and friendship from everyone, but he is not prepared to pay in kind. Hence, in addition to his known opponents, chief among his victims are his closest collaborators as well as his own relatives. A thick skin seems to be the one tested qualification to hold high office in Trujillo's administration. A man may be today a high-ranking cabinet officer and tomorrow a minor official in the same department he headed. Legislators and judges as well as any other "elected" officials must hand their resignations to "the Chief" before taking oaths of office. Soviet-style purges, political trials and recantations are also part of Trujillo's system. Even the members of his own family, whom he professes to love dearly, hardly escape his brutal repression and have been known to take the rap whenever the Generalissimo's own political interest is at stake. When the marital escapades of his internationally known headstrong daughter Flor de Oro ultimately became a source of embarrassing publicity, "the Big One" restricted her to the Dominican Republic, where, disavowed and disinherited, she lives in oblivion.

Late in 1954 an unforeseen incident forced Trujillo to cast still another of his kin in the role of scapegoat. A savage, cold-blooded, example-setting assassination "while trying to escape" of ten young prisoners, supposedly working in an army shooting range, awakened with sudden intensity the quietly dormant Dominican conscience. The youths had been sentenced a few days earlier to prison terms ranging up to thirty years for a gruesome hold-up of a Canadian-owned bank in the city of Santiago. The criminal undertaking had already left a death toll of two bank employees and two policemen.

To pacify the horrified citizenry, Trujillo promptly demoted the Chief of the Staff of the Army (who happened to be his own nephew Major General Virgilio García Trujillo) and expelled from the force the military commander in Santiago, Colonel Ludovino Fernández. A commission of prominent lawyers was appointed to investigate whether Colonel Fernández could be indicted for, of all crimes, genocide. However, the commission never made a report of its findings and a few months later Fernández was reinstated and promoted to the rank of brigadier general.

With equally fantastic detachment Trujillo has made high office a stepping-stone to an almost unbelievable scheme of personal enrichment. In Trujillo's mind the Presidency is just another opportunity to be exploited not only by the incumbent but also by the 150 or more Trujillo relatives billeted on the country. In the Army alone there are six generals whose names are Trujillo. So bold and systematic has been the plundering that according to conservative estimates the monthly income of the tax-exempt Trujillo clan surpasses $3 million.

Under the new *trujillista* rules of ethics every action is judged, not by standards of right or wrong, but solely from the standpoint of whether it is in the interest of the ruling clique. Trujillo regards himself, therefore, above all laws—man-made or God-given—and believes them poppycock. Even the Russian czars—who would permit no man to reduce their absolute power—respected the Criminal Code and sometimes permitted their actions to be tempered by a regard for public opinion. Not Trujillo. He goes further—he reserves the right to complete and absolute power, irrespective of any law that may be passed by Congress.

Let us not imply that "the Big One" is a man without morals. Quite the contrary. He feels a missionary urge to look down upon his subjects' behavior with a zeal sometimes verging on prudishness. The Benefactor adheres to the loftiest moral standards, provided they are to be observed by other people. Hence, he frowns upon somebody's else gambling, excessive drinking, ostentation and even smoking (his aides cannot smoke in his presence). He abhors "rock'n'roll" and has issued directives for all government employees to belong to Catholic associations. If virtue is measured by the absence of "minor" vices, Trujillo qualifies as a virtuous man. He does not smoke, play cards or shoot dice. Currently he does not get drunk frequently, yet his liking for the strong *Carlos Primero* is an ingrained part of Dominican folklore.

Were further proofs needed of the divorce between words and actions within Trujillo's scheme of things, they could be provided by the words and actions of "the Chief" and his close relatives. "How fortunate are those who go through life without ostentation," wrote Mrs. María Martínez de Trujillo in her *Meditaciones Morales*. While deep in her moral meditations the gracious lady probably did not realize the broad gap between her own exalted words and Trujillo's palaces (more than thirty in all), Trujillo's thirty-five automobiles, Trujillo's strings of race and polo horses, Trujillo's yachts, Trujillo's hundreds of uniforms, Trujillo's jewelry, Trujillo's lavish parties, and Trujillo's fabulous display of wealth.

That the Benefactor is not bothered by his own inconsistencies is shown by the unparalleled ardor with which he prosecutes minor graft and corruption among lesser officials of his Administration, whereas he remorselessly exacts a ten per cent rake-off from every contractor of public works. He frowns upon an Army officer owning a gasoline service station, whereas his big business ventures monopolize large sectors of Dominican trade and industry. Trujillo would throw in jail any Government official guilty of misappropriating public property, but he and the Government are so nearly one and the same that it is most difficult to estimate the extent of his own personal holdings.

The Benefactor is also a very sensitive man when it comes to any criticism of his person. Upon learning of the mildest attack upon himself or his policies, he is always ready to cry out—"libel!" Conversely, he feels no qualms about descending to the depths in defaming a fallen enemy.

Although many of the aforementioned practices are part of the manipulation of the "big lie," which has become a necessary element of the power wielded by Trujillo, much is the product, as well, of "the Big One's" acute megalomania. The Generalissimo loves to play the role of World Statesman. His ego is enhanced by the flattering accounts in the Dominican press of his alleged triumphs on the international stage. For instance, Spain's admission to the United Nations (the result of a world-wide package deal worked out by the great powers) was hailed by Dominican editorial writers as Trujillo's single-handed accomplishment.

Trujillo, however, is not entirely fooled by his own propaganda. This explains his seemingly strange statement to *Time* that "if there can be said to be any tragedy in my destiny, it is that a man of my great capabilities has been required to waste them, in a sense, on such a small country."

He has strongly denied he ever said this. In a public speech he said: "If I had been given the choice of being a famous conqueror in other lands or an obscure soldier working for the happiness of the country where I was born and which I love, I would have rejoiced in the opportunity to offer my life for the Dominican people."

THE TERROR

1. EVER SINCE RAFAEL L. TRUJILLO'S ADVENT TO POWER ALL the principles of democracy and freedom cherished by human beings have been swept away in the Dominican Republic. Today there is no liberty in the sense in which Americans understand these words. In its place is a grim, all-pervading substitute: terror, under which arrest and imprisonment without trial, exile, and death—as well as Government-inflicted poverty and ever-dreaded starvation—have been the fate of thousands of people whose only crime was reckless criticism of the ruling clique.

Terror expresses itself in most varied forms in Trujilloland. It is patent in the institutionalized arbitrariness—paired with unsurpassed ruthlessness —prevailing in high government levels, as well as in the absence of the normal guarantees providing for proper enforcement of constitutional civil rights. It is in the methods of thought-control and brain-washing which characterize the educational system and guide the functioning of Dominican communication media. It is also clear in the relentless effort to starve enemies and "indifferents" into ideological conformity. Moreover, it is evident in the all-penetrating activities of a multiple-branch secret police; in the refusal to permit any but fervid, safe *trujillistas* to leave the country; in the constant encouragement of spying and denunciation in all walks of life; in permanent large-scale witch hunts, arbitrary penal retributions, and the harshness of the places of confinement.

In Trujillo's case, terror is not the work of a sadist or the product of unrestrained bloodthirst. It is rather a grim means to achieve a pre-established end. It is the result of planning and organization aimed at keeping power at all costs.

So imbedded in Trujillo's mind is the concept of terror as a prop of Government administration, despite the fact that the last vestige of all active internal opposition to the regime was finally wiped out during the late Forties, it has never been reduced in intensity. Under the conditions of quiet so much advertised by Dominican press agents, terror might seem a total anachronism. Nevertheless it is there, although nowadays it is used more as a prophylactic agent than as an instrument of suppression. Trujillo subscribes to the theory that a little insubordination may eventually lead to a lot and, therefore, the flowers of liberty had better be cut while still in bud.

After twenty-seven years of continued repression, terror no longer takes the bloody forms it did at the outset. More refined methods of punishment have evolved. Yet arbitrary arrests are still commonplace; and topping the list of chastisements is the relentless economic pressure that leaves whole families without means of livelihood—many times in retaliation for actions committed by one of its members living on foreign soil. Thus, when this book was first announced, the Trujillo regime answered by accusing the mother and the aunt of the author—respected ladies of advanced age—of distributing communist propaganda. Thereupon a campaign of vilification began against the private school in which my mother was employed as a teacher, with the purpose of denying her a productive occupation.

Today, as much as yesterday, a man arrested for actual or imaginary offenses may be shot or hanged (the rope is Trujillo's favorite method of execution) in a prison backyard. Kidnappings, murders and mysterious disappearances are as much part of the system of repression as they were in the early days of the regime. Cases of quiet disappearance are still common, so common in fact that people have coined a graphic phrase to apply to a man who leaves his home never to return. They simply say: "Se perdió" (he got lost), and everybody understands.

Although nowadays for reasons of foreign public relations blood is not usually spilt in public, a few particular cases, called "examples," are sometimes described in the press or otherwise made public knowledge. These "examples" are intended to keep the edge of terroristic weapons from becoming blunt with disuse. As a rule they are executions of obscure individuals, reported to the police for having talked too much while drinking or for being guilty of some other minor political sin. Nevertheless, the shape these "examples" take is repulsive. "A particularly grisly form of reminder," reported a reputable American magazine, "believed original with the Dominican Republic is that of the hanging body."

Suppose, added the magazine story, an enemy of the Government in Barahona disappeared from his accustomed haunts. "The police know nothing, and nothing appears in any newspaper. The wise do not inquire too closely into his fate. But some days later inhabitants of San Pedro de Macorís or Samaná, at the other end of the island, are shocked to see a body hanging in some sufficiently public place. There is no identification, of course, for no one in town has seen the person before."

Occasionally people of high social standing meet death for disagreeing with the regime. This happens when the Government wants to set a particularly pointed example. R. Donato Bencosme, a former provincial governor, is one of the recent cases. Formerly an opponent of the regime, Bencosme (a brother of the Dominican exile of the same name who was shot to death in New York in 1935 by a member of the Rubirosa family on orders from Trujillo) was persuaded to collaborate with the regime four years ago and appointed Governor of Espaillat Province. Late in 1956, following a press campaign of invective and defamation against his person, Bencosme was demoted. He was tried for activities against the "public order," convicted, thrown in jail. On February 20, 1957, when everyone thought he was serving his prison term, it was reported in *El Caribe* and *La Nación* that Bencosme and his chauffeur had met death in an automobile crash.

Understandably enough, the attitude of Dominican society toward these outrages is one of utter fright. Sometimes men, driven by desperation, sacrifice themselves—committing heroic acts of protest against the unbearable abuses of the authorities. Few, however, are ever brave or foolish enough to impair for idealistic reasons and principles the security and welfare of their children, parents and dear ones. Trujillo made this discovery early in his career and since then has exploited it for his own benefit. Economic and moral pressure brought to bear upon innocent third parties has become one of his most effective weapons.

Knowing Trujillo's willingness to resort to ruthlessness with the weapons of terror at his disposal, Dominicans have learned never to discuss politics in public places, or in the presence of children, servants or strangers. Children are always chased away before any controversial political issue is discussed. In this connection I remember the unanswerable question put by a particularly bright Dominican youngster to his father. "Papa," he asked, "how come that when we talk of Trujillo in school we always cheer, whereas when you do it here at home it is always in a whisper?"

When questioned about the Generalissimo himself, the people's attitude changes. With alacrity they will give an enthusiastic standard answer: each one will profess deep love for the Benefactor. Even the few who in the privacy of their homes dare to indulge in the most bitter criticism of the regime will act in public places as its most enthusiastic supporters.

This uncritical support of the Trujillo regime—in which foreigners sometimes join—is hardly calculated to induce people to trust each other. In the light of what transpires in the public statements of loyalty printed by the Dominican press and distributed through the propaganda outlets of the regime, citizens have grown suspicious of everyone else and tend to look upon acquaintances, neighbors and outsiders as actual or potential agents of the dictatorship. Trujillo has been able to create a climate of suspicion and mutual distrust, highly convenient for his ends.

Hallett of the *Christian Science Monitor* pointed out that those who have been in the country for some time in business or other fields of activity say they do not know whom they can trust. "Anybody may be a spy," he said. "Any foreigner here for some time finds that certain topics of conversation related to politics are taboo in talking with Dominicans."

Dominicans now display a craven desire for personal security and financial well-being, a readiness to conform and a willingness to delegate all decision to bureaucratic authority which is shocking. Civic responsibility is lacking altogether, and indifference and apathy are standard reactions to the most outrageous official abuses. "What is grave," wrote Jesús de Galíndez analyzing the situation, "are not the illegal arrests or even murders; what is grave is the total destruction of the spirit of a nation."

Yet, if the people fear Trujillo, the latter in turn betrays in his procedures an acute dread of his repressed subjects. Not only is the Benefactor the most closely guarded ruler in the world, constantly surrounded by bodyguards and special troops, but he is constantly watching his closest associates.[1] The Benefactor coerces and intimidates even his dreaded henchmen. Duplicity, informing, forgery, blackmail, extortion, as well as all manner of weapons for psychological warfare, are among the preferred instruments of terror. People remain at liberty, conduct business, or hold government or private posts only as long as "the Big One" permits them.

Repressive measures are not confined to enemies or alleged enemies of the regime. Not even devoted service saves those who somehow displease "the Chief." As a result, fear and anxiety are shared by all classes—all the way from Cabinet Minister down to the lowliest peasant. There are innumerable examples of men capriciously transferred overnight from a comfortable Cabinet berth to a bunk in jail. At one time or another "subversives" have been found in grocery stores, within the army, in government ministries, in newspaper offices, in the University, in factories, in trade unions, in social clubs—in fact, everywhere except under the bed.

Some of the examples defy credibility. A young newspaperman, Teófilo Guerrero del Rosario, reporter for *La Nación* and correspondent for the American magazine *Vision* and the Cuban publication *Carteles,* was condemned to two years in prison in November 1956, for the crime of plotting with the Red movement. All that the prosecution's evidence proved

---

[1] George Beebe, Managing Editor of the *Miami Herald,* who interviewed Trujillo late in 1957 had this to say about this subject: "In a 15-minute wait at the palace, an assortment of guards and attachés came into the waiting room, and I could feel their searching eyes trying to detect any bulge of weapons that might be on my person."

was that Guerrero "wanted to go to Puerto Rico" where he expected to find a better job with a newspaper.

Government officials have lost their posts after being accused of having money in American banks. A Vice-Rector of the University lost his position when he was charged with having stated that graduates should be sent abroad for further study on the basis of academic standing rather than political reliability. An engineer, Emilio Montes de Oca, went to jail because his son, then living in Puerto Rico, spoke disrespectfully of the Generalissimo. Prior to his release, Montes de Oca had to publicly disavow his scion.

It would be senseless to deny the effectiveness of Trujillo's terror. As one of the fundamental props of the regime it has been employed so successfully that Dominicans feel they cannot escape "the Big One." They know he is constantly watching them and they have no hope for an independent existence apart from the regime. Their hearts have been hardened and their characters softened so that they no longer have any will power.

Everyone living in the Dominican Republic (nationals and foreigners alike) has a serial number. Upon reaching the age of sixteen, every resident must carry at all times a card called *Cédula Personal de Identidad* (Personal Identification Card), which besides its number, includes the name, age, civil status, occupation, race, address, picture, fingerprints and other information about its possessor.

A person needs the *Cédula* for practically every act of everyday life: to travel inside and outside the country; to get a driver's license; to cash a check; to apply for a marriage license; to register at the University; to appear in court either as counsel or as party; to practice a profession; to get and hold employment (employers who hire people without the card are subject to severe penalties); to vote; and to be buried.

On election day the citizen takes his *Cédula* to the voting booth where it is stamped *votado,* meaning that the person has complied with his electoral duty. As Herbert Matthews observed, failure to vote is "tantamount to flaunting opposition to the Generalissimo." Since no one wants to be thus branded, Trujillo always gets a tremendous *si* (yes) for his one party ticket. Even Dominicans living abroad show up on election day at their respective embassies or consulates to stamp their *Cédulas.* Other people send telegrams from abroad to be on record as having been out of the country should someone question the lack of the electoral stamp on their cards. Questioned about the peculiar electoral system, Government officials graciously explain that it should be copied by all democratic countries—it is impossible to commit electoral frauds, because no one can vote twice. Of course, they never say that those who fail to vote *once* are liable to visits by the secret police.

Every year a stamp must be attached to the *Cédula,* showing that the bearer has paid his per-capita tax, which is a sort of rudimentary income tax. This tax, based on personal gross wealth plus monthly income, is figured on the basis of a cumbersome, highly unscientific method of computation. Taxpayers are divided into thirty-five categories for the purpose of assessing. The minimum a person must pay is $2 and the maximum may reach $15,000,000 a year. The Benefactor and his family, the military, and women with more than twelve children are exempt from this tax, but for other Dominicans not to have the current tax-stamp in their *Cédulas* is as bad as not to have the card. Penalties range from heavy fines to jail sentences up to five years. When a person passes away, relatives must show his stamped *Cédula* before a burial license may be issued.

For almost as many purposes as the *Cédula,* Dominicans are required to present a secret police document known as the "certificate of good conduct." Unlike the *Cédula,* however, the certificate (supposedly issued by the provincial governors) may be refused to those who are not *persona grata* to the Government. For instance, as a rule people with relatives, however distant, listed as enemies of the regime cannot qualify for possession of one of these documents unless they themselves are cooperating with the Government. This, in turn, means that the person is unable to travel out of the country, practice a profession, or even manage his own business.

By Act of Congress the right of any citizen to practice his profession as a lawyer, physician, dentist, architect, engineer, chemist or pharmacist is subject to the unconditional judgment of the President of the Dominican Republic. Prior to the beginning of the practice of a profession, university graduates must apply for a Presidential *exequatur.* Upon receiving the application the President decides, after a thorough review of all factors concerned, political or otherwise, whether the candidate is acceptable or not. If a graduate is suspected of being either a "subversive" or not a good enough *trujillista* he may be barred altogether by the withholding of the *exequatur* or required to recant his "indifference" toward the regime.

Due, however, to the fact that the *exequatur* is issued on a permanent basis, and may only be canceled after cumbersome public legal procedures, the regime resorts to this type of punishment in very few cases, and only when publicity is deemed wise either because of the personality of the culprit or the gravity of the situation. For routine punishment of professionals, a far simpler method has evolved. By another Act of Congress all professions now have their *colegios,* or professional associations, to which every university graduate must belong. The strictly controlled, powerful *trujillista* organizations issue each year, upon payment of a small fee, a card which authorizes the bearer to legally perform his work during the ensuing year. The card may be withheld by the *colegio* officials—all handpicked Trujillo associates—without any explanation. Sometimes they don't even bother to refuse the card—its issuance is merely delayed indefinitely. In the meantime, if the applicant tries to practice his profession he may be, and usually is, prosecuted.

The defense of any alleged "subversive," even in a civil case, is sufficient to place a lawyer under suspicion and sometimes to bring about the end of his practice. Even in those cases where for reasons of his own Trujillo allows a court-appointed lawyer for the defense, attorneys as a rule cast themselves in the simple role of pleaders for mercy and show a marked inclination to avoid conflicts with the prosecution. There have been cases of over-cautious defense attorneys turned prosecutors.

Furthermore, the system of licenses is not limited to the liberal professions. To perform any business activity or trade; to act as agent or correspondent for a foreign publication, news agency or business firm; to sell insurance or to work as a traveling salesman, people must register with the Government. The authorities have no legal right to refuse registration, but the catch, of course, is that the procedures may be delayed at the will of the authorities, and the applicant is in no position to carry out his normal activities lest he be accused of illegal practices and thrown in jail.

Moreover, no man who has suffered political imprisonment after being properly convicted by a Court may expect, after his release, to qualify for any business, trade or profession. He has to go through a long period of his life legally deprived of all civil rights. This means that he is absolutely disqualified from the exercise of any function in the State as well as any position of trust, authority or management in private business or industry. It is in effect a sentence of economic exile from society.

Americans sometimes show disgust with the exaggerated loyalty checks and security measures through which federal government employees must go. They would certainly feel better if they knew what a prospective Dominican Government employee has to do in order to secure a job. Almost all applicants for subordinate posts are required to fill out a form prepared in 1945 by the *Comisión Depuradora de Empleados Publicos* (Commission for the Purging of Public Employees). This document— a sworn affidavit of eternal loyalty to the Generalissimo—is a masterpiece of totalitarian political thought-control. Its signers must give in it detailed explanations of their lives and the lives of their relatives, friends and acquaintances.

In addition to inquiries concerning the activities of relatives and acquaintances known to be opposed to the regime, the questionnaire presents the following questions:

"What political work have you done?

"Give details of your cooperation with the present government:

"a) Political rallies attended? b) Political rallies not attended? c)

Propaganda made in favor of the Government? d) How many non-political articles have you written? e) How many political articles? f) How many talks, lectures, and speeches have you delivered on themes of interest to the Government? g) What other manifestations of loyalty have you made? h) Do you punctually attend *Te-Deums* at patriotic festivities, politico-cultural ceremonies, meetings, agricultural reviews, committees and subcommittees of the *Partido Dominicano?"*

Trujillo himself once sent a personal circular to all public employees asking them whether they had had "any conversation with persons who are enemies, opposed or indifferent to the Government." Then "the Big One" asked his servants what efforts had they made "to attract such individuals into our (*trujillista*) ranks." Ominously enough, Trujillo's letter ended by asking those who had not done any "attracting" the reasons why. However, not even compliance with these requests is enough to ensure permanence in a Government post. At frequent intervals, a thorough investigation is conducted by a high official with the title of *Coordinador de Empleados* (Coordinator of Employees). This official keeps a stern watch over the morals, politics and, sometimes, the efficiency of the Government labor force.

To make sure that the objects of his benefactions won't stray from the path he has ordained, Trujillo has set up army check points every twenty-five miles on roads throughout the country. Against the chance that somebody might try to drive through them, huge bumps have been placed in the road before each one. It would practically be suicide to drive over them at any speed faster than a crawl. The *Cédula* must be displayed at every check point, and the driver must give his name, residence and destination point.

The Dominican constitution guarantees, without any reservations whatsoever, the safety and inviolability of the mail. As a routine matter, however, practically all letters are opened in transit. This mail censorship permits the secret police to pry into the innermost lives of Dominican citizens, looking for the faintest hints of rebellion, non-conformism, or even dangerous thoughts. The secret police's overzealousness in this matter sometimes carries them to ridiculous extremes. On one occasion a package of books was mailed to me from the United States and, as usual, its contents had to go through a routine inspection. One of the books was an English-language, anti-Communist treatise dealing with the relations between Church and State in the Soviet Union. Unable to read English the secret police agent in charge of censorship at the customs house decided that the word "communism" on the cover of the book was a good enough reason to warrant the impounding of the package. After hearing that my books had been seized, I called up the Chief of Police who, upon my simple explanation that the book was against, not for, communism, lifted the ban. Had I not at the time been a high Government official, and hence in a position to be listened to, I would have lost not only my books but perhaps even my liberty.

Radio and telephonic communications are tightly controlled as well. Wire tapping is commonplace, and no Dominican will ever talk about anything more important than the weather over a telephone. Every morning Trujillo receives in his office a report on inter-urban and international telephone calls put through the day before. To check international radio and telephonic communications in the whole Caribbean area, the Dominican Army operates a superbly efficient monitor service. Also monitored are the contents of all Caribbean and United States short-wave radio news broadcasts, and Army stenographers make up bulletins to be circulated within a very exclusive group of Government dignitaries. Sometimes Trujillo himself picks up choice tidbits from these bulletins and sends them to the newspapers for publication. Secretly monitored telephone conversations over the international frequencies are also reported in "confidential" bulletins to the Generalissimo, thus allowing him to keep abreast of interesting developments, political and otherwise, within his zone of influence. There is certainly no privacy in the Dominican Republic, or for that matter in the entire Caribbean area. The Army is in charge of jamming all foreign broadcasting stations over whose microphones systematic anti-Trujillo campaigns are conducted. For years several radio stations were kept from the Dominican listeners entirely.

Furthermore, peasants are tied to the land and ordinarily need a government permit to move from one place to another or to change their permanent places of residence. This system of near-bondage has been devised with the object of preserving within certain zones of the country much needed man-power required by the fast-expanding Trujillo sugar empire. Yet, if any tract of land, no matter its extent, is ever needed for the expansion of the Generalissimo's sugar plantations, then the forced uprooting and transport of peasant communities is effected without a qualm. There exist estimates that several thousand people of all ages were evicted from their own land without any legal procedure whatsoever when the enormous Trujillo-owned *Rio Haina* sugar plantation was in process of development.

In a manner reminiscent of Soviet decrees, the Dominican Government also prescribes what farmers should grow. Recently the tillage of cotton was declared of "high national interest" due to the fact that the Generalissimo had entered upon a large-scale textile operation.

As already pointed out, Trujillo learned early from his Marine teachers that to succeed, a military regime must keep the population disarmed. Aside from a passport, the hardest thing to get in the Dominican Republic is a permit to carry arms. This is only granted after a thorough check of the background, political reliability and associations of the applicant. Then the gun must be bought from the National Army on presentation of a written authorization issued by the Secretary of Security. If by any chance the permit is revoked the gun must be returned to the Army without delay. Both the Army and the Department of Security keep complete records of guns' specifications as well as the identity of their owners. A yearly fee of $100 must be paid by the licensees. Legal penalties for carrying arms without a permit or for possessing them under the same conditions are severe, but usually people caught red-handed just disappear.

Some of Trujillo's directives border on the ludicrous. Heavy fines are imposed on those who smoke while riding in a car; every official document, including applications for passports and import-export licenses, has a line in which one must fill in the number and date of his affiliation in the *Partido Dominicano;* it is a punishable offense to wear khaki trousers and shirts of the same color and it is against the law to carry your coat over your arm.

No photograph of the Generalissimo may be put on sale without its artistic merits being checked and approved by the Secretary of Education and Fine Arts. Toilets must be installed (and bought from the hardware monopoly controlled by the Trujillo family) even in thatched roof huts. Municipal ordinances subject festivities other than strictly family affairs to a $2 permit issued by the local police. Another law forbidding poor people to enter Ciudad Trujillo in bare feet has brought about, according to *Time,* a new form of business enterprise—renting shoes at stalls just outside the city limits. "On the hottest afternoons, men wear jackets and ties in the streets of Ciudad Trujillo because El Jefe likes it that way," noted an American reporter.

Why do people take all this without even passive resistance? There are many complex answers to this simple question. The truth is that inside the country no one seems to care for politics or how the country is run. Terror has produced such apathy that there are very few people with the moral or physical courage to risk life, fortune and relative security by open or covert rebellion or even independent political thinking. Even mild criticism of the regime is a one-way ticket to certain disgrace—if not death—and there are very few people willing to face that creeping, all-embracing (never seen but always felt) punishment called social ostracism.

Trujillo has a talent for practical psychology. Thus, periods of intense repression are followed by strange lulls, during which nothing seems to happen within the country. "A policy of firmness does not exclude, however, the use of generosity after any trouble has been ended," wrote official biographer Lawrence de Besault. "When President Trujillo believes that there is repentance and a desire to change on the part of the guilty, he uses the power of pardon granted him by the constitution of the Republic, and his arms open to welcome those who have been converted to the cause of justice."

As with the change-of-pace of a baseball pitcher, these tactics allow Trujillo to keep his enemies and subjects off balance. This slackening of pressure not only lets off potentially dangerous steam but lures people into a false sense of security and brings about a "thank heavens, all is over" frame of mind. It arouses false hopes in those who otherwise might be driven by despair to frantic acts of rebellion.

The amnesties, invitations to exiles to return home, pardons of political offenders, paroles, etc., not only serve a public relations purpose in making Trujillo appear as a forgiving man but also attain the more important end of inducing the people to believe that through good behavior they may stave off persecution. So Dominicans vie with each other in an effort to show loyalty to the regime and to bid for a safe place in the *trujillista* order of things. Even people who have been humiliated and unjustly punished by "the Big One" instead of rebelling would rather wait patiently for the forthcoming moment of pardon. "Only the corpses are without hope of being pardoned," says an expression that goes the rounds among collaborators and former collaborators of the regime.

These periods of relative calm, during which offenses against the regime are forgiven and apparently forgotten, do not last long. After a while terror comes back in full swing, lest people become restless and start asking for real freedom or get ideas that they can do things in their own ways. Terror is for Trujillo a sort of straitjacket he cannot throw away permanently if he is going to stay on top.

As a result of international pressures arising from the Galíndez-Murphy affair, the country is now going through a new spell of terror.

2. In accordance with the standard practice of dictatorships, Trujillo has organized an efficient system of espionage. The Benefactor considers essential for the defense of his regime the knowledge of the opinions, intentions and actions of all residents of the Dominican Republic as well as Dominicans living abroad. During twenty-seven years of keeping tabs on enemies and potential enemies of the regime the different branches of the Dominican secret police have evolved into one of the most ruthless terroristic organizations in the Western Hemisphere.

Millions are spent to maintain the operations of an espionage network. A vast assortment of agents, recruited from all walks of life (including reputable professionals, politicians and former FBI and Central Intelligence Agency operators as well as gangsters, criminals and hoodlums) work around the clock both inside the country and outside the limits of the Trujillo fief. Consequently, to date no other Latin American regime is so well informed as the Dominican dictatorship of the situation prevailing either within its own boundaries or in neighboring countries, including the United States.

The role of the Dominican intelligence network has become known because Trujillo and his associates seem to derive pleasure in boasting about it. The Dominican Republic is probably the only country in the world whose leaders do not feel any qualms about spying on other countries. Dominican newspapers have printed news about the return to the country of alleged secret agents operating in Cuba, Haiti, Guatemala and other countries. Trujillo and his aides brag about how much they know about everybody else and proclaim the supposedly excellent cooperation they lend to foreign law-enforcing agencies. The international news agencies' dispatches filed in Ciudad Trujillo occasionally contain grave imputations against the heads of foreign Governments attributed to the Dominican Army Intelligence. At least once the reckless accusations provoked a grave international incident, which was investigated in 1954 by the Organization of American States upon request of the Costa Rican Government. The charges made by the Dominican espionage agency that President José Figures of Costa Rica had given haven to European Communists could not be substantiated before the international organization.

Despite this and other setbacks the Dominican authorities persist in advertising their undercover activities within other sovereign states. "The Dominican Republic admits to having an efficient intelligence system and has made available its information on the international Communist conspiracy to the United States," asserted the present Dominican Ambassador in Washington, Manuel de Moya Alonzo, in answer to an interview given by the author of this book to the *New York Times,* in which was expressed the belief that Dominican Government agents had kidnapped and murdered Dr. Jesús de Galíndez.

Later Trujillo himself explained, in an interview in the *New York Herald Tribune,* September 8, 1957, that the Dominican Government had put in the hands of the United States State Department "much information" concerning the alleged existence of a "Caribbean Comintern" with its headquarters in the Soviet Embassy in Mexico City and other "major Soviet bases" in New York City, Miami and Puerto Rico.

A flagrant example of *trujillista* trespassing on the prerogatives of the investigative and law-enforcing agencies of other lands is the so-called private investigation of the Galíndez disappearance, now being conducted with Dominican Government funds under the direction of the American attorney Morris Ernst. After refusing cooperation to the proper American authorities the Trujillo regime suddenly announced in July 1957 that it had retained a U.S. public-relations man, two U.S. lawyers, and a batch of former FBI and CIA agents, as well as other private dicks, for the avowed purpose of making a full-scale inquiry.

That the "investigators" are doing more than looking into the Galíndez affair was publicly revealed by Angel Ramos, publisher of *El Mundo,* the leading newspaper of Puerto Rico, and President of the Executive Committee of the Inter American Press Association. Ramos announced during the meeting of the IAPA in Washington in October 1957 that the Executive Committee of the Association had resolved not to intervene "in an investigation into the Galíndez Affair which is being financed by Generalissimo Trujillo." Ramos added that the office of Morris Ernst called the Secretary of the IAPA "requesting certain information which, in our opinion, has nothing to do with Galíndez. The Committee was consulted by the administrator and agreed not to give any information to the investigator paid by Trujillo, believing that an investigation conducted at the request of Generalissimo Trujillo and financed by him might reach conclusions of a doubtful suspicious nature."

Unfortunately, although the findings of the Dominican secret police are not always correct, the *trujillista* bragging about the existence of an enormous apparatus of espionage in and out of the country is not empty. Trujillo maintains what an American reporter has aptly called "one of the most tortuously conceived secret-service systems in the history of espionage."

The Dominican secret service is not one but many agencies, completely separated one from the others, but all performing their duties with crushing ruthlessness if not always efficiency. The existence of this split-personality secret police best illustrates "the Big One's" guiding principle of "Divide and Rule." Separated into at least six different branches, which check upon each other as much as they watch the rest of the people, the Dominican Gestapo keeps a vigilant eye upon the citizenry and brings swift punishment for the slightest deviation from *trujillista* discipline.

Topmost in the Dominican espionage echelon is the brand-new Secretariat of State for Security, created by Trujillo July 1, 1957. Appointed by the Benefactor as first Secretary of Security was Major General Arturo Rafael Espaillat, 35, a Dominican citizen who graduated from West Point in 1943. Between his graduation and 1956, Espaillat rose from first lieutenant to brigadier general and acquired within the country the dubious fame of being one of the toughest Trujillo henchmen. In May 1956 Espaillat left his post as Under Secretary of the Armed Forces and head of the War Department intelligence branch to become Consul General in New York City. A year later he scampered home after the U.S. State Department had sent a note to the Dominican Government asking that Espaillat waive diplomatic inmunity "in order that he should be amenable to the usual and lawful procedures in matters of investigation and trial" in the United States. The unusual request was made after the State Department had officially announced that it had sufficient evidence to indicate a link between the disappearance of Galíndez and the American pilot, Gerald Lester Murphy.

Back home Espaillat was promoted to Major General and assigned to the seemingly powerful job of head of Security. Then, with Espaillat's status settled, Trujillo got around to answering the U.S. State Department note. The Dominican note stated that it would be "improper" for a man of Espaillat's high station to face a judicial process in a foreign country.

As head of Security,[1] Espaillat bosses an army of some 5,000 policemen and spies. He holds command over the national police, special police and the intelligence service at home and abroad, including the United States. He also has under his control the most dreaded of the so-called special services—the "Spanish Police," a corps of about one hundred tough former Spanish secret-service men, well-trained in Nazi and Spanish methods of repression. This group has been operating in the Dominican Republic since the beginning of 1956 on a sort of "lend-lease" agreement with the Spanish Government of Generalissimo Franco. Also under the Department of Security are the "Veterans" and other strong-arm squads recruited from the ranks of ex-convicts, dishonorably discharged army personnel, slum hoodlums, countryside bully boys and parolees. Reasons for selecting persons with such backgrounds are found in Trujillo's conviction that men with suspended convictions hanging over their heads are likely to prove willing tools of terror.

The Secretary of Security is also in charge of all matters concerning the issuance of passports as well as the enforcement of immigration regulations. It was Major General Espaillat who handled with celerity the deportation of the Jehovah's Witnesses after the sect was declared outside the law by Act of Congress in July 1957.

Major General Espaillat is also endowed with power to enforce all regulations concerning registry of foreign agents and companies, the expediting of arms permits, the "public vigilance of suspicious foreigners," surveillance of lucrative gambling operations, the application of the press law and newspaper censorship, and control of all organizations, meetings and public movements. The enforcement of security at international conferences held in the Dominican Republic is under Espaillat's jurisdiction as well.

All embracing as his duties appear to be, Major General Espaillat does not hold a monopoly on spying. Vying with him—and keeping an eye on his own activities—are at least six other police organizations such as the Army Intelligence (to which are ascribed many of the discoveries of

[1] Espaillat was recently transferred from the Cabinet to the post of Inspector General of the Navy.

"Communist" activities in foreign countries announced in press releases by the regime); the Naval Intelligence; the Inspectors of the Presidency (a small group responsible only to Trujillo whose cardinal task is to watch closely the activities of the high officials of the regime, including the heads of the other undercover agencies); the National Palace bodyguards (a counterpart of the American secret service, whose chief is the notorious former Consul General in Manhattan Felix W. Bernardino, who appears in public functions a step behind the Generalissimo), and last but not least the large corps of informers and inspectors of the *Partido Dominicano*.

La 42 was disbanded a few years ago and its boss Miguel A. Paulino reintegrated in the Army with the rank of full colonel, but the "Veterans" —a similar organization made up of former soldiers and officers the majority of whom have been kicked out from the armed forces for common crimes—act as executioners when the kangaroo courts of the secret police pass judgment on alleged opponents of the regime.

For university students there is a special espionage service. Charged with this highly specialized chore is the Prefect's corps of the University. Under the leadership of a former prizefighter and graduate of *La 42* the prefects keep tab on student activities, checking friendships (in and out of the university), habits, hobbies and political leanings.

By far the most conspicuous duty of the different Dominican security agencies is personal protection of the Generalissimo against would-be assassins and plotters. In their line of duty they consider every resident of the country a suspect and people live—whatever their station—under perennial surveillance. As a result, one of their normal functions is the detection, investigation and cataloguing of the political opinions of citizens as well as residents from other countries.

Although all the police agencies act with a mailed fist, their techniques of investigation are not very sophisticated. They work upon the assumption that every man is actually or potentially "subversive" and rely for their information upon material received from undercover agents, neighbors, servants and personal enemies of the persons under investigation.

Dominican detectives write down all sorts of gossip about what people supposedly said or what they were suspected of having done. Most of the carefully preserved information relates to personal habits and life, and when deemed convenient the contents of these dossiers are sifted for use in letters to the editors of the newspapers.

All in all, the dossiers are the foundation for the police classification of people into two sweeping categories: "cooperators" (those who willingly collaborate with the regime) and "subversives." To be classified as a "subversive" a person does not have to be an open or even a covert enemy of the regime. Many of those included within this category are people who sincerely do not care for politics and might even turn out to be "cooperators" if they were given the chance. This arbitrary division of Dominicans into two different groups provides a clue for the seemingly strange remark made by a "pro-Trujillo Dominican" to Milton Bracker, correspondent for the *New York Times,* that about ten per cent of the country's population, or nearly 260,000 persons, should be reckoned as "subversives."

In many instances the police classify a man as "subversive" to put pressure upon him and eventually force him into giving up a business or professional career and joining the ranks of active supporters of the regime. If this is the case, the longer an "indifferent" (as the police call those who neither oppose the regime nor collaborate) holds out, the greater the inconveniences he has to suffer. If he does not surrender within a reasonable time, his name is transferred to the list of "enemies of the situation." As all "enemies" are considered "communists," the real coloring of the political ideas of a man does not make much difference to the secret police. In their lists all "enemies" are Red. However, there is a further classification: there are "active" enemies and just plain enemies. The latter are allowed to live relatively in peace. To be sure, they are forbidden to travel abroad, practice their professions or be seen in the company of foreigners, but they are not thrown in jail or killed, unless caught in an overt act of rebellion. Their plight is somewhat similar to that of the "untouchables" under the ancient caste system of India. As soon as a man is classified as an "enemy" the police quietly slip word to his friends and business associates of his new status. If by any improbable chance someone chooses to disregard the hint, the police lose no time in making plain—on an "or else" basis—that they would appreciate "friendly" cooperation in their dealings with the "enemy." Thereupon the marked man is fired from employment, dropped from business and professional firms, unobtrusively dropped from social clubs and subjected to whatever other measures of retaliation are suggested by the authorities. Almost identical procedure—sometimes accompanied by a splash of publicity—is followed in cases involving Government officials cast out of the Benefactor's favor.

The "active" enemies are worse off. Still, to be labeled "active" a man does not need to indulge in overt opposition. It is enough either to have been affiliated in the past, however loosely, with some opposition movement; to have been charged with persistent criticism of the regime or to have steadfastly rejected *trujillista* overtures for collaboration. People who have lost a close relative through any repressive action of the regime are always included within the "active" category, since there is the belief that they may become bitter and inimical forevermore.

Whenever the regime considers it necessary to bring the populace to heel, so-called "examples" are drawn from the "active" group. In accordance with political winds or caprices of "the Big One," the "actives" travel back and forth from home to jail. If, after a reasonable number of jailings, they do not come out as vocal supporters of the regime the chances are that they will disappear, be "suicided," or meet a fatal road "accident."

Strangely enough—this is one of the most peculiar characteristics of the Trujillo regime—the group of "active subversives" has proved to be one of the largest recruiting grounds of high Government officials. As a rule, members of this group have been at one time or another the brightest intellectual figures of the country, promising young men and prominent members of the old aristocratic classes. Through force, blackmail or bribe, Trujillo has successfully appealed to fear, hope of personal advancement or even baser instincts of human nature to recruit and rally around him the natural leaders of public thought.

The lure of public office, after a brief visit to a jail, is sometimes powerful enough to gain converts. Many of Trujillo's earliest close collaborators came to Government straight from the infamous *Nigua* prison. Famous among these is Dr. Manuel de Jesús Troncoso de la Concha, former opponent turned collaborator and elevated later to puppet President. On July 23, 1930, Dr. Troncoso was arrested and arraigned for alleged violations of the Penal Code. He recanted and thereupon was released and appointed Rector of the University. "Then years later," points out Jesús de Galíndez in his book, "Troncoso de la Concha will be President of the Republic."

The Benefactor unquestionably derives special satisfaction in appointing either ex-enemies or would-be opponents to his close circle of advisers. Doubtless Trujillo derives a sadistic pleasure in humiliating men of a certain character and dignity forced by the sheer weight of terror into collaboration and making them carry out publicly policies and directives they oppose at heart. Besides the Benefactor's sadistic impulses, this policy obeys practical considerations. It is Trujillo's belief that there is no better way of giving the coup de grace to a formerly stubborn opponent than to force him finally into close, open collaboration with the hated regime.

Knowing that all men have weak spots, Trujillo seldom fails in his efforts to entice the people he wants on his side. He stops short of nothing, be it bribe, threats, blackmailing or cajoling. Finding an opponent's weaknesses is just a matter of time, patience and careful investigation.

The method, moreover, is not limited to the drafting of outstanding political figures, professionals or businessmen. Whenever the dictator hears that a member of the younger generation shows exceptional talent or gives promise of becoming a man of prominence, the latter is approached with a tempting offer. Those who refuse to become sycophants are soon taught a bitter lesson by long imprisonment or continued persecution. Out of jail, they go jobless and see the best years of their lives wasted in what seems a fruitless, hopeless resistance. With the passing of time most of them give up and join the ranks of active supporters of a dictatorship they abhor. In this way the latent patriotism of Dominican youth is corrupted and, what is perhaps more tragic, the ideals of integrity, dignity, liberty and freedom become perverted.

So effective has proved this method that there is hardly a man of social and economic standing in the country who has not lent his collaboration to the regime one way or the other. This, in turn, totally disables them for further activities as Trujillo opponents. Knowing this, the Dictator drops them after a tour of duty (whose length depends on the amount of adulatory work performed); and totally discredited and destroyed as potential serious competitors, they are sent home to brood.

The threat of publication of their statements and adulatory correspondence with the Benefactor (always carefully filed) keep the former opponents turned *trujillistas* in check. In the few cases in which a man shows courage enough to reassert his temporarily lost ideals, the smashing propaganda machine of the Dictatorship is put to work against him. The cost of defiance is always tremendously high both morally and materially. If lucky enough to escape from Trujillo's reach, the man will find himself the subject of much scorn and vicious persecutions brought about by the hideous techniques of the Big Lie.

In such cases the first step of Trujillo's propaganda is to turn the new enemy into a controversial figure. This is done through the printing of pamphlets and other derogatory literary efforts, the spreading of gossip, all sorts of accusations and rumors intended to discredit the opponent. Usually, the breach with the regime is attributed to selfish motives of the former collaborator and his abandonment of the camp of *trujillismo* is sometimes ascribed to fear of legal procedures on account of disreputable activities such as embezzlement, graft, tax evasion, thievery and so forth. Somehow Trujillo manages to find a receptive audience for his charges and at times convinces people (especially those who ignore the facts of Dominican life) they should waste no sympathy on the object of his scorn.

Trujillo usually gets his effects through the adroit exploitation of the facilities of international news agencies whose correspondents in Ciudad Trujillo are hand-picked newspaper editors or former journalists who will transmit the official releases as they receive them without daring to indulge in a dangerous check of their veracity. If the accused exile answers back and yesterday's story blows up, there are always new charges to bury the refutation. Without moral reservations "the Chief" allows his press agents to use arguments such as this:

"Mr. So and So was an arrogant *trujillista* when on top. Why didn't he raise his voice then to denounce the regime? Why did he observe in silence the abuses he nows condemns? Now, after he has grabbed a lot of money and is running away from justice; now, after he and Trujillo have fallen out because of his treacherous unpatriotic conduct, is when Mr. So and So discovers that Trujillo is a tyrant. How are you going to believe a man who just a few weeks ago was praising Trujillo?"

This, of course, is completely false, though the falsehood is hidden under seemingly irrefutable logic. The truth, however, is that neither this man nor any other Dominican could say otherwise while in Trujillo's grip. They have always known that Trujillo is a tyrant, but deprived of their right to say so within their own country, if they are going to preserve the security of relatives as well as that of associates and accomplish any good by remaining alive, they must wait for the relative safety of foreign soil to speak their minds.

For domestic consumption, however, Trujillo does not dare to follow this approach. Inside the country people know enough not to be fooled by his propaganda. Furthermore, anyone accused of stealing money from Trujillo or of cheating him in any way is regarded as a sort of hero, although people will not dare to proclaim it. To force people to turn their backs on former collaborators it suffices to publish in the newspapers an item stating that So and So has become a "traitor" and has gone back to the "communist party" where he belongs anyway.

This name-calling mania has been carried to comic extremes. For instance, a University professor, Ing. José Ramón Baez Lopez Penha, was dismissed following the accusation that he had criticized in front of his students a new government rent tax. Prior to dismissal, a letter was planted in *El Caribe* calling the wealthy, conservative engineer (whose fortune had been made as a result of profitable government contracts) a Red. His alleged "communist leanings" were no obstacle to reinstatement, following an abject recantation.

Regulated from morning until night, his opinions dictated by law, his movements and conversations watched, his employment often subject to the consent of the dictatorship, it is hardly surprising if anyone who disagrees with Trujillo's opinion of the benefits of his regime turns his eyes to other freer lands. During the early days scores of the ablest men emigrated, but nowadays the right to exile is denied to most opponents.

One of the most carefully controlled matters is issuance of passports to travel abroad. Any attempt to leave the country without a regular traveling document is severely punished. There are widely known cases of people who have lost their lives because someone else accused them of seeking a way to leave the country. Pedro Naar Rivero, a young newspaper reporter employed by *El Caribe,* mysteriously disappeared in June 1954. It was later known that the police had picked up Naar after intercepting his correspondence applying for a post on a Cuban newspaper. The inquiries made by the management of *El Caribe* met with a bland statement by Anselmo Paulino, Trujillo's righthand man, that Naar had crossed the border and interned himself in Haiti. This never happened.

The life of Dominican exiles, harassed by the long arm of the dictatorship, is not easy, but despite its inconveniences there are men, many of them formerly prominent, who have risked the loss of wealth, comfort, family life and social standing rather than remain in the country, their lips sealed and their movements noted. One of the most inspiring examples of successful resistance to Trujillo's terror is provided by the case of one of the best-known Dominican criminal lawyers, Dr. Ricardo Roques Martinez, now in exile in New York City.

Dr. Roques' story has not been told yet in full and it may not be told since it would endanger the security of many people living in the country. This much may be said. In 1947, during the period immediately preceding the abortive invasion of Cayo Confites, Dr. Roques was engaged, as one of the underground leaders, in the organization of several cells of the forthcoming movement of internal resistance. Tipped off by one of Trujillo's secret agents, he learned that orders had been issued for his apprehension and murder. He promptly contacted the underground groups under his leadership and their members took him into hiding.

During the next four years—a long period of anxiety—Roques lived with the secret police on his tail, moving from one place to another, many times using most extravagant disguises. During this seemingly endless period, Roques lived in at least seven different places; for several months he was restricted to the narrow space between a high wardrobe and a wall. Not once was he betrayed by the people in whose hands he put his own life.

Finally, his friends spread the rumor that he had passed away and, surprisingly, Trujillo believed it. Taking advantage of the fact that the police had relaxed their vigilance as a result of the death rumor, Roques' friends decided the time was ripe to smuggle him out of the country, a risky operation they achieved by means that are still kept secret. After a long ordeal Roques reached a French Caribbean island at the end of 1951; from there he went to Costa Rica and finally to New York City where at present he is the representative of the anti-Trujillo party, *Vanguardia Revolucionaria Dominicana.*

The remarkable feature of this story is that no one ever betrayed Roques. Many innocent people were tortured by the police during their frantic search of the revolutionary leaders. Many people knew Roques' whereabouts and some of them were imprisoned and tortured but they never admitted any knowledge. Roques' former legal secretary, Abelardo Acevedo, was beaten to death by Army officers in the Ozama fortress. This time, however, they picked the wrong man, since Acevedo knew nothing about his employer's underground activities.

The Roques story—and its accompanying anecdotes of unselfish devotion to a cause by humble members of the working class—will undoubtedly make one of the fascinating chapters in the hitherto unknown history of Dominican "freedom fighters." This and other tales will disprove the baseless theory that Dominicans are a people without backbone.

In 1954 the Benefactor forced through Congress a resolution denouncing the Inter American treaties on the Right of Asylum. Since then the Dominican Republic is the only Latin American nation which does not recognize this imbedded principle of Inter American international law.

Fear of the scrutiny of the secret police is not exclusively Dominican. Foreigners find it exceedingly trying to live in Trujilloland. A visitor may not be conscious of being followed as he is conscious, for example, in countries behind the Iron Curtain. However, a visitor soon realizes that the Government meant it when it charged General Espaillat with "public vigilance of suspicious foreigners." And any foreigner is considered "suspicious" until proven otherwise.

Surveillance, though very subtle, starts upon arrival. The immigration authorities have a long list of names of people not allowed under any circumstances to visit the country. If the visitor's name is not on the list he will be warmly welcomed and let alone to do whatever he wants. The taxi he takes down to his hotel is nevertheless driven by a man whose duty is to report to the police any suspicious movement of his fares (in order to keep their union cards and consequently the right to work, chauffeurs must perform as agents for the secret police).

Once in his hotel room the guest will be closely watched. His telephone will be tapped, his mail opened and a record of his appointments and visitors carefully made for the police. The chances are that he will not have a moment of privacy, though he probably won't know it, since there will not be hatchet-faced policemen around. The personnel of the hotel will be very nice, but almost without exception they work for the secret police. (Most maids, waiters, bartenders and doormen are British subjects from the West Indies who, being illegally in the country, are given the choice of becoming informers or deportation to their crowded islands.)

Permanent residents of the country know however the extent of the surveillance and are always careful what they say and where they say it. Even diplomats consider it wise to discuss confidential matters outdoors. If further proof were needed that the eyes of the police do not make distinctions between nationals and non-nationals, the Dominican newspapers printed on September 28, 1956, an official notice advising all foreigners they should present themselves during the first four days of each calendar month to the nearest police precinct. They were asked to bring their identification documents plus two photographs—one profile, one front. A few days later the police reversed the order without explanations. The new advertisement simply said that the Security Service had provided them already with all the needed information.

Not even the Diplomatic Corps accredited in Ciudad Trujillo is exempt from the terror tactics of *trujillismo*. Diplomats are treated in almost the manner other people are and the regime applies to them as much pressure as to ordinary mortals. Even they "are expected to speak favorably of the Generalissimo," reported a correspondent for *U.S. News & World Report.*

Herbert Matthews, veteran correspondent of the *New York Times,* pointed out that for the visitor, especially a newspaperman, "certain little things are immediately obvious or ascertainable." When your telephone at the Hotel Jaragua is picked up, he asserted, there is the unmistakable buzz that indicates that it is tapped. "It is known," he wrote, "that some of the rooms have microphones in the radio, and a newspaperman has to expect to be put into such a room. When he sits in the dining room or bar or any part of the hotel with a low ceiling, it is safer to talk in low voice."

Matthews added—and very correctly indeed—that a guest of a hotel "may be positive that his mail and telegrams are censored. At the airport coming in, a search is made for newspapers and magazines containing derogatory references to the regime. *Time,* for instance, has been barred four times since December (1952 to March 1953)."

Foreign corporations and individuals are not even free to hire their own employees. Under an Act of Congress every Dominican must get Government permission before working for a non-national employer. This law is double-edged. It, in effect, enables the Government to select a foreigner's employees—even his housemaids. It also enables the regime to forbid employment by foreigners of Dominicans who are out of favor, thus closing one of the few opportunities of livelihood left to blacklisted families.

Small wonder that under such relentless pressure outsiders conduct themselves in the country almost in the manner the helpless nationals do. As a result, the same wide gap of distrust that divides Dominicans separates foreigners from one another as well as from local society. Suspecting that outsiders are always either under Government surveillance or on the regime's pay-roll, ordinary Dominicans shun them, especially those who speak their own language. They know that if detected talking with someone who afterward may commit an indiscretion or make an unwelcome remark, they will be accountable to the police, whether it is their fault or not. Furthermore, they never know who might be an agent provocateur for Trujillo under the guise of an inquiring innocent tourist or newspaperman. As Dominicans say, *"en bocas cerrades no entran moscas"* (Flies do not enter into closed mouths). This is what makes it so difficult for visiting newspapermen to assess the actual situation within the country. And so risky at times, it should be added, since the chances are that people will report to the police any political questions put to them. Milton Bracker of the *New York Times* reported that a question he asked a Dominican journalist was known to Trujillo within twenty-four hours.

In a country where guarantees against encroachment on legal rights are in practice void, there is little a man can do to look for redress. There is, to be sure, an elaborate judiciary, since the regime has taken pains to keep the external trappings of democratic rule. But the judiciary is a mockery and the judges are trusted hirelings.

However, as Trujillo hates to let people know that he is not loved even by a handful of "subversives," political trials are not very frequent. Occasionally, someone is publicly tried as a "Communist"—the preferred political charge against critics of the regime—but this is done to spotlight Trujillo's relentless effort to eradicate the "Red menace." The great majority of political offenders are dealt with in other ways. Those who are not suppressed outright by the military or secret police are accused of rape, homosexuality, drug addiction, tax evasion, embezzlement, murder and other non-political acts. Thus, Trujillo can make good his claim that there are no political prisoners in Dominican jails.

Anyway, inside a jail there is no difference between one kind of prisoners and the others—all are brutally treated. Discipline in the jails is always harsh and cruel, although there are few known cases of physical torture of political inmates. This, however, is due to the fact that not many of the people thrown in jail are conspirators or possessors of information of any value. In the cases in which confessions are required the most brutal beatings are administered, as in July 1957 with the members of the religious sect, Jehovah's Witnesses. As a rule, however, the Benefactor kills rather than tortures.

Yet, even without recourse to physical torment Trujillo's jails are gruesome enough to break the resistance of any prisoner. The shock of being torn from their families and placed in vermin-infested cells, usually without any knowledge of the charges, must obviously cause mental torture to any but the most callous. Threats of hanging and other grisly forms of death, as well as uncertainty about the fate of relatives and dear ones, is sometimes enough to accomplish Trujillo's desired end of assuring future collaboration from most of the "subversives." Those with enough will power to resist are soon converted, through undernourishment and overwork, into miserable ragamuffins.

3.

WERE IT POSSIBLE TO ARRAIGN TRUJILLO BEFORE A WORLD Court to answer for the crimes he has instigated, the charges would add up to an indictment so damning that even "the Big One" might well shrink from attempting a defense at the bar of international public opinion.

No account of the terror tactics of the Dominican regime will ever be complete without mention of its chamber of horrors. Trujillo's list of murders is endless. In a country where capital punishment was constitutionally abolished in 1924, executions have been perpetrated by the thousands. Yet their exact number will always be a matter of conjecture. The only one who knows—Trujillo himself since not even his executioners live long enough to tell tales—doesn't do any talking.

Intelligent propagandists for the regime stress that Trujillo is "mild" nowadays and that gone are the days when any enthusiastic *trujillista* could shoot without hesitation anyone suspected of opposition to "the Chief." It may be that open and brazen murders and other outrages that might rouse indignation abroad and keep tourist trade away have ceased to be performed. Nevertheless, every policeman, every soldier, every spy is still a law unto himself and is authorized to deal arbitrarily and without fear of punishment with the rest of the population. *La 42* has been ostensibly licensed, but its remaining members (many have disappeared in the rough-and-tumble of twenty-seven years of terror) hold high command in the armed forces, important government posts and even diplomatic representations. Perhaps opponents of the regime are not beaten or murdered in the streets any longer—they are simply removed from sight quietly.

Not all the murders committed in latter days may be classified properly as political. Occasionally, repression has stemmed from baser motives than the heated passions of political controversy. Many an innocent person has been disposed of on account of greed and many a private feud has been settled in blood. It is a commonplace in the Dominican Republic that when Trujillo was rounding up the gigantic acreage for which he is now famous, the land he could not buy from legitimate owners, he acquired later from their defenseless widows.

One of the most shocking cases of murder for greed was perpetrated in 1947 on the persons of a couple of wealthy refugees, the Austrian Otto Smolensky and his wife, the Belgian Baroness Marie Louise Smolensky.

The Smolenskys had been living in the Dominican Republic since 1937 on a large farm called *El Ranchito,* located in the rich agricultural province of La Vega. In March 1947 *La Nación* reported that the bodies of Otto and Marie Louise had been found in the wreckage of their automobile at an isolated spot on the road between the city of La Vega and Ciudad Trujillo. No details of the causes of the accident or the circumstances surrounding it were printed. After the scanty original news story the case was never mentioned by the press, despite the fact that the victims were prominent in local social circles.

It was, however, a matter of public record that on the day of his death Otto Smolensky had closed the last of a series of financial transactions intended to liquidate his holdings in the country, which he was leaving to take up residence elsewhere, presumably in the United States. On that date he sold *El Ranchito* to Virgilio Trujillo Molina, eldest of the Trujillo brothers, and was paid with a certified check allegedly issued by a Ciudad Trujillo bank. Upon signing the bill of sale and other documents, the couple had drawn a large amount of their own cash from their bank account in La Vega and with the Baroness's jewelry among their luggage had set out for Ciudad Trujillo, where they were supposed to take a plane and fly out of the country.

They never reached the capital city. A few hours after their departure from La Vega some motorist saw their car at the bottom of a ravine and reported it to the police. Rescue parties found the bodies of the couple, but no mention was ever made either of the sums of money or the jewelry they were known to be carrying.

Listed by the police as an "accident," the matter was promptly put to rest. Dominicans, however, were not fooled by the police explanations— the brief public mention of the "accident" fell into a too well-known pattern to pass unnoticed. Bit by bit, pieces of evidence were dug up and through the grapevine the real picture took form gradually. The truth is that when brother Arismendy "Petan" Trujillo Molina, another member of the Family, heard that the Smolenskys were going to take the road loaded with liquid assets, he quickly schemed to retain the loot in the country. Thereupon "Petan" sent for a group of hand-picked gunmen, headed by a trusted executioner, José Cepeda, and entrusted to them the job of intercepting and killing the travelers and robbing them.

Although the hold-up was successfully carried out, Arismendy was not to enjoy the spoils. When the Benefactor heard of his effrontery, he summoned brother "Petan" and peremptorily ordered him to hand the plunder over. His conscience eased by this move of exalted justice, "the Big One" ordered the case closed. Thus, inquiries made by the heirs of the Smolensky fortune concerning their legacy in the Dominican Republic failed to receive a satisfactory answer. No accounting was ever made of the inheritance. Nor, thus far, have diplomatic representations on behalf of the Smolensky family produced results. The case was the perfect double-play: Virgilio Trujillo (whose check was never cashed) to Arismendy Trujillo to Rafael L. Trujillo.

Sometimes it is not necessary to own property to get oneself disposed of. Just to know about an act of spoliation may be fatal. In 1945 Dr. Jorge Alejandro Nin, a young lawyer, perished, according to the newspapers, in a road "accident" while on his way to take the post of District Attorney of his home town of Barahona. Also reported dead in the same accident was the alleged chauffeur of the car, an aggressive leader of the Drivers Union whose intransigent nature was not agreeable to the authorities. Although known to few people at the time, two days before the published date of the "accident" Nin had been arrested by secret police at the law office he shared with another lawyer now in exile in the United

States. Only a few hours earlier Nin had confided to his colleague that he was deeply worried. A few days before the police had questioned him concerning accusations made by an informer. Nin had been charged with stating at a party that Trujillo had robbed his father's salt mine in Barahona province. His appointment as District Attorney came after he had been arrested.

Sometimes the lives of the intended victims are mercifully spared by the always "generous" Benefactor. Then they are only accused either of "communist activities" or of a common crime. Late in 1955 "the Big One" decided to build a polo field for his sons on someone else's property. Accordingly, he ordered the Government to expropriate the plot of ground for reasons of "social interest." Apparently dissatisfied with the Government assessment, the legal owners of the land dared to criticize it in front of third parties. Two of them, Enrique Apolinar Henriquez and his brother Abad, were promptly accused by the Dominican Attorney General of "communist activities." Later Enrique was brought to trial and sentenced to a jail term for the crime of having introduced into the country an expired ticket of the lottery of Puerto Rico.

The recent attention paid by the American press to Trujillo's terror has forced certain changes in the tactics of the publicity-conscious Generalissimo. He has become more cautious and sophisticated, and, as a result, an ever increasing number of political crimes are covered up under the mantle of accidents or suicides. Today the preferred method seems to be "suicide for remorse," whereby a prisoner after "confessing" guilt to a particular crime states in writing that he is giving up life voluntarily as a matter of self-punishment.

One of the last instances of "suicide for remorse" with which I had to deal as editor of a Dominican newspaper was that of Goico Morel, accused of killing a small merchant under grisly circumstances. Under the police third degree Goico finally confessed to murder. The next day, Goico, a nephew of Emilio Morel, one of Trujillo's early collaborators who later turned exile, was found hanging in his cell. According to the police, he left a note saying that because of remorse he had decided to dispose of his own life. The police, however, did not explain in this case, or in any other, why the only people with access to pen and paper in a Dominican jail are would-be suicides.

A thorough examination of Dominican newspaper files will produce countless examples of news stories, released by the police, dealing with this type of punishment. So frequent, in fact, is this type of case that I finally ordered my subordinates at El Caribe to discontinue printing examples of them. They continued to be printed in La Nación.

One of the most peculiar cases of "political suicide" occurred late in

1949. One morning the police announced that Dominican sailors had fished out of the muddy waters of the Ozama river, in Ciudad Trujillo, an automobile belonging to a young physician of American origin, Dr. Enrique Washington Lithgow. His body had been found inside the car. Further investigation, the police asserted, lent support to the theory of suicide.

The truth, however, as ascertained by reputable Dominicans whose identity cannot be yet revealed, was the opposite. Lithgow, a civilian cancer specialist at the service of the military hospital, was under police investigation at the time of his death. He had been accused of confiding to someone who turned out to be in contact with the police that he had found out that Trujillo was suffering of cancer and had only two years to live.

Even though inaccurate, Lithgow's diagnosis proved to be his personal undoing. Shortly after his conversation with his confidant he was picked up by secret police as he was leaving a private clinic where he worked. The police agents, who were waiting inside his car, drove him off for his last ride. Twelve hours later his body was recovered from the sticky bottom of the river. A strange footnote to this case was provided by the Dominican authorities themselves. Shortly thereafter they issued a certificate of death by "accident" at the request of interested parties, for the purposes of insurance payment.

Not long afterward, on the morning of June 2, 1950, a truck was found smashed and burning in a ravine at *El Número,* on the coastal highway west of Ciudad Trujillo. In the charred wreckage were the bodies of five men and an old lady. The wreck was duly reported by Dominican newspapers as an "accident," and no details concerning an investigation were ever released by the National Police.

Missing after the "accident" was the truck's owner, Porfirio "Prim" Ramírez Alcantara, commission merchant and brother of Trujillo's bitter foe and exile leader Miguel Angel Ramírez, one of the military commanders of the abortive revolutionary attempts of Cayo Confites and Luperon.

This "accident" might have remained an absolute mystery, had not the truck driver survived long enough to talk with a member of the Ramírez family. Juan Rosario, the driver, asserted that Ramírez' truck had set out the night before from Ciudad Trujillo to San Juan de la Maguana with a load of wheat. The driver was accompanied by Ramírez himself, an alternate driver and three helpers. At the last minute they took aboard another man and the old lady who asked for a lift.

Four kilometers from the capital they made a routine stop for checking at a military post. A sergeant demanded that the truck convey six soldiers to the bridge over the Nizao river, between Trujillo's home town of San Cristóbal and Bani a few miles further west. Upon arrival at the bridge the truck was surrounded by a group of Army officers and soldiers headed by Lieutenant General Federico Fiallo. While the soldiers pointed their guns at the occupants, Fiallo asked them to step down.

Ramírez was the first to jump out from the truck to inquire about the display of force. He was attacked with clubs, the surviving witness said. Apparently the soldiers were under orders not to use firearms, thus to be able later to simulate an accident. However, Ramírez put up strong resistance to his assailants. An abled-bodied six-footer, Ramírez knocked General Fiallo down and grabbed a club away from an officer, knocking down with it three other men (one allegedly died). General Fiallo who was back on his feet finally ordered the soldiers to open fire and Ramírez fell, his body riddled with bullets.

Since the shooting had not only messed up the original plans of simulating an accident, but had also been heard by people living in the neighborhood, the soldiers left Ramírez' body at one side of the road and hurriedly took the other occupants of the truck to *El Número,* an isolated spot farther down the road. There the innocent bystanders of the freshly committed crime were beaten to a pulp, drenched with gasoline and thrown back on the truck. After setting the vehicle on fire the soldiers dumped it into the ravine.

Badly wounded, the driver Rosario somehow managed to pull himself from the burning truck. After the soldiers left he crawled to the road and dragged himself several miles from the carnage. Finally he found a parked truck, whose driver, not knowing the nature of his "accident," agreed to take him to the nearest hospital in the city of Bani. There, Rosario lived long enough to tell the tale of the fateful night and, fortunately enough, to a physician, brother of his employer, Dr. Victor Manuel Ramírez, who, advised by the professional grapevine, reached the hospital several steps ahead of the secret police. Rosario's life could not be saved. As soon as the police caught up with his sensational escape they appeared at the hospital and, though rather belatedly, they disposed of him right then and there.

These were not the only victims of the mass murder. One of the assailants, a police sergeant named Alejandro Menéndez, happened to be a friend of Dr. Ramírez. Bothered by conscience he went to see his friend and not only told the story of the night before but warned the doctor regarding further attempts against the life of other members of the Ramírez family. Apparently as one of the participants in the crime the man was being closely watched by the police, because, upon return to his precinct, he was arrested. The same night his body was delivered to Mrs. Menéndez. She was told that her husband had hanged himself with his own tie.

Thereupon the whole Ramírez family took refuge in foreign embassies and eventually escaped from the country. With them they brought out the gruesome story, which Dominican exile organizations used to file an official protest with the United Nations. In the bill of particulars the Dominican Army was charged with willfully ambushing and massacring Porfirio Ramírez and his companions, a fact the Government denied.

As the exiles had asked a formal U.N. investigation on the ground that it was a violation of human rights, the Benefactor decided to play safe. He demoted General Fiallo and quietly made some of the lesser executioners disappear. Furthermore, he put his trusted aide at the disposal of the Attorney General for indictment, when and if necessary.

Fiallo's disgrace did not last long. Soon Trujillo reassured himself that nothing would come out of the exile's protest to the United Nations and he appointed the former General to the Cabinet post of Secretary of Public Works. (Later Fiallo was restored to the Armed Forces with the rank of Colonel, Chief of the National Police.)

These, nevertheless, are simply a few of an endless series of incidents. They are individual, isolated cases. This, however, does not mean that Trujillo is not capable of mass slaughter as well.

One of the worst massacres of Dominican underground opponents took place in 1949 at the time of the abortive revolutionary attempt known as the Landing of Luperon.

This revolutionary movement had been planned in close cooperation between a main exile organization and important sectors of the still partially organized underground. By means not yet clear, Trujillo managed to plant as a sort of liaison officer between the two plotting groups one of his stooges, the late Captain Antonio Jorge Estévez.

Jorge, who a few months later was going to meet death in Cuba in a new attempt to perform espionage work for the Dominican Government, provided the Generalissimo with all manner of details about the forthcoming uprising. Knowing beforehand the revolutionists' plans, their prospective landing points, the strength of their forces and the identity and location of the internal resistance groups, all Trujillo had to do was sit and wait. Airtight plans were made in advance to meet the forthcoming emergency and to ruthlessly suppress not only the invasion forces and their allies but also all groups and individuals who were on the lists of recalcitrant opponents of the regime.

Upon hearing on the night of June 19, 1949, of the landing of a PBY plane with a revolutionary party on board in the coastal town of Luperon, Trujillo set in motion his machinery of repression throughout the country and in a matter of hours hundreds of political suspects, whether connected or not with the plot, were killed or imprisoned. Although the official communiqué about the happenings on that night of the long knives mentioned only the names of two civilian casualties—Fernando Spignolio and Nando Suarez—it is a well-established fact that in the opposition stronghold of Puerto Plata alone executions were counted by the hundred.

Long after the revolutionary attempt had been crushed the secret police was still rounding up alleged plotters. The mass executions seemingly had the intended effect since it was years before any organized resistance to Trujillo was to break out again. Even the last reported attempt against Trujillo's dictatorship, in June 1956, is still a baffling mystery to discerning Dominicans. Although not a word was printed by the local press a news story leaked out through Dominican censorship to the effect that the Generalissimo had narrowly escaped assassination. According to these press reports which originated in Washington, a purported plot to blow up the Benefactor and his entourage during the inaugural ceremonies of the new Church of the city of Moca had been uncovered and had misfired at the eleventh hour.

A bomb had been planted, it was asserted, in the Church which Trujillo was scheduled to visit. However, shortly before zero hour one of the plotters lost his nerve and tipped off the authorities. Several arrests were made and the bomb was quickly removed.

To date the details of the plot remain mysterious but reliable Dominican sources feel inclined to believe that the plot was conceived by Trujillo himself and hatched by his *agents provocateurs* in an effort to bring about a favorable climate for the ruthless suppression of the increasing number of discontents, who were getting too bold in their criticism of the rampant inflation and extravagant spending in the World Fair. In the manner typical of *trujillismo* right after the discovery of the plot a press campaign of insults was carried out against those whose names had been associated with the abortive attempt, particularly a youthful lawyer named Dr. Rafael Estévez Cabrera and other members of his family. Estévez was called a "professional thief" and "arsonist," and a letter to the editor of *El Caribe* bluntly accused his fiancée, a member of an aristocratic family from Santiago, of being pregnant as a result of illicit sex relations with the lawyer. Other members of the family were accused of murder and other common crimes. Thus far, all efforts to ascertain the whereabouts of the male members of the Estévez family have met with failure.

Trujillo does not limit the application of terror to his own fellow citizens. "The Big One" has been responsible for the suppression of the lives of several citizens of the United States. Two Puerto Ricans have met death during the Era of Trujillo: Eduardo Colom y Piris and Juan N. Miranda.

The best known of the two cases is that of Colom y Piris, since documents pertaining to the investigation conducted under prodding of the U.S. State Department have been published in the collection of papers entitled *Foreign Relations of the United States*. This American national, then 18, was arrested April 29, 1933, in San Pedro de Macoris by Lieutenant Sindulfo Minaya Benavides, of the Dominican Army. The Puerto

Rican youngster had been accused by a police spy of having spoken disrespectfully of President Trujillo. No one ever heard of him again, but according to an affidavit sworn by his mother (who visited prisons and government offices for many days in order to discover the fate of her son) the boy was shot on May 1, 1933. Puerto Rican press reports quoted Colom's mother as stating that appeals to the U.S. Consul in Santo Domingo brought only general assurances that her youngster was safe. The case, however, aroused such an intense public outcry in Puerto Rico that strong diplomatic pressure was exerted upon the Dominican Government in an effort to get a satisfactory explanation.

Under pressure by the State Department the Dominican authorities finally came out with an explanation: Lieutenant Minaya, the alleged author of the murder, had been arrested and would be brought to trial soon. They, of course, denied all political implications but shortly afterward informed the U.S. Legation in the Dominican capital city that Minaya had been shot "while attempting to escape" from the San Pedro de Macoris prison. The U.S. Government was by no means satisfied with the bland explanation and kept the heat on Trujillo until the Dominican Government agreed to assume responsibility for the crime and made a diplomatic settlement. Consequently the mother of the murdered boy received a $5,000 indemnity.

Trujillo, on the other hand, got away with impunity in the case of Juan Miranda. The latter, a long-time resident of the country, where he was highly respected and had worked both as a teacher and a farmer, was murdered by a group of soldiers in his residence in Barahona province, shortly after the killing of Colom. Miranda's case did not arouse as much attention as the previous one, probably because the unfortunate professor did not have a living mother. No diplomatic representations were ever made that I know of, and the whole affair soon sank into total oblivion.

A few years later the international character of the gangster-style operations of the Generalissimo was to be clearly underlined again by the cold-blooded assassination of an American clergyman: Reverend Charles Raymond Barnes, Minister of the principal Episcopal Church in the Dominican Republic.

An affable man, Barnes had performed his religious duties in the country with charm and understanding, becoming in the process well-known and liked by Protestants and Catholics. He had converted his church, located on one of the main thoroughfares of the city, into a center of civic activities in a way the Trujillo regime has always frowned upon.

On the morning of July 27, 1938, Barnes—who as a bachelor lived alone in a house next door to the church—was found dead, lying in a pool of blood, in the middle of his own bedroom. The discovery of the minister's body, shot and badly beaten, was made by his maid when she came to work. The crime caused consternation within Dominican society and a chill of horror struck the foreign colony.

Without awaiting for a diplomatic representation, the Dominican authorities announced at once that they were opening a thorough "investigation." The Government solemnly asserted that the majesty of the law would be upheld and the culprits punished. Shortly afterward the alleged author of the crime was produced. According to the police reports he was the minister's house-boy, a Puerto Rican named Diaz.

The police told the press that upon his arrest Diaz had confessed killing the clergyman because the latter had made homosexual advances. Through the ensuing trial Diaz stuck to his story and the Court found him guilty of the charge of manslaughter and sentenced him to a prison term. Diaz was then sent to jail, never to be seen again.

The real story behind Barnes's murder is one with sinister political overtones. It seems that Barnes had smuggled out of the country a few letters, addressed to friends and relatives in the United States, giving vivid accounts of the massacre of Haitian peasants ordered by the Generalissimo a few months earlier. Inadvertently, Barnes sent part of his correspondence by way of the regular Dominican mail service. Intercepted by the *trujillista* postal offices the letters were turned over to the secret police. Upon reading the minister's mail, Trujillo ordered his military aides to bring Barnes to his presence at his country retreat of *Hacienda Fundación,* in San Cristóbal.

What happened during the fateful interview only God and Trujillo know. Barnes, however, came out of the conference a condemned man. The details of Barnes's actual liquidation remain buried under a maze of contradictory versions which place the execution either on Trujillo's farm or in the victim's home. Also a mystery is the seemingly willing confession to the murder by the house-boy. The theory that Diaz was, in all likelihood, bribed with the offer of a large sum of money coupled with the promise of freedom within a reasonable length of time seems plausible. However, if that was the case, Diaz paid dearly for his foolish greed.

The story of the Reverend Barnes did not end with the conviction of the Puerto Rican house-boy. Already shielded by the travesty of justice, the Dominican newspapers soon afterward showered upon the late clergyman all manner of libelous accusations.

THE ARMED FORCES

1. ON THE SUNNY MORNING OF AUGUST 15, 1957, CIUDAD Trujillo's George Washington Avenue was the scene of the most brilliant military pageant ever staged by the Dominican Armed Forces. Although announced as part of the program of festivities on the occasion of "little brother" Héctor's second inauguration as President of the Dominican Republic, the parade of more than 30,000 men was really in honor of "big brother," the Commander in Chief of the Armed Forces, Generalissimo Dr. Rafael L. Trujillo, who stole the show from his puppet.

For three hours regulars and conscripts passed in review for the benefit of foreign diplomats and military attachés, distinguished visitors from other lands, high Dominican officials and a throng of several thousand citizens. From a couple of comfortable reviewing stands (one especially reserved for the Generalissimo and a handful of relatives and selected aides), the guests of honor admiringly observed the martial bearing of the trim soldiers and marines marching by with impeccable precision. Flattering comments followed the passing of the superbly trained infantry regiments; the tight chugging ranks of the motorcycle scouts; the mobile antiaircraft guns; the efficient transportation and communication units; the field artillery and the scores of lumbering tanks. A few miles off, deep in the restless Caribbean Sea, more than twenty units of the powerful Dominican Navy maneuvered, while overhead the frightening drone of the potent engines of the British-made jet planes (Vampires) and other aircraft of the Air Force deafened the audience. A large part of the impressive array of equipment was American, inherited during and after the Second World War or bought from third parties. (Part of the American fighter planes were acquired from Sweden, and it was recently announced that the Dominican Government was closing a ten-million-dollar deal with Japan for the transfer of American Sabre Jets.)

However, few of the foreigners watching this colorful, elaborate display of force were aware that almost none of the erect, spruce draftees mingling with the well-trained, hardened professional soldiers knew how to fire the rifles they were carrying. Trujillo who likes to boast of an army of more than 100,000 men, does not dare to teach his soldiers to shoot. For Dominican conscripts (compulsory military service has been in force since 1947) basic training is limited to drilling. "The Chief" knows that if it is necessary he can always complete the unfinished job of training his soldiers in a few weeks. "At any rate," a high ranking Army officer explained to me, "we have enough combat-ready professional troops to hold down any front for a good many days."

The tough, cunning Generalissimo was taught early by his Marine tutors that the most effective way to ensure absolute obedience is to take away from the people the means of attack. Trujillo carried the principle to its logical conclusion. In army garrisons outside the capital, for example, stocks of ammunitions are always kept low. Not only are draftees almost entirely ignorant about weapons, but civilians are not allowed to carry arms of any kind. Even high Government officials are not permitted to own a gun without special authorization. People sometimes "get lost" after being accused of illegal ownership of a pistol.

Even though the conscripts exhibited by Trujillo in parades are not real soldiers, the regular armed forces are known to be strong enough to defeat singlehanded any combination of two other neighboring military forces. The Dominicans are so far ahead of their closest neighbor Haiti that there is hardly basis for comparison. Apart perhaps from Venezuela, the Dominican Republic has the best-trained, most powerful armed force in the Caribbean.

The real strength of Trujillo's military establishment is a closely guarded secret, but few doubt that if pressed Trujillo could make good his boast of putting 100,000 men on a war footing. Still, the best available data show a standing army of about 14,000 men. Another 60,000 have received a seventeen weeks course in basic military training. According to Nanita's biography of Trujillo, the "selective service carries on its rolls the names of 467,704 citizens (between the ages of eighteen and thirty-five) who freely volunteered to register."

The comparatively huge size of the Dominican Army can hardly be related to any danger from outside. This extravagant military might would be of limited if any value in the event of a nuclear world war. Under the existing inter-American peace arrangements and safeguards against aggression it would be of doubtful value even for a localized conflict. Its major function—as is the case with other Latin American armies—is internal rather than external.

The Dominican Navy has a strength of 3,000 men and thirty-four combat and auxiliary vessels, including two former British Navy destroyers and several Canadian-built frigates and corvettes. The importance of Trujillo's naval power is brought into sharp focus by the fact that the Dominican Navy is bigger than the Mexican and could easily overpower any other naval force in the area, with the exception of Venezuela's. This disturbing situation has not been overlooked by the United States. In order to restore at least a semblance of balance of military power in the region, America has been forced at times to encourage limited-scale armament races.

Although himself an Army man, Trujillo has always shown a marked predilection for the Navy. "The Chief" seems to derive a particular satisfaction from playing the role of Admiral of the Fleet. As such he is frequently photographed wearing a naval uniform. When some particular problem irks him, the Generalissimo takes to the sea and thoughtfully strolls on the bridge deck of the *Angelita,* once famous in American society columns as Mrs. Joseph Davies' *Sea Cloud.* There is also the presidential yacht *Presidente Trujillo,* a converted frigate, considered one of the most luxurious ships afloat.

The sole glorious feat of the Dominican Navy is the capture of *El Quetzal.* This ship, a former U.S. landing craft, set out on July 25, 1951, flying the Guatemalan flag, from the Cuban port of El Mariel with a cargo of avocado trees for Puerto Livingstone, Honduras. Four days later she entered the Dominican naval base of Las Calderas escorted by one of Trujillo's warships.

For over three weeks nothing was heard of *El Quetzal.* Then hell broke loose. On August 24, the Cuban press front-paged a sensational story: Dominican warships in an unprecedented act of contemporary piracy had "captured" the ship in Cuban waters and her captain had been tortured to make him say that he had gone to the Dominican Republic voluntarily. Almost simultaneously the Dominican newspapers hailed with banner headlines an official statement reporting that Lieutenant Pedro Alfredo Brito Baez and First Machinist Nelson Alcides Brito Salomón had returned to the country and reported to serve in the Dominican Navy, after completing a tour of duty as Trujillo's naval intelligence agents in Guatemala and Cuba. With them they brought *El Quetzal* in an effort to prevent her being used in "subversive activities" against the Dominican Republic. The other nine crew members (six Cubans, three Guatemalans) had been interned pending trial in Dominican courts.

El Quetzal had a strange story. Bought in 1947 by Dominican revolutionists and baptized *El Fantasma* (The Phantom), she had, after several close escapes from American and Cuban authorities, taken part in the abortive invasion of the Dominican Republic from Cuba known as the "Cayo Confites affair." In the only naval action of that ill-fated revolutionary adventure, *El Fantasma* had intercepted and captured off the Cuban coast the Trujillo-owned sailing boat *Angelita* (not to be confused with the Generalissimo's yacht of the same name nor with a cargo ship mentioned at the time of Galíndez' disappearance). When the Cuban army broke up the invasion before sailing off for Santo Domingo, *El Quetzal* was seized and subsequently taken to the naval base at El Mariel. Three years later she was returned to her legal owner, the exiled Dominican leader Miguel Angel Ramirez. This devolution to Ramirez was a corollary of a Cuban-Dominican settlement, worked out through the mediation of the U.S. Ambassador to Cuba, Robert Butler, whereby the *Angelita* went back to Trujillo. After reconditioning his boat, Ramirez registered her under the Guatemalan flag and planned to start a shipping business. Trujillo, however, held a personal grudge against this particular ship, because of her previous activities. Tipped off by his Chargé d'Affaires in Cuba, Dr. Felix W. Bernardino, about the date and itinerary of *El Quetzal's* maiden voyage, the Benefactor saw an opportunity to even the score.

While still in Cuban waters *El Quetzal* was met by a Dominican squadron, under the personal command of Admiral César de Windt Lavandier, Chief of Staff of the Navy. The surprise operation was executed so quickly that Brito was captured without time to finish a radio message to the Cuban authorities, warning of the presence of Dominican warships.

Lest someone should doubt the authenticity of their printed story, the Dominican authorities produced Lieutenant Brito at a local press conference. He appeared in a brand-new white uniform. I attended the conference as a correspondent for the Associated Press and International News Service and vividly recall him—calm and poker-faced—recounting how, having completed the secret mission entrusted to him by the Dominican Navy, he had "voluntarily" decided to surrender the ship to his country's Navy. He also said that he had grown tired of serving "international communism," although the reasons for this apparent contradiction with his other statements were never explained. At the time Brito did not show signs of having suffered physical torture, but it is generally understood that, despite his seemingly candid statements to the contrary, he did not have any part in the betrayal of *El Quetzal*. Obviously, after his capture he was convinced that should he play ball with Trujillo, his own life and the lives of numerous relatives held as hostages would be spared. Upon publication of Brito's story the Cuban newspapers changed their tune and bitterly accused him of having always been a secret agent sent to spy on Dominican exiles in Guatemala and Cuba.

Whatever the truth is, the Cuban Government promptly instructed its diplomatic representative in Ciudad Trujillo to intercede for the Cuban nationals. So did the Guatemalan regime through the Uruguayan Government, since normal diplomatic relations with the Dominican Republic had been interrupted a few years before. However, direct negotiations failed to produce results. The Cuban Government then decided to put the dispute up to the Inter American Peace Committee of the OAS. As it turned out, the Guatemalan Government of Jacobo Arbenz failed to press, for reasons not clear, the matter of the ship's illegal capture. Consequently the dispute was limited to the treatment and final disposal of the Cuban and Guatemalan nationals imprisoned by the Dominican Republic. What followed was a bitter, involved, inconclusive judicial wrangle. In the interim the Cuban Chargé d'Affairs left his post in Ciudad Trujillo and went home because, as officially reported in the Cuban press, Trujillo gave him a thorough personal dressing down, studded with profanity and insulting remarks about the then President Carlos Prío Socarrás.

Meanwhile the Dominican courts were busy. First they condemned *El Quetzal's* crewmen, including the Britos, to thirty years in jail for subversive activities. However, the contradiction between the court's stand and the official version that secret agent Brito had turned over the ship of his own volition soon became a source of much embarrassment. Thereupon a Court of Appeals reversed the original decision, acquitting the two Dominican sailors, who were also promoted in rank by the Navy. Finally Trujillo acceded to the release and deportation of the foreign crewmen. *El Quetzal* and the Britos were kept by the Benefactor. No one knows the whereabouts of the Britos, but it is very doubtful that even Trujillo could now produce them for another press conference.

Today the most powerful—and the youngest—of the services is the Air Force, with more than one hundred combat and training planes, at least one-third of which are jets. A corps of some 3,000 élite troops, including motorized units, stationed ten miles outside the capital city, at the San Isidro base (considered one of the most complete and efficient bases in the Caribbean area) rounds out the offensive power of the Air Force.

The impact of U.S. military aid may be plainly noticed in this branch of the services, trained and practically created by Americans as it is. Ever since the Dominican Republic entered into a Mutual Assistance Pact with the United States in 1953, Dominican Air Force personnel have been learning to fly, shoot, drill, and even think American-style. A team of American advisers has been close to the Dominican Air Force Chief of Staff, Lieutenant General Rafael L. Trujillo, Jr. So close, in fact, that there was a widespread supposition that Trujillo, Jr., had become a "captive" of his American counselors, at that time led by an aggressive U.S. Air Force Colonel named Samuel Hale. Moved by these rumors the Generalissimo stepped in and appointed an Acting Chief of Staff of the Air Force in May 1957. Young Rafael was shipped with the rank of Colonel to the United States to study at Fort Leavenworth, and Colonel Hale was quietly removed from his highly sensitive post; but American influence is more marked in the Air Force than in any other branch of the service. The Army, for instance, is being trained by a group of Spanish officers who arrived in the country early in 1956.[1]

By treaty rights Trujillo does not have trouble getting arms from the United States, but he wishes, nevertheless, to be self-supporting in this matter. His five-million-dollar small arms and ammunition factory, *Armería E.N.,* assures a permanent source and leaves a surplus for export.

The arms factory idea sprang from a diplomatic incident back in 1945, when Spruille Braden was Assistant U.S. Secretary of State for Latin American Affairs. On November 29, 1945, the Dominican Government, through its Ambassador in Washington, Emilio García Godoy, asked the State Department for an export permit to obtain an exorbitant quantity of arms from Winchester. A month later, on December 28, 1945, Braden handed García Godoy a note with an added aide-mémoire. The latter made these points. It was impossible to see why the Dominican Government wanted so many arms unless it intended to use them against a neighbor or its own people. It was the policy of the United States to co-operate fully *only* with governments that were freely elected. Democracy did not exist in the Dominican Republic either in theory or in practice.

Trujillo was taken aback by this complete about-face by the State Department, considering its usually nice behavior toward his government. Denied the right of lawfully buying arms in the United States, the Benefactor resorted to smuggling. Soon the American authorities were on his tracks. In Augusta, Ga., Karl J. Eisenhardt and three others went on trial in Federal District Court, charged with the theft of machine guns from a United States Army depot in April of 1947. The FBI had also discovered that planes purchased by Eisenhardt from the War Assets Administration had turned up in Ciudad Trujillo without the required export licenses. Eisenhardt, who had been a special adviser to the United States Embassy in Venezuela during the war (he resigned under a cloud), told the court that the stolen machine guns had been bought and paid for with money "belonging to the Dominican Republic," for the purpose of "repelling invasion."

In the meantime Presidents Eurico Gaspar Dutra, of Brazil, and Juan D. Perón, of Argentina, had extended a helping hand to their friend in need. In Brazil alone Trujillo bought seven million dollars' worth of ammunition and equipment. Alarmed by the size of such purchases, the left-of-center Government of Venezuela, then involved in a bitter feud with Trujillo, charged that these large quantities of military supplies were destined to further the ambitions of Venezuelan exiles gathered in the Dominican Republic. A formal note of protest was filed with the Brazilian

---

[1] A significant fact is that after young Trujillo's removal, a group of Dominican air cadets have been sent to France to study.

Foreign Minister, who promptly dismissed the whole issue with an unconvincing explanation. No heavy armaments were involved, a Brazilian Foreign Office spokesman said, and the weapons had been sold with the understanding that they were to be used only for internal police purposes. Though Venezuela was not convinced by this explanation, Trujillo retained his arms.

The game went on endlessly, and it was a costly one. The stage was set when Alexander Kovacs, a mysterious Hungarian refugee, appeared in Ciudad Trujillo with a very appealing scheme. He offered Trujillo the establishment of an arms factory to manufacture, among other weapons, a light machine gun whose patent he controlled. No mean businessman himself, Trujillo immediately saw the immense possibilities of the proposition. The factory was promptly erected in Trujillo's hometown—San Cristóbal. Kovacs and his beautiful, young platinum-blonde wife, Rose, became prominent members of official circles, lavishly honored by the Dictator with titles, medals and wealth.

For almost three years the plant was operated by Hungarian and Italian technicians (recruited after careful screening by Kovacs himself) under the utmost secrecy, disguised as a "zipper factory." The common workers were Dominican soldiers. Local people in the know used to call it the "candy factory."

Gradually the secret leaked out. The biggest bang occurred when a young Hungarian employee named Gyula Kemeny escaped in June 1950 and took refuge in Cuba. Upon arrival in Havana he made grave charges against the Trujillo regime, which, he said, kept Italian and Hungarian workers under conditions reminiscent of those existing in the infamous labor camps of Siberia. He asked for an investigation by the United Nations agency dealing with refugees.

According to Kemeny, the majority of the workers employed at the *Armería* were being kept on the job against their will. Kemeny said: "They are prisoners because they cannot leave San Cristóbal and cannot receive or send letters."

Describing the plant, Kemeny said that some 800 or 1,000 light machine guns were made each month under the Italian Bereta patent. Also some heavy machine guns were manufactured as well as a large number of accessories for German Mauser rifles. He talked about impending plans to produce large quantities of rifles, since "one of Hungary's most famous inventors and manufacturers of rifles" had just arrived in Ciudad Trujillo. The Hungarian added that the plant had a German-made smelter and that at least part of its output was packed for mysterious shipments.

Upon publication of Kemeny's story in the *New York Times,* the Dominican government at once replied, charging the Hungarian with being a "communist spy" who had been "discharged from the arms factory for that reason." The arms factory was too solid a fact to be denied.

Nowadays Trujillo can buy all the arms that he wants from foreign sources, but he keeps the factory going anyway—just in case. With the years the *Armería* has become one of the most impressive show windows of Dominican military might, and a must for visiting American generals and admirals. The Hungarian and Italian technicians live under much better conditions, although complaints are not unheard of. Lately the *Armería* has invaded the *field* of normal business, and gone into the manufacture of barbed-wire and air-conditioning equipment. Imports of barbed-wire were severely curtailed by official decree, and the purchase of such an article in foreign countries was subject to licenses issued by *Armería's* director, Major General Alexander Kovacs. The air-conditioning units are sold under the trade-mark of *"The Benefactor."* These unorthodox activities have given rise to the question of ownership. Though this is not clearly established, the factory appears to be government-owned. At least its expenditures are listed in the Dominican government budget.

How can a small and relatively poor country support such a military establishment? The answer is simple. From the outset the regime has dedicated the largest single item of its budget to military considerations. Their allowance has increased with the years, both in absolute amount and in relative importance. Of a total budget of $122,728,500 for 1956–57, the armed forces were allotted $28,685,110.87, or almost twenty-five per cent of the Government expenses. This sum does not include money set aside for the purchase of heavy military equipment, such as planes, ships and tanks. Such inventories are never published. Nor does it include the million dollars which—according to the well-informed *Washington Post*—the Dominican Republic was scheduled to receive in military aid from the United States during the same fiscal year.

2.

THE GLARING CONTRAST BETWEEN THE DIRE POVERTY OF the masses and the prosperity of the military caste is one of the distinctive features of the Dominican Republic under Trujillo.

The military are the pampered children of the regime and no effort is spared to keep them happy and ready to hold down the people. They enjoy all kinds of economic benefits. Officers' pay is relatively good and, by hook or crook, the majority manage to become gentlemen farmers. Their homes are among the most luxurious in the capital and other important towns. Jobs are fairly secure, promotions rather swift, prestige and power almost unlimited, and opportunities for graft are many and various. Many of the most lucrative offices in the Administration, such as the General Directorship of Customs, have been at one time or another in the hands of soldiers. As a result, the military have evolved into a sort of arrogant, contemptuous aristocracy.

Creatures of Trujillo's creation, however, even the highest ranking officers, are not allowed to forget that they owe rank, social position, wealth and successful careers to the magnanimity of the Benefactor. They are not permitted to become influential in their own right or to form dangerous cliques. Every now and then, fearing his bully boys are becoming too big for their breeches, Trujillo shakes up the structure of command. After one of these clean-ups it is not at all unusual to see the former head of the Navy serving as chief of the police, or a former lieutenant general functioning as a colonel. About fifty per cent of the officers above the rank of colonel are either related to "the Chief" by blood or marriage or are cronies from the old Constabulary, but, kin or no kin, friend or no friend, Trujillo doesn't trust them very far.

The military's standing as a class, however, has not always been so high in the Dominican Republic. Once upon a time, writes Abelardo R. Nanita, "being a soldier was like having the plague." The state of the Army was one of "perennial shoddiness, disorder, filth and chaos."

Sumner Welles writes in *Naboth's Vineyard* that the Dominican military forces had never merited public confidence, much less popular respect.

Even Nanita admits that the "troops were recruited from among the dregs of society and were for the most part unemployed farm laborers, professional idlers, or village bullies without any education or social contacts with their fellowmen, who had not yet acquired any habits of cleanliness and personal hygiene."

This description shows well the conditions the American occupation authorities had to cope with when they began to organize a Constabulary, in preparation for an eventual withdrawal. To be sure, the Military Government strove hard to eradicate the ancient Dominican idea of military duty. They sought to replace it with a new concept of the function of military forces. Along these new lines, great efforts were devoted to the creation of a nonpartisan Constabulary, trained in the theory that it would be a corps solely concerned with the execution of the law and removed from politics.

In the process the Americans ran into unexpected, serious difficulties. Drafting privates was a relatively easy task, but it was found to be almost impossible to recruit officers. Due to a deep-rooted sense of pride—and to a natural repugnance to collaborate with occupation forces—educated Dominicans refused to join the Constabulary (*Policía Nacional Dominicana*). Only hardened thugs and slum hoodlums applied for induction.

The elements of danger in such a situation soon showed themselves

openly. The nonpartisan force envisaged by its creators failed to materialize. Under the lenient eyes of President Horacio Vásquez, the American
dream backfired badly. Three years after the Marines' withdrawal the well-
trained, well-organized National Army they had left behind had fallen
under the absolute control of an ambitious, unscrupulous officer, determined to use the techniques learned during his period of training with the
American forces as a means to satisfy a long-repressed hankering for unrestricted personal power.

Lacking the deterrent of a long-established military tradition, Trujillo
could easily develop the force into a docile agent of his boundless ambition. Adroit manipulation of the commissioning of officers, as well as of
promotions, allowed the General to pack army rosters with people entirely acceptable to him. Rigid internal discipline was enforced and officers
were not permitted vacillations in their pledges of personal loyalty to Trujillo. The few officers who showed any independent strength of character
were separated from the service. Yet, as long as their loyalty was unwavering, the faithful were given security and protection, even to the point of
protection from prosecution in cases of common crimes.

A short time after Trujillo took over the presidency, he set out to assert
the privileged position of the Armed Forces. The military were lavishly endowed with prerogatives tantamount to those of an occupation Army. Naturally, they became arrogant. Then and now soldiers are cocksure and certain of the importance of the military caste. Even privates look down upon
the entire civilian population as potential lawbreakers. When a soldier fights
a civilian, the former is usually right. In the rare instances in which a soldier is tried for an offense against a civilian he is always brought before
sympathetic military jurisdiction.

To stamp the seal of respectability upon his army, Trujillo induced in
1931 a group of scions of aristocratic families to join as second lieutenants.
It may be assumed that at the same time "the Chief" wanted to inflict one
more humiliation upon the same people who, a couple of years before, had
scorned Army officers, including Trujillo himself.

Trujillo's triumph over the aristocracy was short-lived this time. Forced
to abandon their former style of living, the young socialites found them-
selves unfitted for military careers and, one by one, left the Army within a
short time. By 1956 only one of them was still in active service, Colonel
Salvador Cobián Parra, and even Cobián was marked for oblivion. On
November 1 of that year, the United Press belatedly reported from Ciudad
Trujillo that Colonel Cobián (wrongly listed as still holding the job of
Chief of Dominican Intelligence) and his civilian subaltern Andrés Avelino
Tejada "killed each other in a duel." The story added that the duel was
fought, according to close associates of both men, "over personal mat-
ters." The Dominican newspapers, however, never mentioned the alleged

duel. In their October 28 issues, both *La Nación* and *El Caribe* printed the story of Colonel Cobián's death, "yesterday at midday," as if it was the result of natural causes. Reading the local press it is impossible to find even a passing reference to Mr. Tejada. For domestic purposes he did not exist. For the same reasons Cobián's funeral was an elaborate state affair with President Héctor Trujillo and high government officials in attendance. Though absent, the Benefactor sent a tribute of flowers. Adding to the general confusion over the affair, Dominican newspapers had printed on the day of the Colonel's death the full text of a presidential decree, effective October 26, appointing the notorious "hatchet man," Lieutenant Colonel César Augusto Oliva Garcia, to be Cobián's successor in the post of National Security Chief. There the matter rested for months.

Then, to deepen the mystery, the U.S. State Department, in a diplomatic note addressed to the Dominican Foreign Office on March 12, 1957, pointed its finger towards Colonel Cobián. The Colonel, said the State Department, was one of the high Dominican officials with whom the American flyer, Gerald Lester Murphy, had been very well acquainted, while Murphy was serving as a pilot of the Trujillo-owned *Compañía Dominicana de Aviación*. All this has given rise to pointed questions, still unanswered and perhaps unanswerable: What did Cobián know about the Galíndez disappearance? What kind of connections did he have with Murphy? Why was he demoted first and then killed? Who was Tejada?

A happier story, thus far, is that of another member of the group of draftees to which Cobián belonged. Porfirio Rubirosa took advantage of the opportunity to launch his remarkable career as an international lover. While serving in the Army, Rubirosa met and married Trujillo's daughter, skyrocketing himself into wealth and international intrigue. Since then Rubirosa has been very close to the Benefactor, as well as his son Rafael, enjoying privileges few Dominicans have ever dreamed of.

Trujillo, however, did not lose hope of converting his unruly soldiery into a refined social élite. Throughout the years there has always been a heavy sprinkling of uniforms at official social events. Still, the Armed Forces officers apparently have not yet learned how to conduct themselves in society. Five years ago, Trujillo's birthday party was an all-out military affair to which civilians were not invited. The National Palace was the scene of a brilliant formal ball, to which commissioned officers in full-dress uniforms took their beautifully gowned wives. Three days later *El Caribe* printed a story—written at the National Palace—stating that the distinguished guests of the Generalissimo had stripped the mansion of all its silver and table linen. "There you have the reason why civilians were not invited," the cynics commented.

Endowed with special privileges, the military practically do as they please, provided, of course, they do not show political ambitions of their own. They do not recognize authority other than Trujillo's. Wherever there is a military commander, the civilian authorities are relegated to a subordinate role. Although forbidden by the Constitution to engage in partisan politics (they are barred from the voting booths) army officers are always photographed presiding at political rallies and other ceremonies organized by the Dominican Party.

Finding the doors of political aggrandizement closed, at least for the time being, smart officers usually employ their energies to achieve easy financial advancement. Graft is widespread. Officers' salaries, though not low by Dominican standards, are supplemented by other sources of income, especially "gratuities" from private citizens interested in furthering illegal schemes. There are influential posts of command that can be used to shake down businessmen and exact tribute from them. Up to the time Trujillo himself took control over the whole industry, these posts were mainly located in the vicinity of sugar mills. The managers of the American sugar properties used to pay army officers what was called an *iguala* or monthly fee, in return for "labor peace," protection against certain governmental inconveniences and other significant favors—such as "bumping off" potential trouble makers! Short of fixing taxes (the only thing Trujillo does not allow anyone to tinker with) there is practically nothing the "sweeping boys," as the military men are privately called, cannot do for their protégés. The amount of the *igualas* collected by these self-styled industrial peacemakers goes from a few hundred to several thousand dollars, according to the kind of services rendered.

"Protection" for gambling establishments and houses of ill-repute makes up, outside Ciudad Trujillo, another sizable source of income for commanding officers. In the capital, "protection" is monopolized by one member of the family: Captain Romeo "Pipi" Trujillo Molina. Gambling, though illegal—save for the National Lottery and a few chartered casinos —is allowed to thrive for the benefit of the military class.

Trujillo and his family find in the Armed Forces still another supplementary source of income. They employ Army personnel, not only on guard duties in their homes, farms and other properties, but also for menial labor. Army enlisted men drive the trucks (sometimes Army property) at the sugar plantations owned by Trujillo. Soldiers take care of the cattle herds and stables at *Hacienda Fundación* and other farms of Trujillo's. Free Army driving is provided for all the Trujillos and no house is ever built by them without the help of the Army's Corps of Engineers.

The most coveted post in the Armed Forces is that of Quartermaster General. Two years at this post—that is the usual time allowed to each officer—is enough to make its holder rich, even after splitting the spoils with President Héctor Trujillo. (According to reliable information—and my own private experience—ten per cent of every Armed Forces financial transaction must be set apart for brother Héctor. When *El Caribe* bought, in June 1955, a folding machine from the Army printing shop, I had to pay ten per cent in advance. The Quartermaster General graciously declined his share as a token of friendship.)

A letter printed in *El Caribe* on January 3, 1956, gives an idea of the magnitude of this graft operation. The letter, never answered or denied in any manner, charged former Colonel Perdomo with stealing $2,000,000 while serving as Quartermaster General. Cited as source of the information was one who should know—a former Quartermaster General—Brigadier General Máximo ("Mozo") Bonetti Burgos.

Theoretically, the military are forbidden to engage in business activities while on duty, but many officers are active partners or shareholders in profitable business ventures. Their favorite fields of investment are real estate, service stations, transportation, and farming. The last is considered the most suitable investment, since the officers can always count on using convicted criminals as farm-hands. Ironically enough, this sort of modern slavery is highly regarded by its victims. Convicts like to be sent to the officers' farms as *presos de confianza* (trusties), for there at least they have the chance of getting nourishing food. (It is known that out of the twenty cents a day normally allowed by the Government for a prisoner's food, Pedro V. Trujillo Molina receives an eight-cent cut. There is also, of course, the cut the officer directly in charge of the jail takes.)

No business deal is too small for the top brass. The current Chief of Staff of the Navy, Rear Admiral Rafael B. Richardson, was once temporarily dismissed from service after being publicly charged with selling Navy footgear to civilians.

Why does such a supposedly rigid disciplinarian as Trujillo condone these corrupt practices? Or, at least, why has such a great monopolizer not monopolized graft for himself?

Aside from the fact that he once engaged in such endeavors—and still does occasionally—Trujillo finds them highly convenient as a means of keeping, under threat of punishment, guilty officers tied to his regime. Trujillo's careful study of the character and behavior of his underlings has convinced him of the urgency of maintaining on the statute books the prohibition against engaging in business ventures. Whenever an officer falls into disgrace, "the Chief" unearths his subaltern's crimes and lets the sword of the law descend upon the head of the guilty one. Though possibly belated, the punishment is usually lethal.

In March 1956 Dominican courts gave a thirty years' stretch at *La Victoria* to a former army major named Segundo Manuel Imbert, who only a few years before had been riding high in the northern part of the country as Trujillo's favorite trigger boy. Imbert had been indicted, along with a group of "veterans," for the murder, nine years before, of a minor leader of the Sugar Workers Union. Although his co-defendants pleaded guilty to the charges and the depositions of a long array of witnesses for the prosecution provided damaging evidence against him, Imbert, with contemptuous detachment, denied the crime. Luis Espinosa (the hanged union leader) he said had committed suicide. But, murder or suicide, the case, as unfolded in court, told an almost unbelievable tale of collusion between law-enforcing officers and the otherwise respectable officers of a large private corporation to block a $100,000 claim Espinosa was pressing, on behalf of the sugar workers, against the then American-owned *Central Montellano*. It was not explained during the trial why, with so much evidence against the culprits, the authorities waited so long to act.

The security of Trujillo's regime must rest on some mass-power factor —if not a highly specialized political police force or parliamentary organization, then the armed services in general. Being a military man Trujillo has chosen the latter, though not completely discarding the other alternative. Making the military the instrument of his terror was facilitated by the fact that, as an inheritance from the Constabulary, the Dominican Armed Forces are legally empowered with police duties and are considered both the guardians of external sovereignty and of internal order. (This explains why officers always carry side arms, even when off-duty, a thing that strikes foreigners as an unnecessary display of force.)

From the outset of the regime Army officers have been guilty of the majority of the political crimes committed against Trujillo's foes. The present top brass is almost fully made up of notorious hatchet-men whom the people identify with murder, thuggery and corruption. The Army as a whole bears part of the responsibility for the horrible massacre of 15,000 Haitian peasants in October 1937, as well as for less well-known atrocities against the Dominican people.

Soldiers, however, can derive other pleasures from their careers than killing political opponents. For instance, those officers who like to travel can always get assignments to missions abroad. Sometimes, the post of military attaché is used as a sort of gilded exile for officers in disgrace. (Until July 1957, Captain Homero Lajara Burgos, a former Rear-Admiral and Chief of Staff of the Navy, served as Dominican Naval Attaché in Washington. Lajara's habit of writing home about matters in general—over the Ambassador's head—did presumably finally cost him his sinecure.)

Ever since he succeeded in grabbing power, "the Chief" has been apprehensive that somewhere in his military set-up there is a latter-day Rafael ready to do to him what he did to Vásquez. For this reason he is continually pulling the carpet out from under his subordinates. Under Trujillo's stern eye constant reshuffles make certain that no one will ever have enough influence to build a following of his own.

Military officers fear—as much as civilians—the letters to the editor section of *El Caribe*. Following the appearance of such letters, usually charging officers with improper conduct and behavior unbecoming to their lofty status, "investigations" are opened and as a rule the accused ones are acquitted by their fellow officers. Occasionally, however, some officer marked for punishment is dismissed under a cloud. The action is announced in pompously worded communiqués from the Defense Department. Invariably, the alleged culprit is back in uniform a short time later. (It is considered dangerous to keep these characters unemployed for long periods.) This method of punishing now and forgiving later is another of the Machiavellian devices used in keeping the people off-balance. Knowing that at any moment the Benefactor can throw the crumbs of forgiveness in their direction, the chastised officers and officials patiently wait the moment of pardon. Their will-power broken, they have no alternative but to wait in abject submission.

One can repress but not entirely suppress human ambitions. Whatever his other accomplishments, Trujillo has not yet found a way to uproot such human frailties as greed and longing for power. Several times "the Chief" has been forced to ruthlessly suppress movements, even conspiracies, directed against him from within the Armed Forces. Luckily for him, for one reason or another, none of these plots has ever advanced beyond the preparatory stage. On each occasion, punishment has been administered quickly and without mercy. There have been cases of civilian conspirators—even participants in plots to kill the Generalissimo—whose lives "the Chief" spared for reasons of his own. Equal clemency has never been shown to members of the Armed Forces.

Even though always ending in disaster, the list of military plots is impressive. Among the earlier military conspiracies, and perhaps the best known of them all, was the one led by Colonel Leoncio Blanco. This man, a perfect specimen of the hoodlum-officer of the old *Policía Nacional Dominicana,* had caught Trujillo's eye for his bravery, ruthlessness and cruelty. Promotions were fast for Blanco and soon after Trujillo took power the Colonel was assigned as military commander of the wealthy Barahona Province near the Haitian border. The post assures control over the lucrative gambling operations in the region's vast sugar plantations. A seemingly inexhaustible flow of money came in those days from the smuggling of Haitian laborers across the border. (American sugar mill operators paid ten dollars, to be divided between Trujillo and Blanco, for each one of the several thousand sugar cane cutters illegally brought into the country every year at harvest season.) Merely a sideline for Blanco was the income from the contraband of large quantities of highly-prized Haitian rum.

What happened next is not clear, but after a brief visit to Barahona in 1933, Trujillo suddenly had Colonel Blanco relieved of his post, transferring him to a subordinate position at the Ozama fort in the capital. There, it was thought, the Colonel could be closely watched. Whether Blanco was already plotting when Trujillo demoted him, or whether his disgrace was due to Trujillo's jealousy upon hearing some shouts of "Long live Colonel Blanco" during his visit to Barahona, is part of the mystery. In any event, late in that same year rumors started along the grapevine that Colonel Blanco, Brigadier General Ramón Vásquez Rivera, a former Chief of Staff of the Army, and other officers had been placed under arrest.

Apparently, only by sheer luck had Trujillo discovered in time a well-organized plot against his life, headed by his former favorite, Leoncio Blanco. The Colonel, it seems, had the setting all ready for a daring coup. He had enlisted the help of a large group of Army officers, all of whom proved faithful to their pledges to the bitter end. However, despite all the precautions and safeguards, a fatal mistake was made by none other than Blanco himself. Fearful that Trujillo might escape on his personal yacht, Blanco conceived the idea of winning Captain Andrés Julio Monclús, the ship's commander, to his side. After listening to the Colonel, Monclús agreed to lend a hand—but only in case Trujillo took refuge on his yacht. Ten minutes later Colonel Federico Fiallo (one of the most dreaded of Trujillo's henchmen) came to the yacht looking for Blanco in a hurry. Thinking the plot had been discovered and that Fiallo was seeking Blanco to arrest him, Monclús' nerves failed and, without being asked, he spilled the beans. Though his interest in Blanco at the moment was for quite a different reason, Fiallo took Monclús with him and both tattled to Trujillo. "The Chief" swiftly closed in.

Within minutes Blanco was thrown in jail and subsequently murdered. General Vásquez Rivera, who seemingly was not an active participant in the plot (though he had heard about it and did not report it), was spared this time. Separated from the service, Vásquez was sentenced to five years in jail, then pardoned and sent out of the country as Consul General in Bordeaux, France. Recalled later, he was imprisoned, and in 1940 it was announced that he had committed suicide in his cell at Ozama fortress. The other officers implicated in Blanco's conspiracy were shot, with the exception of Rafael L. Trujillo Martinez's godfather, Major Anibal Vallejo, at that time Chief of Staff of the new Air Force. Though badly tortured Vallejo was magnanimously pardoned by the Benefactor and released from prison. Later he was named to a position in the Public Works Department as Inspector of Roads Construction. One day it was announced that the former Major had met death at the hands of a group of Haitian squatters, during one of his inspection tours near the border. Then the long hand of the Generalissimo reached out for practically every member of the Vallejo family, who were shot or stabbed to death within a short period. To Anibal's widow he gave a job in the Labor Department.

For all practical purposes Blanco's plot is the biggest military "inside job" Trujillo has had to cope with, but one that was far more significant, at least for ruthlessness in dealing with it, was the so-called "tank detachment" conspiracy.

Organized in 1946 by an ambitious young officer who had studied abroad, Captain Eugenio de Marchena, the conception of this plot was fairly simple. While passing in review during military exercises which the Generalissimo was expected to attend, the tank under Marchena's command was supposed to blast the presidential stand away. Shortly before zero hour, someone talked. A few hours before the parade, Trujillo clamped down on Captain de Marchena and his men. The whole tank outfit—sixty men in all—were silently transferred to isolated outposts on the Haitian-Dominican frontier in the small towns of Pedernales and Loma de Cabrera. Not long after they had taken up their new posts, the conspirators were stabbed to death, all on the same day. Only Marchena was not killed on that occasion. Held as a prisoner and taken from camp to camp as an example to other officers, he was executed a year later.

It is a soldier, a noncommissioned officer, to whom Dominican folklore attributes the status of Trujillo's Public Enemy Number One. The saga of the legendary sergeant Enrique Blanco (no kin to the Colonel) is a story Dominican countrymen pass around in whispers. Sometime during the middle Thirties, Blanco, a sort of Robin Hood, impelled by an inordinate hatred for Trujillo created a one-man reign of terror against the Army. For months this elusive one-man revolution kept hundreds of soldiers on a war footing in the rich agricultural zone of the Cibao valley. Only when all the Blanco family and hundreds of farmers had been butchered in reprisals, did the Army manage to drive to suicide the fearless sergeant. The soldiers who did not dare to get close to this man while still alive, for fear of his deadly marksmanship, took his body with them through the streets of several towns and villages, displaying it on a truck. Blanco's almost incredible feats are kept alive in the words and music of a *merengue* known by many but sung by none.

Probably there is as much discontent within the Army as there is in other walks of life, but the Blancos, de Marchenas and Vallejos seem merely forsaken names tossed long ago on the scrap heap. The military are as well-tamed as the rest of the Dominicans and they are much more frightened.

Still, if there is a faint ray of hope, it must be looked for in the Armed Forces. Of course, nothing can be expected from the generals (of which the Dominican Army has a larger number comparatively than any other army in the world); they are so enamored of their wealth and property, and too involved to be trusted. Moreover, they are so afraid of popular vengeance that they dare not risk any change.

However, not all the officers, especially the younger ones, are seasoned hoodlums or illiterate underworld characters, haunted by fears and burdened with crimes. Among the newer promotions are men who, under other circumstances, would have behaved as decent human beings. They cannot feel proud of themselves. It is our hope that whenever the country as a whole turns against the regime, as is bound to happen, these younger officers will meet the challenge and help with an orderly transition to a popular, representative form of government.

THE DOMINICAN PARTY

"IN THE DOMINICAN REPUBLIC," RUNS A WELL-KNOWN JOKE, "ANY number of political parties may exist, subject to one condition—that one party is in power and the rest campaign from jail." The one on top is Trujillo's own party—the *Partido Dominicano.*

This joke indicates the degree of political freedom existing in the country. The Dominican Constitution's elaborate bill of rights to the contrary, this is a modern one-party dictatorship. Unlike its Soviet counterpart, however, the *Partido Dominicano* is not an integral part of the State and does not run the country.

Outwardly, the *Partido Dominicano* looks like the political party of a free nation. But a careful examination reveals such resemblance to be purely accidental. First, despite its seemingly democratic structure, the Party is only a subservient instrument of Trujillo's will. Second, lacking a genuine popular foundation, the Party does not have to cater to the electorate with platforms and promises—it just tells the people how and when to vote. It also tells them how to behave in the presence of its Supreme Chief (*Jefe Supremo*): Generalissimo Trujillo. "Pause before the Supreme Chief with chest uplifted and right hand on heart" instructs a notice published on September 23, 1937, by the then Chairman of the Party, Daniel Henriquez Velazquez.

Popular cooperation is not one of the things Trujillo craves, nor does he look with favor on any genuine political interest on the part of the masses. However, the rank and file are of tremendous use for the Party, particularly at the frequent parades and "spontaneous" demonstrations staged to glorify "the Chief." On occasion the Party membership is herded into convention halls to rubber-stamp Trujillo's decisions. These meetings are held to give a smattering of democracy to the Party's procedures, but in reality the delegates are confronted with a bizarre set of rules that make it impossible for them to disagree with "the Chief's" wishes. "The Dominican Party demands from its members loyalty, enthusiasm and discipline and consecrates and proclaims the principle of the Presidential reelection," states Article 5 of the Party's Charter. According to Article 43, Trujillo has the exclusive right to appoint the Party Chairman and all paid employees of the organization; to authorize all Party expenditures and exercise the power of veto on Party resolutions, object to Party candidates and punish disloyalty. His authority as Supreme Chief is "undiminishable and untransferable," says the same article. Article 27 states that the Party's Executive Board "cannot dispose of anything which conflicts with the decisions of the Supreme Chief." At least four other articles make no bones about where the final judgment on Party matters rests and assure that Trujillo's will is final and that only his voice can be heard on Party councils. Accordingly, despite the Party's elaborate by-laws and its large bureaucracy, nothing is ever done without Trujillo's approval. "The Chief" not only lays down the political line —he has to be consulted even on minor administrative details. The situation is particularly obvious in financial matters. Only "the Chief" keeps tabs on the financial records of the Party, which are never the subject of public reports. Apart from a few close associates of Trujillo, no one in the Dominican Republic has ever seen the Party's balance sheets, a fact that makes it one of the most private political organizations in the world.

This fabulous political party has been in existence since 1931. Founded by Trujillo shortly after his first inauguration to cut short the wavering coalition rule brought about by the downfall of the Vásquez regime, the *Partido Dominicano* soon monopolized the country's political activities. In order to expedite his Party's task, Trujillo dissolved, absorbed or proscribed all other existing parties.

Once "the Chief" had uprooted the influence of the old chieftains, he entrusted the Party with the mission of spreading the new gospel of *trujillismo*. Its Charter stressed as a main function "to sustain, propagate and put into effect the patriotic creed of its founder (Trujillo)."

Within a year of its creation the Party claimed control of 80 per cent of the electorate. Not an extraordinary exploit considering the favorite method of proselytizing: to throw the recalcitrants in jail and leave them there until they had signed up. This original method of recruiting has since given way to more subtle ones, but the Party has not grown weaker with the passing of time. On December 31, 1956, its enrollment showed a total of 1,452,170 members. As reported in the 1957 annual Convention, 55,889 persons joined the organization during the preceding year.

Membership figures include males as well as females, since the Party is open to *all* Dominicans over 18 years of age. After Trujillo's extension of the suffrage to women in 1942, the Party established a separate feminine branch and hence all its lists of candidates for elected posts have contained a sprinkling of women. The feminine element, however, has never been of much consequence in Party affairs and the separate set-up did not last long. Gradually, the women's section merged into the main body of the Party and currently is another of its regular bureaus. The distinction of heading this particular bureau has fallen upon a bevy of Trujillo's private procuresses. Yet, not all of its heads fall into such category. The present incumbent is Mrs. Amada Nivar de Pittaluga, a nice, fat lady, whose main qualification for the job is close kinship to one of the Benefactor's most durable favorites—Lina Lovatón Pittaluga.

Apart from a faint, brief challenge by the extreme left in the middle forties, the Dominican Party's monopoly has gone undisputed in the political field. Even this short period of competition was fomented by Trujillo himself. Late in 1946 Trujillo arrived at a deal with the Cuban Communists and, as a result, a group of exiled Dominican Red leaders returned from Cuba and other countries to form the *Partido Socialista Popular* (communist). Though hitherto both parties in this strange deal have kept secret its details, there are grounds to believe that Trujillo had promised free reign to the Reds inside the labor movement, in exchange of the latter's assurances of mild political opposition.

Why did Trujillo indulge in this risky game? This has been an enigma. Those who know point out that the Dictator had a two-fold aim in mind. On one hand, he wished to present the brand-new *Partido Socialista Popular* as an example that political freedom existed in the country, and, on the other, he sought to prove that only the despised Communists were in opposition to him. Eventually Trujillo outlawed the PSP.

The wind of post-war liberalism had not yet blown itself out. So, in deference to vogue, Trujillo resolved once again to set aside his highly successful one-party system.[1] With recent bitter experience still in mind, Trujillo settled for an alternative—the creation of "opposition" parties of his own.

The appropriate signals were then given to chosen collaborators. "No sooner said than done" and two new parties came into existence—the

[1] I have refrained from mentioning the so-called *Partido Trujillista*. Hitherto no one knows the reasons behind the organization of this party but in preparation for the 1942 elections the Dictator entrusted his personal dentist, Dr. Jose Enrique Aybar, with the job of forming this political group. Apparently the *Partido Trujillista* was never meant to be a rival political organization, but rather a club of the political élite within the framework of the Dominican Party. Its only active drive was an alleged "depuration" or purge campaign conducted through a group of University students known as the *Guardia Universitaria* (University Guard). Cabinet members and other high officials went through the humiliating experience of being questioned by young University students about their personal loyalty to "the Chief." After the purges were completed almost everyone was a member of both parties, which then proceeded to nominate Trujillo for President. After the common victory at the polls the new party promptly folded up.

Partido Laborista (Labor Party) and the *Partido Nacional Democrático* (National Democratic Party).

Decidedly, the three-party system was a smash hit. Overnight the Dominican Republic became a safe "democracy" and Trujillo could show his own "loyal opposition" to visiting journalists. Quietly the parties held what amounted to private conventions and their lists of candidates were made public on March 31, 1947. The Dominican Party as expected nominated Trujillo for President. Then everybody retired to the sidelines to wait for election day. The labor candidate, however, almost derailed the smooth scheme. As head of the Labor Party's ticket there had been chosen a Francisco Prats Ramírez, a member of the Dominican Congress for the *Partido Dominicano,* who just a few months before had composed a lyrical birthday stamp for the Benefactor. The pre-electoral campaign was quietly proceeding as scheduled without unnecessary speeches or appeals to the voters, when it suddenly took an unexpected turn. Prats Ramírez had forgotten himself and signed with other fellow Congressmen a petition favoring Trujillo's reelection to a fourth term. Though the slip caused a lot of official embarrassment it did not influence the electoral returns. A pro-Trujillo landslide was announced on May 16—"the Chief" was in again with 92 per cent of the vote. (The Dominican Party was officially credited with 781,389 votes, the National Democratic Party with 29,765 and the Labor Party with 29,186). Nevertheless, Dominicans were not through with their "opposition" candidates. The announcement that Mrs. Consuelo Prats Ramírez, wife of the defeated Labor Party presidential candidate, had won the only labor seat in Congress provoked a sharp comment which speedily spread throughout the country. In Spanish *"consuelo"* means "consolation." So Dominicans consoled themselves by calling the newly elected Congresswoman "Mrs. Consolation Prize."

Though successful, the experiment has not been repeated. The "opposition" parties were promptly buried. So deeply buried that four years later, in 1951, when an American journalist asked the Chairman of the *Partido Dominicano* about the country's political system, the Dominican politician scratched his head in a vain effort to remember the names of the alleged opposition parties. "He (the Chairman) called in an assistant who likewise scratched his head in vain," wrote Theodore Draper in *The Reporter.* "It took a little research outside the office to produce the information. 'They are so small, they do not count,' Señor Tolentiono (the Chairman) explained good-humoredly."

Always a scrupulous observer of the letter of all Constitutional canons, Trujillo would not think of disregarding the electoral provisions of the Dominican Magna Charta. To help affix the sanction of the people's approval to Trujillo's power, the Party still provides hand-picked lists of candidates. However, in recent elections all pretense at democratic procedure has been thrown overboard and the *"trujillista"* ticket is always rewarded with 100 per cent of the vote. "Not even dictators such as Hitler or Stalin, Mussolini or Franco would have dared to announce such unanimous results," wrote Jesús de Galíndez.

Yet, even for rigged elections people need advice. As election time approaches, the Party's propaganda machine is put to work telling the constituents how to vote. Since no one in his senses would ever contradict the official Party's directives, the job is not difficult. Without much electioneering (usually a few newspaper articles and a handful of rallies are enough) the Party achieves wonderful results. In the elections for members of a Constituent Assembly held on November 13, 1955, all the votes cast— 1,182,455—were attributed to the Dominican Party passive candidates.

In preparation for the 1957 presidential elections the Party conducted another of its peculiar campaigns. First, it went through the ritualistic proceeding of offering the nomination to the Generalissimo who with the air of a demigod refused it. (His 28-year-old son, Rafael, Jr., was not available either for the Vice-Presidental slot.) On "the Chief's" recommendation the Party turned then toward the faithful and obedient incumbent Héctor B. Trujillo, who agreed once more to play the puppet. For the recently recreated post of Vice-President the selection fell upon Dr. Joaquin Balaguer, a mild-mannered, soft-spoken intellectual with a long record of service to Trujillo. Reasons for the Vice-Presidential selection are not clear. However, in a formal statement addressed to the Party the Generalissimo stressed the point that he was choosing Dr. Balaguer because of his desire to reward a deserving youngster. Cynics state that at 52 Balaguer is hardly a youngster. But Balaguer, they recall, is the author of an adulatory paper entitled "God and Trujillo," which he read at a formal session of the Dominican Academy of History.

The electoral campaign was not a lively one. Neither Héctor nor his running-mate delivered a single speech, nor, for that matter, did any of the candidates for elective posts. Party organizers and professional agitators were put in charge of the electoral chores. There were huge parades and rallies, and much speech making. However, any one unfamiliar with the Dominican political scene would have been misled into believing that the man up for election was the Generalissimo. All the rallies, all the speeches, all the banners, all the slogans featured him. Only secondarily were the candidates mentioned. It did not make any difference. Last May 16 practically the entire adult population—the halt and the blind included—poured into the booths to elect the Dominican Party ticket.

The Party's card is part of every Dominican adult life. Official documents such as applications for passports, for import or export licenses, for marriage licenses, for certificates of good conduct, for enrollment at the University, all have a line in which the applicant must fill in his membership number and date of affiliation with the Party.

Membership in the Party by itself does not guarantee employment. Patronage is Trujillo's exclusive prerogative and one of his most adroitly employed weapons. Not even minor local offices escape "the Chief's" personal grasp. Moreover, in this, as in many other matters, there are no set rules. The Generalissimo's whims are as much of a deciding factor as the aspirant's record of loyalty to the Party. Trujillo guards so jealously this prerogative that to handle patronage he has several special aides, who are in no way connected with the Party organization.

Occasionally the Party swings over the heads of its members the club of expulsion. Cautiously administered in the past, the punishment is now employed with increased frequency. The most recent victims have been several former close associates of the Benefactor, whose personal displeasure they had provoked. Usually the disciplinary action has no permanent effects. After a certain length of time a pardon is granted and "the Chief" graciously welcomes the disciplined members back into the fold. But, before securing parole and therefore the possibility of regaining their means of livelihood, the alleged culprits are forced to recant most abjectly. Their letters confessing past errors and political sins are printed in full in the newspapers as an example for all. Then the Generalissimo magnanimously grants the requested absolution. The Benefactor's gesture is usually accompanied by flattering editorials written in the National Palace.

Trujillo is a lover of eulogies. To feed his hankering for praise the Party has been converted into a ready-made instrument of adulation. A great deal of money, time and effort is spent by the Party to keep up the continuous flow of adulatory literature which feeds Trujillo's ego. Radio, television, newspapers and loudspeakers work in a concerted effort, selling Trujillo's "glorious achievements" to his weary fellow citizens and to the world at large as well. The Party sponsors all kinds of literary ventures to present Trujillo in a favorable light. These are the activities which have earned for the Party a special mention in the newest Trujillo Constitution as a "vehicle of culture."

Part of the Party's propaganda activity is, likewise, the staging of gigantic mass rallies. Cooperating in full force with the Party along this line always can be found Government departments, schools, labor unions, civic groups, social clubs, chambers of commerce, Rotary Clubs, Masonic Lodges, religious associations, farmer groups and Boy Scouts. On such occasions the speakers' platform is shared by the pick of the *trujillista* supporters. As a rule the oratory is channeled toward adulation for "the Chief." Sometimes, however, the speakers shower abuse on those in the political doghouse. Their "traitorous" activities "against the Fatherland" as well as their alleged "communistic" leanings are denounced with gusto, particularly since the speakers know that if they do not put enough vehemence in their attacks they are liable to be accused of "lacking in *trujillista* fervor"—an unpardonable crime. It should be added that often today's accuser is tomorrow's accused, and vice versa.

On the sidelines the Party performs still another important task. It gathers information about every living soul in the Dominican Republic. With the purpose of giving a helping hand to the official secret police agencies, the Party keeps in its files complete records of the private and public life, background, habits, personal character and political leanings of each Dominican citizen of any importance and of foreigners residing permanently in the country. Based upon data collected by informers, the dossiers contain unevaluated and unsupported evidence compiled from rumors, malicious gossip and plain hearsay.

For its gossip-gathering activities the Party hires a large number of people. Its paid informers are called "inspectors." Other undercover agents work on a part-time basis; still others spy just for fun. To encourage the latter sort, the Party spreads the word that what they call "good services" are well rewarded. Yet, the bulk of information comes from the servant class. To keep going this valuable source of information the Party organized several years ago a so-called "School of Maids." Located at the Ciudad Trujillo headquarters this informer's training center operated for several years disguised as a school for "domestic science and home economics." It was discontinued about five years ago when the Party authorities discovered that its "graduates" were subject to a nation-wide unorganized boycott. Participants in this really spontaneous movement of silent protest were not only foes of the regime but also some of its best friends and collaborators. After all, no one likes to be spied on!

Aside from being the watchdog of the political and personal mores of its members, the Party is also a kind of guardian angel, spending a modicum of its takings on charities, always performed in "the Chief's" name. Each donation, such as a sewing machine for a poor widow or a wooden leg for an indigent invalid, is accompanied by a kind letter supposedly straight from the Benefactor. The newspapers receive lengthy releases praising the Generalissimo's "proverbial generosity," which they run sometimes accompanied by photographs of the "grateful, lucky beneficiaries." As a result, Trujillo is deluged with requests, ranging from sets of musical instruments (usually granted) to barber's chairs (sometimes denied).

Supposedly to carry out this and similar programs, the Party has assured itself of a regular income of several million dollars a year. An idea of the size of the Party earnings might be gathered from the fact that, aside from the contributions it exacts from its members in business, it has been receiving since 1931 ten per cent of the monthly pay of each person on the

Government's payroll. This tithe, bringing over $2 million a year, is automatically deducted and turned over to its treasury.

Moreover, the Party has been engaged for years in highly profitable business ventures. Though no one knows for sure what happens to the loose change, it is assumed that at frequent intervals the money collected by the Party is transferred from its treasury to Trujillo's own personal pockets. Otherwise, after 26 years of successful operations, the amount of liquid capital in the Party's treasury would be staggering.

One thing Trujillo's stern eye has not prevented is corruption in the Party's bureaucracy. As in other branches of the regime, the Party officials receive cuts and commissions from the people dealing with them, from printing shops to office equipment suppliers. Stories of corruption in the Party appear frequently in the newspapers. R. Paíno Pichardo, one of its last chairmen, was fired from his post at the beginning of 1956, after the press printed charges of malfeasance of funds set apart for the Party's building at the International Fair.

Even if the Party does not wield real power, it is conspicuously present everywhere. Its modernistic quarters, worth in excess of $3 million, are a prominent feature of 54 cities and towns across the country. These buildings, with the organization's royal palm insignia prominently displayed, are usually the best and most comfortable in each locality. Called "Party Palaces," they are easily recognizable since, apart from small variations, they look much alike in all cities—they are copies in minor scale of the sumptuous national headquarters in Ciudad Trujillo. Their common characteristic: the same gleaming white stucco fronts and the identical quotations from Trujillo's speeches in raised letters. Carved in each palace's façade, in big, glittering characters, is the slogan of the Party: *"Rectitud, Libertad, Trabajo, Moralidad."* (The words have been chosen not for their meaning but for the reason that their first letters from the initials of Trujillo's complete name: RLTM.) Also adorning the palace's fronts are such Trujillo's sayings as: *"Mis mejores amigos son los hombres de trabajo"* (Workingmen are my best friends), and *"No hay peligro en seguirme"* (There is no danger in following me).

Each first floor is arranged for the normal business of the Party—offices, reception halls and auditorium. The latter is particularly important because one of the Party's main activities is the so-called *"conferencia"* or compulsory indoctrinating one-night course on Trujillo's patriotic deeds. The second floor is another thing. Few ordinary party members have ever set foot on them. There are luxurious living quarters in them, always ready for the boss to use. Access to them is forbidden even to local chieftains. For trespassing many a man has lost a sinecure.

Real estate, however, is not the Party's main business. It is a fact that its investments in all business were reported to exceed $6 million in February 1957. One of the Party's exclusive provinces was until fairly recently a broadly-publicized social welfare program—the giving away of free milk and shoes to the needy. Actually, while receiving all credit for this piece of political charity, the Party not only was not putting a cent of its own in but was making money. The funds to carry out the program were provided by the Dominican Government. The milk, in its turn, was bought from Trujillo's dairy monopoly (*Industrial Lechera C. por A.*) and the shoes from the Dictator's own shoe factory (*Fadoc*). Furthermore, a few years back the Party was active in building houses for low-income families. Again the Government provided the funds and the Party made the profits on the sales of the houses. The Party also provides medical care for ailing elders and sick children—in the Government's hospitals and at the State expense. These are just a few of the ways in which Trujillo exploits the rich possibilities of combining business and philanthropy.

The Party likewise has done well for itself in straight business ventures. Its investment specialities are publishing houses (it once owned outright the daily *La Nación* and was until 1954 the second biggest stockholder in *El Caribe*); but its tentacles reach out to other fields according to Trujillo's desires. (Recently it provided the capital for a vegetable growing corporation in the mountain resort of Constanza.) All Party financial investments are sure bets. When a business is not profitable enough, it is promptly unloaded. As a money-making proposition the Dominican Party is certainly a unique institution and perhaps the only political organization in the world operating at a profit. But the Party's earnings represent only a minor part of Trujillo's income.

MATERIAL PROGRESS

1. ONE OF THE MOST SUCCESSFUL PARTS OF THE TRUJILLISTA propaganda is that which deals with material progress and the development of the country's natural resources. With the help of long columns of statistics, Trujillo's eulogists do not miss an opportunity to show that Dominicans never had it so good before and that Santo Domingo is one of the most progressive and wealthy countries of Latin America.

The Benefactor himself, as is shown by his own statements, revels in long accounts, usually written by his own press agents, of the "prodigious strides" made under his personal guidance to achieve the splendid transformation of the country from a backward tropical hell-hole into an advanced modern nation.

There is much truth and much mere propaganda in these glossy accounts of progress. It would be childish to deny that, for better or worse, "the Big One" has played an important role in the latter-day economic development of the nation. But, while Trujillo's share in spurring economic advances has been overemphasized by his propagandists, for obvious reasons the selfish motives behind Trujillo's economic policies have been overlooked by his partisans and left in the hands of his enemies. The resulting lack of balance in the different approaches makes it another of those things concerning the Benefactor in which it is almost impossible to achieve objectivity.

There are, to be sure, enough proofs to show how much the standard of living has improved throughout the country under Trujillo's rule. It is, however, too early to assess properly the lasting effects of Trujillo's so-called enterprise, imagination and resourcefulness upon the future course of Dominican progress. Trujillo's economic policies are seemingly aimed at granting ample incentives to the enterprising spirit of business, but as in practically everything else the Benefactor has been often guided by expediency and self-interest.

It is impossible, on the other hand, to determine whether the progress of the country would have been greater had it been governed by a democratic regime during the last twenty-seven years. The obvious advantages of a dictatorship in making trains run on time, averting strikes and forcing people to work hard are too well-known to be repeated here, although in Trujillo's case it might be pointed out that despite the fact that he had been in power since 1930 it was not until the early forties when the Dominican Republic, as many other Latin American nations, began to gain a full measure of prosperity. Even today, while the picture is not as gloomy as it was twenty years back, it is not as rosy as claimed by the tourist leaflets. The country with its 19,000 square miles and 2,698,126 inhabitants is still a partially developed land. The wealth of the Dominican Republic, notwithstanding tax exemptions and sky-high tariffs intended to stimulate industrial growth, is almost exclusively derived from its agricultural products, chiefly a few cash crops. More than 80 per cent of the working population is engaged in agricultural activities and more than 90 per cent of the country's exports comes from plantations and farms.

Nevertheless, a walk through the streets of the capital serves to demonstrate material improvements in a variety of ways. Old buildings are being demolished. Broader avenues and four-lane highways are in process of construction and tall new buildings spring up alongside as if by magic. The building boom, however, though it helps the Trujillo-owned cement monopoly, is not a cause but a result of prosperity. The good times are due to the solid price of coffee, sugar, tobacco and cocoa in foreign markets—they alone accounted in 1956 for 86.8 per cent of the total value of national exports. Important as well, although to a much less degree, are rice, corn, bananas, tropical woods and vegetables. The large foreign trade, independent of any action on the part of the Government itself, has been largely responsible for the current prosperity.

These favorable factors, however, would have meant little for the administration and the people as a whole had not the Government taken certain steps to ensure the following: First, the adroit manipulation of the sizable reserves of foreign exchange accumulated during the last decade of rising prices, in order to bolster not only the official monetary policies but also certain sectors of the national economy. Second, the repeal, through a Constitutional Amendment passed in 1934, of the prohibition imposed upon the Government's power to tax export commodities, which had been inserted in the prior Constitutions under pressure from foreign interests. This amendment alone made it possible for the regime to lay its hands upon large amounts of cold cash that had been unavailable to previous administrations.

It seems fair to conclude that the chances are that as long as the foreign buyers of Dominican cash crops keep on paying the current high prices there will be prosperity in the country. Or, at least, a semblance of prosperity, since many of the external trappings of material progress are deceptive in a country where wealth and property is highly concentrated in the hands of a small élite. The situation is further complicated by the fact that in most cases political and personal criteria are the determining factors of the majority of the important movements of the regime in the fields of trade, agriculture and industry. Most of the so-called efforts to increase production or to create new sources of wealth and welfare are circumscribed to spheres in which the Generalissimo is personally interested. Nonetheless, the opinion of many of Trujillo's detractors to the contrary, even under these conditions some of the widely advertised prosperity has trickled down to the masses.

It has been said, and properly, that upon the fortunes of a few crops lie the hopes of the Generalissimo for carrying out his most ambitious plans for the economic development of the country. This Trujillo knows well. So well, in fact, that he himself has linked his personal and political future with that of the largest of Dominican agricultural activities—the production of sugar and its by-products.

Largely controlled by Trujillo-owned corporations (twelve of the sixteen active factories belong to them) the Dominican sugar industry has increased production during the last five years, assuming definite leadership among Latin American exporters, second only to Cuba. By Decree of the President of the Republic its production for 1957 was fixed at 993,172 short tons. However, due to the existing U.S. legal system of import quotas and tariffs which makes concessions in favor of Cuba and Puerto Rico, the two main Caribbean competitors of the Dominican sugar industry, the Dominican industry is forced to sell outside the protected and highly lucrative American market in what is known as the "world" or "free" market. As there is a marked difference of prices between the two markets, under normal conditions, Trujillo—Mr. Sugar himself in his own country—has been making strenuous efforts to convince the American Congress that it should apportion him a larger share of the high-priced U.S. market. His lobbyists spare neither money nor influence in their struggle to assure Dominican sweets a place beside Cuban and Puerto Rican sugar in the American heart.

Exalted words about justice (most of them justified, strangely enough) are uttered time and again to cover the selfish motives of the sugar merchant named Trujillo. "Unlike other Caribbean countries we have never enjoyed the economic aid and protection of the great industrial nations," asserted the Benefactor in a press interview. "All that we have done we have done alone. But if there is one thing that we have asked—and will continue to ask—it is more equitable treatment in reference to sugar, our principal product. While the Dominican Republic buys most of its imports

from the United States, restrictive laws prohibit the sale of more than five
per cent of our production. Because of this discrimination the Dominican
Republic is forced to sell its sugar in markets where at present it brings
35 per cent less than it would in the United States. This situation is prejudicial to the Dominican Republic. It is also prejudicial to the best interests of North American manufacturers from whom we buy our imports
and points up the necessity of reconsidering economic arrangements between the United States and Latin America."

These high-sounding words were echoed by the *trujillista* financial
wizard and manager of Trujillo's personal interest in sugar, Dr. José María
Toncoso Sánchez, who said: "The Dominican economy is a sugar economy. Cuba and Puerto Rico sell in the U.S. market, which is protected.
They sell for $5.50 in the U.S. what we sell for $3.10 in the international
market. . . . The only reason we fight for a higher sugar quota from the
United States is to have more money for the people."

This concern for the attainment of stable and profitable sugar markets
would be commendable had it stemmed from genuine patriotism. The
Dominican Sugar industry, after all—even now as a Trujillo quasi-
monopoly—is responsible for 44.2 per cent of the country's total volume
of exports. It also employs 73.7 per cent of the working population and
pays 67.7 per cent of the salaries and wages. Despite the fact that most
of its large Trujillo-owned sector is tax-exempt, the sugar industry is one
of the main sources of fiscal revenues.

On the other hand, the sugar industry is not, and has never been, a
national industry in the pure sense of the word. Before Trujillo took it
under his personal control it was operated by large foreign corporations
intent only on producing sugar cheaply and making big profits when possible. Under the monopolistic hands of Trujillo the industry is not used
for social progress but as a means to assuage the thirst for power and
wealth of its insatiable owner. Trujillo's invasion of the sugar production
field has brought about calamitous changes in the economic structure of
the country as well as in the forms of land tenure. Wages have been
lowered and a great deal of the work in "the Chief's" plantations is done
by a new class of slave workers recruited from soldiers, prisoners, unemployed city dwellers and so-called "vagrants." "The Big One's" land-
grabbing activities to round up his large sugar properties have laid the
foundation for a *latifundia* system evident in the growing concentration of
the best agricultural tracts in the hands of the Benefactor and a few of
his relatives and henchmen. The ensuing decline in the number of farms
and small holdings is responsible for dangerous proletarianization of
hitherto independent farmers.

Next to sugar, the second largest sources of Dominican wealth are
coffee and cocoa. For several hundred years large amounts of these prod-

ucts have been exported to the extent that a type of cocoa has received the name of "Sánchez," the principal export center in the country. On account of high prices in the foreign markets, production of cocoa and coffee is rapidly increasing. In 1955 coffee took second place among Dominican exports with $28,402,357, followed by cocoa with $23,889,261. Here again we find the ever-grasping hand of the Benefactor. It is estimated that from each dollar that these two crops bring into the country, either Trujillo personally or his Administration takes out a sixty cent cut, leaving the rest to be divided among planters, laborers, intermediaries and exporters. The Benefactor as honorary member of the export cartels of such products, to which all importers are forced to belong, shares a part of the profits without any risk on his part.

Wealthy as it is, the Dominican Republic is no agricultural paradise. There are areas, especially in the famous Cibao Valley, where land is so rich and the climate so equable that very little human effort is required to produce a crop and several crops may be grown in one year, even though outmoded farm techniques are stiill employed almost without exception. Yet, other parts of the country need irrigation and still others are what might be literally called desert. To bring these areas into production the Government has been furthering much-talked-about irrigation projects and through another of the many Trujillo-owned corporations is offering the services of farming machinery to the peasants. However, the high cost of this service impedes most of the farmers in making use of it.

To say that great strides have been made is no exaggeration, though there is much to be done yet. It has not been an easy job either, since traditionally Dominican resources were inadequately used and widespread poverty seemed to be endemic and ineradicable. Hence, it must be admitted that the present methods of developing the country's natural resources are a step away from the more pernicious economic habits of the past, when Dominicans would invest only in real estate or mortgages and shun investments in productive enterprises.

The fact that during many years Trujillo could not show any real progress is not entirely his fault. He took power in 1930 in the middle of a world economic crisis, at a time when the Dominican national income had dropped to $7,000,000; exports had sunk to less than $10,000,-000; the foreign debt stood at $20,000,000 (plus an internal funded debt of several million more), and customs—traditionally the chief source of revenue—were in American receivership.

By 1934, owing to a revision of debt payments, things started to improve. An Emergency Law of October 23, 1931, diverted to government expenses $1,500,000 from customs revenues which up to then had been pledged to service the foreign loans.

From then on Trujillo felt free to put into practice his conceptions in the economic field. The upswing, however, did not come until the war and post-war years. The first big jump in Dominican trade, from $31,000,-000 to $50,000,000, took place in 1942. Since then Trujillo has been able to manipulate yearly favorable trade balances amounting on occasion to as much as $20 million. (In 1956 the country's exports were $126,480,-542 whereas imports were $108,092,125.) National income is estimated currently at $542,678,100, or roughly a per capita income of $226 a year. The foreign debt was paid off in 1947 and the country does not owe a dollar to any foreign banker or Government. (The internal debt, however, has been growing fast in the last four years. In July 1956 it reached the all-time high of $120,659,255.) National budgets have been in surplus since 1931 and the one for 1957–58 (largest of all) was figured at $131,525,000. The Dominican gold peso remains firmly at par with the United States dollar, even though at the end of 1955, as a result of the unbridled spending on the World Fair project, exchange reserves dipped 20% and have not wholly recovered.

New industries—most of them developed since World War II—turn out a wide array of commodities (many formerly imported), such as glassware, cement, textiles, air conditioning equipment, steel articles, barbed wire, batteries, asbestos materials, paper bags, paints, fertilizers, beer and other alcoholic beverages, peanut oil, nails and cattle feed. The traditional industries (such as sugar, meat packing, rum, cigarettes, dairy by-products, soap, and matches) have also been enlarged and modernized. Industrial progress is further showed by these statistics: In 1935 there were 1,076 manufacturing establishments employing 20,301 people and turning out 16.3 million dollars' worth of produce. In 1954 there were three times as many establishments with three times as many employees, producing articles worth more than $162,000,000.

Behind this boom there is a lot of Government intervention. The Government intervenes from start to finish in the process of establishing a new enterprise in the country. If the project is considered "satisfactory" to Trujillo himself or those of his associates whom he has put in charge of that operation, the matter is referred to the proper Government authorities and a contract is signed between the company and the State specifying taxes, tariff exonerations, extent of the investment and other pertinent points.

As a result, practically all of the principal industrial enterprises now in operation within the country have been established by Trujillo himself or by people in partnership with him. A few have been started by the Government itself and later, if proven profitable, turned over to private interests, usually those in which "the Big One" has his hand. "Government policy is to operate industries new to the country," points out a friendly publication, "until they have demonstrated the ability to go it alone. Financial support is then withdrawn and operation turned over to private management. Strong government protection of the firm, either Dominican or foreign-owned, incorporated under Dominican laws, continues; so far in practice, it might be said that complete separation is never quite made."

Unable to free themselves from government controls, Dominican businessmen are at the mercy of Trujillo's caprices. The Benefactor can make or destroy them and knowing it they show, like the rest of the Dominicans, insecurity and timidity in their everyday doings. According to the aforementioned publication: "There are few countries in the world where commercial and industrial activity is so thoroughly blended and coordinated with Government. That, of course, could be both an asset and a liability. . . . It might even be said that with good government relations no foreign firm loses money in the Dominican Republic." What the magazine failed to explain was that "good government relations" mean total surrender to the Benefactor's will.

The close ties between Government, Trujillo personally, and foreign or domestic private interests is best demonstrated in the standing projects for the exploitation of the mineral wealth of the country. Outside agriculture, nature has not been very prodigal with the country, but nonetheless efforts are being conducted to tap the mineral reserves of the country, believed to be varied but limited. All concessions, save those for exploitation of bauxite, have been granted to corporations owned by Trujillo or in which he has a stake. These enterprises have been engaged since 1947 in an intensive exploration and evaluation of the nation's resources, which it is said have revealed the existence of deposits of gold, salt, iron, bauxite, sulphur, gypsum, chrome, copper, cobalt, graphite, titanium, lime, nickel, platinum, asbestos, and uranium. Some coal has also been reported.

Although the extent of the iron deposits has not been fully estimated, these are being worked since 1952 and it is believed that sufficient high-grade reserves exist to continue shipping 20,000 tons a year to the United States plus supplying a local steel industry for many years. Exploitation of the iron deposits was started in 1953 by an American corporation named *Minera Panamericana* by virtue of an arrangement with the Trujillo corporation *Minera Hatillo*. As officers of the American corporation at the time there were a former U.S. lieutenant general, W. Larsen, and a man who had just been relieved of the highly sensitive post of Naval Attaché of the United States Embassy in Ciudad Trujillo, Lieutenant Commander Harold Thompson Mejías. Suddenly the Larsen-Thompson group was dropped in favor of a new group of American capitalists.

As result of this new partnership one of Trujillo's persistent dreams has been reactivated—the search for oil. Although scientific studies show a faint possibility of oil deposits, these have not been located, despite the fact that the Dominican Government has spent a fortune prospecting.

The only non-Trujillo mining operation in the Dominican Republic is conducted by Alcoa Exploration Company (a subsidiary of the Aluminum Corporation of America) in the bauxite fields of Cabo Rojo, on the south coast. The contract under which those operations are being conducted was announced in May 1957 as a "far reaching step in the program set under way by Generalissimo Rafael L. Trujillo for the Dominican Republic's economic progress." William B. Pawley, whose suggestions served as a basis for the new Dominican laws on investment, hailed the signature of the contract as a step evincing confidence in the Dominion Republic as a field for foreign capital investment.

Pawley, whose official capacity is that of "honorary adviser of the Dominican Republic's Bureau of Mining," added that the Alcoa contract should encourage other investors to stake large amounts in the development of the country's mineral and oil resources.

Obsessed by the idea that one of his missions on earth is to make the country known to the outside world, Trujillo believes that spectacular building is the way to achieve his aim. Consequently, the Benefactor has embarked the Administration on an ambitious, expensive and seemingly endless program of construction. This embraces the building of new ports, superhighways, airports, bridges, irrigation works, public buildings, churches, housing projects, electric stations and factories. It must be said that the accomplishments have been many and that more can be expected as long as the country maintains its present enviable financial position and its four cheap-labor crops sustain themselves in the dollar markets.

However, advances along other lines in which Trujillo also appears to be interested are not so apparent. Increased efficiency has been achieved in the Administrative machinery, but to judge by the content of the many Trujillo-sponsored letters to the editors which appear in the daily press corruption is rampant and inefficiency hampers the normal development of plans for the development of the country.

Despite the obvious shortcomings of the human element engaged in carrying out Government programs, great progress has been brought about in public health, sanitation and education. Every city and town of importance has its own aqueduct (one may usually drink water directly from the tap) and the capital and Santiago have excellent sewage systems. About forty modern hospitals have been built and much is being done to tackle the problem of endemic diseases such as hookworm, tuberculosis, malaria and syphilis. Solid cement block homes are slowly replacing thatched huts that were standard housing for centuries. Although some slum clearance programs have been announced, there is much to do.

Those who, aware of the limitations of Dominican economy, have seen the conspicuous display of wealth in the World Fair and other new projects may well ask: Where does the money come from? A satisfactory answer cannot be given without resorting to a long-drawn-out recital of many factors already mentioned, but a simplified explanation boils down to one word: taxation.

Taxation makes true the most extravagant dreams of the dictator; it is a weapon for the destruction of the most hated enemies of the regime, and is the supreme principle of fiscal policy within the Dominican scheme.

Dominicans are today the most taxed people in the world, though, strangely enough, there are few direct tributes. There is not an income tax, at least as Americans know it, and the cumbersome and unscientific corporation tax is extremely low by any standard. Taxation, however, amounts to a crushing capital levy. High excise and export tributes, along with some unique taxes on production and inventories, eat up, within the high-income groups, the margins of capital which otherwise could be used for further economic development and expansion of trade and manufacture. A maze of indirect tributes, leaning heavily on necessities and other articles of everyday consumption, puts a heavy stress upon low-income groups and increases the cost of living, thus fostering inflation.

2.   AS HERBERT MATTHEWS REMARKED, "TO UNDERSTAND THE Dominican Republic one must study it like a coin—first one side and then the other." We have seen one face of its tremendous economic progress. Before examining the other, we should point out that the effects of prosperity should not be measured merely in terms of tons of concrete poured or miles of roads built, but also in terms of human satisfaction. Put through this latter test, Trujillo's so-called prosperity and progress prove a dismal failure. A very small portion of the population shares in the much-advertised material progress.

Perhaps the country is no longer the hemisphere's poorhouse. Perhaps Government revenues are high and strides have been made "that have taken nations centuries to accomplish." Perhaps the country, once the most backward in Latin America, now is in the vanguard. Perhaps people are acquiring more luxuries as well as taking a fancy for those things which are not truly necessities. (For example, last year the number of radios in the country was estimated at 58,000. There were about 2,000 TV sets and 7,150 automobiles.)

Moreover, Ciudad Trujillo, showplace of the dictatorship, is a clean, modern city as well as a fast-spreading one. Its streets and markets are spotless; its stores well stocked; its night life, if not actually gay, is not devoid of charm, especially for those who like gambling; its traffic is orderly and its courteous and well-mannered inhabitants look content and busy. The eulogies (daily reprinted by the local press) that junketing journalists heap upon the city are factual and well deserved. This much, of course, is true, but it is far from the whole truth.

The full story is quite another thing. The stark truth, despite all the alleged new bright spots, is that for the average citizen the basic realities are still the same as in the pre-Trujillo days, when not worse in certain cases. A peasant economy based on four cheap-labor crops prevails as always. Two-thirds of the population still produce little, consume little and buy practically nothing. Although there is basically no unemployment—and almost everyone works and works hard—this happens because, in the last analysis, everyone works first of all for the regime. New industries and so-called new sources of work have proved to be no deterrents for the rampant inflation choking the working classes, who earn 80 per cent less than their North American counterparts and must pay living costs as high as those of the United States if not higher.

It may be that a clean market place is better than a dirty one and that a wide street is preferable to a narrow one, but there is little consolation in seeing fine supermarkets and broad avenues as near to filthy slums and dire poverty as they are in Ciudad Trujillo. And, certainly, markets stocked with luscious fresh vegetables that few people can afford to buy are unadulterated window dressing. Neither the elegance of the city's shops nor the beauty of its buildings can hide the fact that just a few blocks away live people who cannot buy even a pair of shoes. The multitude of the begging, the unclad and the underfed defy police regulations and all efforts to legislate wretchedness out of the well-groomed *trujillista* fief. Notwithstanding the high-sounding prohibitions of the Trujillo Labor Code, barefooted children sell newspapers and lottery tickets late at night in the city streets. And tourists are accosted in front of restaurants, theaters and other places of entertainment by children who repeatedly plead: *"Gimme fi cen."*

The truth is that this situation is not the sad plight of a few remnants of an ignorant lower class incapable of assimilating progress. Except for the few rich who daily get richer while they enjoy the good graces of "the Big One," in the Dominican Republic today the poor get poorer and the gulf between grows larger. Caught in the trap of high prices and scant incomes the salaried urban middle class—the clerks, some professionals and most heads of Government departments—whose pay checks are sometimes mortgaged three months in advance—lives a precarious life, always in the grip of money lenders and grocery creditors.

Outside the cities conditions are much worse. A few minutes' ride beyond the capital city limits will show there is not much real or fake progress. It the tourist is not lost in contemplation of the gorgeous Dominican landscape, he cannot miss on both sides of the road the miserable dirt-floor huts in which Dominicans have lived since ancient times. Nor will he fail to notice the hundreds of undernourished children running naked with their bloated bellies.

The unbelievably poor live side-by-side with the astoundingly rich. The literate live side-by-side with those who can neither write nor read. The assessment of $226 per capita income, even if correct, may not mean much in a country where wealth is concentrated in so very few hands. (A recent banking statistic shows that seven accounts representing the 0.9% of the total number of accounts make a 27.54% of the total amount of deposits.) Were it possible to subtract the huge wealth of the Trujillo family and divide the rest of the national income among the remaining members of the Dominican population, there is no doubt that the per capita income would be reduced by perhaps as much as $150. Moreover, total national income expressed in money terms is misleading since, unlike more economically advanced countries such as the United States, a considerable part of the economic activities, especially in the agricultural sector, are carried on without the medium of money. A good part of the total national output of goods is never sold in the market for money.

A better idea of the actual income of the average Dominican is afforded by the minimum wages officially set by the Government agency in charge of such matters. The level of salaries for unskilled labor still varies between $26 and $78 a month in those industries and occupations covered by social legislation. (The labor code provisions are not applicable to farms with less than ten workers nor are they enforced at the sugar mills owned by Trujillo.) Notwithstanding a labor code provision setting forth the principle of "equal payment for equal work," women are still paid lower wages than men. There are occupations in which the females are still paid from 90 cents to $1 for an eight-hour work day. And it is possible to hire either a maid or a cook for $15 to $20 a month. In an upper bracket a good bi-lingual stenographer may be employed for $150 a month. This of course is a far cry from the not so distant days when a dairyman declared before the Minimum Wage Commission that as late as December 1945 he paid to his *peones* 30 cents a day plus food.

In the meantime the price level in the Dominican Republic is the same —when not higher—as in large American cities such as New York. The average Dominican, depending on a few staples for his daily diet, is bewildered when he goes to the market and is asked to pay 84 cents for a dozen eggs. In a country that still depends on kerosene to light more than half its homes, people are forced to pay 31 cents a gallon. Low-grade gasoline is 43½ cents a gallon in Ciudad Trujillo (higher inland), a fact which, coupled with the fact that a license plate costs $180 a year, accounts for the low number of cars.

It is miraculous the way in which middle-class housewives make ends meet when they have to pay from 14 to 17 cents for a pound of rice, the basic staple of Dominican diet, 15 cents for a pound of refined sugar, and 17 cents for a pound of beans. A pound of fish costs 45 cents and Grade B meat sells for 85 cents a pound. Better meat is unavailable outside of the tourist hotels and large restaurants, because the best quality beef is exported by the Trujillo monopoly. The price of a pound of lard is 44 cents and the consumer must pay 52 cents for a pound of the only available edible grease: peanut oil. A package of domestic cigarettes—properly branded *Benefactor*—costs 40 cents. Whenever bought outside the black market, American cigarettes cost 85 cents a package. To emphasize the plight of the average city dweller, it only remains to point out that a small modest unfurnished three-room apartment rents in Ciudad Trujillo from $90 to $120 a month.

Expert opinion to the contrary, low salaries have not acted as a deterrent for inflation. Extravagant Government spending in unproductive public works such as the $40 million World Fair and the luxurious living of high Government officials and other members of the upper classes, have fed the inflationary trends as much as in places where the wages of organized labor contribute to the rise of salaries. Dominicans, unlike people in democratic countries, must suffer in silence the steady mounting of the cost of living.

Trujillo's monopolistic practices, the lack of any new substantial foreign investments and the withdrawal of large amounts of foreign capital during the last four years, the swollen bureaucracy, the complex taxes (many of which cost more to collect than they bring in) and the immense budgets have begun to catch up with the economy. At the end of 1955 an economic slow-down was clearly apparent, so much in fact that the Government operations were momentarily affected at the beginning of 1956. With characteristic ruthlessness Trujillo promptly resorted in February of that year to his favorite method for balancing the budget—salaries were slashed, personnel reduced. No one knows how many people were discharged from Government departments but their number must have been considerable because the Government—in order to insure the official agency in charge of loans against a big loss—felt itself compelled to allow one-month severance pay to the fired employees to be turned over in payment of their debts to the *Monte de Piedad*.

Dominicans had to swallow in silence the bitter medicine. Fortunately for the rest of the people, this stopgap measure seemed to be enough to save the day for the Government. Clouds were further dispelled by a new injection of foreign exchange pumped into the country by cash crops. At the end of 1956 the price of sugar bounced up to its highest level since the Korean War and coffee and cocoa held up on their own heights. As a result, the crisis was soon past and by the month of August, 1957, it was possible for the regime to announce officially that trade and production figures for the first six months of the year presaged the most prosperous twelve-month period in the history of the Dominican Republic.

Riding the wave of its greatest economic boom, the Dominican Republic shows nonetheless a strange patchwork of economic and social contrasts. Engrossed in its eye-pleasing programs of urban public works the Government has neglected to employ its revenues in more productive projects of social improvement to combat poverty and backwardness.

On the other hand, stifled by the enormous growth of the ever-expanding public economy, private enterprise is lagging far behind. Tax-ridden and strictly controlled, the private sector of the Dominican economy does not dare to make a move without previously receiving the go-ahead signal from the Government authorities. Depending on the regime for the allocation of their resources, the leaders of private industry have let many opportunities pass beyond recall.

The dependency of private business on the Government is not totally unjustified. Many an enterprising businessman has been ruinously forced out of business for trespassing into a field exploited or coveted by the Benefactor. Moreover, credit facilities are almost monopolized by the three existing Government-owned banks (only two other banks—and they are Canadian—operate in the country), which—with the exception of the Central Bank—supposedly conduct business along the lines of traditional private credit institutions. However, the *Banco de Reservas* and the *Banco de Crédito Agrícola e Industrial,* with combined assets of over $200 million, have deviated from their avowed purpose of alleviating the problem of inadequate credit facilities in the country and have turned into instruments of Trujillo's control over the economic, social and political life of the people.

Behind their businesslike fronts the Government banks cover up one of the most unscrupulous systems of political blackmail ever conceived. The Government banks are run by politically minded, rubber-stamp boards of directors, whose members are appointed by the President of the Republic. These boards are empowered with authority to steer the national credit policies, but in practice they limit themselves to carry out directives handed out by the Benefactor or a group of his closest aides. Credit applications are approved or rejected not only on the basis of their merits but in accordance with the applicant's political credit-rating with the secret police. Once the credit is granted it is always used as a weapon to keep debtors within bounds of political subservience.

No wonder business prospects look gloomy, especially for those engaged in small retail trade. The curtailment of the free flow of trade has brought about a marked fall in retail sales which in turn has forced many merchants, large and small, to resort to desperate measures to get rid of their accumulating inventories. Newspaper columns have been full of advertisements of *baratillos* (special sales), something to which Dominican businessmen traditionally resort whenever faced with the threat of a business recession.[1] The same columns have been reporting a larger number of business failures than usual, particularly in the interior. And, more significant still, is the fact that during September and October businessmen of all sections of the country were invited to mysterious special conferences at the National Palace with the Secretary of State Without Portfolio, Virgilio Alvarez Pina.

The rosy picture is blurred as well by the fact that there is all too evident a tendency within unskilled groups of laborers to go back to low-productivity occupations. An exceedingly high number of people are now engaged in the sale of lottery tickets, street peddling and boot blacking, which in any Latin American country is the first sign of impending economic trouble. To dispel rumors spreading out of the country to the effect that Dominican workers were having a tough time, the Government announced, through its Secretary of Foreign Affairs on September 24, 1957, that currently "unemployment was at only one-tenth of one per cent of the population; the salary index at 348.9 and the general price index at 235.5, using 1945 as a base year."

That the Government statistics give a false picture is proved by the growing official concern with the problem of unemployment. During the last year several official bureaus of employment have been opened throughout the country and all jobless people are under obligation of registering there with indication of their names, trades and addresses. It could be, however, that, as many of Trujillo's detractors say, these bureaux have nothing to do with unemployment and are in reality recruiting centers of forced labor for the Big One's sugar plantations. According to these accounts, whenever it is necessary the police round up city unemployed and after convicting them of vagrancy pack them off to work in the sugar mills.

Recently, moreover, newspapers have printed official notices advising foreigners that prior to securing employment they must obtain a special card issued by the Government. The Governor of the National District, where the capital city is located, periodically prints advertisements and

---

[1] In a country where there is practically one season the whole year there is hardly the need for a change of styles or for the easing off of last season's inventories at the end of the summer or winter.

makes statements to the press "inviting" farmers—who have lately migrated to the capital in great numbers seeking salaried employment—to go back to their former places, lest the authorities punish them for violation of the official regulations forbidding countrymen to settle in cities without a Government permit.

In addition to these disturbing factors, there are further proofs to show that Trujillo's ill-conceived economic programs have caused many social dislocations and have created added hardships, particularly for the white-collar workers. Usury is rampant and people pay the highest rates of interest known to any Western country. Money lenders have sprung up apparently from nowhere and even the Government has embarked on the business of lending money to its own employees. The *Monte de Piedad,* a government-owned glorified pawn shop, bails the government labor force out of economic difficulties at the interest rate of three per cent per month—36% a year. Collateral for the loan is the employee's next-month salary which is sent directly to the *Monte* by the National Treasurer. The Government interest rates, however, are not the highest in force. According to a letter to the editor printed in the January 3, 1956, issue of *El Caribe,* the prevailing rates of interest vary between ten and twenty per cent monthly. These, of course, are illegally collected, but by Act of Congress the finance houses are authorized to charge, for loans up to $500, a legal rate of four per cent monthly. For mortgages and other commerical transactions the Dominican Civil Code decrees an interest of 12% annually. Clients of the large banking firms still can get money at rates varying between four and a half and seven per cent annually.

This seemingly contradictory maze of evidence is what makes risky any type of prediction about the future course of Dominican economy. It would be utterly ridiculous to deny that Trujillo has put forward some strenuous and imaginative efforts to raise the standards of productivity of the country. All things considered, and without leaning backwards to indulge in any wishful thinking on whether the country would have been better or worse off without Trujillo, it must be admitted that Trujillo's long tenure of power is marked by some constructive fiscal, monetary and economic reforms *but also by a perilous concentration of wealth and means of production in the hands of a few greedy individuals.*

EDUCATION FOR TYRANNY

1. ALTHOUGH NEVER STATED IN COHERENT FORM, TRUJILLO'S views of the role of education within an authoritarian system of government nevertheless constitute a contribution to the political philosophy of totalitarian dictatorship.

As conceived by Trujillo, the goal of education is to provide the means of subduing people into meaningless conformism. This idea that the proper aim of the school is to prepare the masses for blind acceptance of the propaganda line of the clique in power—it could be defined as education for tyranny—is by no means the invention of the Benefactor. This conception, which reduces education to a simple political prop, is shared to a large extent by almost all contemporary totalitarian regimes, especially those behind the Iron Curtain. Yet, in framing the actual machinery for its implementation few rulers have exceeded the cunning and insight shown by the Generalissimo.

Unlike the classical Latin *caudillo,* who for the perpetuation of his power relied largely upon the ignorance of his subjects and therefore feared the effect of education upon the dark masses, Trujillo has exhibited a perceptive understanding of the possibilities of education as a vehicle of political control. Looking toward Europe, beyond the jungle of Latin American politics, the Generalissimo found that contemporary fascist and communist dictatorships had shattered the delusion that education and expertise make those who acquire them proof against self-deception or political prejudice. Very often, by blunting natural common sense, education actually increases gullibility.

Studying totalitarian systems of thought-control, Trujillo learned how to use educational devices on the largest possible scale to strengthen his regime. Moreover, in the process of taking over and adapting totalitarian conceptions of education to the conditions of his own country, "the Chief"

made a few improvements. While in other countries the systematic glorification of every achievement of the regime is guided by the desire to perpetuate an idea, however wrong it may be, in the Dominican Republic
it is ruled almost exclusively by considerations of egotism, self-interest
and selfish attachment to power and wealth on the part of the absolute
ruler.

To a people like the Americans, who regard universal education as a
necessary basis for democracy, the fact that Trujillo is building innumerable schools and has passed laws requiring compulsory school attendance
for children over seven years of age, may possibly mean that despite Trujillo the country is undergoing a healthy change toward democratic procedures. This is an opinion shared by such a keen observer of the Latin
American scene as Professor Dexter Perkins (no Trujillo lover), who
expresses it in *The United States and the Caribbean*.

After giving credit to Trujillo for showing "much interest in the schools
of the country," Perkins asserts that at the present time "there is a dis-
gusting amount of servile praise of the dictator in the public schools." So
far so good, but then Perkins errs in his interpretation when he says that
"this is a very different thing from the exaltation of a system, and it would
be fairer to say that President Trujillo, by his extension of a system of
public instruction, is preparing the way for the downfall of the kind of
regime he represents than to regard him as the founder of the Fascist
state, or as the embodiment of the Fuehrer principle."

The concept of Trujillo as a passing Latin dictator without roots in the
past or projections into the future and preparing his own undoing by the
education of his people is not corroborated by facts. To begin with, the
Benefactor is perhaps stronger today than ever before and seems to be
very much a permanent fixture of Dominican politics.

Education does not seem to be conducting the people toward democracy. Under Trujillo its sacred purpose of enlightening has been perverted
and it is being employed to foster among people who are taught to read
propagandist text books a new myth of Trujillo as a God-given blessing.

A man who does not want to leave judgment to posterity is impatient
lest his self-praise be lost for lack of a literate people. Thus, Trujillo has
urged upon his followers the necessity of helping other people to become
literate. "No demonstration of support or praise will be as highly gratify-
ing to me this year (1955)," said he, "as the cooperation which may be
given me in order that every single Dominican, whether from the cities
or the most distant villages, may learn to read and write and may receive
the benefits of that basic education which will make him fit to participate
actively in our public affairs with a keen awareness of his constitutional
rights and duties."

Under the prodding of Trujillo, all those associated with him must show their friendship by undertaking the task of teaching other persons how to read and write. "If each one," pointed out the Benefactor, "resolves to contribute in some way to the success of this far-reaching campaign against illiteracy which is about to be launched in order that every single Dominican may read the words of the anthem where the glories of our land are sung and follow the prayers through which the blessing of the Almighty are beseeched, I am sure that we will then be able to realize fully the ideal to which I have dedicated myself this year which has been named after me by a thankful people: to conquer illiteracy and wipe it out entirely from this new nation."

Why he waited twenty-five years to launch an all-out war on illiteracy Trujillo did not explain. Nor did he indicate that the national anthem he was referring to was at the time undergoing a thorough re-writing by his own private secretary in order to include his feats in it. Nevertheless, the campaign was launched under the name of "Trujillo Literacy Program." By Government orders all employers canvassed their workers to find out which ones were illiterate and thereupon were asked, on a voluntary-or-else basis, to install in their plants, or at least to pay for them, anti-illiteracy units.[1]

The current emphasis on education has reached a point now where people are being compelled to learn how to read and write, even if they don't want to.

Whereas in 1930 there were only 526 schools of all kinds, with 50,800 pupils, at present 4,419 schools are functioning with a registration of 423,424 students. In addition, 289,249 persons are attending anti-illiteracy centers. The current budget for education alone is approximately $10 million, an amount, according to the Foreign Minister, Porfirio Herrera Báez, "equivalent to the total national budget in 1930." Comparisons are always odious and this one must be particularly hateful to the Benefactor, but without as much fanfare the neighboring island of Puerto Rico, many times smaller than Santo Domingo, and with a population slightly larger, spends two and a half times that sum for the same purpose.

Without denying the great progress in the way of carrying out a full-fledged educational program, it seems that in the Dominican Republic the most substantial advance has been made in the field of statistics. Many ciphers are released to show the annual reductions in the rate of

[1] One of Trujillo's habits is that of assessing businesses for civic improvements in their immediate area, in addition to their normal tax obligations. So, when in preparation for the festivities of the 24-month long "Year of the Benefactor of the Fatherland" the public lighting of Ciudad Trujillo was improved, the full cost of the project fell upon the merchants and landowners of each neighborhood. Similarly, many shops and offices in the downtown zone were requested to put up electric signs. Upon each inaugural ceremony the local press gave credit for the improvements to the "genius of the Generalissimo."

illiteracy, the growth of schoolroom facilities, the extent of the welfare programs for students (a free breakfast of chocolate and bread in some urban institutions), the extension of the curricula and other minor accomplishments. Little is said in official documents of the acute shortage of teachers and the almost insuperable problem of persuading teachers to dedicate their lives to rural education. With the help of these Government statistics published by the Department of Education, Murray Kempton calculated for the *New York Post* that for 20 years, up to 1956, "the Trujillo government had been reducing illiteracy at a rate of 1.3 per cent a year." Furthermore, in 1956 after years of intense activity 45 per cent of the people still could not write and read. Predicting, however, an early triumph of the crusade against ignorance for which the Benefactor had asked the active support of even those who do not share his "political philosophy either because they have been unable or unwilling to rise to the level of my patriotic ideals," the Minister of Education asserted that in five years the illiteracy rate would be no higher than 18 per cent.

Lost in this maze of ciphers and press releases, few people were probably aware of the fact that the year when the Generalissimo made his resounding pledge to teach every Dominican to "read the words of the anthem where the glories of our land are sung" a slash in the appropriation of the national budget for education took effect. In his message to Congress about the 1956 budget brother Héctor made a terse announcement of the reduction without superfluous explanations or even a word of regret. The amount of the cut was not stated, but a significant fact was that in the same message the "president" reported an increase in military expenses.

Puzzling contradictions such as this come to the surface, without causing any embarrassment to the regime. Without a free press, they are soon buried under a new pile of fresh optimistic statistics.

But even if the Dominican Government spends three times more in arms than in education, instruction is still free and theoretically compulsory. Each year, at the beginning of the new courses the authorities put on an all-out drive to enforce the laws on public instruction. For a few weeks attendance in classes is fair, then it rapidly declines.

Various are the reasons for the high incidence of truancy. The main one, however, has an economic basis. Parents, who themselves in most cases have had no education, will not force their children to attend school, because they believe it is more important to have them at work in the fields or selling lottery tickets and newspapers. For people who have to work hard during the day in order to eat in the evening, five or six hours a day in a schoolroom seems a sheer waste of time.

In addition, other reasons for the lack of appeal of the educational program may be found in its consistent efforts to mold oncoming generations to the *trujillista* creed. Students in all grades are taught that Trujillo knows nothing but wisdom, sponsors only benevolence and is infallible. They are thoroughly indoctrinated in the single-purpose principle that loyalty to Trujillo (whose person is identified with that of the Fatherland as its Father and Benefactor) comes before love of family and home. As part of the brain-washing, the Generalissimo's personal flag (a complicated pattern of five stars mingled with the blue, white and red of the national emblem) flies in each school beside the Dominican flag and students of all ages are employed to swell the crowds at political rallies, church ceremonies and other "civic gatherings" in homage to "the Big One."

The hero-worshiping cult of Trujillo's personality is the *leit motif* of national education. As Murray Kempton pointed out, "another fruit of learning, unmentioned but hardly objectionable to the old man, is the opportunity, even the compulsion, to read about all his glories."

The amount of printed material on the life and achievements of the Benefactor in use in the schools is enormous. The authors of the majority of school texts—be it mathematics, geography, hygiene, cooking or history—undertake to prove that the Trujillo regime is the most truly democratic of all forms of government. Starting with the premise that the Generalissimo is a man of genius—the incarnation of the nation's soul—they maintain that at each moment he perceives through his matchless gift of divination the popular will and wastes no time in turning his absolute power to its immediate fulfillment. Sometimes the authors go a step farther, and assert that "the Chief" forecasts the popular will before it takes form, thus making unnecessary its formulation by the people. And it is at times written that Trujillo knows better than the people themselves what they want or what they ought to have. Thus it is not up to the people to think at all.

For example, the alphabet is learned in public schools in a "civic primer" whose author is "the Chief" himself. A few sentences of this "primer," taken at random, offer the best illustration of the manner in which the school is utilized as breeding ground for informers and other future professionals in denunciation. "The President works unceasingly for the happiness of his people," reads one. "It is he who maintains peace, supports the schools, builds the roads, protects all forms of labor, helps the farmers, favors industry, keeps up and improves the harbors, supports the hospitals, encourages learning, and organizes the army for the protection of all law-abiding citizens.

"If you should find in your home a man who wishes to disturb order, see that he is handed over to the police. He is the worst of evildoers. Criminals who have murdered a man or stolen something are in prison. The revolutionary who plots to kill as many as he can and steal everything he can lay his hands on, your property and that of your neighbors—he is your worst enemy."

Still another paragraph: "Peace is the greatest benefit we can have. We should sustain it by our conduct as peaceful men and women and by prosecuting those who try to end it.

"You should see in every revolutionist an enemy of your life and property. In a time of disorder there is no protection nor security. War among brothers is the worst calamity the Republic has suffered."

This primer has been in use in Dominican schools for twenty-five years and is the most circulated text-book in the country. Millions of copies have been printed at Government expense and freely distributed not only among children but also among farmers and urban laborers.

There is another book whose reading is compulsory in the schools—Mrs. Trujillo's *Moral Meditations*. Teachers are supposed to offer it as one of the best examples of national literature, and as a work of moral philosophy that has earned universal acclaim. For the glorification of these literary efforts, the regime has instituted "Books Day," to be celebrated every year. On this occasion, as stressed by *La Nación,* on April 25, 1956, every school has to prepare a special program intended to bring to its pupils the benefits of outstanding examples of Dominican literature, such as the writings of Trujillo and his wife.

The brain-washing operation continues on Mother's Day, Father's Day, Independence Day, and so forth. Then homage is paid to different members of the Trujillo family. On Mother's Day, for example, school children are instructed to write little essays not on the virtues of mother-hood in general but on the exemplary ones of Trujillo's mother, Doña Julia Molina.

Indoctrination efforts do not stop in grade schools. They occur on higher educational levels, including the University of Santo Domingo. Under Trujillo the ancient Dominican University has been thrown into a black pit of moral degradation, professional mediocrity and academic serfdom.

Quartered in a $5-million housing project known as "University City" the University of Santo Domingo has made fantastic material progress during the Era of Trujillo and now boasts in its modernistic buildings equipment and gadgets of the most advanced model. Its academic standards (though low) are good enough to mass-produce lawyers, physicians, dentists, engineers and architects ready to mind their own business and make an honest dollar in their professions.

Ever since 1934 when the faculty of the University bestowed upon the Generalissimo an honorary degree in all its disciplines (the only person to hold such an honor), the University has been an honorary degree mill with an exceedingly fast turnover. From Nicholas Murray Butler, President of Columbia University, who traveled to the Dominican Republic to receive his honorary degree in the middle thirties, to Vice President Richard M. Nixon, who received his in 1955, a host of distinguished American citizens have been honored by the *trujillista* University. The most recent ceremony of this kind was held, according to the monthly magazine of the Dominican Embassy in Washington, D.C., to award the degree of *Doctor Honoris Causa* in the Faculties of Philosophy and Law to two American legislators: Senator George A. Smathers, of Florida, and Representative Kenneth B. Keating, of New York. Equal honors have been awarded to the representatives of the foreign governments who during their tour of duty in Santo Domingo have shown a "friendly" attitude toward Trujillo. Because in the fulfillment of his high office he "earned the abiding affection of the Dominican people" the University thus honored, before departure, former U.S. Ambassador William T. Pheiffer.

As a professor of the University (a title awarded to him despite the known fact that he never set foot in a school room higher than the elementary grades), "the Big One" feels special affection for the University. He has chosen the enlightened center of Dominican high learning as a suitable sounding board for the deliverance by important visiting scholars, diplomats and intellectuals of highly complimentary speeches and lectures about himself. When the former Brazilian Ambassador, Paulo Germano Hasslocher, delivered his much-translated eulogy of the Benefactor, the latter sat on the rostrum, his face beaming, during the hour-long exercise in genuflection by the official representative of a great nation.

Outside these activities the University of Santo Domingo, unlike its counterparts all over Latin America, is a quiet place. Professors as well as pupils seem to have been cast in a pattern of silence, subservience and conformity.

Even professors talk in whispers during the class periods as if ashamed of being heard. And there are reasons to believe they should, since on certain subjects such as history and philosophy the Rector's office supplies the professors with directions for lectures prepared in accordance with the current party-line. Thereupon student spies are planted in the classrooms to insure that the professor follows without dangerous deviations the official outline. "I can always tell who they are," said one professor. "They take notes at the wrong times."

Controversial subjects are avoided, even subjects so alien to partisan politics as the personality and character of the Founding Fathers of the Republic or the life and work of the great Latin American scholar Eugenio María de Hostos, who in the last decades of the nineteenth century introduced modern methods of teaching.

The case of Hostos deserves attention. After being a hero to Dominicans of the past four generations, Hostos, by Trujillo's order, is undergoing downgrading. For reasons yet unknown *El Caribe* opened in the middle of 1956, on suggestion from the Benefactor, a symposium designed to revaluate Hostos' role in Dominican culture. After the first answers were printed it was obvious that the regime was involved in a move to destroy the high reputation of the revered scholar. A few of his remaining disciples were selected to tear to shreds the glory that surrounds Hostos' name.

Cynically Dominican university students say that they don't want to be heroes like their Cuban counterparts. To hide his inner fear and anxiety the Dominican student grows an outer shell of sneering indifference, which seemingly makes him insensible to the normal currents of life that elsewhere renders youth rebellious and idealistic.

Today students are too young to have known anything but life under Trujillo or too well indoctrinated by years of extolling the excellences of the Benefactor or too scared to engage in the risky game of political opposition. Yet the Government does not relax its vigilance. Trujillo knows that the Latin American universities are often hotbeds of democratic and other radical ideas and he does not want such a thing to happen in his own. Stringent security regulations are ruthlessly enforced and every student is under an around-the-clock surveillance by fellow students, wardens, prefects, professors and outside informers. "The University of Santo Domingo is unique for two things," wrote Murray Kempton. "It is the oldest in this hemisphere and certainly the only university in the West where an applicant needs a certificate of good conduct from the local police chief for admission."

The last vestiges of intellectual freedom gone, Dominican students' favorite activity appears to be that of paying homage to Trujillo and placing around his neck costly trinkets such as the "Collar of Democracy," a diamond-studded jewel they gave the Benefactor in 1951.

This, however, was not always the case. Occasionally, the Benefactor has had more than his normal share of trouble with the students. In 1930, the University took the leadership in the fight for Freedom and soon became known as one of the main foci of opposition to military rule. Through their mouthpiece the *Asociación Nacional de Estudiantes Universitarios,* or ANEU as it was known, the students took a firm and at times intrepid stand against the trigger-happy storm troopers of the military regime.

Fearing that student opposition might become the spark that set off the feared libertarian explosion, and aware that the history of Latin American nations is dotted with incidents in which apparently minor student movements have grown into full fledged revolutions, Trujillo decided to crush at gun-point the ANEU-organized political rallies of protest in the capital.

Shortly thereafter ANEU was dissolved, and those of its members who stood firm in their opposition found it increasingly hard to earn a livelihood. The overwhelming pressure upon these people was not released until they recanted or left the country. Measures were then taken that were designed to prevent open student opposition happening again.

Knowing that, notwithstanding the fact that many of the students engaged themselves in political activities out of sincere idealism, there was a great majority of crackpots and conscious or unconscious opportunists hankering for public attention, Trujillo trained his big guns on the latter, and then tried to seduce them with offers of government jobs and the hint that profitable careers were in store for them. This became known as the "sweet approach."

The balance in favor of Trujillo's methods—either the terror or the so-called "sweet approach"—is a precarious one, so precarious in fact that in 1945 a simple democratic wind was enough to upset peace and quiet anew within the University. Under the influence of World War II and the democratic principles of the United Nations Charter an intense preoccupation with political and social problems set upon University student circles. Under the guidance of a group of liberal-minded professors, such as Dr. José Antonio Bonilla Atiles, then Dean of the Law School, Dr. José Horacio Rodríguez and Dr. Moisés de Soto of the Law School, and others whose names cannot be mentioned since they still live in the country, large groups of students with aspirations and democratic ideas had an opportunity to get together. The newly created University Theater afforded the opportunity for meetings outside the stroke of the secret police ax. During rehearsals the bases were laid for what a few months later evolved as a powerful underground movement.

As a result, the clandestine movement of *Juventud Revolucionaria* was born. The aim of this organization was to bring to the Dominican people a democratic form of government. The movement did not last long inside the University, being soon suppressed in ruthless fashion.

Its existence, nevertheless, brought about new, more stringent methods of control over the University. Professors as well as students are since then under fresh suspicion. A cloud of silence rests upon them.

2.   NEVER BEFORE IN THE HISTORY OF THE DOMINICAN Republic have there been so many works printed, busts cast, pictures painted and music composed than at present. Yet this vast literary and artistic output has failed to furnish the world a single work of excellent, enduring quality.

The absence of social liberties, moral tolerance and creative freedom, coupled with twenty-seven years of censorship, propaganda and terror, have dried up the sources of Dominican imagination and have thrown a gifted, sensitive people into an abyss of collective negation.

Literary and artistic performances lack spontaneity and dignity. The only written or spoken expressions of ideas upon which intellectuals may safely indulge are those in praise of the Benefactor or in denigration of his enemies. The most exalted examples of literary acumen are those comparing the Generalissimo with the lightning, the mountaintop, the sun, the eagle, volcanic lava, Pegasus, Plato and God. "He (Trujillo), like God, created from nothing on the seventh day a splendid and brilliant Fair of the Peace and Brotherhood of the Free World," wrote in *El Caribe,* November 8, 1955, the foremost Dominican philosopher Andrés Avelino.

Dominican intellectuals are frozen into dogmatism. Their horizons have been narrowed to such extent that they have grown to regard themselves unworthy of the social sciences and pay almost no heed to the humanities. Historical studies are preferred but this happens only because they afford either an escape from the present or an opportunity to make political hay out of distortions of the past intended to further current political interest. Thus, a lot of crypto-historic essays and more ambitious enterprises as well have received the accolade of the Dominican Academy of History, the super-censorship board. Blessed by the Academy there is in circulation a lot of historical trash, whose only merits is to follow with despicable subservience the party line as set in the National Palace. In the meantime some of the most valuable works on Dominican history are proscribed. Sumner Welles' *Naboth Vineyard,* one of the most authoritative histories of the country, has not been read by more than a few score Dominicans. A Spanish translation of this monumental history, printed some years ago by the publishing house of *El Diario,* of Santiago, was not allowed to circulate. It is said that Trujillo strongly objected to those revealing passages in which the author explains why the Americans were unable to outfit the Constabulary force with the right kind of officers.

Fiction has become an almost forgotten genre. Intellectuals find little room for creative work of the kind necessary for good, uninhibited, satisfactory fiction. Short stories are sparsely published, but during the last fifteen years no more than three full length novels have been written and for that matter the last one to come out is only a fulsome, pseudo-historical profile of life under "the Chief." Its author, Pedro Verges Vidal, was a member of the dreaded corps of Inspectors of the Presidency.

Poets—always abundant in Latin America—have not been extinguished, but they seem unable to turn out anything but worn-out clichés. Currently they spend a great deal of time concocting rhymes to sing the glories of the Generalissimo; an album with their best *trujillista* verses is in process of publication by the highest cultural center of the country, the *Ateneo*

Dominicano. The poets have also given a share of their poetic lode to the cultural prowess of Mrs. Rafael L. Trujillo, Sr., as well as to the beauty and talents of her daughter Queen Angelita I. As *Time* pointed out, "the No. 1 occupation of Dominican intellectuals is writing flowery tributes to the Genius of Peace, Hero of Labor and Paladin of Democracy."

To reward the ceaseless efforts of the artificers of the written word Trujillo has established, in the manner of the American movie industry, his own "Oscars." These awards for excellence in artistic and literary fields are given the names of different members of the Trujillo family. There is, for example, the yearly Rafael L. Trujillo Prize, which is bestowed upon the author of the best book, Dominican or foreign, dealing with any aspect of the "portentous work of government of the illustrious leader of the Dominican people." Other prizes, supposedly intended to foster the cultural advancement of the country, are awarded each year to the best political article, the most acclaimed literary work, the most important didactic book and the most outstanding volume of verses. Few Dominican intellectuals, however, have been considered worthy of the awards. In 1955 the prizes of the contest for the best poems and hymns composed in honor of Queen Angelita—large lumps of cash amounting to $25,000—went to a handful of prolific Spanish writers whose entries were counted by the score. And, in spite of the fact that the local output of political literature exceeds in quantity anything the wildest imagination could conceive, the award-winning press eulogy for 1956 was one written by Trujillo's most consistent foreign admirer—the Venezuelan historian and politician J. Penzini Hernández. Originally printed in *El Universal,* Caracas, and later reprinted freely by the domestic press and as a joint paid advertisement placed in U.S. publications by the Dominican Press Society and the Dominican Information Center, the prize article, entitled "Assault by Slander," is for tone and content one of the best examples of *trujillista* prose.

Prizes are not the only means of promoting belles-lettres in the country. The Benefactor is a Maecenas who bountifully pays for books, pictures and symphonic scores. Young authors need only send "the Chief" their songs of praise to see them in the public light. Newspapers—notwithstanding the fact that while editor-in-chief of *El Caribe* I made an effort to deny posterity much of this sort of literature—are under compulsion to give protective shelter, whatever their merits, to all written expressions of the art of pleasing the Benefactor.

There are many examples, admiringly told by Trujillo's aides, which illustrate the various modes in which "the Chief" attends to the cultural needs of his people. According to a story recounted by a former Secretary of Education to Murray Kempton, once upon a time the Benefactor heard that the Dominican side of the frontier with Haiti was cluttered with citizens who did not even know the National Anthem. Upon receiving such a frightful piece of news "the Big One" acted quickly. "I want musical instruments in every school on the border. Go to the United States and buy 25 Steinways" was the peremptory command of the Generalissimo. Thereupon the Minister made the trip and brought back the pianos which, reportedly, were acquired for $5,000 apiece. The story, however, had an ending entirely different from that told by the Minister to Kempton. On the border there are not 25 music academies. The pianos were taken to the frontier, no doubt, but once there it was found they could not play by themselves. Since it was more difficult to find 25 pianists than an equal number of pianos, the latter were left to deteriorate in the battered school houses of the border.

On another occasion the Generalissimo was informed that a new press officer of the American Embassy named Francis Townsend had published once, as a result of a collegiate interest, a volume of translations into English of the works of several Dominican poets. Trujillo was also told that the book was out of print, so he promptly directed *El Caribe* to publish, at Government expense, a new edition of Townsend's book. "The Chief" ordered an adequate introduction to the volume by one of his aides, Otto Vega; the preface credited the enterprise to "the suggestion of that great leader and generous Maecenas who is Generalissimo Dr. Rafael L. Trujillo."

However, a minor difficulty had to be ironed out before publication. Dr. Townsend, unversed in the mysteries of Dominican politics at the time he made his selections, had included certain authors whose political ideas ran counter to those of the Benefactor. The "generous Maecenas" was in no mood to let appear in a book he was paying for the names of people who, however lofty their afflatus, were his enemies. Eliminated from the anthology, with or without Townsend's knowledge, were two poets of stature now living in exile. Carmen Natalia Martínez and Pedro Mir.

Art exhibits, concerts and lectures in fine arts—most of them under the Administration's sponsorship—are daily occurrences, but all have a common feature: a lack of the gaiety and spontaneity that mark artistic gatherings everywhere else. The spiritless productions of artists and musicians, although at times flawless from a technical standpoint, show a strange frigidity and a lack, according to John Fischer, editor of *Harper's,* of the "exuberant artistic flowering, for instance, which is so notable a characteristic of the disheveled Haitians who occupy the other half of the island."

Connected with Trujillo's boundless ambition to play an important role in the international field is the intensive use of cultural, historical and educational congresses which in rapid succession have been staged in the Dominican capital since 1956. Starting with the celebrated Congress of Catholic Culture held early in 1956 with the attendance of a host of prominent clergymen and laymen, each of these gatherings has been employed as effective sounding boards for the international display and glorification of every achievement of the regime.

In the presence of such notable figures of the Catholic World as Francis, Cardinal Spellman, Trujillo has made use in these "cultural" gatherings of all known propaganda devices on the largest possible scale, to prostitute their avowed purposes in every way so that they may contribute to the strengthening of his regime. Many resolutions have been put through with the sole purpose of making the rest of the world swallow the regime's propagandist pap. Thus, the full Assembly of the Second Hispanic-American History Congress, held in October, 1957, approved, on the initiative of Dominican historian César Herrera (a brother of Rafael Herrera, current editor of *El Caribe*) a resolution which condemns the activities of intellectuals who have betrayed the cause of Hispanidad in order to enter the ranks of international communism.

According to a United Press dispatch Herrera asserted that the "archetype of those subjects," with respect to the Dominican Republic, is the author of this book. "Ornes," said Herrera, "after proclaiming, in innumerable articles published in *El Caribe,* his adhesion to Christian culture and his rejection of the Marxist ideology, betrayed these principles and associated himself with Communism."

It is totally consistent with Trujillo's belief that the only non-Communists are those who proclaim their devotion to his cause in a uniform way. For him a Communist is anyone who criticizes his regime.

The truth is that like all dictators throughout history Trujillo is no friend of culture and education in their genuine sense.

Intellectuals, under Trujillo, are still permitted to exist; but they are compelled to write the prescribed brand of literature. Trujillo has suppressed all independent manifestations of culture and learning in favor of a single official brand developed under the tutelage of the dominant clique. Intellectuals are under compulsion to direct their work to a single end— the maintenance of the Generalissimo in power.

In order to produce a perfectly uniform type of intellectual, the regime has taken firmly in hand during the years all artists and writers, especially members of the young generations, supervising them step by step, until the more useful and adaptable are finally enrolled in the *trujillista* ranks. The others, called "Unassimilables," are suppressed and utterly destroyed morally if not physically.

Initial intellectual surrender is no guarantee of survival. It is true that spineless intellectuals seem to have a place assured in Trujillo's realm as long as they behave in accordance with the capricious norms set by the regime. Life for Dominican intellectuals is a succession of scares—they fear to displease the master at the helm and, above all, they fear their talents may betray them into some expression of forbidden truth, some flash of candor, which may sound their death knell. Neither reputation nor brilliant work confers security. Distinction is all too often a sad prelude to extinction.

Enclosing themselves in a sort of ivory tower a few intellectuals have been able to escape Trujillo's dominance inside the country; others, more fortunate, have left the country to try their wings where there still are open spaces. Those who remain in the country very rarely have been able to maintain anonymity. The hand of the dictatorship sooner or later reaches out and then comes the moment for the fateful choice. What is worse, while in retirement these passive rebels condemn themselves nevertheless to intellectual sterility, since to publish a non-political work or not to mention Trujillo's name in an article, book or any other literary exploit simply means suicide. It is not strange, therefore, that intellectual life, outside of shallow political moments, is sunk into a coma.

This was not always the case. In the past Dominican writers, philosophers and poets have competed with distinction in the market place of ideas. Dominican were such revered figures of Latin American letters as Pedro Henríquez Ureña, philosopher and philologist, Fabio Fiallo, poet, and Americo Lugo, historian.

Young Henríquez Ureña left the country during the American military occupation to settle in Cuba, Mexico and Argentina where he made a brilliant reputation. In 1930, at Trujillo's request, Henriquez went back to Santo Domingo. He accepted an appointment as head of national education and immediately set upon the task of bringing about much needed reforms of the educational system. Instead of opening new schools as Henriquez was advising, Trujillo chose to close them, giving as excuse the urgent need to stabilize the battered national budget. After months of fruitless efforts, Henriquez resigned his post (a crime Trujillo never forgives a collaborator) and went back to his teaching job in an Argentinian University, where he died years later.

So well-established was Henríquez' prestige all over Latin America that Trujillo did not dare to attack him openly while alive. Even after Henriquez' death Trujillo paid tribute to his memory, naming one of the buildings of the new University City after him.

Yet one day the long-awaited opportunity to even the score showed itself. In August, 1956, a Dominican lady, Flérida Nolasco, printed in *El Caribe* as part of a series a eulogistic piece on Henríquez Ureña. The Benefactor himself, under the pen name of Lorenzo Ocumares (one of his favorite ones for signing anonymous letters to the newspapers), wrote a letter to *El Caribe* stating that although Henriquez had been a man of "great learning and an eminent figure in Latin American literature," those talents had been of no use to his own country. Then the writer went on to accuse the late scholar of taking advantage years back of his post as director of Dominican education to plant "the sick seed of the Communist doctrine in the minds of student groups."

Fabio Fiallo, a romantic poet of no small stature in Latin American letters, and a man who has been compared by French critics with figures of worldwide reputation like Tagore, had led a full and respected life until he clashed with Trujillo.

During the American occupation Fiallo's writings and stand for the liberty of his country, brought him into conflict with the censorship regulations of the military. An article, whose language was particularly objected to by the Marines, was studded with expressions such as "martyrdom of the Fatherland," "chains," and "this cruel civilization which came to us through the back door with fixed bayonets in a dark night of deceit, surprise and cowardice. . . ."

This was considered too much by the authorities and Fiallo was charged with two violations of the Executive Order prohibiting the setting forth of doctrines "tending" to incite the masses to "unrest, disorder and revolt." Fiallo's ensuing trial and sentence to three years in prison by an American military court under the occupation status erupted into a *cause celebre*. "To most Americans," Knight wrote, "the 'poet patriot' was a passing headliner in the press, but his trial in 1920 made the *Yankees* about as loathsome as possible to the Latin peoples of the two hemispheres."

The second time Fiallo was thrown in jail things were different. Someone had had the idea, early in 1931, of secretly distributing a handbill with a reprint of one of the poet's articles slashing the Dominican Quislings during the American occupation as the "catspaws of the foreign invader —prosperous in their new connection and sneering in their attitude toward the cruder days of independence."

Incensed by the obvious reference, and not knowing the identity of the real perpetrator of the profanation, "the Chief" decided to make an example of the author. This time, however, no incensed protests were filed and unlike the days of the American occupation no photographs showing the handsome old man in stripes were smuggled out of the prison. Not even a mock trial was staged. Everything happened in a very private way and very few people, if any, knew outside the Dominican Republic what was going on.

Upon release Fiallo was not hailed by an enthusiastic crowd at the prison's gates. Quite the contrary, people avoided him for fear of political contamination. His heart broken by the indifference, complacency and cowardice of his terrorized compatriots, the old poet died shortly afterward. No posthumous homage was paid to him.

Americo Lugo's story is perhaps sadder than Fiallo's. A colleague of Fiallo during the nationalistic campaigns of the American occupation period, Lugo was a genuine scholar, who had devoted his life to the study of history. His prose, terse and brilliant, had honored many foreign publications and his ability as a lawyer had given him fame and fortune. Already an old man, Lugo decided by the time Trujillo started his regime of terror to retire from public life.

For years Lugo managed to steer his way out of political entanglements with Trujillo. The day came, however, when Trujillo thought it was time his feats were included in Dominican history books and naturally enough he wanted this done by the best talent available.

Trujillo approached the old scholar with a frank offer to publish a history with no strings attached. A contract was signed between the Government and Lugo and the latter set himself to the task. On January 26, 1936, Trujillo let the cat out of the bag in a casual way, during a political speech in the small town of Esperanza some 150 miles from the capital. Reading the press reports, Lugo came upon the knowledge that in his capacity as official historian, he has been chosen to write the "history of the past as well as the present."

Lugo wasted no time. He wrote a lengthy letter to the Benefactor, flatly challenging his statement that he was an "official historian." The letter made also plain, in strong and dignified terms, that under no circumstances was Lugo going to write any "history of the present."

Lugo's letter, as can be imagined, was never printed by the Dominican press though there is evidence that it was sent to the newspapers by its author. Nevertheless hundreds of copies were circulated through underground channels. As a result the newspapers delivered smashing attacks upon the aging scholar, without revealing, of course, the real reasons. Congress promptly rescinded the contract and Lugo fell into the category of a "subversive." His house besieged by secret policemen, stripped of all his properties, through tax assessments and phony law suits, Lugo died a few years later. His last years were spent in isolation (no person would dare to visit his home) and poverty, but he stood his ground with real courage, facing indignities and humiliations without budging. He never gave in to Trujillo's pressure, with the result that his name is secretly revered by Dominicans as an exalted symbol of opposition.

THE SERVILE PRESS

1. THE DOMINICAN REPUBLIC HAS THE FEWEST DAILY PAPERS of any independent nation in the world. At present there are only three in Trujilloland. They have a combined circulation—dailies and weeklies together—of less than 45,000 copies.

Startling as it seems, this stunted development is quite natural. Freedom of the press has not existed outside the statute books since the early days of 1930. "Its last manifestations in the electoral campaign of that year were stifled by terrorism, *La 42* and the post-electoral arrests," wrote Jesús de Galíndez in *The Era of Trujillo.*

Nearly six years of almost unanimous vocal opposition to the over-thrown Vásquez regime, at the cost of heavy financial sacrifices, exhausted the newspapers' reserves of energy and capital. With perhaps the single exception of *Listin Diario,* the newspapers were on the verge of collapse in that year of 1930. Now, faced with the already mounting pressure of an expanding dictatorship, the press was too enfeebled to meet the challenge and carry on. Soon Trujillo discovered how to profit from this dismal state of Dominican journalism.

"The Chief" found out that by paying lip service to the causes championed by the journalists it was relatively easy to win over to his side some honest but short-sighted editors. Where double-talk was not enough, more subtle means were employed. Government jobs, juicy official printing contracts—up to that point monopolized by *Listin Diario*—outright subsidies and bribes, mixed with an occasional threat, usually did the trick and assured the allegiance of the more "practical and realistic" publishers.

Less than six months after taking power, Trujillo had been able to bribe, coerce or cajole into his service the biggest names of Dominican journalism. Those he could not reduce fast enough into submissiveness, were either thrown into jail, forced to leave the country, or murdered. Many a free-thinking editor came out from a short visit to Trujillo's dungeons converted into an enthusiastic supporter. The story of Emilio Reyes illustrates the fate of the more stubborn ones who, regardless of Trujillo's efforts to coerce or corrupt them, stood up and fought. Editor of a small weekly and a man of deep-seated principles, Reyes insisted on continuing to write the truth as he saw it, despite ominous warnings from the local authorities. One day, after printing an article particularly critical of the Administration, Reyes was imprisoned in his home town of Azua. Whereupon it was announced that Reyes had been killed "while attempting to escape," as he was conducted under arrest to the capital.

Among all the papers *Listin Diario* took the longest to capitulate. At the time one of the oldest Latin American dailies, it had passed through its most glorious period during the days of the American military occupation. True then to the responsibilities of a free press, *Listin* conducted a courageous campaign for the restoration of the trampled-upon Dominican liberties. Never a crusading newspaper, however, *Listin* soon after the American evacuation aligned itself with the most reactionary wing of the clique in power. For its unconditional, almost slavish support of the Vásquez Administration, it became the center of bitter journalistic controversies, losing in the process much of its well deserved earlier prestige. Nonetheless, when Trujillo took power *Listin* still was the most influential Dominican newspaper.

Associated as it was with the old landed aristocracy, *Listin* could not readily acknowledge "the Chief's" glorious leadership. Its venerable columns were closed to the pack of hacks Trujillo was already supporting.

Trujillo's tactics to dislodge *Listin* were simple enough. First, all printing contracts were withdrawn, and subsidies passed over in favor of other publications. Second, the dreaded thugs of *La 42* were directed to assault the newspaper's quarters. (A member of the Pellerano family, owners of the daily, was murdered under mysterious circumstances by an alleged personal enemy.)

Under the overwhelming power mustered by the new Administration, *Listin's* resistance weakened (its opposition became nominal, tapered to a mere whisper), but nothing short of all-out surrender would satisfy the Dictator. It was left to "the Chief" to administer the *coup de grace*. Upon his orders the paper's publisher, Arturo Pellerano Sardá, was imprisoned. What happened next is a matter of conjecture. Shortly afterwards released, Pellerano announced—almost two years in advance—that he and his newspaper would support Trujillo's reelection at the ballot of 1934. Thereafter the regime could not find a more loyal ally than *Listin*. In reward, Trujillo channeled all the windfalls back to the paper and as a token of friendship made it, like all others, house organ and singer of his praises.

Then followed a period of peaceful coexistence—on Trujillo's terms, to be sure—between the regime and the press. Dominican newspapers looked like Trujillo's patrimony. The Benefactor's word was the publishers' gospel on what to print and whom to hire.

Nevertheless, by 1939, the Generalissimo was itching to try out a paper of his own. During a trip abroad, someone "sold" him the idea that a publishing house was an exceedingly profitable venture. Why then should other people make the money he could easily pocket?

With the help of a Chilean newspaperman, Daniel del Solar, whom he had met in the United States, Trujillo set out to start a journalistic empire. Del Solar, however, was not to see the project materialize. Shortly before *La Nación* was ready to go to press with its first issue, he was unceremoniously dropped from the scheme. A Dominican journalist, Rafael Vidal, took over as editor and publisher.

La Nación, the first Dominican newspaper printed on a rotary press, made its entrance on February 19, 1940. Being the first local daily to subscribe to the three big American news services, *La Nación's* pages were filled with world news, articles on current events, comics, pictures, sports and women's page features. Collaboration was solicited and even paid for. Even in its praises of the Benefactor the newcomer showed, at least in its initial stage, more restraint than its colleagues.

Notwithstanding its technical excellency *La Nación's* reception fell short of enthusiastic. To make it a going concern there was needed something more than high editorial quality. To fill the widening gap between steadily mounting expense and almost nonexistent revenue, Government advertisements were diverted toward the paper; businessmen were instructed to patronize it to the exclusion of other media, and state employees were forced to buy subscriptions. (So strictly were these rules enforced that there were instances of families receiving three and more issues.) This crushing economic pressure, ruthlessly applied under Trujillo's personal direction, promptly decimated the already thinning ranks of Dominican journalism. Reduced to only four in the capital (*Listín Diario, La Opinión, Diario de Comercio* and *La Tribuna*), and two in the interior (*La Información,* of Santiago, and *Diario de Macorís,* of San Pedro de Macorís), even these remaining newspapers soon started to fold.

The first casualties—between 1940 and 1942—were *La Tribuna, Diario de Comercio* and *Listín Diario.* The former had never been much of a paper. *Diario de Comercio* was a subsidized sheet at the service of the Italian and German legations. (It closed right after Pearl Harbor, following the inclusion of its publishers in the American "black list.") *Listín Diario,* however, was another thing. Although in its declining years it had evolved into a mouthpiece of foreign fascist groups, mainly of the Spanish *Falange, Listín's* death was a sad event, not merely for what the material loss of such an old enterprise meant but also for what it had been before becoming a captive of vested interests and then of Trujillo's dictatorship. Whatever its journalistic sins or virtues were, the passing of *Listin* marked the final eradication of all vestiges of a romantic era of Dominican journalism.

La Opinión continued for a few years as *La Nación's* sole competitor in the capital. Founded as a magazine during the middle twenties by a French national, René de Lepervanche, this afternoon daily, unlike *Listin,* had never opposed Trujillo nor was so servile in its laudation of the Dictator. Considering the circumstances, it was quite a lively newspaper.

Late in 1945, in the face of a particularly severe barrage of criticism originating in American liberal spheres, and—what was even more inauspicious—in the usually restrained U.S. State Department, the Benefactor conceived a clever maneuver to extricate himself without risking an iota of his absolute power. Since most of the criticism was leveled at his tight control over the press, "the Chief" created a "free press" of his own.

One day Trujillo's Secretary of the Presidency, Julio Vega Batlle, called upon the Editor of *La Opinión,* José Ramón Estella (a Basque married to the daughter of the late Lepervanche) and solicited his cooperation to a Government plan for a "moderate opposition campaign." [1] The Administration, explained Vega Batlle, wished to contrive such a campaign and was willing to subsidize the editor personally for his collaboration.

Fearing a trap, Estella did not accept the proposal right away. He requested an appointment with Trujillo himself for further discussion. At the ensuing conference—granted without delay—the Benefactor blandly asked the editor to go ahead with the plan as expounded by his aide. Estella made it clear he was not accepting the proffered payment. Moreover, in order to start the proposed campaign he requested, within the acknowledged bounds, guarantees of absolute freedom of action. Trujillo agreed, on the one condition that *La Opinión* refrain from attacking either himself or the Army.

The following weeks were ones of frantic labor in the *La Opinión* news room. Inspiring civic campaigns followed one after the other; the "inside" story of world events and dramatic local episodes found their way into the paper's columns. In a matter of days, *La Opinión* turned into a crusading journal, invading the broad fields of social problems, labor conditions, the cost of living, and, of all things, racial discrimination. It was, as an observer pointed out, "trying to drink it all up in one gulp." For the first time in sixteen years Dominicans had the chance to read something resembling a real newspaper and their reaction was genuine excitement.

It was too good to last. Early in 1946 in the midst of the flurry, the

---

[1] Of this peculiar incident I have first hand knowledge because I was at the time the managing-editor of *La Opinión*.

former Vice Rector of the University of Santo Domingo, Dr. José Antonio Bonilla Atiles, paid a visit to the editor's office. He had brought a letter he wanted to be printed. Addressed to a group of prominent professionals who were beating the drums of reelection almost two years in advance of election time, the document suggested that the Benefactor was not the only possible candidate. Bonilla urged his colleagues not to be hasty.

The letter did not contain any personal attack on the President. Yet it was the first time that anything directly connected with Trujillo himself had been brought up. A brief editorial conference was held to discuss Bonilla's request. Then Estella decided by himself to print the letter.

Publication of Bonilla's letter created a great deal of confusion. People did not know at first whether he was acting on his own counsel or whether he had been instructed to set off a trial balloon. In official circles—where people knew better—some measure of resentment was shown, but not enough for the paper to really worry about. Aside from a few discreet official inquiries no action was taken either against the newspaper or against Bonilla.

Yet, an upheaval was bound to happen. *La Opinión's* next issue came out with another controversial document. Bonilla's letter had touched off a minor campus explosion at the University Law School, where he taught Administrative Law, and a group of about sixty students had signed a message endorsing the professor's stand. Having printed the first letter, Estella had no choice but to continue. The Government now became alarmed at the students' intervention and there was an explosion.

Pressure was brought to bear upon the students, their parents and relatives. Consequently, many signers recanted. Another letter was hastily prepared at the National Palace for students to sign and send to *La Opinión*. They had been tricked, the official manifesto asserted, because never before publication had they set their eyes on the document printed by the newspaper only a day ago. The students had been made to believe, the Palace's version of the incident went on to say, that they were signing a petition to the University faculty pleading for a reduction of tuition fees. Why such a petition should be made almost eight months ahead of the beginning of the next term was never explained. With those who refused to join in the recantation movement the Government showed patience, tolerance and understanding. However, when the next registration period started, they were flatly refused the right to register. A new wave of recantation followed.[2]

"Moderate" opposition was tossed overboard as a result of the students' letter. On this occasion Trujillo did not bother to receive the paper's

[2] My sister, Maricusa Ornes, lost her chance to graduate at the University of Santo Domingo Law School, on account of her reiterated refusal to recant.

editor nor did he ask Estella's cooperation. A brief telephone call from the Palace was enough. A campaign of insults and vilification was started in all newspapers against Dr. Bonilla. The courageous professor—following an abortive attempt on his life by one of Trujillo's thugs, Colonel Apolinar Jáquez—took asylum at the Mexican Embassy and shortly thereafter went into exile with his family.

The Bonilla occurrence was the grand climax of Trujillo's journalistic farce. Its ending, however, was anti-climactic. The Benefactor made a fair offer to the Lepervanche family, who, after selling their property, packed up and left the country. A few months later *La Opinión* merged with *La Nación*.

Ciudad Trujillo had achieved by 1947 the dubious distinction of being a one-newspaper capital. Yet, by a strange twist, "the Chief" was no longer the owner of *La Nación* when the process of elimination was finally consummated. He hates headaches, at least business headaches, for the sake of a few thousand dollars. And a newspaper is a very tricky piece of property. Newsprint shortages during the war years, lack of skilled labor and other complexities plaguing Dominican journalism proved too much for the Generalissimo's forbearance. To relieve his mind of the petty problems of everyday newspaper management, "the Chief" disposed of the property—at a profit no doubt. The shares of stock were transferred first to the *Partido Dominicano* and then, in 1946, to Senator Mario Fermín Cabral. In 1957 Trujillo took over *La Nación*.

In 1947 the talent for enterprise of an American promoter, Stanley Ross, proved overpowering enough to persuade the Benefactor he should put his money anew in a newspaper. Ross prevailed upon Trujillo that this time he needed a different sort of house organ. It was agreed that to identify *El Caribe* (as the new publication eventually was baptized) with the regime would be a mistake. Foreign consumption—a thing always dear to "the Chief"—was the *leit motif*. The new paper should be "independent, non-political" and, unlike the rest of the press, should not use so many laudatory adjectives preceding mention of the Benefactor's name. In *El Caribe* the Generalissimo would be called simply "President Trujillo." This, and the introduction of the technique of basing news stories upon a mixture of half truths, innuendoes and outright lies (until then Dominican newspapers had been plain, unsophisticated liars), were going to be the upstart's major contributions to Dominican journalism.

A dummy corporation was founded to carry out the new formula. Stanley Ross appeared as President of the corporation and editor of *El Caribe*. Notwithstanding all efforts to conceal the identity of the real owner, everybody knew who had invested the required half million dollars to start the paper. Lest there be any mistake, doubts about ownership were further dispelled at the outset by the fact that most of the names in the original list of stockholders were of people in Trujillo's employment, including his then personal business manager, Bienvenido Gómez. "I supplied the necessary funds for the appearance of the great newspaper *El Caribe,* on April 14, 1948," said Trujillo for the benefit of the Inter American Press Association, in October 1956.

Unquestionably *El Caribe* revelled in the use of the lie as an instrument of policy. Shielded behind the presumptuous motto "at the service of the Antillian peoples," the new daily set out in a big way to break the few rules of ethics still in use in local news rooms. The *Foro Público* (letters to the editor section)—one of its most successful innovations—was shortly being employed to bludgeon Trujillo's friends and foes alike, with anonymous slanderous missives written at the National Palace. Its new style of journalism, full of distortions and suppressions—some big, some little—usually crude, occasionally clever—promptly established *El Caribe* as a freewheeling, spectacular newsmonger.

Ross rose from obscurity to dazzling notoriety, but *El Caribe* proved to be, despite ceaseless promotion and self-advertised big circulation, a money-draining proposition. After eight months of a fantastic, injudicious and wholly extravagant spree of unchecked spending the paper had sunk deep in the red, the deficit over $100,000. Trujillo's ax fell on Ross's head. "The Chief" appointed his then right hand man, Anselmo Paulino Alvarez, to take over *El Caribe.*

Under Paulino's stewardship—which lasted from January 1949 to February 1954—*El Caribe* was reshaped to fit the role of unquestioning supporter of the Trujillo regime. The new book of house style threw out as a useless sham the Ross-imposed restraints in the use of adjectives before Trujillo's name. It was considered less sophisticated but more frank and honorable. However, those of the Ross-devised features which had proven their worth as instruments of political repression were carried on and sometimes improved. Trujillo himself, through his collaborator at the helm, took a direct interest in setting the political line of the newspaper.

Paulino did not know anything about the actual running of a newspaper. But he and Trujillo knew where and how to get people who could help them. This time I was the chosen target. The fact that I was quietly practicing law did not save me. I had retired from journalism in 1946 when, freshly released from a *trujillista* political jail, I had refused to put my byline to an article praising the Benefactor, as requested by the new publisher of *La Opinión.*

Now, however, Trujillo needed an editor to take Ross's place and that was all, despite my past record as a "subversive." When I tried to avoid the issue, Trujillo sent me word that I should remember what happens to stubborn opponents. Then, under further threats of pressure against myself, my blood relatives and in-laws, I was left with no choice but to assume the post of editor in chief of the newspaper, which in spite of its impressive name was a totally subordinate and technical position from which I exerted no influence whatsoever on the political conduct of the paper. I do not try to justify myself. Maybe I could have held out against Trujillo and still stay alive and free—free, but unable to work and support my family; free, but unable to travel out of the country; free, but unable to publish any of my writings, however non-political, and free, but unable to mingle with old friends.

It was a "shot gun wedding" bound to end in divorce. In the interim, however, as editor of *El Caribe* I had to write many *trujillista* editorials (some with my by-line), although all the lead articles, particularly those attacking foreigners, were always dictated at the National Palace, and most of the time Trujillo himself edited their text.

To say that I disagreed with the editorial policy of *El Caribe* and with the things I was myself writing, would certainly sound now as a very flat piece of self-justification. In February, 1954, I had the opportunity to buy *El Caribe*. To indemnify himself from his losses during Ross's administration of the newspaper, Trujillo had sold the corporation, two or three years before, to the Dominican Government. (A few shares of stock had been left in the hands of the *Partido Dominicano* to manipulate the corporation directorship.) At last Paulino's turn had come and he was already slated—though no one suspected it yet, least of all himself—to fall into disfavor. The Benefactor was quietly engaged in the task of wresting power from his favorite's hands. *El Caribe* was put up for sale, and I submitted the highest bid. With the help of a personal loan made by the Bank of Reserves (of which at the moment I was a director), I paid in cash the required purchase price of $634,455.61, obtaining ownership of every one of the corporation's 1,165 shares of stock. To keep the dummy corporation going I put ten of those shares in the names of my wife and other relatives and personal friends.

I had then the quixotic idea that as the owner of *El Caribe* I would be able to change—gradually of course—the low character of the newspaper. By then I had had enough contact with Trujillo, but I was still under the illusion that much of what happened in the country was due to the fact that the Generalissimo, surrounded by self-seekers and sycophants, did not have the right people around him nor did he know everything that his subordinates were doing in his name. That I was one hundred per cent wrong I now readily admit: each Dominican newspaper, regardless of ownership, in order to subsist has to dance to Trujillo's queer tunes. And those tunes are his, no one else's.

To be sure, I was the owner of the newspaper. No one ever told me how to handle its finances; how much newsprint I should buy or have in stock; how many pages an issue should have. On editorial matters, however, things were different. Trujillo kept on acting as if the newspaper had never changed hands. After a while my wife (who reluctantly had approved of my venture into *El Caribe's* ownership) and I had our definite second thoughts. The outcome was just a matter of time.

Before taking our final decision to break away from the poisonous environment in which we were submerged, a full year and a half of bitter uncertainty, anxieties and frustrations were to elapse. A totally unforeseen accident was going to rescue us from under Trujillo. One day I got into trouble with the Benefactor because of a minor misprint in *El Caribe*.

The contretemps that got me into difficulty involved a caption. On October 27, 1955, a picture in *El Caribe* showed a crowd of flower-bearing school children placing their bouquets at the base of one of the 1,800 busts of Trujillo. Beneath was a caption informing my readers that the little ones were putting their blossoms on the Benefactor's "tomb." The error, an obvious minor newsroom mix-up, became serious only because of "the Chief's" power and idiosyncracies. To put Trujillo's immortality in doubt is the worst conceivable offense to his ego, and offenses do not go unpunished in Trujilloland. Fortunately, before the misprint appeared, my wife and I had arranged a trip to the United States to attend a meeting of the Inter American Press Association in New Orleans. And, although the big guns of the National Palace's propaganda office had already started firing against me, we left the Dominican Republic, as scheduled, on October 28.

Apparently, in the confusion of the moment, no one had issued instructions to detain me, a rather difficult decision in any case, since Trujillo, the only one who can make up his mind without fear of the consequences, was not around. Three or four days before, he had gone to Kansas City on a family trip which included a $200,000 series of cattle and horse deals.

During the days following our arrival in the United States I had an opportunity to read the Dominican press, and what I saw there about myself did not look reassuring. A campaign of personal vilification against me had started in *La Nación*. Among the printed material, moreover, there was a very amusing letter attacking me but addressed to none other than Trujillo's little brother Héctor, the President. That, by the way, showed the unusual importance attached to the incident, since Héctor's chief function is not to punish political offenders but to wear out the carpets of the National Palace hurrying from the western wing of the huge building to the eastern side, where big brother gives orders and rules.

My role as one of Trujillo's publishers had always been disturbing to my wife and me. Now our sense of disgust increased, and after a great deal of deep inner conflict and mutual consultation we decided the time for a decision had finally come. No matter what, we would not return to the Dominican Republic.

Before the final breach, however, I made a trip to Kansas City from New York City, where I had gone, and personally informed the Generalissimo that I was not going back. I offered him, as a peace gesture, my newspaper for sale, and he politely asked me to write him a letter to that effect, which I did several weeks later, on December 14, 1955. During our Kansas City conference Trujillo was very nice. He went out of his way to give me the impression that he would be pleased to let bygones be bygones and that he was not kicking me out. He seemed unable to grasp the whole meaning of my decision and appeared totally at a loss trying to understand why anyone could react in such a way to a few insulting letters sent by him to a newspaper.

The letter I wrote Trujillo upon his request has since been passed around as a proof of my "treason" and of my alleged abortive attempt at "blackmailing" the Benefactor. Trujillo's propagandists, as well as Stanley Ross, say that I wrote the letter to extort $100,000 from Trujillo in order to buy a Spanish-language daily in New York, and that, when rejected, I turned against the Benefactor, suddenly finding that the "eternal and absolute loyalty and friendship" that I had sworn for him in the same letter "was no longer eternal, loyal nor friendly."

The letter does not bear out these allegations. Its chief purpose was to remind the Benefactor, perhaps too diplomatically, that I was not going back to the poisonous climate of the Dominican Republic where I had been born and lived all my life; where most of my relatives reside and all my property is located; where I had enjoyed a profitable law practice, owned the largest newspaper, held a high government position (Vice President of the Development Commission), had been a bank director and otherwise had standing and was entitled to certain advantages. Furthermore, I refused to recant, making plain at the same time that I was not returning because the unhealthy environment of my native land was no longer bearable to me. Only incidentally did I offer my newspaper for sale or mention any other business transaction.

It is unfortunate that with only a few days out of the country I had not had time enough to disengage myself from the peculiar mannerisms which form part of the present Dominican way of life and so I still had to write my otherwise frank letter in the language peculiar to all communications to the Benefactor if an answer was to be forthcoming. Somewhat needlessly I told Trujillo again what I planned to do with the money in the event of the sale of *El Caribe*. Morover, as I would need additional capital had I bought *El Diario de Nueva York,* I so advised him of this. I did not, either in my letter or in any other document, nor in any other way, try to "sell" Trujillo on any editorial policy had I bought the aforementioned daily.

Trujillo answered that he was not interested in buying newspaper properties, either in his own country or abroad, and as it was Christmas time he wished me "health and prosperity." Thereupon he illegally assumed control over my newspaper without paying for it.

Upon his orders, decrees were issued stripping me of every post and medal I ever had. In the manner reminiscent of Nazi and Communist techniques of smearing former public officials cast out of favor, my family and I were publicly libelled in the most vicious way. My own newspaper under its brand-new Trujillo-appointed management joined the pack and printed disgraceful stories and cartoons. Professional, political and social organizations declared me *persona non grata*. I was even asked to return the keys of Ciudad Trujillo, which had been granted me in an apparently thoughtless moment. This I could not comply with since the keys had been removed, together with many other little mementoes, by Trujillo's own secret police during their search and subsequent occupation of our home. Finally, my father, Germán Ornes, a respected lawyer and former professor, was imprisoned and condemned to two years in prison on trumped-up fantastic charges of drug addiction.

What has happened since with *El Caribe's* property is an involved *trujillista* operation. For months I did everything within my reach to assert my rights. The Inter American Press Association (IAPA) in successive decisions recognized me as the legitimate proprietor and legal representative of *El Caribe*. Trujillo's contentions that there was a private dispute between a debtor (myself) and a creditor (the bank) were rejected as baseless. Meanwhile, in the Dominican Republic nothing was done, though the usurpation of my legitimate rights was maintained by the regime.

Suddenly the Banco de Reservas de la República Dominicana announced in the press the transfer of its creditor rights to an American-owned construction outfit doing business in the country: Elmhurst Contracting Co. Then without ever getting in contact with me and without paying heed to my repeated efforts to fulfill my obligations and exert my ownership rights, Elmhurst foreclosed on the property. Neither Elmhurst nor the Bank of Reserves ever answered one of the letters written to them in my behalf by my American attorney, R. Lawrence Siegel. This attitude prompted Siegel to point out in a letter addressed to the IAPA that in his experience he had "never met or heard of anything comparable to the Bank (of Reserves)-*El Caribe*-Ornes situation."

"It is incredible," said Seigel, "that a responsible financial institution will conduct its affairs with a depositor so as not to acknowledge his request for information concerning his bank account and so as not to comply with requests for delivery of his bank statements and cancelled checks. It is unbelievable that a creditor-bank holding paper for a balance of a principal sum which has been reduced to the amount of $489,000.00 by the debtor after making all previous payments in time would not be amenable to the requests on the part of the debtor and his attorney for a conference regarding the payment of such debt." He finished by saying "but all of these inconceivable and astonishing things did occur here."

2.   DOMINICAN JOURNALISM IS AN ENDLESS EXCURSION INTO hagiography.

Editors and columnists daily come close to putting their hero, Generalissimo Rafael L. Trujillo, on a par with the Deity. Reading the Dominican press without any other acquaintance with Generalissimo Trujillo's activities and policies would give one the impression that the Benefactor combines the creative mind of a Copernicus with the inventive one of a Marconi, that he has the military genius of an Alexander the Great combined with the statemanship of a Talleyrand. On April 4, 1957, in a single paragraph of an article printed in *El Caribe,* Trujillo was called "the Great, Saviour of America, Orientator of the World and First Anti-Communist of the American Continent." His birthplace, San Cristóbal, has been compared to Bethlehem.

Nowhere in the world, except perhaps in the Soviet Union, has journalism become so degrading. Regardless of ownership, each newspaper is a conveyor of Trujillo's propaganda and a willing tool of the Dictator.

Trujillo constantly encourages distorted editorials and articles as well as slanted headlines in the press. This, along with outright misrepresentation in the offerings of the radio network owned by brother Arismendy Trujillo, is the daily fare of Dominican public opinion.

There is no other press but Trujillo's press. Thus, what is printed in the newspapers is the most reliable index to official purpose. Each article and editorial, as well as most of the news stories, are the direct or tangential expression of government policy. News about government and political activities is always presented in strict conformity to the text of the official press releases. Reporters, no matter how much they know about a particular news item, will never write a story until told to do so. Then, they do not dare to make any independent check on the pertinent facts. So, the general outlook of the Dominican press, as set forth by the capital publications, represents Trujillo's policies as faithfully as Moscow's *Pravda* and *Izvestia* represent the Kremlin.

There is no overt government censorship, although the Secretary of Security is empowered to impose it whenever he sees fit. There is no official authority or censorship bureau to which journalists must resort in order to check on the publication of their stories. There is no need for them. The actual situation was summarized years ago by an editor as one of "edit at your own risk but be damn careful what you print." This accounts for the formulation of a strict, unwritten voluntary code of self-censorship. Nevertheless, in all editorial and composing rooms there are always informers ready to report any dangerous deviation from the "line."

The standing set of directives, established for many years, makes everything fit into grooves. In a given situation the newsmen know exactly what to write. One of the unbreakable dogmas, of course, is that the Benefactor can do no wrong. However, Trujillo feels himself so well entrenched nowadays that there are very few editorial "taboos" actually in force. Papers print foreign dispatches about workers' strikes, civil rights legislation, democratic upheavals, longing for freedom among other peoples, revolutions and overthrowing of dictatorial governments, all unheard-of examples of news reporting under any other totalitarian dictatorship. Editors do take pains to softpedal stories about foreign university student strikes, but only because "the Chief" fears they might instill perilous thoughts in his own students.

But on local matters, to keep their jobs editors must sing the *trujillista* tunes over and over. In the news rooms and editorial sanctums the prevailing habit is to write only what is good for Trujillo. "Dominican journalists' main difficulty is to find a new adjective; he who finds a new idea is already a genius," wrote Jesús de Galíndez. With a nice touch of irony, and doubtless with an unconscious vengeance as well, Dominican editors' originality is being revealed every Monday, for several years now, in an identically worded *El Caribe* front-page headline reading: "Public Hail Trujillo at the Race Track."

Cynicism is rampant. There are very few journalists who in private would not talk sarcastically of Trujillo's megalomania or otherwise deride the salient features of the regime, but they will never say a word in public, because there is too much fear in their hearts. Shabbily treated by the regime (with a few exceptions among publishers), and most of them badly paid, newspapermen feel themselves the neglected stepchildren of the system. Yet they know that it is not possible for a publisher, editor or writer to earn his living and continue to defy the regime.

There is a residue of humor left. Trujillo may have been able to force them to write what he wants, but he has not succeeded in making them take those things seriously. An old-time joke in *El Caribe* illustrates this point. Every Sunday afternoon on his return from covering the exploits of the then undefeated and seemingly invincible polo team led by Lieutenant General Doctor Rafael L. "Ramfis" Trujillo, Jr., the sports editor would be received by his fellow writers with a unanimous "Who won today?"

Under the circumstances the fare which Dominican newspapers serve their readers is boring. Preferential treatment is given to political rallies where civic, business, labor and professional groups pay homage to "the Chief's" exalted policies, as well as to lengthy and repetitious reports on the country's economic development, cleanliness and progress; the initiation of public works; the educational advances and the health improvement programs. Banner headlines are usually reserved for stories of the unveiling of busts of the Benefactor, his mother or his little brother Héctor. In June, 1956, the inauguration of "President Trujillo Street" in the city of Santiago was a lead story of *El Caribe* requiring the pens of two reporters.

One of the main tasks of the *trujillista* press is to paint a happy picture of life under the guidance of the Benefactor. Calamities and pessimism have no place in the jolly frame of Dominican journalism. Squalor, poverty and sickness among Dominicans cannot be shown in print.

Nevertheless, local news about crime and accidents are reported quite freely—almost in the way in which American newspapers cover such happenings. Except—and here we find another Dominican peculiarity—when a mysterious crime or "accident" is involved. Then the papers, if printing the story at all, adhere without deviation to the not always logical police version. This accounts, at times, for some peculiar reading, as in the occasion, in 1949, when on orders from lieutenant general (later police colonel) Federico Fiallo the newspapers printed a picture showing a silk stocking and a bottle of whisky conspicuously over the charred ruins of an automobile. The purpose was to give credence to the police version that the Architect Trene Pérez (well known as a recalcitrant "indifferent") had lost his life in an accident, while on a drinking spree with an unidentified female whose body was never produced.

Hardly ever are editorial comments printed in the monotonous pages of Dominican newspapers. And, whenever printed, they either consist of syrupy accounts of Trujillo's latest accomplishments or of bitter denunciations of the Benefactor's enemies. In the latter case the initiative always rests upon the Generalissimo himself. The dirtiest ones are personally dictated by him. Moreover, even in the rare instances in which a new idea is suggested by an editor, he feels obliged to ascribe its origins to "the Chief's" storehouse of thoughts.

On occasion editorials are employed to create an artifiical demand for measures the Government has already been contemplating. Whenever the Benefactor wants to impose new taxes or harsher economic controls, he plants editorials, articles and letters reproaching businessmen for their selfishness, greed and other sins. Suddenly big words like "profiteering," "popular welfare" and "creeping inflation" are unearthed. People in business are made to appear as vampires of their fellow-men's blood. The same energy and ingenuity is shown by the press in denouncing those people the Generalissimo is interested in stamping out of business in order to take over their coveted enterprises. Then names appear in print. Otherwise the press just gives a general picture of the immorality, lack of patriotism, wickedness and selfishness of the merchant class.

Under the pressure of the intense press campaigns the Government appears submissive to public demand and soon thereafter a presidential message is sent to Congress calling for remedial legislation, which is promptly passed.

Dominican papers subscribe to one or more of the American news services and provide their readers with an ample amount of foreign information. As a rule, they do not slant the agencies' reports, unless directed by the Palace. Whenever relations with another nation go through a period of strain, the local press receives, straight from Trujillo's offices, a number of stories on economic distress, political unrest, official corruption and communist activities in the "enemy" country. During part of 1956 and 1957 a campaign of this sort was conducted against the government of Puerto Rico. Cuba had been an earlier victim.

A "must" are reprints from foreign publications eulogizing the Benefactor. The press prints long dispatches under foreign datelines showing how favorably the Generalissimo's achievements are viewed in other countries, especially in the United States. "The Chief" is always willing to pay well for this kind of publicity, so well in fact that Ciudad Trujillo has become a known pot of gold for adventurous and unscrupulous foreign publishers and reporters. The Dominican Government once paid over $100,-000 for publication af a "special issue" of a third-rate Mexican magazine called *Auge*. The issue—later reprinted in English—never circulated in Mexico.

At the same time, uncomplimentary foreign comments are kept out of the newspapers. Except for those few with access to the foreign press, Dominicans first learned about Galíndez's disappearance and Gerald Lester Murphy's murder when their government decided to provide its own slanted versions of certain aspects of the two cases. "The daily newspaper *El Caribe*," said the *New York Times*, August 13, 1957, "has not printed a word about the hiring of Mr. (Morris) Ernst and former New York Supreme Court Justice William H. Munson to investigate the (Galíndez) case. Nor has mention been made in print of the hiring of Sidney S. Baron, a public relations man, as press agent for the Government."

This brings us to an amusing feature of Dominican journalism—the practice of publishing the Government's version or rebuttal of suppressed news stories. Occasionally Dominicans find themselves reading heated editorials on matters that were never given to them as straight news. For example, the accusations leveled against the Trujillo regime by Representative Charles O. Porter (D.-Ore.) have not been printed in the Dominican Republic. However, there have been many insulting editorials and articles in *El Caribe* and *La Nación* against the courageous American Congress-man as well as derogatory analysis of his motivation. "It is apparently necessary to rebut the charges you don't publish in a country where every-body knows they aren't true anyway" was Murray Kempton's caustic com-ment on the queer situation.

Sometimes, stories about important events are delayed for weeks and even months. In 1956 the latest Cuban-Dominican controversy did not find space in the Dominican newspapers until the mediation team of the Organization of American States advised both countries to directly nego-tiate a settlement. Then the Foreign Office communiqué was printed as if it were a normal follow-up on a story everybody had been reading about in the newspapers. No background material was ever printed.

In a normal edition of a Dominican newspaper, Trujillo's name is men-tioned as often as one hundred times, usually preceded by his full titles and several adjectives. But whenever a so-called "special edition" is printed (a thing that occurs three or four times a year, on occasions such as the Benefactor's birthday), adulation knows no limit. Every corporation —foreign or domestic—every merchant, every professional association, cultural or social organization, consistently buys space (ranging from a quarter to a full page) to congratulate "the Chief" and to testify their love for him. These editions are opportunities for out-of-grace politicians or citizens accused of "indifference" toward the regime, to find an easy way of advertising their all-out support of *trujillismo*. On the birthday edi-tion of October 24th, 1956, thirty-three Trujillo-owned corporations bought space to congratulate Trujillo.

Needless to say, under Trujillo the life of an editor is no bed of roses. Editors get angry summons from the National Palace for a variety of causes—from a displeasing item in the Social Column to a misplaced word in the lead editorial.

A Dominican editor must always be careful to whom he gives hos-pitality in his columns. Porfirio Rubirosa, for instance, is good copy for editors anywhere else but in his native land. Although he has issued the famous Dominican lover a permanent diplomatic passport to promote his country abroad, the Benefactor is too jealous to allow too much publicity in his own press to a Dominican known better than himself in the interna-tional sets.

At the time of Rubirosa's marriage to the fabulous American heiress Barbara Hutton, Dominican newspapers were permitted a fair coverage of the affair. One afternoon, however, I received in my office of *El Caribe* a telephone call from the Palace, and the favorite in turn told me "the Chief" was inquiring whether there was not more "constructive news" than the antics of Rubirosa and his bride. The hint was taken and the

Rubirosa-Hutton romance was cut short—at least for the readers of
El Caribe—a few weeks ahead of its actual ending.

The term "constructive news" has an elusive meaning in Dominican
journalese. It can be either anything in praise of the regime or a particularly vicious attack on its enemies. All kinds of news are constantly
suppressed for not being "constructive" enough. For lack of "constructive-
ness" big news events like the massacre of 15,000 Haitians on Dominican
soil in 1937 are still waiting to be reported in full by the local press.

At regular intervals Trujillo invites the press to formulate "constructive" criticism, but the invitations are wisely acknowledged as empty gestures. Nothing ever comes out of the suggestion except, perhaps, a few
surreptitious jokes.

My second experience with a non-constructive story also involved
Rubirosa. Months after his separation from Miss Hutton, our Romeo came
back home to invest part of the loot in a confiscated cocoa farm (which he
later sold back to the Dominican Government for $800,000) and to par-
ticipate in a series of polo games.

A moderate amount of publicity was allowed. Yet the respite was going
to be short-lived. It ended the day after one of my sports editors had the
happy idea of interviewing Rubi at a cockfight. Although treated as a
normal sports feature, the story had shattering repercussions. Trujillo
personally took exception to the fact that Rubirosa had been quoted as
saying that prior to this occasion he had never attended a cockfight. A
letter to the *Foro Público,* sent by messenger from the National Palace,
called the hero of our story a liar. He should remember, the document said,
that he had been brought up among gamblers and had spent his early life
next door to his father's cockpit. The editor of *El Caribe* (myself) was
bluntly queried on the amount of money received to promote Rubirosa.
Neither Rubirosa nor I bothered to answer the letter, an unheard-of thing
in a country where people rush to answer whenever their names are mentioned in the dreaded section. With that we spoiled Trujillo's fun.

With such effective *de facto* control of newspaper writing hardly any
legislation is needed. A press law has been enacted, however, but it is
rarely enforced. Its main features are of an administrative character, providing for the registration of publishers and editors, as well as the daily
deposit (a provision strictly enforced) of two copies of each edition at
the Secretary of Security's offices. The law is a sharp razor to put out of
business any publication, if it is desired to do so.

Another law, of April 1933, declares that anyone who might by his
writings, letters, speeches or in other ways spread "information of subversive character, injurious to the authorities or defamatory of the government" should be tried as a common criminal.

On March 26, 1947, Trujillo signed law No. 1387, whereby any person of Dominican nationality who with the purpose of defaming the Republic or its institutions spreads false and malicious news among foreigners residing or passing through the Dominican Republic, or who transmits such news abroad by any means of communication, will be condemned to from two to three years in prison. If this offense is repeated, the offender is liable to the maximum penalty of the law, which is five years in prison. Foreigners found guilty of violations of this act may be summarily deported from the country by decree of the Executive.

Act No. 4602, passed by Congress in December 1956, provides for the registration of agents and correspondents of foreign publications and news services. Since registration can be withheld by the authorities at will, this insures the government absolute control over the representatives of the foreign press permanently stationed in the Dominican Republic.

With or without this act, the predicament of the American news gathering services in the Dominican Republic is not enviable. Outwardly there is no censorship for outgoing news. The correspondents of the news agencies can file whatever stories they want without prior presentation to the authorities. (Usually upon request from the government the cable offices supply copies of dispatches.) However, the news services are systematically exploited for Trujillo's purposes, and find it difficult to report impartially unfavorable notices of the regime.

The problem stems from the fact that the news services do not consider the Dominican Republic newsworthy enough to warrant the permanent stationing of regular correspondents. Hence, they have to rely upon "stringers," who usually are highly placed local journalists (sometimes even government officials). Upon the judgment of these men rests the filing of local news with an international angle. In accordance with their ingrained habits they always play safe and only file those stories released for foreign consumption by the National Palace. Whenever they receive a query from their main offices, this is promptly passed on to Trujillo's office where the answer is prepared. Frequently the "stringers" are directed by Trujillo to exploit certain facts in a manner carefully calculated to serve the political aims of the regime. Occasionally the Government files the stories directly, sending a copy of the message later to the correspondents.

Unknowingly, as in the case of the controversy between Costa Rica and the Dominican Republic in 1954, the news services have been used at times as tools of international friction. In the Costa Rica instance a news dispatch from Ciudad Trujillo (attributed to the Dominican Army Intelligence Service), accusing the Costa Rican government of harboring European communists, originated a bitter international incident before the Organization of American States. The ensuing investigation proved that the Dominican Government could not back its baseless charges. Had the news agencies had regular and independent correspondents in Ciudad Trujillo, unafraid to check the facts, they would have discovered beforehand that the explosive story was based on unwarranted hearsay gathered by Stanley Ross.

The situation could be remedied easily if the American news agencies would enter into a "pool" arrangement and send down a regular reliable correspondent. I know that a "pool" arrangement, in which one or a few newspapermen represent the rest, is only justified when there are grave problems hampering the free gathering of news. It is my judgment that such a situation exists in the Dominican Republic. That sort of arrangement is entirely justified if the news services are really interested in serving their clients unslanted news from the Dominican Republic.

The same problems are faced on the radio-broadcasting field. There, though a few privately-owned radio stations still operate, the biggest network *La Voz Dominicana* (which includes television and other media of entertainment as well) is another of the Family businesses. This radio and television network gives most of its time to news programs, which faithfully reflect the government line.

In spite of the fact that many people doubted the wisdom of investing in television in a country where relatively few could afford receivers, and where other more basic improvements were needed, the Dominican Republic was one of the first Latin American countries to exploit that medium of communication. Brother Arismendy, with the help of heavy government subsidies, undertook the difficult operation. Nowadays there is no doubt of television's popularity with those who can afford sets. (According to reliable information there are about 3,000 sets in the country.)

Although the whole operation cost the Dominican Government about $2,000,000 a year, it is considered worthwhile in prestige.

3.

"Now you are coming down to the Dominican Republic; just one thing please: stay out of the *Foro Público*." This was the only advice tendered by an American corporation official to his wife, who was joining him in Ciudad Trujillo.

However good it might be, the counsel was rather academic because it could scarcely be followed. The honor, or the disgrace, of appearing in the *Foro Público*—the letters to the editor section of *El Caribe*—depends entirely upon "the Chief's" whims.

Every morning, with fear in their hearts, Dominican officials and other prominent citizens and residents of the country read this section before anything else. The appearance of anyone's name is a sure sign of imminent trouble for that person. Begun apparently as a bona-fide column of letters from readers, the *Foro Público* soon was corrupted into one of the most feared weapons devised by the Benefactor in his relentless quest for new means to subjugate people to his will.

Trujillo chooses friends and foes indiscriminately as targets for attacks printed in this section. The letters, though often caustic, are not always accurate. Discerning Dominicans know that they are the Benefactor's way of informing the public about the current direction of his caprices.

If such slanderous and vindictive material were to be submitted to any newspaper of a free country it would be considered the work of a neurotic and tossed into the wastebasket. Yet in the Dominican Republic it is not only printed, but Cabinet members who are mentioned in such letters feel obliged to write long and elaborate explanations and even apologies. Actually, they are under compulsion to do so in accordance with a Dominican Party directive, but in obeying they grovel in the most abject language. Those who do not apologize, or explain, or are not abject enough when doing so, are kept continually under attack until they conform to the acceptable form of answer. After the humiliating process is completed, they are usually fired, or perhaps they are transferred to some minor post which they dare not refuse. Sometimes, if they perform their acts of personal obeisance with conspicuous humility, they are pardoned, and their retraction and repentance accepted—at least until another time.

Why are people so filled with fright at the appearance of their names in the *Foro Público?* Simply because they are aware that the letters printed are all written in the National Palace and that they are under personal attack from the Benefactor. As editor and later publisher and owner of *El Caribe* I know who was the author of the majority of the letters published in the *Foro.* I know, as do many Dominicans, that Trujillo himself dictates many of those letters, the rest being written by his most trusted aides in the Palace, including highly placed figures in the Cabinet.

As a rule, the printed letters complain about laziness, idleness, graft, alcoholism, malingering, thievery, sexual deviations, infidelity and moral turpitude among public officials, businessmen and members of the social set. Whether the accusations are true or false is not really important. The charges of vice and corruption, even those levelled against persons high in the regime's hierarchy, are taken by the people as matter of fact occurrences. This disturbing fact, which mirrors current social conditions, reveals the lethargic state to which Dominicans have descended. Most people appear to draw the obvious conclusion that such excesses are inherent in the nature of the prevailing system, and that there is nothing to be done about it. If but a minute part of these shocking accusations were justified, the Trujillo regime would be one of the most corrupt in history!

There are reasons to believe, however, that many charges are trumped up and used by Trujillo to discredit actual or potential enemies, collaborators in disgrace as well as business competitors. Yet certain accusations appear to be true. Although many of the victims are already marked for sacrifice for reasons other than those stated, many times the charges seem to be based upon truth, particularly those concerning subordinate government employees, against whom political lies are hardly needed as reasons for removal.

Usually dismissals and even court procedures follow the publication of charges in the *Foro*. Let us not get the wrong idea, however. If Trujillo becomes incensed over corruption to the extent that he takes part of his time to order such letters to the editors, it is not because he has higher ethical scruples than any democratic ruler. It is simply because a corrupt act is a propitious windfall that helps him to offer a circus to his audience by lashing and taking to the sacrificial stone the alleged culprits.

Trujillo is so pleased with his devilish toy that the job of selecting the material for the letters became for a while his main hobby. He has even written letters thanking *El Caribe* for the so-called moralizing effects of *El Foro Público*. Brother Héctor, the President, has done likewise. Lately, however, Trujillo's interest in the *Foro* has lessened, apparently because he is kept busy by more pressing issues, such as the Galíndez-Murphy case and the one-man crusade of Representative Charles O. Porter.

The importance of the *Foro Público* in Dominican life is so great that there has appeared a new slang expression: *forear,* meaning, to make someone appear in the *Foro. Foreado* is the person whose name has appeared in the column. The signer of the letter (as a rule a fictitious name) is called the *forista.* Sometimes the made-up name of the signer is a combination of names of real persons who might have some bearing upon the letter's subject.

El Foro became so successful after its introduction in Dominican journalism by the American newspaperman Stanley Ross, that *La Nación* soon started its own section entitled *El Lector Dice Que* (The Reader Says That) to occupy a place in the unsavory forum of name-calling.

The device of the published letter is at times used by Trujillo to manufacture "public opinion" in support of some specific policy. A chain reaction is started which usually takes the form of an *encuesta* or "symposium." When the first letter answering a particular question posed by the newspapers (always under orders from the National Palace) carries Trujillo's signature the matter is very simple. "The Chief's" suggestions are followed by a flood of flattering letters, praising the brilliance of his ideas. On Trujillo's cue the same people who had written letters against the institution of the Vice-Presidency fourteen years before, wrote in 1955 news letters clamoring for its re-establishment. It's quite another thing when the Generalissimo's stand is not clearly stated at the outset. Then the *encuesta* drags out for days with little or no response, until the floodgates are opened by the publication of a letter signed by someone the people consider authorized to give a hint about "the Chief's" ideas upon the subject submitted for discussion.

People have asked me, over and over again, what would be the lot of a publisher who refused to print such material. Well, the publisher crazy enough to do such a thing would be cooking his own goose. Upon refusal he would surely occupy a vermin-infested cell in a jail. "The Chief" would then print not a letter, but an article, with the rejected material plus some addenda, under the publisher's by-line. In the meantime the news of the publisher's jailing would be suppressed. When the storm finally broke into print neither the publisher nor the person he was trying to protect with his refusal would be spared. The publisher would be accused of some common crime that had no connection with the real issue. And, worse yet, the third party—the person originally under fire—would never know that his friend fell into disgrace and went to jail because of him. Probably he would feel very happy that a scoundrel, who three days before was attacking him, finally had been exposed for what he was—a common criminal. This may sound unbelievable—but so is Trujillo.

EVERY TRUJILLO A KING

THE BENEFACTOR, LIKE NAPOLEON, HAS PACKED THE GOVERNMENT with his close relatives. To impose his kin upon his harassed people he has spurned both ethics and traditions and has made a mockery of the due process of law. To help the Trujillos to rise and accumulate wealth, while denying such an opportunity to many others, the Benefactor has followed a course that found few precedents in history. He has made presidents out of brothers; although a sworn enemy of the Dominican aristocracy, which he secretly admires, he has converted daughters into shining queens; he has made distinguished lady writers out of wives and a "paragon of the womanly virtues" out of his own mother. His children and other relatives are generals, ambassadors and ministers; they also are black marketeers, speculators and profiteers who have waxed rich during the Era of Trujillo.

There is no question that Trujillo has always been thoughtful of his large family, which includes his parents, his ten brothers and sisters, scores of nephews and nieces, both legitimate and illegitimate. He has transformed the whole country into a field of exploitation for anyone named Trujillo. As has been aptly said: "The brothers export, the brother-in-law imports, and the head of the family, naturally, deports." There is not a poor Trujillo in the Dominican Republic. With the booty from the country Trujillo has even fed his numerous mistresses and their relatives as well as the mistresses of his brothers and children.

Trujillo's father was José (Don Pepe)Trujillo Váldez. Don Pepe, an obscure post-office employee from San Cristóbal, had as his only source of pride the fact that he was the son of a Spanish police officer, José Trujillo Monagas, who for unspecified difficulties left Havana, where he was stationed, and came to the Dominican Republic, where he met a native beauty named Silveria Váldez. Soon thereafter Trujillo Váldez went back to his country, leaving behind Silveria and her offspring in dire poverty. Although Silveria lived to be 105, she never recovered from that sad state.

Until his boy took power Don Pepe had led an obscure life in his home town. A jovial, good-natured person, who had never been anything better than a postal clerk, he was regarded by San Cristóbal society as something of a failure. When Rafael entered political life, things changed overnight and Don Pepe was "elected" a member of Congress. Soon he was holding court in the middle of an increasingly large number of former cronies and patronage seekers as well as court fixers. Yet he was destined to be the member of the Family, as the clan is known by the Dominicans, who enjoyed least the power and wealth heaped upon them by Rafael's sudden rise. Don Pepe began to indulge too late in life in physical pleasures and could not rival his own son in the art of love. He died on June 10, 1935, and his son's administration decreed ten days of national mourning. Don Pepe's body was buried in one of the chapels of the Cathedral of *Santa María la Menor,* built by the Spaniards four centuries before, where is also buried Christopher Columbus. Ever since one of the legislative rituals most strictly observed is the performance of a yearly Mass on the anniversary of his death. Clad in immaculate white, the whole government and diplomatic corps attend the Mass and the placing of wreaths on Don Pepe's tomb.

The Benefactor's mother is Julia Molina Trujillo, better known to sycophants as *Mamá Julia.* Busy with the care of her ever-increasing, never prosperous household, Mrs. Trujillo did not have much time for anything else. By the time Rafael joined the Army she had left her home-town and was living in *Villa Duarte,* one of the capital city's poorest quarters. It was her address that Rafael gave in his induction papers.

Nowadays one sees frequently on newspaper front pages photographs of Doña Julia receiving delegations of people from all walks of life who are eager to pay their respects to the matriarch of the Dominican Republic. She has been awarded by Act of Congress the title of First Lady of the Nation and she is also known as the *Excelsa Matrona.* On Mother's Day the Dominican students must write small compositions about her virtues and all festivities of the day are dedicated to her as the embodiment of all that is good in Dominican womanhood. She is eulogized "for your rich treasure of eminent virtues; for your exemplary virtues of a woman born to be a symbol of the purest moral and spiritual values . . . ; for having given the Republic its greatest statesman and the world one of its most signal workers for its political reorganization."

The old lady has never accustomed herself to the homages that started to fall upon her after more than sixty years of obscure life.

Trujillo's immediate legitimate family is not large. It is formed by his third wife, Mrs. María Martínez de Trujillo, and his three children, Lieutenant General Rafael L. (Ramfis) Trujillo, Jr., 28; María de los Angeles del Corazón de Jesús (Angelita) Trujillo, 19; and Leonidas Rhadamés Trujillo, 17.

The daughter of parents who came to the Dominican Republic from Spain, Doña María is entitled by Act of Congress to the title of First Lady of the Nation as is Trujillo's mother. Aside from her now rare public appearances alongside her husband and her inroads into the literary field, Doña María stays out of the limelight. She is constantly eulogized in high-flown language, but somehow she is not promoted as much as the rest of the Family. One reason for this might be her once ambiguous relationship with the Generalissimo.

For a man who is constantly proclaiming his high moral virtues, the Benefactor has led a far from exemplary moral life. He has been married three times and has generally conducted himself, in and out of marriage, in a manner far from pure in the eyes of the Catholic faith he claims to profess so devoutly.

Trujillo's marriage with his second wife, Bienvenida Ricardo, was scarcely launched when "the Chief" took a fancy to the beautiful María Martínez, by whom he had Ramfis in 1929. María who has grown stout was in those day a real beauty with the features and charm that have made Spanish womanhood famous. She also had a genuine knack for business. The combination was explosive and no sooner had she linked her lot with that of the rising General than she was managing the lucrative laundry concession of the armed forces, to which soldiers were obliged to pay a sizable portion of their monthly wages.

After Trujillo took power in 1930 Doña María discovered that the Government had a lot of pending bills. Thereupon she established a new business. "The Government employees," points out Albert C. Hicks, "were to receive their long overdue salaries out of Government funds, but by way of María who, for the service she rendered them, was to receive a percentage. The proportion she took ranged from 75 to 80 per cent. As for the merchants hung up with unpaid bills—here, too, a settlement was to be made. For her commission, María took a paltry 60 per cent of the value. Thus, within a year's time this delightful lady had cleared for herself in the neighborhood of some $800,000."

About the same time María acquired the almost bankrupt *Ferretería Read* and out of the decaying business grew one of the most prosperous hardware concerns in the whole country. A simple commercial venture was not satisfying enough for grasping María Martínez. She soon branched out and invaded the loan shark business, but, of course, with the security afforded by her closeness to government circles. Her so-called *Banquito* (small bank) began advancing to government employees a month's salary at the rate of 5% monthly. Instead of paying its employees the Government would pay the *Banquito,* thus assuring a steady clientele to the shrewd businesswoman. (Years later she sold for an unspecified amount of money the good will of her *banquito* to the Government itself.)

By 1935 Bienvenida Ricardo, the second wife, was a useless household decoration to the President. He sent her on a protracted trip to Europe and while she was out of the country an astounding piece of legislation was rushed through Congress. On February 20, 1935, Congress approved a bill making five years of childless marriage a ground for divorce. For his inspiration the devoutly Catholic Generalissimo went far afield from Dominican tradition—in some manner he became aware of an Oriental custom which dictates that any Islamic husband whose wife does not bear him children within the five years after their marriage may repudiate his mate in favor of a new and possibly more fecund woman.

The first to take advantage of the new law was the Generalissimo himself. Bienvenida Ricardo was removed quietly from the contemporary capital scene. But the Islamic-Dominican legislation which had freed her Catholic husband was of no benefit for her. Although her marriage to Trujillo was legally dissolved she was in no sense a free woman. For Bienvenida Ricardo there was no chance for a new beginning even had she wished one. Years later, after she was no longer the Dominican First Lady, she bore a child whose name is Odette Trujillo.

After his second divorce Trujillo married María Martínez, who since "shares, understandingly and loyally, the President's worries and joys," as Nanita stresses in his biography of "The Big One." But if she ever thought that as the First Lady she was going to assert any influence on the political life of the country there was a bitter disappointment in store for her. Writes Nanita: "Her share in the President's public life is not of the publicity-seeking kind indulged in by other women of high station who have taken a hand in politics."

Although she is politically powerless, Mrs. Trujillo has proven to be a nuisance to many of her husband's collaborators, especially newspaper editors. Since she still takes great pride in her past beauty, utmost care has to be taken whenever her photograph is going to be used to illustrate stories. The editors play safe by using cuts fifteen and twenty years old. But news stories are really tough. Photographers are carefully instructed not to snap close-ups of the First Lady nor to take pictures of her full round body or her profile. Since many times she is photographed alongside her husband and the latter wants as many of his pictures in print as possible, sometimes wrong pictures of the First Lady slip into print. Then the cultured and charming lady is likely to burn the wires with invective that the patient editors have to put up with silently. Fortunately Trujillo is an understanding man when it comes to his wife's foibles and he does not pay much attention, if any, to her complaints against the press.

Her temper aside, she is a woman of no small culture and charm. According to Nanita, "her lofty idea of her vocation as mistress of her own home and of her station in society and in the world at large is reflected in her literary articles in her popular and justly praised book entitled *Meditaciones Morales* (Moral Meditations), and in her successful play *Falsa Amistad* (False Friendship)."

As an author of distinction Doña María has been compared to the great masters of literature. A front page story of *La Nación* of April 20, 1956, asserts that Mrs. Trujillo's name is already associated with the nobility of the letters. Her writings, adds the story, "like the flow of the sources of Christianity are comforting beacons that educate and stimulate in a way that reminds readers of the serenity of St. Teresa de Jesús." On the other hand, about her literary prowess a more sober critic, Murray Kempton of the *New York Post,* had this to say: "She is the author of a play, about which loyal Dominicans of taste concentrate most of their public enthusiasm on the elegance of the costumes in the last act, and of *Moral Meditations,* a collection of *pensées* which the official literature describes as occupying that empyrean plane side by side with the works of Norman Vincent Peale. Both were ghost-written by José Almonia, the Generalissimo's former secretary. In the Dominican Republic Doña María is customarily described as the first lady of Caribbean letters."

Doña María has not gone without her share of trouble with the Benefactor. No sooner had he married her than he felt an urge for new mistresses. In 1937 he chose a beautiful and aristocratic *señorita* of Ciudad Trujillo's high society, Lina Lovaton, whom he "elected" Queen of the Carnival. Miss Lovaton was for years to come number one contender for Doña María's position. One day, however, the aristocratic señorita was shipped hurriedly to the United States in the company of her Trujillo children, following an abortive attempt at assassination.

In the early fifties there was much talk in the Dominican Republic about a final rift between the Benefactor and the First Lady and a divorce was suggested. Doña María once more decided to take the bull by the horns and clearly served notice to her estranged husband that she was not going to put up with any divorce nonsense. Murray Kempton who during his visit to the Dominican Republic heard the common version of what happened wrote in the *Post:* "At this moment of crisis, Doña María, in the privacy of the nuptial chamber, pulled a gun and announced that she would put a hole in him (Trujillo.)" Knowing that his wife meant what she was saying, the Benefactor set aside permanently his divorce plans. In 1955 he finally got a Papal dispensation to marry Doña María in accordance with the Catholic rites.

Ramfis, the Crown Prince of the Dominican Republic, has been generously endowed by his father since his early years. On April 17, 1933, when he was three years old he was declared by official decree a Colonel in the National Army, and the military and civil authorities were instructed to "render him all considerations befitting his position." When Ramfis turned four the whole cabinet attended the birthday party at his mother's place, despite the irregular situation then existing. The newspapers printed long stories and photographs of the semi-official ceremony. In 1936 he was declared "Protector of the Poor Children." Upon reaching the age of eight he earned the military merit medal "for exceptional virtues that he has shown at an early age."

Prior to this Trujillo had, according to Nanita, given a proof of his unbounded love for his son, when the latter "was stricken, at the age of seven, with a serious illness that endangered his life. There was no question of any restraint in his demonstrations of affection for the boy, and there seemed to be no ameliorating the worry he felt." Finally, the eulogist proclaims, the seemingly endless hours of anguish and prayerful hope were rewarded with the child's complete recovery.

When Ramfis was nine he was "promoted" to the rank of brigadier general. For several years honors were heaped upon him by the hundreds. Bridges, parks, hospitals, schools and roads were named after him. Postage stamps were issued to publicize his face and the newspapers reserved for him the most extravagant compliments. Then, at the age of fourteen, in 1943, he unexpectedly resigned his rank on the ground of youth, a discovery that was hailed by the Dominican press as a most precious demonstration of selflessness. *La Nación* published on September 5, 1943, letters from two cabinet members (R. Paíno Richardo and Manuel A. Peña Batlle) congratulating Ramfis.

Following his resignation as a general Ramfis entered the Army as a cadet. Six years later he was a captain, law student and distinguished turfman. At the end of 1949 he was appointed an inspector of diplomatic missions with the rank of Ambassador. He was then twenty.

He became an honorary lieutenant colonel in 1951, a colonel in 1952; a brigadier general the same year and despite the fact he cannot pilot a plane and papa does not allow him to fly he was made Air Force Chief of Staff in 1953. He received a Doctor of Law degree (without ever having gone to classes at the University) and his promotion to major general at the same time. He is now a lieutenant general. In the month of August, 1957, Ramfis, who had been relieved unexpectedly of his duties as Chief of Staff of the Air Force a few months before, was shipped to the United States to study, at American taxpayers' expense, at the Army's Command and General Staff School at Fort Leavenworth, Kansas.

General Trujillo assumed the rank of colonel while at school. With him to take the same course went one of his childhood pals, Lt. Col. Fernando A. Sanchez. The presence of Trujillo, Jr., at the American Army

Command and General Staff College was sharply questioned by U.S. Representative Charles O. Porter, who wrote a letter to the Secretary of the Army, Hon. Wilber M. Brucker, in which he said that he found it "hard to rationalize making this wonderful training available to men who will use it to oppress their own peoples and who will never be able to contribute anything substantial to American defense." The Army's reply to Porter, signed by Brigadier General J. E. Bastion, Jr., Deputy Chief of Legislative Liaison, is a masterpiece of evasion. The only thing that clearly comes out is that under the Mutual Security Act of 1954, as amended, "the Dominican Republic is eligible to receive military assistance. The Dominican Republic requested and was allocated two spaces at the Command and General Staff College." Furthermore, stated General Bastion, "the Department of the Army provides training at United States Army service schools only to those countries which have been declared eligible for such training under Presidential directives, the Mutual Security Act of 1954 as amended, and Department of Defense policy directives."

Ramfis is hot-tempered, brash and rude. In general he acts in public as a spoiled brat, ever ready to rally to papa's side at the slightest provocation. At official functions he remains apart, aloof.

In his private life Trujillo, Jr., seemingly is following in his father's footsteps. He has been married twice to the same girl, Octavia Ricart de Trujillo. During their two marriages the couple have had five children. Like his father, Ramfis plays for all it is worth the religious angle while in the Dominican Republic, but out of the country he acts the playboy. Society columns have associated his name with several glamorous feminine names of the American smart set, including that of Peggy Howell Taylor, former wife of hotel and shipping magnate Dan Taylor and present wife of wealthy young industrialist Carl Dahlberg. Peggy was a well-chaperoned guest aboard the luxurious Trujillo yacht a couple of winters ago in the Bahamas, according to society columnist Charles Ventura.

The handsome, six-foot Lieutenant General Trujillo, Jr., is a great sportsman as well. June 5, his birthday, is celebrated in the Dominican Republic as the Day of Sports. His sportsmanship, however, is peculiarly revealing. He is never satisfied except to win, so to humor him no one dares to defeat his side at any game. He is a dedicated polo player and the team he leads—the Ciudad Trujillo—went undefeated during several years, even against the most noted foreign poloists. When people started to wonder what kind of supermen played on Trujillo's team, Ramfis deigned to lose a game once in a while.

Through Ramfis, Trujillo hopes to maintain his dynasty in power after he has gone. A recent amendment to the Dominican constitution lowered the eligible age for the Presidency to twenty-five and following this measure there was, for several months, a movement to draft Trujillo, Jr., as running mate of his uncle Héctor in the elections of 1957. In a letter addressed to the President of the *Partido Dominicano,* Ramfis declined the honor. As reasons for his decision he gave his desire to stay in the armed forces as well as his purpose to earn merit by his own efforts. Rumor has it, however, that he was mad because his father did not offer him the Presidency right away.

Trujillo seemingly wants to pave the way for Ramfis to succeed him, but he hesitates to give the boy the required power to insure smooth continuity. Moreover, notwithstanding his admirers and good-wishers, foremost among them his father Rafael, Sr., Ramfis has not developed, as he certainly will need to if he is going to perform the role papa has in mind for him (but only when he is already gone), qualifications of kingship.

People who know him well doubt he has the prudent judgment, moderation and, above all, the patience he will need to carry through the period of instability and even chaos that will necessarily follow his father's death, even if this event occurs peacefully and in bed. There is another factor against Ramfis. Although his father may claim a certain degree of popularity among the masses, due to the ceaseless cult of his personality, there is no proof that Ramfis shares in any degree that ascendancy.

Trujillo has brought up his younger son, Rhadamés, somewhat more conservatively—at eleven, he was only an honorary Army major. Like his elder brother before him, Rhadamés also resigned his commission to become a cadet, which he is now in the Air Force. As is the Trujillo custom, his name graces streets, parks and buildings. Moreover he has been unanimously elected president of honor of a number of youth recreation clubs and at this writing a beauty contest is being prepared in his honor. He boasts the finest stable of race horses in the island and his entries in cattle fairs have earned a high percentage of first prizes. He has been listed as the owner of the famed Trujillo farm *Hacienda Fundación.*

Currently Rhadamés studies at the Kemper Military School, in Boonville, Missouri. On October 21, 1957, *El Caribe* printed a letter addressed to the Generalissimo by the President of the School, Major General Joseph P. Cleland, praising Rhadamés as an "excellent and outstanding" youngster.

If Ramfis is the unofficial Crown Prince, daughter Angelita has been officially crowned Queen in ceremonies that rivalled those put on in European monarchies.

Trujillo lavishes most of his affection upon Angelita, a pretty brunette. When the International Fair was inaugurated in December 1955 the only person who was allowed to compete with the Benefactor himself for a little share of the popular acclaim was Angelita. She was crowned Queen Angelita I by her uncle Héctor in a regal ceremony attended by the diplomatic representatives accredited to the Dominican government.

On her way to the throne Angelita I paced—followed by a retinue of hundreds of courtiers—along a mile of red carpet. When the moment of the coronation arrived, as *Time* described, "scurrying attendants brought a jeweled scepter for her hand and a diamond-studded gold crown for her head." Dominican intelligentsia wrote poems for the occasion, bearing such titles as "The Only Angelita." As a further example of the Byzantine extravagance Trujillo heaps over this child, two hairdressers were flown down from New York all expenses paid, to set her royal coiffure the day of the coronation. Their fee: $1,000. To earn that, as one beauty magazine reported, all they did was to invert Angelita's pony tail. Dominican society chroniclers described the Coronation ball, offered by President Héctor Trujillo, as the most outstanding social event of the Western Hemisphere.

The young lady has on her record, however, a minor diplomatic storm between the Dominican Republic and Great Britain. When she was only fourteen years old, her father appointed her Ambassador for the Coronation of Queen Elizabeth II in 1953. The British Foreign Office politely declined to acknowledge her credentials. The whole thing was hushed within the Dominican Republic, until it was let out by British Ambassador Stanley Gudgeon. His indiscretion about this slight suffered by the Benefactor's daughter cost him his post. Gudgeon had issued a few checks bearing his signature at a Dominican gambling casino and Trujillo promptly turned them over to the British Foreign Office.

The usual number of parks, streets, hospitals and schools have been named after Angelita, including one of her father's yachts, but the young lady never had a happy look. She has suffered her share of physical misery, having undergone several operations for a strange back ailment. Worst of all, perhaps, is the fact that for years she was a secluded person, whose public appearances were strictly controlled by her father. Rumor among Dominicans was that no suitor would be allowed to approach her, since her possessive father considered her too good for any Dominican and was hoping for a blue-blooded cavalier from the old European aristocracy. Suddenly at the beginning of December 1957 was announced the engagement of beautiful Angelita to an obscure Air Force major—Luis de León Estévez. The marriage took place on January 4, 1958, and from all corners of the world presents were showered upon the couple. Among the gift senders were fellow dictators Francisco Franco, Marcos Pérez Jimenez and Antoine Kebreau. The latter sent from Haiti a special plane to bear the gift.

If Angelita is the Queen the other legitimate daughter (and the eldest of all the childen), Flor de Oro, has become the pauper. Strong-willed, not totally devoid of tropical, mulatto charm, Flor has acquired fame for her marital escapades.

Popular, vivacious and possessor of a well defined, strong personality, very much like her father's, Flor is perhaps the only Trujillo who dares to stand up to the Benefactor. A spendthrift habitué of New York and Paris café society, she was called home a few years ago and forbidden to leave the Dominican Republic by her father, obviously displeased by her antics and frightened by the damage Flor's emancipated ways was doing to his precarious prestige.

The Benefactor became so angry at Flor that he had a law passed allowing a father to disinherit and disavow his children, which he immediately did to her. She now lives in complete obscurity with her mother Aminta Ledesma on the outskirts of Ciudad Trujillo.

Trujillo has other children, but being born out of wedlock, they are kept on the sidelines. However, they all have a right to the name and in accordance with new laws have a right to the Generalissimo's estate.

In their own ways Trujillo's brothers are little dictators by themselves, although they are dwarfed by the tremendous shadow of the Benefactor. As long as they respect his dominant position, Trujillo allows the rest of the clan to act very much as they please but he does not have any intention of letting anyone replace him. For trespassing some of his brothers have tasted the bitter flavor of the exile life, although never for long and always in grand style.

"Little Brother" Héctor Bienvenido (Negro), the "president," is probably Rafael's closest collaborator, but even he is not permitted to share either genuine power or prominence with "Big Brother." For instance, the Dominican press publishes long lists of the Generalissimo's engagements, but not of the President's. Rafael's picture almost invariably appears on page one, but Héctor's only on rare occasions. The Supreme Chief heads the receiving line at state receptions, the Chief Executive follows. The dictator is played up over his brother even in official Government propaganda disseminated abroad—so little regard does Trujillo have for ordinary political etiquette. Yet, if nothing happens to the Benefactor within the next four years the chances are that "president" Héctor will continue his humiliating daily walks from one wing of the National Palace to the other to receive instructions and carry out orders for his brother.

Héctor, now 48, is a swarthy, homely, mild-mannered, cultured man of no small personal charm, who has lived all his life under the protective wing of the Benefactor. His blind loyalty to the Generalissimo is well known and he will never dare to disagree with his brother's policies. Héctor has gone as far as calling brother Rafael, in an official presidential speech, his "father." If he has a mind of his own he has certainly achieved the feat of concealing it.

Héctor joined the Army at the age of eighteen, in 1926, and began to get rapid promotions four years later, when brother Rafael took power. During that time he had been preparing himself to enter the University of

Santo Domingo where he intended to study dentistry. This he never did. During the early days of the regime he was a military attaché in several European capitals, while his brother tested unsuccessfully the reliability and political acumen of elder brothers. Finally Rafael decided to try the youngest brother. The "little brother" was in the long run entrusted with the most important and perhaps most difficult task of the regime—control of the armed forces. He successively served as chief of the staff of the National Army and Minister of War, Navy and Air, before being "elected" to the Presidency when brother Rafael decided to step out, in 1952, to play the bigger, loftier role of Super Chief of State.

There are people who think, even inside the Dominican Republic, that if left alone Héctor would follow a more moderate course than Rafael. This is a difficult thing to ascertain. There is no doubt that Héctor is mellower than Rafael and has a genuine sense of humor. But there have been periods in which Rafael has gone out of the country and left Héctor in charge. At those times terror has not been relaxed in any form.

Lately the legend of Héctor's mildness has been put back in circulation by people highly placed in Dominican official circles. One of them told Milton Bracker, of the New York Times, that "the president is important."

To clarify the statement the following exchange ensued:

"When the visitor asks, 'Because of the Constitution?' the officer says: 'To hell with the Constitution. As a transformer.'

"And he makes clear that those in the highest circles around Generalissimo Trujillo are so terrified of the ire or displeasure of the Jefe (Chief) that a 'transformer'—literally a device to step down a voltage that can destroy—is important to those who feel they may have risked that ire."

I do not share the "transformer" theory about Héctor. It is true he cannot be blamed for the brutal tactics of his big brother, but there is no proof that he would act otherwise had the opportunity of ruling entirely by himself come unexpectedly. I believe that a much better appraisal of Héctor's role is that of Theodore Draper, who wrote: "Yet Héctor was always the younger brother who did not have to fight to get ahead. He did not have to develop the ruthlessness and cunning of the older brother. Héctor is considered a rather shy, pleasant and moderate person. The question is whether he will develop his brother's more brutal qualities if he has to stand alone."

Like other members of the Trujillo clan Héctor combines the talents of a prosperous businessman with those of a gentleman farmer. He shares ownership with J. M. Bonetti Burgos of one of the most lucrative Dominican monopolies—the peanut oil manufacturing concern, which sells about 80 per cent of the edible oil consumed in the country. Besides accumulating money (unlike Rafael he is stingy), Héctor's only known hobby is to collect shoes, of which he has hundreds of pairs.

The "president" lives at his mother's home although he has another residence on his enormous estate of Engombe, a few miles north of the capital. He is an inveterate bachelor, but for the last twenty years has been engaged to Miss Alma McLaughlin. According to Milton Bracker: "a popular explanation for the protracted engagement is that the Generalissimo, having both a wife . . . and a living mother, feels that another First Lady—i.e., the wife of the President—would complicate protocol."

This can hardly be the case since Trujillo has already managed successfully such a situation before. During the period 1938–1942, when the two puppet presidents of the time were married men, there were three first ladies in the country. Nearer to the truth is another version, given to Bracker by a Government official, that "it seems unlikely the President will do so while their mother is alive."

The "president's" fiancée is a daughter of Charles A. McLaughlin, a longtime Trujillo crony who first came to the country as a U.S. Marine Sergeant in 1917. He became a Dominican citizen in 1956 and is a Colonel in the staff of his future son-in-law. He also acts as proxy of the Benefactor in a number of business enterprises. He now presides over the corporation that "bought" the formerly Government-owned Jaragua and El Embajador hotels, in partnership with a subsidiary of Pan American World Airways.

Unquestionably Rafael trusts Héctor enough to leave him at the helm when he goes on extended tours abroad. It is doubtful that he would do this with his elder brother Virgilio. In the early days of the regime Virgilio occupied high ranking positions, but it seems that instead of obeying he tried to do some thinking for himself. Rafael has the idea, however, that he does not need around him men with independent minds or excessive ambitions of their own. Virgilio's tinkering with the administration of civil justice coupled with an obvious jealousy of Rafael's absolute power made him an uncomfortable partner, but "the Chief" put up with this patiently until he discovered with no small chagrin that, taking advantage of his position as Minister of Interior and Police, Virgilio was reaching into every accessible *trujillista* domain, tirelessly wooing political chieftains and army leaders, trying to establish a machine that would owe allegiance only to him.

That was too much. Thereupon Virgilio was promptly assigned to a diplomatic mission and sent abroad to brood. For several years he performed as his brother's Minister to the French Government in what proved to be a very gilded exile. For Virgilio Trujillo the Dominican Legation in Paris turned out to be a business blessing. There, even if he was miles away from any possibility of taking the longed-for big step to ultimate power among Dominicans he was, nevertheless, in an excellent position to continue his search "for a fast buck."

Hitler had already created the refugee problem when Virgilio arrived in Paris. Then came the Spanish Civil War. The Dominican Legation was swamped with requests for visas made by people seeking haven in the New World and willing to pay any price for a small stamp on their passports. Those with considerable means found in Virgilio a man who could give service even if he charged a high price.

Capitalizing on human suffering behind the cloak of an alleged humanitarianism, one of the most repugnant rackets was established by the Trujillo brothers in Paris—the selling for exorbitant prices, either in cash or jewels, of Dominican passports and visas. Both brothers were in partnership again, but not for long. The visa factory soon got Virgilio in hot water with "big brother" again. Not because the Benefactor objected to the questionable activities, but because he thought Virgilio was cheating him of his share of the spoils. Virgilio was dismissed summarily; he decided that it was safer to stay away for a while. Later he came back and a reconciliation took effect, but when Virgilio started acting anew as "Mr. Supreme Court," taking away business from the boss himself, he was again shipped out of the country—this time as an Ambassador, Inspector of Embassies and Legations.

If Héctor is self-effacing and Virgilio untrustworthy, Arismendy, another of the Trujillo boys, is more than a phenomenon; he is a portent. He is a man who moves fast, even for a Trujillo.

Petán, as he is better known in the country, is all kinds of things to all men and, moreover, at all times. He is an army man (lieutenant general); a patron of the arts (owner of the largest chain of radio broadcasting and television stations); a gambling kingpin (as owner of a night-club casino); big businessman (in the import and export field); and a clever manipulator of shady business deals and protection rackets. He, too, has cherished dreams of taking for himself all that wonderful power that Rafael holds. He too discovered that it is all right with Rafael if one of his kin is not particular about the means of acquiring riches, but it is quite another thing if one of them sets his eyes on political power.

Before learning his lesson, Petán had to suffer a bad experience. In 1935, taking advantage of the fact that the Benefactor was sick in bed, Petán hatched a plot to win power. Warned by his Secret Police, the Generalissimo acted with ruthlessness and speed. Of all the conspirators the only one spared was Petán himself and this only because the army commander in charge of the mopping-up operation thought wise for his future safety to warn Petán in advance. Without bothering to say a word to his fellow conspirators, Petán took refuge, literally speaking, under his mother's bed. A few days later as an extra safety measure he took a plane to Puerto Rico.

After a cooling off period, Petán promised to behave and mind thereafter only his own business. Rafael then pardoned his brother and allowed him to engage in the very reputable activities of promoting the cultural and artistic progress of the country through a multiple million-dollar radio and television empire.

On the sidelines Petán built up a very profitable organization to oversee what is called in the Dominican argot the export of *frutos menores,* that is to say a combination of vegetables, poultry and other agricultural products. In accordance with this set-up every exporter must take Petán as a partner or at least pay him tribute for his "protection," independently of the payments they have to make the Benefactor himself through other organizations. Otherwise Petán gunmen wipe out the recalcitrants with the precision of a Detroit assembly line. Currently, Petán exacts a few cents on each stem of bananas exported from the country by any corporation or individual (with the exception of the big American corporations), and $1 for every box of plantains. Exporters of poultry pay him a flat rate of $10,000 per year for a permit to stay in business. Each truck that passes through the town of Bonao—Petán's stronghold on the Cibao road—must pay a fee.

Slowly but inexorably Petán's interests have broadened until they have come to include control of the garment industry, slot machines, gambling casinos and loan shark rackets. *La Voz Dominicana,* Petan's radio network, is not only a big propaganda outlet the Trujillo regime uses to give "the full treatment" to foreign governments and enemies of the regime. It is also the vehicle of one of the most lucrative international numbers rackets, which operated by a mobsters' syndicate spreads out through the length of the Caribbean. The "hoods" in Havana, Panama and Caracas sell numbers in combination with a seemingly harmless *Voz Dominicana's* raffle supposedly intended as a giveaway of small prizes to its Dominican audience. The syndicate rigs the daily winning numbers in their own favor and then cable them to Arismendy who dutifully announces them over his radio station. This peculiar racket—known in Panama as *La Dominicana* —produces a weekly income to Petán figured in five ciphers. This, however, is by no means all profit for Petán. Part of the proceeds have to be turned over to the Benefactor himself, who has a pronounced allergy to the sight of other people getting too wealthy, even his own brothers. The latter appear as a front in many businesses and rackets ultimately owned by the Generalissimo.

If we wish to grasp the whole meaning of what is happening in the Dominican Republic, let us free our imagination for just a second and let it picture what would happen were people of the ilk of Lucky Luciano, Al Capone, Albert Anastasia and their relatives, good as well as bad, to take over the White House.

There are other brothers and sisters also in business. General Pedro

Trujillo is one of the least known of them. He specializes in settling small lawsuits of the kind the Benefactor would not bother with and controls the charcoal distribution monopoly in Ciudad Trujillo. He is the overlord of all the mess operations in the National Army, but the profits from this very remunerative operation must be shared with brothers Héctor and Rafael. He shares the rest of the Family passion for owning land and for buying it on their own terms.

Then we have Romeo, better known as Pipí. He is a tough who after twenty-seven years of power still acts as in the old days. The black sheep of the family, he never rose above the Army rank of captain, and is not allowed to present himself where decent people can see him, although he was dressed in white tie and tails, for the first time in his life, to accompany brother Héctor at his inauguration as President in 1957. Pipí regulates prostitution and small gambling houses. His activities along these lines have put him at odds with other members of the clan at times. *Time* once printed the following story then going the rounds inside the country: "Prostitutes in the Dominican Republic are called *cueros* (hides). Once Petán slapped a levy on exports of cattle hides. Pipí objected. Their mother, one of the First Ladies of the Land, decided the case. 'None of that, Petán,' she admonished. 'You know the *cueros* belong to Pipí.' "

In all the years since Trujillo has been in power the clan has suffered only one casualty, aside from Don Pepe. Brother Anibal lodged a bullet in his own head on December 2, 1948, although there are people in the Dominican Republic who swear the man was incapable of doing such a thing to himself—to others, maybe.

The truth is however that Anibal was a paranoiac, whose sickness became more accentuated after a tour of duty as chief of staff of the National Army. It seems that instability runs heavily in Anibal's side of the Family, since in the summer of 1957 his son Marcos had to be taken, according to press reports, to a Mexican sanitarium.

Anibal also had his share of trouble with "Big Brother." Rumor has it in the Dominican Republic that he was dismissed from the Army on account of the competition he was giving the Benefactor in the matter of uniforms. Dominicans still recall with inner amusement Anibal's colorful dress uniforms and red capes cut in the best Napoleonic tradition.

Of Rafael's sisters the one who looks most like her brother is Nieves Luisa. She is a business woman and very experienced in all kind of worldly practices. In her youth she emigrated to Cuba and there is no question that she hates to hear about her Cuban interlude. She is now in the renting business. This is a special kind of business peculiar to the Dominican Republic. Since World War II a system of rent control has been in full force. Nieves is in the business of renting homes from their owners at the control levels and then subletting them at her own high levels. If the tenant dares to complain to the rent control authorities the chances are that he will land in jail the following morning, arraigned on charges of "communist activities."

There are three other sisters but these are very discreet ladies indeed. Japonesa, who is the constant companion of her mother, is married to Luis Ruiz Monteagudo, a member of Congress and prosperous business-man (shoes). They are also big landowners. Japonesa is the mother-in-law of Dr. Ramon Berges, currently Dominican Ambassador to France. Her son, Dr. Luis Trujillo, is at present the Secretary of the Presidency, one of the most important cabinet posts in the *trujillista* set-up. This young man is also a lawyer with a large corporation practice.

Marina, another sister, is married to Senator José García, a former major general and chief of staff of the National Army. She is the mother of two army generals: Lieutenant General José García Trujillo, currently the Secretary of the Armed Forces and as such second in line to succeed the President; the younger son is major general Virgilio García Trujillo, who after a long period in the *trujillista* doghouse was reinstated November 1957 in his old post of chief of staff of the Army.

Another member of this branch of the family is Dr. Joaquin Salazar, former cabinet member and ambassador, and now head of a law firm in Ciudad Trujillo. He is the husband of Lourdes García Trujillo. Salazar was recalled in March 1957 from his post as Dominican Ambassador to the United States, and "benched" until assigned to a new cabinet post. Salazar heatedly denies that the flurry over the Galíndez case had anything to do with his replacement by Trujillo's longtime associate, Manuel de Moya. Salazar points out he had been in the foreign service for eleven years, but in Washington's diplomatic circles there is the feeling that he was recalled when the reaction in the U.S. to the Galíndez case got "out of hand."

Another of Marina's daughters, Mireya, is married to an Army general: José (Pupo) Roman Fernandez.

THE LIVING GODS

RAFAEL LEONIDAS TRUJILLO MOLINA HAS LIVED FOR MORE THAN twenty-seven years in an atmosphere of directed, frenetic adulation, created to make him seem one of the truly immortal figures of history.

There is no more lucrative occupation in the country than devising new kinds of homage to the Generalissimo. Yet, as time passes the praise factories find it increasingly difficult to fill their quotas of new forms of adulation and in recent years there has been a pronounced tendency to tedious repetition. For example, although he has never fought a single military battle, "the Chief" has already been awarded two medals for alleged acts of bravery as a triumphant and courageous general. Bejewelled collars (for which Trujillo seems to feel a particular deep affection) have been bestowed upon him at least twice. One of these costly trinkets (perhaps the costliest of its kind in existence) is called the "Collar of National Gratitude." To match it Trujillo has decided to hang democracy around his neck in the form of the so-called "Collar of Democracy," a gift from the University students.

Since Christianity as a way of life took root in the consciousness of the Western peoples no ruler has ever dared to associate his name with the name of God on an equal footing. There have been, to be sure, those who have ascribed divine origin to their right to rule and those who have denied altogether the existence of God and consider religions as the "Opium of the People." But there is no other example of a President, King, Emperor or Dictator who has claimed, as Trujillo now claims, a place alongside that of the Almighty. No other ruler of modern times has ever used, in order to further his own ends, a slogan such as the notorious "God and Trujillo" which appears in neon lights and academic theses in the Dominican Republic.

Moreover, by Act of Congress time is measured in Trujilloland from the Generalissimo's coming to power—1957 is the 28th year of the Era of Trujillo, and laws, official decrees as well as legal documents, must so state. Oaths of loyalty—like the impressive one publicly made by 30,000 workers on May 1, 1956—are rendered not to God but to Trujillo. In 1942 when Congress named San Rafael one of the Dominican provinces it took pains to make clear in the text of the law then being passed that it was an honor to Trujillo himself. No one can ever address Trujillo as "you." It is always "Your Excellency," "Your Honor," "You Lord of the People" and the like.

Trujillo began collecting titles—of which he has several score—early in his career. He was officially proclaimed "Benefactor of the Fatherland" by a Congressional Resolution of November 11, 1932. The rank of Generalissimo of all Dominican armed forces was conferred on him by law passed on May 25, 1933. In 1938 Congress declared him "The First and Greatest of the Dominican Chiefs of State" and in 1940 passed a law giving him the additional title of "Restorer of the Financial Independence of the Republic."

Furthermore, Trujillo is the Liberator of the Nation and the Protector of the Beaux Arts and Letters. By common consent "the Chief" is the country's number one statesman, journalist, hero, teacher, man of justice, guardian of the people and genius of thought. The new Dominican constitution, as amended in 1955, not only consecrates the titles of Benefactor and Father of the New Fatherland, but declares to be "national monuments" all the statues, busts, monuments that the "national gratitude" has erected or will erect to honor Trujillo.

At the entrance of Santiago Trujillo's 13-foot gold-plate statue stares down on the second largest city of the country from the base of the largest monument ever built for a living man. The citizens of Ciudad Trujillo are casting for him a 23-foot-tall equestrian statue, which, according to Murray Kempton, is "the largest of its kind ever built for anyone, living or dead, in 5,000 years of recorded human vanity." There are at least two other gigantic statues in process of erection, one of them in the Benefactor's home town of San Cristóbal.

If Trujillo's statues are still not very numerous in the country, it is because for many years his superstitious nature opposed this kind of homage. The only other living Dominican president who ever ordered a statue of himself, Ulises Heaureaux, was murdered before the monument was shipped from Spain where it had been cast.

Busts, however, are another thing. "The Big One" has never objected to them and to date there are more than 1,800 overlooking parks, streets, colleges, hospitals and offices throughout the country. Sometimes the bust even adorns respectable, law-abiding, police-fearing homes. Judging by the news stories about the Congress sessions it seems that one of the main functions of the Dominican legislature is to pass resolutions authorizing one community or another to erect new busts of either the Generalissimo or some member of his family. The manufacture of busts of "His Excellency" has become one of the most profitable business operations in the country and there is at least one factory, owned by a Spaniard named Dorado, which turns out nothing but busts. There comes to mind the story of another Spaniard refugee sculptor whose main occupation was for years to sell busts of the Benefactor to the municipalities. Noticing that for some time the sculptor was not showing his accustomed activity, a friend of his dared to ask a newspaper reporter whether the Spaniard had fallen out of grace. "No," was the reply. "The trouble is that we seem to have been running out of parks lately."

Though there is a law forbidding giving the names of living persons to cities and streets, during Trujillo's lifetime there have been cities, streets, parks and provinces named after him. In 1932 a province was named "Trujillo" and his home town San Cristóbal was made the capital of it. Then the capital city, always known as "Santo Domingo de Guzmán," the name it was given by Bartholomew Columbus in 1496, was rebaptized Ciudad Trujillo. Subsequently other provinces were named "Libertador," "Benefactor" and "Trujillo Valdez," the latter after Trujillo's father. Even nature has had to pay its homage to the Benefactor—the highest mountain in the Antilles has been named Trujillo Peak, in accordance with a law passed on September 21, 1936.

The dizziest heights of flattery are reached every year on October 24, Trujillo's birthday. This provides the occasion for a national orgy of government-directed adulation. This, however, is not the only holiday proclaimed for Trujillo. There is the "Day of the Benefactor," which is celebrated the second Sunday of January to commemorate the changing of name of the capital city. May 16 is marked red on Dominican calendars on account of the fact that on that day in 1930 Trujillo was first "elected" President. In the religion of *trujillismo* this is like a New Year's Day.

The common people never catch a glimpse of the Benefactor in anything less than an environment of glory. Recently, however, the pageantry has been severely curtailed and the Generalissimo makes almost no public appearances. Ever since some Latins have acquired the distasteful custom of sacrificing their own lives in order to get their fellow citizens rid of unsavory tyrants, Trujillo's only regular appearance, aside from his daily walk in the closely watched George Washington Avenue, is to the race tracks on Sundays, where he is surrounded by a very thick wall of bodyguards.

Yet, when "the Big One" deigns to appear in public—after overcoming a not unnatural fear of being shot at—he comes in view of the Dominican people in well-arranged theatrical settings. The ceremonies then take on the nature of triumphal pageantry and "the Chief's" presence is the signal for orderly cheers from the big claque of school-children, government employees, union members, "veterans" and slum hoodlums.

Of all means of flattery Trujillo prefers pictorial reproductions of his facial features. The Benefactor is so much in love with himself that he regards as the supreme sign of devotion to his person the keeping of one of his pictures. Those who do not have in their homes a lithograph, painting, sketch or photograph of the Generalissimo are liable to be branded "communists." When searching a home the secret police regard the failure to produce a picture of Trujillo as the strongest evidence of lack of loyalty.

The thoroughness with which the Benefactor is humored by his people has brought about a peculiar situation. No matter the place, "Big Brother" will always watch over the people, actually or metaphysically, in the Dominican Republic. "The Big One" is on every wall staring down at his subjects and visitors—benign looking, stern, serious, smiling or enigmatic. The photographs have, nevertheless, a common feature: all flatter the man; not a strange thing, after all, if it is recalled that no picture of "the Chief" may be put on display without prior official verification of its "artistic merits."

From the excellence of drinking water (which is very good) to the modern labor legislation (which is hardly enforced) everything done in the country must be attributed to the Generalissimo. Even the "president" will not send a message to Congress proposing a new bill without first assuring the legislators that he is acting in compliance with the Generalissimo's wishes.

And what is not done by Trujillo is accomplished for him. When the overburdened Dominican taxpayers threw down the drain $40 millions of their hard-earned money in an International Fair for the Peace and Brotherhood of the Free World the only tangible achievement to come out of the project was a sickening process of glorification of Trujillo and his family. The Fair was expected to attract tourists and investment capital to the country, but as *Time* put it, "its essential purpose was expressed by a fair official in a pep talk to English-speaking guides: 'This great international exposition is a tribute in homage, admiration and respect to the illustrious Benefactor.' "

One of the huge murals with Trujillo as the central figure displayed at the armed-forces building was very amusing. The two-part mural depicted on one side Columbus aboard the *Santa María*, and on the other Trujillo on the bridge of a Dominican warship. Read the explanatory legend: "462 years after Columbus' voyage, Generalissimo Trujillo in command of three powerful Dominican naval units, set out on a good-will voyage to Spain."

It has become customary to fill the walls of public monuments and government as well as party buildings with quotations from Trujillo's speeches. "Trujillo Forever" and similar slogans convey the message of the new *trujillista* gospel to the people in short, direct sentences. On stone pillars beside the doors of hotels, public buildings, military establishments and schools, bronze letters say: "Era of Trujillo." Buses, trucks, automobiles, bicycles, pushcarts, even shoeshine boxes are adorned with the ever-present, oft-repeated "God and Trujillo," as well as the more indirect "Trujillo Is My Protector" and "Long Live Trujillo."

The Government hospitals are decorated with signs reading "Only Trujillo Cures Us." At village pumps, "Only Trujillo Gives Us to Drink." Beside each irrigation ditch the posters read: "Trujillo Is the Only One Who Gives Us Water," "Seeds Grow Because of the Water Trujillo Gives Us" or "Crops Are Plentiful Because Trujillo Has Given Us All the Water We Need." These placards are set up, of course, by the "grateful" farmers themselves. They do it, however, on their own free will—or else! Those who do not show the required enthusiasm are denied access to the irrigation facilities by the *Departamento de Recursos Hidráulicos*—always on account of some minor technicality; nothing to do with politics indeed!

Theodore Draper, the American reporter whose perceptive remarks on the Trujillo regime have been frequently quoted in this book, depicts this situation in the following terms: "There is literally not a single shop or business of any kind without a picture of Trujillo prominently displayed. A truck passes and on its bumper is painted: *Trujillo es mi protector*. A flimsy little shack used for selling a few bottles of soft drink bears the sign: *Dios y Trujillo son mi fe*, 'God and Trujillo Are My Faith.' With a broad grin a shoe-shine boy shows off all his English—'Gringo, shine?'—and his box reads—*Viva Trujillo!* It is as if the dictator were everywhere, watching everything, knowing everyone."

The amazing process of deification is by no means restricted to the Benefactor's person. Streets, towns, provinces, bridges, roads, hospitals, parks and schools have been named after his relatives from two generations before "the Chief" to two generations after. There are as many busts of Trujillo's mother as of "the Chief" himself and the trend now is to erect that kind of monument to the "little brother."

Early in his career Trujillo was advised that postage stamps are a good means for imposing one's face without risking painful rebuffs. Right from the outset of the regime the Dominican post offices have had a large stock of stamps bearing Trujillo's face. It also offers a choice of other members of the family. There is one issue featuring *Mama Julia,* another with *Don Pepe's* face. Ramfis' baby face is there for sale also, as well as a whole set with Héctor's homely façade. For the same price, however, buyers have a choice of the prettier face of Angelita.

Trujillo's efforts to gain recognition in international circles have not been always unsuccessful. The University of Pittsburgh, in the United States, bestowed upon him an honorary degree of doctor and more than forty governments, beginning with the dictatorships of Mussolini and Juan Vincente Gomes and ending with the Vatican, have awarded the Benefactor their highest decorations. Wrote Dr. de Galíndez: "I very much doubt that any other tyrant has succeeded in assembling so picturesque a collection of titles, decorations and honorary degrees."

All this may seem elaborate nonsense and I suspect that Trujillo knows it, although sometimes he acts as if he believes in it. In view of his record, however, there is one thing Trujillo has never been able to get rid of even after having reached the demigod status—his "nouveau riche" complex.

During his trips abroad, mainly to the United States, he loves to play a splashy role. In 1952 and 1953 he visited the United States and during his stay abroad the Dominican press dutifully gave a big play to his alleged new triumphs.

Upon that occasion Trujillo was host at a lavish reception in the Mayflower Hotel's Chinese Room and an adjoining ballroom. The decorations included 1,000 red roses; the buffet table was 50 feet long; the service was of gold; champagne bubbled from lighted fountains. "Washington hasn't seen anything like last night for a long time," wrote a *Washington Post* society reporter.

Some twenty months later, in 1955, he visited again the United States and *Newsweek* wrote: "Rafael Leonidas Trujillo Molina and entourage departed from Kansas City, Mo., last week after a three-week visit and left the town enough to talk about for three more."

This time Trujillo showed off in great style. His first move when he got to town was to establish credit at the Commerce Trust Co., whose executive vice president was A. B. Eisenhower, President Eisenhower's brother. With the credit, whose amount was not revealed but was estimated at close to $200,000, Trujillo got down to business. According to *Newsweek* he had gone to Kansas City principally to buy American cattle and cattle-working horses. He also wanted to see former President Truman (as he did at a party given at the Kansas City Club) and while in the city his daughter Angelita underwent a minor operation at the hands of Dr. Wallace Graham, former White House physician.

His departure, wrote *Newsweek,* was something to see. "A reception was held the night before for more than 700 guests, hastily invited by telegram, at which the main feature was champagne from a fountain." Always the parvenu, the Benefactor departed once again from the United States leaving no doubt that for him champagne from a fountain is the utmost expression of refinement.

Worse, however, than his displays of megalomania are the hypocritical shows of modesty the Generalissimo occasionally stages. Thus, not being sure of the domestic as well as international reactions when, twenty-two years ago, somebody or other first tried to change the name of the capital city from Santo Domingo to Ciudad Trujillo he perfunctorily recorded his opposition to the idea and then left the Presidency and went on vacation.

Ever since visitors have been reminded how the Benefactor suffered when the members of his Congress finally voted unanimously to give his name to the oldest city of the New World, founded and baptized in 1496 by Bartoloméo Columbus. It is pointed out that Trujillo wrote a lengthy letter objecting to the proposed congressional measure. He then asserted that the homage filled him with satisfaction and legitimate pride, but he could not accept it because "such a project, for which I personally thank you profoundly, is in frank opposition to one of the plans which I hold most dear as a lover of my country and as a leader—that of keeping the Dominican nation intimately linked with its glorious traditions, which constitute the most interesting pages of the New World Civilization."

Trujillo's followers, led by his erstwhile collaborator Senator Mario Fermin Cabral (slated to receive six years later as a token of gratitude a Trujillo-imposed jail sentence) were not satisfied with their idol's refusal. The rejection of Cabral's plan only spurred their desires to show their deep affection for the Chief. To overrule his objections, a "tremendous" petition to the National Congress was set in motion. On January 9, 1936, it was definitively presented to both chambers of Congress, backed by 599,173 signatures, a third of the population, including newly born children.

This time Congress obliged under popular pressure, although there is no record of anyone trying to verify the authenticity of the names or even bothering to count them. Without consulting Trujillo, who had gone on vacation a few days earlier, the Vice President Dr. Jacinto B. Peynado, acting as Chief of State, signed the law. This was the only time that Trujillo's power proved inadequate, commented Theodore Draper.

No one, even his closest associates, can ascertain for sure whether or not Trujillo believes all the flattery that is poured upon him from all quarters of the country and even from beyond the nation's boundaries. As an all-out megalomaniac Trujillo enjoys deeply all the dancing before the throne. He not only loves all the pageantry and adulation in which he is submerged and which he encourages by every means, but he would not be able to live one day without it. He derives genuine pleasure from hearing his sycophants proclaiming, in public as well as in private, that he is the greatest statesman of the age, the most generous, the most intelligent and the most beloved.

THAT HALF-BILLION DOLLAR FORTUNE

1.　THE DAY RAFAEL L. TRUJILLO WAS BORN (IN WHAT IS AN empty lot today) in the then poverty-stricken small village of San Cristóbal, there was hardly a piece of bread in the squalid Trujillo house. Sixty-six years later the self-styled Benefactor of a country of almost three million inhabitants and of humanity at large, if we are going to believe a host of press agents, stands on his own feet with a fortune of more than $500,000,000 as one of the handful of men who can make a legitimate claim to membership in the most exclusive club in the world—that of the billionaires and near billionaires.

It seems incredible that a man who in 1917 was a simple guard in a sugar plantation in the heart of a backward country should be able to scale in a few years the highest pinnacles of wealth, without ever dedicating a single day to any genuine business activity.

Trujillo's saga is not fable, however. His accomplishment leaves the realm of phantasy the moment it is taken into consideration that, like half the people with fortunes exceeding the half-billion dollar mark, Trujillo is the despotic ruler of an oppressed, underdeveloped nation.

In the manner of the Robber Barons of the earlier American capitalism, the Generalissimo has clawed his way up to the highest levels of material wealth, although unlike those colorful moguls of the heyday of American predatory, unrestricted capitalism, there is nothing heroic in the ascent of the Dominican tyrant to the summit of the "Very Rich Club."

The latter day Dominican tycoon, and the small group of relatives and associates whom he allows for short periods to belong to his court, have exploited the national resources without restraint or heed to considerations of national interest; they have made private capital out of the public domain and used the wealth of the land in every conceivable way to feather their own nests. Judging by the way Trujillo and his acolytes do things, these men have never heard of such a thing as a "conflict of interest." Indeed, there are many points of contact in the respective philosophies of Trujillo and the Becks, Hoffas and et al., although if the teamsters' chieftains are superior to the Benefactor on any point it is that notwithstanding their repeated recourse to the Fifth Amendment they are less hypocritical than Trujillo. Although he would indignantly reject such a comparison, there is no doubt that in practice Trujillo subscribes to Hoffa's famous candid statement to the effect that "either you are honest or you are dishonest. This conflict of interest thing doesn't mean a damn thing unless it means a man's judgment is affected." In other words, as long as you know what you are doing, you are free to do whatever pleases you.

Thus, in the hands of the Benefactor the immense powers of legislation, taxation, customs systems and tariffs, quantitative economic controls and restrictions and so forth, have been used almost exclusively for the furthering of the private interests of his own clan and the small coterie of military and civilian henchmen who surround him. In the fields they have invaded, Trujillo and his men have killed off, sometimes with the help of a very accommodating due process of law, competing and independent business.

Unquestionably, to pile up Trujillo's wealth in a small country of 2,698,126 inhabitants, who make on the average (whenever they work for a monetary salary) a little over a dollar a day, requires special talents. Nevertheless, the main ingredients of the strange compound that made possible such a fantastic accumulation of wealth within such a short time are ruthlessness and sheer lack of scruples in dealing with innocent third parties.

"The Big One" does not recognize nor respect commitments with anyone. Trujillo has compiled an unbelievable record of perjury and misleading commitments. Honesty has never been one of his preoccupations. Extortion has always been one of the resources par excellence of the Benefactor. When he wants a thing he first tries to get it by "legal" means and usually makes, before taking it over, a reasonably fair offer (particularly if the proprietor of the coveted business or real estate is a foreigner), but whenever refused he forgets about paying for it and takes whatever he wants.

With the passing of time Trujillo's extortions have grown to involve such enormous amounts of money that the common citizen no longer recognizes the familiar swindle. It is said, among the many cynics dictatorship has bred in the island, that the Dominican Academy of History is contemplating a new interpretation of the role of larceny in organized society throughout the ages. As a result the Academy is expected to declare formally that larceny is robbery, but grand larceny is glory. Then the Benefactor will be officially declared the most glorious citizen of the nation.

Trujillo's defenders, sometimes at a loss and always short of arguments on this tricky terrain, contend that in the process of enriching himself "the Big One" has also enriched others. They also argue that as a result of the Benefactor's enterprise, imagination and resourcefulness, the country as a whole has gained a full measure of prosperity. The former argument has some foundation, but the latter is totally misleading. It is true that the Dominican Republic shows many signs of outward prosperity, but as explained elsewhere its good times are due chiefly to the solid price of coffee, sugar and cocoa in foreign markets. Moreover, as anyone who has tried to interest Trujillo in any sort of project knows, he only pays attention to those schemes that promise a fast return with a minimum of capital and effort.

It may well be that Trujillo has come to identify his own welfare with that of the country, but the truth is that very few projects which are not directly beneficial for the Benefactor, or that at least promise to bring about definite advantages for him, have ever been undertaken in the country. The reigning family or their proxies figure as stockholders of practically every profitable corporation in the country. As a result every product a person buys in the country's stores, domestic or imported, means, in one way or another, actual cash money in the pockets of the Benefactor.

As a result, very few private new businesses have been started in the country during the last decade. Notwithstanding Government-avowed protection of foreign capital, the latter, especially American, has been withdrawing from the country at an exceedingly fast rate. The trend has not been upset even by the big business enterprises in the mining field started by the Benefactor in partnership with American and Canadian interests. Trujillo is becoming a little concerned over the fact that his monopolistic methods have become a matter of growing international concern. Accordingly he has instructed his close associate and Ambassador to the United States, Manuel de Moya Alonzo, to put up for sale as many of Trujillo's enterprises as he finds buyers for. Thus far all the signs are that Ambassador de Moya has found very few gullible capitalists willing to risk the uncertainties of doing business under the suffocating wing of the Generalissimo.

Prior to Mr. de Moya's efforts, some steps were taken within the Dominican Republic itself to lessen emphasis upon Trujillo's role in the economic life of the country. Jesús María Troncoso, the regime's financial wizard, chairman of the Trujillo-owned sugar corporations and "Gray Eminence" of the Administration, assured a visiting American reporter that "it is absolutely not true that the Generalissimo is as rich as some say he is."

Troncoso also denied that Trujillo owns a single corporation although he admitted that the Benefactor "will contribute capital to any new industry." Then he added: "Trujillo has not one cent abroad. The sugar mills have been sold to the agricultural bank. He leads, after all, a very quiet and frugal life. He lives strictly as a soldier. He walks a lot. He doesn't enjoy the delicacies of life—except perhaps the best horse.

"Why should he need money? He has, after all, power, which is the important thing."

The reporter then said: If Trujillo is not so rich, how come he can afford to keep an empty presidential suite in each of the two largest tourist hotels in the capital city; to hire foreign polo players to teach his sons the sport of princes; to maintain 25 cars, three yachts, 30 houses and 20-odd farms scattered around the republic? By doing so, Troncoso retorted, the Generalissimo is only upholding an establishment "that will be worthy of his country."

Yet Troncoso's statement that Trujillo does not own outright any corporation is partly true. The Benefactor's income flows from many sources and he cuts himself into practically everything, but probably a very small percentage of his investments is in his own name, a fact that makes it very difficult to ascertain with irrefutable accuracy just what and how much he owns and controls. He lets members of his family and close cronies carry the business torch for him. He is fond of dummy corporations in which his favorites in turn appear as stockholders and hold directorships as long as they are in grace. At present there are a few names whose insertion in the board of directors of a corporation is a sure sign that the Benefactor is behind it. First of all, there is his business manager and chief accountant Tirso Rivera, who has an office next door to the Chief in the National Palace. Then there is his brother-in-law Francisco Martinez Alba, who in his turn has a small coterie of his own formed by his in-laws Dr. Manuel Resumil Aragunde, Enrique Peynado Soler and Manuel Alfaro Ricart. The rest are Dr. Jesús María Troncoso Sanchez, Virgilio Alvarez Sanchez, Manuel de Moya Alonzo (the closest personal crony), Charles McLaughlin, Amado Hernández, Yamil Isaías, J. A. Perrotta, Elías Gadala María, J. Mendoza, Esteban Piola, José Delio Guzman, J. M. Bonetti Burgos. This list is by no means static and it changes according to the political fortunes of the people included. There was a time when No. 1 name on it was Anselmo Paulino, who became president of more Trujillo corporations than any other man.

While working on the preparation of his doctoral thesis for Columbia University, Dr. Jesús de Galíndez reached the conclusion that Trujillo's financial activities have the status of an open secret in the Dominican Republic and furthermore "as with all open secrets, it is difficult to substantiate them with sources of information and figures." Under the circumstances any list of Trujillo's holdings is perforce incomplete. A further complication is posed by the fact that it is very hard to distinguish the Dictator's own massive personal income from the Government's income. No one can say accurately where Trujillo's private property begins and the public domain ends. Many a business venture started by Trujillo has been quietly slipped into the Administration's pocket and vice versa. One formula advanced *sotto voce* by

Dominicans to explain the difference is: "If it loses money, it is government-owned; if it makes money, it's *El Jefe's*."

Trujillo's romance with money started shortly after his promotion to the rank of General, Chief of Staff of the National Army. In cahoots with his mistress (currently his third wife) the General organized several schemes to bleed white the Army's budget, and with the proceeds the would-be Benefactor acquired his first farm and laid the foundation of a modest fortune in cash.

By the time he won power Trujillo, although a man of certain means, was far from being a millionaire. On the same day the Vásquez regime was overthrown, Trujillo started the almost unbelievable process of grabbing, grafting and peculation out of which he was to emerge as one of the richest men on earth. "Since 1930," writes official biographer Abelardo Nanita, "all his free time from the cares of government has been devoted to developing large estates where the products of the soil yield a rich harvest and cattle is improved through breeding." This passion for land is shared by the rest of the Trujillo family. With the passing of time, "the Big One," along with his closest relatives, has become the biggest real-estate owner in the country. It is impossible to establish exactly how much land he and his relatives own, but his king-sized *Hacienda Fundación*, originally a 3,000-acre farm, extends nowadays through several provinces. This walled kingdom, guarded by soldiers armed with machine guns, is like foreign territory to unauthorized people.

If there is a thing Dominican rural men really dread, it is the sight in their neighborhood of any one connected with Trujillo's farming organization. They know that after one of those appearances their tenure on the land is no longer secure. Somehow there is the strange but by no means far-fetched notion among Dominicans that the *trujillista* fief has been put together in the first place by devious means and then maintained and developed by a rough arrogance peculiar to the reigning family.

To give Trujillo the credit he deserves it must be emphasized that his management of his farms has been efficient, his earnings good. Wastelands have been turned into grassy pastures, a profitable stable of thoroughbreds has been established, the ranch help (soldiers and prisoners in the majority) have been housed in fairly decent dwellings and the business of the operation has been organized with the efficiency of a large corporation.

Once he had fulfilled his ambition of becoming a gentleman farmer, Trujillo turned his energies to other fields. Tireless and energetic, Trujillo tossed his hat into the industrial ring. As always he covered his low, selfish, and contemptible purposes of enriching himself with high sounding words about national interest and popular welfare. For instance, the establishment of an insurance monopoly was accompanied by the passage of the first piece of Dominican labor legislation—a workers' compensation law. High tariff and restrictive quotas were established in order to create *trujillista* monopolies shielded by inspired manifestations of patriotism and nationalism. Soon the people began to learn to look with suspicion on every project announced in the national interest, knowing that behind each one of them lay the selfish predatory claw of the dictator. Soon Trujillo was the biggest business man in the country, then almost the only one. As *Time* pointed out, "While dictators in many Latin countries have fumbled their way to economic disaster, Trujillo has turned into a brutally efficient businessman. Name of the business: the Dominican Republic."

The assertion that Trujillo's business is the Dominican Republic is not a simple literary figure—it is an inescapable reality. It means that Rafael Trujillo, but not society, reaps the new riches. It means that although privately owned monopolies are specifically forbidden by the Dominican constitution, practically every industry and trade in the country is under the control of a single person. It means that while hundreds of thousands of people live in substandard conditions, the Benefactor, through his multiple interests, takes down a steady $36 million or so a year, with perhaps another $15 million to be divided among the group of proxies who administer the vast empire.

The situation is self-evident in the sugar industry—the backbone of the Dominican economy—in which Trujillo owns, through a holding corporation, twelve of the sixteen sugar mills now in operation. A newcomer in this field, the Generalissimo did not rise to a dominant position until the beginning of 1957, when he acquired the last six of his twelve properties. However, he started his encroachment right after the end of World War II, when he decided that with the riches he had accumulated during the conflict he was in a good position to wage a victorious campaign against the big Wall Street corporations that owned the majority of the plantations. To begin with, he built two sugar mills of his own. One of these new mills, the *Central Rio Haina* on the Caribbean coast eight miles west of Ciudad Trujillo, was planned as the largest sugar factory in the world. Yet, by the time it was completed, a larger one was already in operation in Venezuela.

Located in one of the richest agricultural belts of the country, alongside the Rio Haina, the Trujillo-owned sugar plantations have since been increasingly growing in size and number. Thousands of farmers have been forced to sell their lands at prices below their real value. Those who showed reluctance to sell properties in which they had been settled for generations, were forcibly dispossessed and transported to other areas. Estimates are that at least 10,000 men, women and children were thus transferred and "exiled" to isolated and not fertile enough regions of the country.

Trujillo invested large sums of his own money in the development of his sugar plantations, but in the process he was helped by the resources of the Dominican Government. His new corporations were awarded a general tax exemption for a period of twenty years, most of their cane was planted on lands watered by a Government irrigation project and roads and other land improvements were also built with government funds. Government-owned construction equipment was largely used without charge and Army trucks provided most of the transportation. Mainstays of the labor force were soldiers and convicts as well as cheap Haitian laborers who were kept as virtual prisoners behind barbed wire enclosures.

The sugar industry is no short-term, hit and run proposition. In order to operate efficiently, it requires a large original investment coupled with a sizable amount of working capital. So, by the time the new Trujillo-owned sugar mills were ready to begin operation early in 1950, after completion of the long, tedious spade work required for their purposes, the Benefactor had already sunk in the venture $30 million. In the process he learned as well a few of the facts of life that at the outset had been hidden from him by the promoters who sold him the idea of branching out into the supposedly lucrative sugar industry. Of all major Dominican economic activities none is more vulnerable to the rise of spiraling prices or the blight of softening business in foreign markets than the sugar industry. This fact, in its turn, aggravates a permanent and peculiar state of general uncertainty which prevails within the industry—periods of intense hope are followed by sudden fears of impending ruinous depression, in accordance with the latest fluctuations of an ever-inconsistent foreign market.

"The Big One" is not a man who likes to invest his good money in enterprises whose success or failure depends on matters outside his own control. A man who has turned the government into a vast and succulent barbecue, Trujillo cannot understand that kind of business in which profits are not a sure bet. The venture began to worry him, lest he could not recoup the good money he had already sunk in it. Finally he came up with an ideal solution to extricate himself. He unburdened himself of the heavy load of the sugar mills by discharging it onto the government's shoulders. For an outright $50 million, which he immediately received in cash and government securities, Trujillo sold his sugar properties to the *Banco Agrícola* late in 1953.

"The Big One" chose to disguise his coup behind a mantle of fake generosity and profound preoccupation in the people's welfare. The pillage of the national treasury was trumpeted as the beginning of a far reaching land reform intended to split up all the sugar estates among individual farmers, and bring about bountiful opportunities to the men at the bottom of the economic pyramid.[1]

To set an example and prove that the Generalissimo (who no longer

---

[1] With the help of hindsight, indeed, it is now clear that the operation was devised as a double-edged weapon. It was the beginning of a relentless *trujillista* sniping upon the foreign-owned sugar properties that eventually ended in acquisition of the coveted plantations. The squeeze play, however, was not immediately successful because the U.S. State Department put itself on record as being "deeply concerned."

owned the properties) practices what he preaches, the first land division took place in *Central Rio Haina* and its sister property *Central Catarey*. The Generalissimo put fifty-nine of his former foremen (most of them Army "veterans") in possession of as many big tracts (up to 9,000 acres) of the lands recently acquired by the *Banco Agrícola*, without even requiring from them a token down-payment.[2]

Upon completion of his propaganda maneuver (which earned him flattering press comments), Trujillo permitted himself to relieve the bank from the cumbersome job of operating such a complicated business. He agreed to buy back on easy terms the same properties he had just sold for hard cash. This time, however, he did not show his face. Several dummy corporations were set up to take over without delay the sugar properties. Presiding over the whole empire is the so-called *Corporación Dominicana de Centrales,* a holding corporation whose chairman is Dr. Jesús María Troncoso.

With large amounts of liquid capital at his disposal, Trujillo was in a position to make new inroads into the sugar industry. With calm efficiency and avoiding mistakes as well as unnecessary publicity, Trujillo's hands reached out unto the rest of the privately-owned sugar properties. In the short span of four years he concentrated in his hands the control of this industrial sector. First to capitulate to the Benefactor's "sweet approach," backed by the grim face of "legal" terror, were three small American (*Porvenir, Amistad* and *Montellano*) and one Canadian (*Ozama*) corporations. Then, on January 5, 1957, it was announced that one of the Trujillo corporations, the *Azucarera Rio Haina C. por A.*, had bought for the sum of $35,830,000 the five Dominican subsidiaries of the West Indies Sugar Company. Shortly afterwards, Trujillo added to his fold the *Santa Fe* sugar mill, leaving only four properties in private hands. Of these, three are owned by the Dominican Vicini family and only one is owned by the once preponderant American interests.

Worth at present an estimated $125 million, the Trujillo group controls nearly two-thirds of the 993,172 short tons which the sugar industry was officially authorized to produce in 1957. The corporations belonging to this group (most of which are tax exempt) have the exclusive rights to sell in the Dominican domestic market, where a pound of refined sugar costs fifteen cents. In addition, they have been allotted the lion's share of the exports to the restricted American market.

Sugar is perhaps the biggest investment Trujillo has made thus far in his country, but it is by no means the only large one. Three years ago he worked out a deal with Jacksonville shipyard tycoon George Gibbs, Jr., to set up a

[2] The land reform was a very short-lived one. Lacking capital as well as the know-how and technical facilities to operate independently on a profitable basis, the *colonos* (homesteaders) could not even meet their first interest payment. Shortly afterwards they were all back in their former posts as foremen.

$50 million port and shipyard center at the mouth of the Rio Haina, right next door to the sugar mill. For some unclear reason the partnership between Gibbs and Trujillo did not last long. By the middle of 1956 Gibbs was back home and his name had been dropped from the Corporation's name. To succeed him as head of the ambitious project, "the Chief" appointed as President of the corporation a young Navy officer, Commodore Tomas Emilio Cortiñas. After Gibbs's departure a publicity campaign was launched to stress the fact that the new shipyard, hailed as one of the biggest in Latin America, was a single-handed effort of Dominican capital.

"Puerto Haina is the biggest enterprise Trujillo has yet undertaken to increase the Dominican Republic's national income—which is sometimes hard to distinguish from his own massive personal income," wrote *Time* in the days of the Trujillo-Gibbs partnership, announced as a joint venture in which the American would put up 45% of the capital, whereas 55% would be invested by Trujillo and selected pals.

The erection of a bigger shipyard in neighboring Venezuela, along with the departure of Gibbs and the all-pervading Dominican official corruption destroyed the high hopes placed on this project. Last year Cortiñas was quietly thrown into jail; sick and tired of the big enterprise, "the Chief" "sold" it to the *Banco Agrícola*. Although some work is done and a giant floating drydock is in operation, the outlook is not bright for this costly project. But, if anyone is going to lose, it is not Trujillo. He has already got back his original investment.

Every time that new avenues of profit are open in the economic field, Trujillo and his relatives are the first, and usually the only ones, to take advantage of the situation. Under Rafael Trujillo's leadership, the Trujillo empire grows bigger and more prosperous. Trujillo now employs more than 60,000 workers in his many private factories; he is turning out glassware, edible oils, alcoholic beverages, textiles, drugs, guns—almost everything but heavy industrial machinery.

One of the first monopolies Trujillo undertook to exploit was the salt industry. He discovered that the methods employed by the owners of the salt pits along the Dominican coasts were unsanitary. Moreover, the salt deposits were located in the maritime zone which is property of the State according to Dominican laws. Doubtless the national interest called for a prompt expropriation of all the trespassing, squalid salt-producing business in the country. Thereupon this was quickly done and the *Salinera Nacional,* a company wholly owned by the Benefactor, was given the exclusive rights to produce and sell hygienic salt in the country. In its fifteen years of existence the salt monopoly reaped profits for Trujillo figured between $700,000 and $1,000,000 a year, whereas Dominicans who had traditionally paid, without contracting any disease, one cent for a pound of unsanitary salt, were forced to pay four times that much for the healthy product.

Business and politics are closely linked in Trujillo's case. Always very sensitive to the fluctuation of the political weathervane, the Benefactor saw signs of impending trouble in the democratic winds then blowing along and across the Hemisphere. In addition, he was having opposition troubles of his own inside the country for the first time since the early thirties. He decided it would be wise to make some extra cash fast, so on January 1, 1946, it was unexpectedly announced that the Generalissimo had "sold" to the *Banco Agrícola* the productive salt business for an undisclosed sum.

"The Chief's" choice proved to be a shrewd one. He cleared a large profit and the properties were there to be bought back at any time he should choose. To do this he waited another decade. After taking over the salt con-cession, the Bank invested several million dollars in new equipment to ex-ploit the heretofore untouched Barahona's Salt Mountain, a ten-mile block of solid, almost pure salt with an estimated weight of 500 million tons, which makes it one of the largest salt deposits in the world.

Late in 1955 the Bank turned over to a new corporation also owned by the Benefactor the salt mines and its costly installations. Details of the deal are not available, but the Benefactor is back selling Dominicans the salt they consume and also exporting some 600,000 tons a year. Announcements were made recently to the effect that in the years to come the Salt Moun-tain may become the basis of a major industrial development.

Cigarettes are another Trujillo exclusive and so are the matches which light them. The *Compañía Anónima Tabacalera,* the only cigarette factory in the country and the largest cigar manufacturer, had been in existence long be-fore Trujillo's climb to power. Founded by a cunning Italian businessman, Anselmo Copello, the *Tabacalera* soon edged out competitors, establishing the basis of one of the most remunerative trusts.

When the Benefactor began studying investment possibilities *Tabacalera* had to catch his eye. However, unlike the case of salt, the Benefactor could not find this time exalted reasons to justify a "legal" confiscatory action. Strong-arm methods against the owners were also out of question, since there were too many of them and, besides, quite a few were foreigners. Somehow, Trujillo found a shareholder willing to sell his stock and he established a bridgehead inside the corporation. Little by little he expanded his holdings until the moment came when he and Copello held the controlling interest.

After Copello's death, which occurred late in 1944 while serving as *trujillista* Ambassador to the United States, Trujillo assumed complete con-trol of the property, paying the Copello heirs a fraction of what their inter-est was worth. Yet, there were a few minor stockholders left and their profits were deemed excessive by the Benefactor. Thus, to curb such scandalous profiteering "the Big One" set up a new corporation, *Comisiones en General,* whose shareholders were the Benefactor and a few proxies. *Comisiones* con-tracted immediately for the distribution and selling of the *Tabacalera* production on an exclusive basis and at a very low price. There is no limitation to *Comisiones'* right to fix the retail price of cigarettes.

For years a high tariff had kept American cigarettes out of the Dominican market, since very few people could afford to pay the price of 80 cents for a package. Throughout the years, however, a black market of American cigarettes was developed in complicity sometimes with high customs officers and other officials of the Trujillo regime. For years the Dominican authorities tried unsuccessfully to stave off the spreading of the black market to no avail. Late in 1955, the Benefactor reached the conclusion that if he could not destroy the black market he might better take it over himself. But, since he does not indulge in illegal activities he entrusted his advisers with the task of finding a way to wrest the trade from the "speculators" by proper means. Negotiations were first undertaken with American manufacturers and a series of individual deals were arrived at, whereby *Comisiones en General* was made the sole distributor of the best known brands of American cigarettes in the Dominican Republic. Then, to obviate the obstacle posed by the high prices of the imported cigarettes, a tax exemption was granted to all cigarettes legally imported by *Comisiones*. The death knell at last sounded for the long existing cigarette black market and another source of income for many Dominicans was cut off.

Fabrica Nacional de Fósforos manufactures all the matches sold in the Dominican Republic. This corporation is, however, one of the two monopolies Trujillo does not own outright. "The Chief's" encroachments in this field were contained only because the controlling interest in this firm is held by the Swedish Cartel. Faced with the impossibility of breaking the Cartel's firm hold and unable to start a competing business, "the Big One" contented himself with squeezing Dominican stockholders out of part of their shares and making himself a minor but nevertheless highly influential partner.

The other monopoly in which the Benefactor is but a modest stockholder (20 per cent) is the *Cervecería Nacional Dominicana,* the only brewery at present operating in the Republic. This is another of the pre-Trujillo solid business ventures, founded by American capitalists in partnership with some enterprising Dominicans. When his efforts to buy the *Cervecería* failed, Trujillo bullied his way into the corporation by unfair competition (setting up of another brewery) and gangster-like methods of intimidation.

In practical terms Trujillo's other holdings may be roughly divided into two main groups. First, the "traditional" businesses, that is to say, the first ones which Trujillo put his hands, and next, the most recent ones.

The oldest in the first group is the *Fábrica Dominicana de Calzado* (Fa-Doc), currently managed by Trujillo's brother-in-law, Luis Ruiz Monteagudo. This factory supplies all the footgear for the Armed Forces and other government institutions. The manufacture of shoes in a country where half its citizens go barefooted, is not the kind of business Trujillo likes.

A more promising field is that covered by the lumber as well as cabinet and furniture factories. At present Trujillo owns the largest sawmills and all the existing drying facilities. Lumber exports are controlled and no one is allowed to get an export license without first paying a tribute to the companies owned by the Benefactor. Through the *Industrial Caobera,* which he owns in partnership with one of his former military commanders, Trujillo controls the furniture manufacturing business in the country. This corporation holds a virtual monopoly over the production of mahogany, and the other furniture factories must buy their stocks there.

As one of the largest cattle growers of the country, Trujillo has been interested in the meat industry right from the beginning. In the early forties, with the help of a loan from the U.S. Export and Import Bank, he built a modern slaughter house and meat packing installation in Ciudad Trujillo. Though the slaughter house is Government-owned, it has been operated by Trujillo under a long-term lease. The *Matadero Industrial and Planta de Refrigeración* not only supplies all the meat and by-products that is consumed by Ciudad Trujillo, but it is also one of the largest manufacturers of soap and lard in the country.

A wide group of the new Trujillo-owned corporations operate in the city of San Cristóbal, the Benefactor's home town, which he seeks to transform into a big industrial center. Located in San Cristóbal are the *Armería E.N.,* the $5 million arms manufacturing center founded with Trujillo's money and now operated by the Government. There we find also the *Fabrica Nacional de Vidrios,* the tax-exempt glassware monopoly, that manufactures all the bottles for the local market as well as other articles, and the *Licorera Altagracia,* the cognac factory jointly owned by Trujillo and a few members of his Cabinet.

Modas Miss America, a garment industry with its main center in San Cristóbal, is owned by American interests in partnership with brother Arismendy Trujillo. Operated by another member of the Family there is a hat factory in San Cristóbal, although this could hardly be called a medium sized business.

The *Sociedad Industrial Dominicana* is the sole producer of peanut oil in the country and perhaps one of its most lucrative ventures. Due to the fact that the production of animal fats is limited and the import of edible grease is almost stopped by a cumbersome system of quotas, licenses and high tariffs, the only cooking grease easily obtainable in the country is peanut oil. This fantastic business operation, which turns out a million gallons of oil annually, is under the control of "president" Héctor B. Trujillo, who administers it in partnership with an old crony, José M. Bonetti Burgos.

The *Industrial Dominicana* also produces more than 6,000 tons of animal feed yearly from the peanut residue. Since the Trujillo-owned cattle industry is growing steadily, indications are that the cattle-feed industry will expand considerably in the future.

Since he began his business career, Trujillo has found in transportation an inspiration for many of his greatest schemes. His particular interest in maritime developments received an early boost with the founding of *Naviera Dominicana* a shipping company that, however, never went beyond its modest beginnings. The idea of becoming a shipping tycoon seemingly revived in Trujillo's mind during the early days of World War II. With money supplied by the Export and Import Bank the Dominican government built in 1942 a group of small sailing boats with the avowed purpose of relieving, by transportation of foodstuffs, the plight of Puerto Rico and other small islands of the Caribbean, suffering hardship from the German submarine blockade and scarcity of shipping facilities.

Trujillo realized the possibilities of making a fat profit and bought the ships on terms from the government at a nominal price. Thus, he handled all the Dominican wartime export of foodstuffs to the Caribbean islands, making in the process a fabulous amount of money without risking a penny. Upon termination of hostilities he turned back to the Government, in payment of his debt, the now useless schooners.

The Benefactor then proceeded to invest $3 million of his own in a new shipping corporation, the *Flota Mercante Dominicana,* started as an all-out effort to capture business from the U.S. lines that traditionally have handled the largest share of Caribbean trade. This operation was bound to be unsuccessful. First, the ships bought by unscrupulous agents turned out to be of a type inadequate for the service for which they were intended. Second, the vessels were most of the time on repair and therefore unable to give regular service. The facts that the *Flota* operating costs were only a fraction of those of their competitors (its crews were Government-paid members of the Dominican Navy) and that Dominican exporters and importers had been told to give their trade, when operating, to the *Flota,* were not enough to offset the disadvantages. Caught in a vice whose jaws were inefficiency and corruption, Trujillo solved the problem in a ruthless way. He sent to jail all people involved in the mess and recouped his investment by the always effective expedient of dropping the hot potato into someone else's hands. He first mortgaged the corporation to the *Banco de Reservas* for $3 million, then gave it to the bank to pay the debt.

At the same time Trujillo showed a marked interest in aviation. When an opportunity presented itself at the war's end, he set up the *Compañia Dominicana de Aviación* as an affiliate of Pan American World Airways. For years CDA lived precariously, relying practically on its domestic services and on a few non-scheduled flights to Miami and San Juan, Puerto Rico. Yet, recently plans were announced to move the corporation's headquarters to a new and bigger place and it was said that studies are under way on the possibilities of new regular routes.

President of CDA is one of Trujillo's close associates and his long-time registered agent with the U.S. Department of Justice, Colonel Charles Alston McLaughlin, a U.S. Marines noncommissioned officer during the occupation of the country. One of the leading foreign residents for years, before becoming a Dominican citizen, McLaughlin, in addition to his duties as President of the CDA, acts as a purchasing agent for the Dominican Government in the United States. According to the reports of the U.S. Attorney General, the amounts received by McLaughlin to act on behalf of the Dominican Government during the period 1950–54 were figured at $910,343. Both during 1955 and 1956 he was reported as receiving $7,200 each year. The Attorney General's report does not make clear, however, how much of this money went to McLaughlin himself.

Dominican progress is well advertised by the country's varied public works programs. In port construction the Government, for instance, has spent $40 million since 1930. All the jobs in this field have been awarded to construction companies in which the Benefactor has a financial interest, chiefly the firm of Felix Benitez Rexach.

In 1946 Trujillo promised the low-income classes to build 25,000 new homes for them. Ten years later only 2,500 had been completed, but in order to speed up construction, the Generalissimo put, in 1955, the sum of $2 million into a house construction firm, the *Compañía de Construcciones Ozamas C. por A.*, whose President is Ambassador Manuel de Moya Alonzo.

To complete its numerous projects, which includes a new suburb of the capital city, the *Ozama* has been granted a very liberal credit of several million dollars by the *Banco de Reservas*. To expedite further disposal of the houses as well as to create popular interest in the housing development, Congress passed a law making legal the establishment of private lotteries with houses as prizes. Needless to say that the first and only concession under the new law was granted to *Ozama.*

Last but not least in the long, tedious list of the Family holdings comes the large group of enterprises (with a combined capital exceeding $20 million), administered by the Generalissimo's brother-in-law Francisco Martínez Alba. This group is one of the most powerful industrial combines; its forte is the representation of American manufacturers. It is no exaggeration to say that American businessmen who go to the Dominican Republic soon find out that their firms are represented one way or another by Martínez Alba.

In the United States, General Motors, Chrysler Corp. and Packard fiercely compete with each other; but not in the Dominican Republic. The same happens with Goodyear, Firestone, and many other firms. Down there they are all members of one happy family. Chrysler is represented by Caribbean Motors Co. (which also represents General Electric and scores of large American corporations), whose President is Martínez Alba himself. General Motors has as its representatives Atlas Commercial Co., another Martínez corporation whose highest executive is Enrique Peynado, married to a sister of Mrs. Martínez. President of *Dominican Motors Co.*, representatives of Packard, is another brother-in-law, Manuel Alfaro Ricart. Caribbean represents Goodyear and Atlas Firestone.

Dominican Motors is the smallest of the Dominican big three. A list of the lines it handles will give a fair idea of the size and importance of the components of this group. They are: Allis-Chalmers Mfg. Company (tractors, graders, industrial equipment, cement factories, mills, turbines); General Motors Corporation—Detroit Division—(industrial and maritime Diesel engines, power plants, spare parts); Ingersoll-Rand Company (pneumatic equipment and industrial compressors, water pumps, Diesel generators); the White Motors Company (trucks); Ford Motor Co., Ltd. (Dagenham), England (Zephyr and Consul cars, Fordson trucks); Studebaker-Packard Corporation (Packard cars); Euclid Division, General Motors Co. (scrapers, industrial trucks for mines); Bethlehem Steel Export Corp. (steel, zinc, tin, manufactured steel); Minneapolis-Moline International (tractors and farm equipment); Harnischfeger Corp. (electric welders); Thomson Machinery Co. Inc. (farm equipment); General Refractories Co. (bricks); South Bend Lathe Works (winches, spindles); Link-Belt Speeder Corporation (steam shovels); Kelvinator Corporation (refrigerators, both domestic and industrial); Zenith Radio Corp. (radios, television sets); Amrocta, Inc., (television sets, drilling equipment); Engineering Equipment Co. (winches, mixers, cement mixers); Smith Kirkpatrick-Gorman Rupp (pumps, centrifugates); Universal Road Machinery Co. (conveyors, elevators).

These products are duplicated in each one of the remaining corporations. There is no question that almost every buyer of American automobiles, manufactured articles or industrial equipment is a contributor to the Family pool.

Far from devoting his time to the care of the aforementioned interests, Martínez Alba presides over the operation of a number of other corporations, including the $7 million cement monopoly, *Fabrica Dominicana de Cemento,* which supplies all the products required to maintain the construction boom in the country. And to take further advantage of the boom, three construction outfits have been set up under the presidency of Martínez Alba: *Mezcla Lista, Concretera Dominicana* and *Equipo de Construction.* These corporations have had a hand in almost every public works job done in the country during the last five years. They can, if they wish, outbid competitors, because they are tax exempt and buy cement cheaper than any other firm, but no one bothers to follow that procedure.

The commercial and industrial activities of the ubiquitous Martínez do not end there. He is also president, as a proxy of his sister Mrs. Rafael L. Trujillo, of the hardware near-monopoly *Ferreteria Read C. por A.* Also his worries are: *Planta de Recauchado C. por A.*, the largest tire rebuilders in the country; *Fabrica de Baterias Dominicanas,* the only battery works in the island; *Caribbean Medical Supply,* wholesale dealers in medical and surgical equipment and *Industrias de Asbesto-Cemento,* the only factory for the manufacture of asbestos materials.

One of Martínez' monopolies that has gained some international name lately is the *Laboratorio Quimico Dominicana* (Dominican Chemical Laboratory), producers of all kinds of drugs and miracle cures from quinine to *Pega Palo.* The latter is a concoction extracted from a wild vine of the Dominican jungle, which is prominently advertised on posters placed in the lobbies of the best hotels of Ciudad Trujillo, as well as by the press and radio, as the miracle ("better than Spanish-fly") that gives old men young ideas. Exploiting the populace's century-old belief in the powers of the vine the *Laboratorio* prepared a mixture of the vine and rum and began to sell it in bottles whose labels have an almost pornographic appeal. To introduce this "strict monopoly of the Dominicans" to the American public a promotion campaign of vast proportions was conducted in the United States, with the help of magazines in the *Confidential* league. Hailed by *Confidential* as ". . . the Vine that makes you Virile!" *Pega Palo* was asserted to be the secret of Porfirio Rubirosa's "boudoir triumphs." A sample paragraph: "They (Dominicans) *know* that Rubi's success as the Babe Ruth of the bedrooms can be credited to a seemingly useless vine that grows wild in the forests and jungles of the Republic. They've been using the same stuff themselves."

Then, as *Time* recounted, "a fast-moving Texas insurance man heard about the vine last fall (1956), flew to Ciudad Trujillo." He signed a contract with the *Laboratorio* at a ceremony attended by Martínez Alba himself and by the top health official of the country, Dr. José Soba, who happens to be, in addition to Minister of Health, president of the *Pega Palo* manufacturing corporation.

Bridges was given the exclusive right to buy *Pega Palo* in a rum base for $77 a gallon, provided that he advertise it in the United States as an "advance" achieved in the "luminous era of Trujillo, renowned father of the New Fatherland." On June 6 the newspaper *El Caribe* printed a full-page advertisement showing photographs of one of the shipments by air of the product in five-gallon drums. Trouble was looming ahead. Bridges did not get a Food and Drug Administration clearance, but started selling the stuff only to doctors. Other importers who were able to get the bulk vine into the U.S. were doing a brisk business at $15 a stem. Then the FDA cracked down and seized $1,500,000 worth of shipments. Said *Time:* "Says the U.S. Government after extensive tests: the weed is worthless—except to its promoters." Added the *Miami Herald:* "Privately, though, many Dominicans admit that stories of aged men becoming fathers are hearsay."

Insurance was one of Trujillo's first business loves, but it is Martínez Alba who handles it for him. Since the early thirties they have owned *Compañía de Seguros San Rafael,* which for years held a monopoly in the field of workers' accident insurance. When the Government set up its own system of social security *San Rafael* graciously acceded to selling to the government its profitable accident insurance line for a sizable amount of money. The company kept on doing business in the field of commercial insurance, in which it has a near monopoly. Only in the life insurance line does it face any real competition from long-established British and Canadian firms.

No monopoly is small business, least of all a monopoly dealing with a necessity like milk. In the Dominican Republic the *Industrial Lechera* is the milk-distributing organization through which all milk in Ciudad Trujillo and Santiago must be sold. Since this monopoly was established about twelve years ago the price of milk has been steadily going up from six cents a bottle to the 17 cents it now costs. By law all dairy farms must sell their milk already pasteurized. Since the *Lechera* is the only one with the equipment required by the health authorities, theoretically not a drop of milk can be sold without having passed through its plants. However, sometimes the *Lechera* allows dairymen to dispense with the use of its pasteurizing facilities in exchange for a tribute of two cents on each bottle of milk directly sold to the consumer. Heads of this Trujillo-owned monopoly have been a succession of favorites and high officials, beginning with Anselmo Paulino. At present the chairman of the corporation is Ambassador Manuel de Moya and its general manager is de Moya's brother Miguel.

Lieutenant General Rafael L. Trujillo, Jr., rejected the Vice Presidential nomination because it might interfere with his military career. But he does not see any conflict between business activities and his Air Force duties. He now owns the second largest radio broadcasting chain (the biggest is owned by uncle Arismendy) and the paint manufacturing monopoly *Pinturas Dominicanas.* Following in his father's footsteps, Trujillo, Jr., does not show his face. The radio corporation is administered by a host of his cronies and the paint factory by his long-time associate and preceptor, J. Antonio Perrotta. For a time this corporation looked as if it might be one of the few *trujillista* business failures, but the U.S.

Department of State obligingly agreed to allow the Dominican Government to raise the customs tariffs on imported paint, which it could not do without such an agreement in accordance with international agreements. In July 1956 the new tariffs went into effect and since then the sailing has been good for the *Pidoca* paints. Perhaps the Dominican paint market is not big enough to warrant a complaint by American paint manufacturers; nevertheless, in helping the consolidation of an ailing monopoly, the State Department set a dangerous precedent.

In addition to all this, the Benefactor has invaided recently the field of textiles. In partnership with a businessman from El Salvador, Elias Gadala María, "the Big One" has set up a group of corporations to manufacture cotton textiles as well as sisal bags and ropes. As a result big cotton plantations are being developed in several parts of the country. To force farmers to produce the raw material in the quantities needed by the new industrial empire, the Department of Agriculture has declared the cultivation of cotton a matter of "national interest" and has set aside large portions of land where cotton must be grown to the exclusion of everything else. Peasants who disobey these directives are heavily fined and their properties confiscated and put in the hands of more pliant people.

Reasons of space forbid a thorough analysis of other *trujillista* trusts such as the $3 million *Chocolatera Industrial* which operates one of the biggest chocolate plants in the Hemisphere; the *Marmolera Nacional* in charge of exploiting the marble quarries, and the several construction outfits that on a permanent or provisional basis do business for Trujillo and his relatives. Land development in Ciudad Trujillo is a new field being opened with Government assistance. A $6 million project was set under way in November 1957 in the northwest sector of Ciudad Trujillo.

Even though the known mineral resources of the country are nothing to keep a mining tycoon awake, mine concessions are of permanent interest to Trujillo. One of his companies, *Minera Hatillo,* controls the iron ore deposits as well as practically all the mining rights of the country, with the exception of bauxite. Recently the Benefactor went into partnership with a group of American and Canadian capitalists for the exploration and eventual exploitation of the oil, nickel, iron, uranium and other deposits under his jurisdiction.

Gold has been produced in substantial quantities and the mine of Pueblo Viejo, one of Trujillo's concessions, still promises a good reward if rationally exploited. Present production, however, is only about $250,-000 annually, but Government geologists believe it could be expanded considerably. Most gold in the country comes from the river beds where it is washed by poor farmers and women, who are forced to sell their entire output to Trujillo's agents at prices arbitrarily set by the latter.

All this is merely a rough estimate of Trujillo's holdings. It does not comprise what the Benefactor has invested in foreign lands, of which there is no record available nor possibility of making an accurate assessment. *Time* said on August 7, 1950, that "Trujillo's foreign holdings, according to impartial sources total about $100 million—half in Puerto Rico, half in the U.S."

2. RAFAEL L. TRUJILLO'S SHEER VITALITY, HIS UNBRIDLED ambition and audacity, are plain in the long list of commercial, farming and industrial enterprises that, either in his own name or in the names of close relatives and henchmen, constitutes his expanding empire.

Trujillismo is something that goes beyond the mere grasping by a ruling clique of all available opportunities to appropriate a great fortune out of the mostly untapped natural resources of the country. These things, one way or another, have been in greater or lesser degree commonplace whenever an audacious, unscrupulous group of freebooters, be it a political party or a family, has secured hold of the machinery of government.

What makes the Dominican situation particularly abhorrent is the sheer corruption and hypocrisy that pervades the actions of Trujillo and the small group of men who carry out his ill-fated policies. They think of themselves as a natural élite, with the élite's prerogative of fixing standards and imposing its own brand of morality upon the society over which they rule. They think of government as a tidy piece of machinery, performing with the efficiency of a modern leviathan all the functions needed for the satisfaction of their appetites and invading every citizen's life with legislation in behalf of their favored grabs.

Trujillo has exacted a high price for his services. Yet, more than the amount of wealth he has taken out of the country, a thing which will perhaps prove to be less injurious than it is generally thought (since many of the productive enterprises the Generalissimo has created will be there long after he is gone), what is really disturbing is the utter degradation evident in all walks of life. With "Operation Big Swindle" in full swing for the last 27 years, government has been turned into a permanent exercise in thievery, embezzlement, bribery, blackmail and all the known unlawful devices evolved by contemporary lords of the underworld. Trujillo is in a position to make regular levies on businesses ranging from sugar mill brothels to foreign construction firms, and to arrange deals with a wide variety of foreign and domestic promoters. For residents of the country going along with "the Chief" means rich franchises and contracts, positions of prestige and power (though never permanent), and, above all, security from the hostility of Rafael Trujillo.

Under the toxic morality of the Benefactor, Dominican business and political life has taken on the virtues of the bawdy house. Unhampered by any checks or legal restraints, Trujillo brazenly misuses the country's wealth. So completely does he think of high office as an opportunity to be exploited that he has billeted an estimated 150 relatives on the country.

This pattern of freebooting was cut out by the Benefactor early. While still only chief of the Army, Trujillo began building up an organization which included several score of strong-arm men and moved into the protection rackets, enforcing underworld laws among gambling and prostitution houses. One of his specialities was the illegal introduction of Haitian workers, who were "sold" to the sugar companies at $10 a head.

As easy money rolled into the Family kit, "the Big One" began handing out huge quantities of money to buy outside symapthy and inside loyalty for his regime. He soon became one of the last genuine free spenders. Under the deluge of Trujillo's money ethics have shown, both within and without the country, a remarkable flexibility. When critics become bothersome, as happened after the disappearance of Jesús de Galíndez, "the Chief" easily obtains eminent businessmen, clergymen and U.S. Congressmen willing to issue statements praising him as an outstanding statesman of the free world.

The plundering has become so bold and systematic that it amounts to a regular levy of millions of dollars a year. For instance, to keep the wolf from his door, the Benefactor has established a rake-off of 10 per cent on every public-works contract awarded by the Government. This glaring fact came unexpectedly to the knowledge of the United States Senate in the course of a routine tax investigation during July 1957. The Senate Finance Committee then learned that the Lock Joint Pipe Co., a New Jersey construction firm, had charged off as a non-taxable business expense a bribe of $1.8 million, paid to get a sewer and water construction job in the Dominican Republic. Reportedly eighty per cent of that sum went to Rafael Trujillo himself. Questioned by members of the committee in secret session, the Internal Revenue Commissioner Russell C. Harrington said, according to press reports, that the State Department had applied pressure upon his office to allow the construction firm to deduct the bribe from its income tax. He was quoted as saying that his office took action on the matter only after the State Department had put itself on record with a plea that it was a proper deduction. The *Des Moines Register,* in a copyrighted story written by Fletcher Knebel of its Washington Bureau, showed how the "tale of international under-the-table financial intrigue" was unfolded under questioning by a group of senators headed by John Williams (R., Del.).

Although the senators emphasized that "the only direct evidence linking Trujillo to the bribe thus far was the State Department's insistence that Internal Revenue challenge the deduction," said the newspaper, it was evident that the New Jersey corporation won its Dominican building contract through the good offices of a British subject. The latter was identified later as being Mr. Albert Rogers, a brother-in-law of the current Dominican Ambassador to Washington, Manuel de Moya Alonzo.

Prodded by the senators, whose temper was described by *Newsweek* magazine as "close to boiling mad," Harrington testified that the Lock Joint Pipe Company had been told by the British subject that they "could swing the deal" by padding the bill $1.8 million to be divided between him and the Benefactor. Still more disturbing was the assertion, attributed to Harrington, that in Trujilloland such bribes were "an ordinary and necessary business expense."

This revelation at a moment in which Trujillo was under fire in the United States for other reasons, lifted a good many eyebrows but nevertheless failed to gain the national attention it deserved. Trujillo kept right on with the main business of collecting not only from Lock Joint Pipe Co. but from every corporation or man who did any kind of business with the Administration. To get an idea of how much Trujillo has made just in his cuts from public works contracts, it must be born in mind that, according to the Benefactor himself, since 1930 the Administration has spent $360 million in public works, which means a $36 million kickback for Trujillo on this item alone. Then comes another ten per cent on everything the Government sells or buys. The custom of taking a bribe is such an ingrained habit by now that there have been cases in which "the Big One" has loaned money to friends supposedly without interest only to request later a ten per cent cut on anything that is bought with the loaned sum. Even his own construction firms must pay to the Benefactor the ten per cent kickback at the moment they are awarded a contract.

No wonder public works receive a high priority in the Dominican Republic. There are cases in which Trujillo's profits in a public work go beyond the ten per cent kickback. In a hospital, for instance, even if he does not handle its building through one of his construction outfits, Trujillo always make a handsome profit. Upon signing the contract with the builders he gets the customary percentage. Then his monopoly sells the cement and *Ferretería Read* sells the steel. Since contractors are forbidden by one of the anti-monopoly Dominican laws to operate the concrete mixing equipment, they have to buy the mix from *Mezcla Lista*. If trucks, steam rollers or tractors are needed there is a good chance that these are bought from *Caribbean Motors Co*. Then when the hospital is finished it is equipped and furnished by *Caribbean Medical Supply*. Once it is under operation the medicines, drugs and other supplies are sold by the Trujillo laboratory.

From the outset another favorite method of the Trujillo family to secure hard cash has been that of buying cheap from the Government and then reselling at fantastic prices. There are cases in which the same property has gone back and forth from the Government to the Trujillos several times. There is a farm named *Altagracia Julia* which no one ever knows for certain who owns at a given time.

Legally or illegally (mostly the latter), all agricultural and industrial production is either directly controlled by Trujillo or his family, or has to pay tribute to them. The existing duplicity of legal taxation and private assessment of business accounts for the high cost of living. Businesses like bakeries, for example, which Trujillo has not deigned to take over directly, must pay protection to remain open. For each sack of flour which is used, bakeries pay Trujillo a flat amount.

Gambling has been legalized in the big tourist hotels and in the Trujillo-owned night clubs. The concessions of the lucrative casinos are awarded to those who pay the best prices not to the Government but to the Benefactor. For years the Generalissimo took the giant's share from the National Lottery proceeds. For almost 23 years the lottery was leased to Ramon Saviñon Lluberes, the largest urban real estate owner in the country and Trujillo's brother-in-law. Then, without any explanation, the lottery was put in the hands of the Government. During the time Saviñon administered the concession no figures were ever made public on lottery profits. An idea, however, of the magnitude of this business is afforded by the fact that in the national budget for 1956 the revenues from the lottery alone were figured at $6 million for that year. Protection of illegal gambling (rampant in the sugar properties and other industrial centers) is shared by Trujillo with his military commanders. In the capital city, however, anything connected with the number rackets as well as protection to houses of ill repute and other centers of vice falls within the jurisdiction of brother Romeo "Pipi" Trujillo.

Sometimes "protection" is given by the Trujillos to people who do not need it. There is the racket of the law suits intended to despoil people of their property in accordance, of course, with due process of law. Many times the Trujillos content themselves with intervening in a law suit already started on the side of one of the parties, in exchange for a fee. Occasionally, however, they start their own law suits. So widespread is this practice that Dominicans call brother Virgilio Trujillo "Mr. Supreme Court."

Trujillo's most fabulous opportunity to make millions came with World War II. The entry of the country in the conflict made necessary the imposition of a series of controls over exports and imports. Supposedly devised to aid in a more effective distribution of inadequate supplies, such regulations were promptly turned by Trujillo into a racket to line his own pockets. Nothing could be either exported or imported, not even a needle, without a license and to secure such documents people had to pay the Benefactor, through the official "controls," a certain amount of money, depending upon the size of the shipment. No receipts were given nor any record was ever kept of the transmissions, but without a visit to the control offices no goods could be moved off the docks. Before long Dominicans knew these offices as the *Aduanitas* (little customs houses).

The system was kept in full force (except for American businessmen who after a diplomatic protest were relieved of the obligation to visit the *Aduanitas*) during the War. At the end of the conflict the system was discontinued to be reimposed again for a few months during the Korean War.

After all controls had been legally lifted, the *Aduanitas* kept on taxing the exports of coffee and cocoa. Finally, the system was thought to be undignified and too obviously copied from gangsters. To substitute for it, two export cartels were formed among coffee and cocoa exporters. The Generalissimo was made an honorary member of both with the right to reap a profit without sharing in the risks of the operations. To this day, however, whenever an independent cattle raiser ships his livestock to foreign lands, Trujillo collects from four to five dollars per head of cattle.

Trujillo firmly believes that insurance policies are taken out to be collected. Thus, whenever any of his factories or other business installations is becoming obsolete, unprofitable or in any manner more a liability than an asset, a mysterious fire breaks out. The modern mills of the peanut oil factory were built upon the charred location of the former factory. Then, last year, sisal stocks were perilously accumulating in the warehouses of the Azua plantation faster than orders came in from the foreign clients. One day a fire destroyed them and *San Rafael* paid the insurance money without further investigation.

Arson is also employed as a method to get business competitors out of the way. Another recent fire, in which the usually efficient firemen of Ciudad Trujillo were seemingly unable to save anything, destroyed beyond repair the only paint factory in competition with Trujillo, Jr., *Pinturas Dominicanas*. This time the destruction was total and no better factory was built upon the ruins. The business had not been insured. Short of capital (the entire business was estimated at $5,000), the owners were unable to raise the high premium asked by *San Rafael*.

The Benefactor's methods for liquidating losing ventures have been tried even on an international scale, sometimes successfully. At the end of World War II the Dominican government acquired a discarded Canadian liner. Named the *Nuevo Dominicano* the ship was reported to be the beginning of a new national merchant marine. Its operation, however, soon proved uneconomical. Trouble accumulated until "the Chief" decided to get rid of the ship without losing, of course, the original investment.

First he sold the *Nuevo Dominicano* to a Miami syndicate, one of whose members was the Dominican Consul General in that city. These people did not operate the ship long. In October, 1953, they dispatched the *Nuevo Dominicano* on ballast to Ciudad Trujillo, supposedly for repair. Then it was announced that she had been lost off the Cuban coasts. No sooner had the news of the *Nuevo Dominicano* wreck been received than the Dominican Government filed a $1.3 million claim with the insurance broker, through the *San Rafael*. The case was taken over by the Government because, it was asserted, the alleged new owners had not complied with their obligation of making a down payment. The original claim was filed in the United States through the Florida law office of Senator George Smathers. The underwriters started their own investigation of the shipwreck and despite all kinds of pressure brought to bear upon them by the Dominican Government, its lawyers and diplomatic representatives refused to pay. Then Trujillo hired the services of the British law firm of Hill, Dickison and Company, in the month of June, 1954, and a law suit was started against a group of underwriters headed by the firm of H. G. Chester, of London. The underwriters served notice they would fight to the bitter end and appointed as their lawyers the firm of Walston and Company.

After some spade work, pre-trial examinations and shadow boxing, Trujillo's attorneys left the matter in abeyance and it is doubtful that the matter will ever be pressed to an open trial by the Dominican Government. This refusal of the underwriters to comply with the Trujillo regime's claims is highly significant since the insurance people are not known for any love for litigation.

There is evidence that "the Big One" does not shy away from consorting, when occasion warrants it, with known figures of the international underworld. Although the charges that Trujillo is a regular partner of the great figures of America's gangland should be discarded in all probability as just another figment of the imagination of those writers who tend to associate almost everyone with Lucky Luciano and Three-Finger Brown, the fact is that occasionally Trujillo is not totally innocent.

It is a well-known fact that many of the most dangerous fugitives of justice have found refuge in the Dominican Republic, provided they have enough money to meet the price set by the Benefactor or willing enough to put their talents at the service of the cause. Recently one of America's most wanted men spent a rest period under "the Chief's" protective wings. He is Edward W. Curd, of Lexington, Ky., identified as Frank Costello's "bookmaker." He has also been accused of being a top figure in basket ball scandals and is under a federal indictment for income tax evasion.

According to an Associated Press dispatch in the *Miami Herald* on June 10, 1957, since 1952 Curd's wanderings, with T-men on his tail, "have taken him from the U.S. to Canada, the Dominican Republic, Cuba and finally the Bahamas." After being exposed by the Kefauver Committee, reported the AP, Curd left the United States and headed for Canada. "After three years there he was afraid the T-men were getting close, so he sailed on a freighter for the Dominican Republic—Trujillo's domain in the Caribbean."

Serge Rubinstein, the man who nearly wrecked the national economies of France and Japan, and who rigged scores of phony deals in the United States, was at the time of his mysterious assassination involved in deals with the Trujillo regime, through the Development Commission, for the chartering under Dominican laws of a bullion bank. This institution was going to operate in Europe, where there are hundreds of people willing to pay any premium provided they can convert their fortunes into solid, legal gold coin.

Trujillo and his associates control three-quarters of the country's means of production and maybe a greater share of the national income. On the other side are the downtrodden Dominicans, who produce little, earn less and consume almost nothing.

☒ ☒ ☒

"PERFECT BOY SCOUTS"

LIKE BOY SCOUTS, THE MEN AROUND TRUJILLO HAVE TO DO their daily good deeds in order to remain in the good graces of their lord and master. Usually what they did yesterday, and much less the day before, does not make much difference. They have to prove themselves anew everyday, and no matter what kind of response they get from the object of their fawning, they must keep on with an unabated show of loyalty. Every public servant is bound forever to the Benefactor, and, however distinguished his past or present services, he is not supposed to expect anything in return.

Trujillo expects this blind loyalty from his subordinates, but he does not pay back in kind. It is said that "the Big One" is a man who neither forgets his enemies nor forgives his friends and that he has heaped more personal indignities on his cronies than on his foes. It is never a beautiful thing to see men betrayed and destroyed by those whom they serve or by their closest friends and associates. Yet this is an almost daily spectacle.

As a result there is a frightful scarcity of men of character in Trujillo's retinue. Only "yes men," ready to bend, swing and dance to any tune, are capable of resisting for long the unceasing pressures brought to bear on his collaborators by the Dominican dictator.

Ever since he succeeded in treacherously snatching power from a man who trusted him, Trujillo has been apprehensive that somewhere within the ranks of his own followers there is a man ready to repeat the story. In all the Era of Trujillo, no chum had been closer to "the Big One" than Secretary of State Without Portfolio Anselmo Paulino Alvarez, who from 1947 to 1954 was the second most important man in the Dominican scheme of things. Neither before nor after had anyone been so powerful as Paulino grew to be, nor so devoted a servant of "the Chief." No one did so many different chores for the Benefactor—from buying his daily bread to troubleshooting for him in foreign lands. No Dominican knew more secrets about Trujillo than Paulino. One day, however, with no warning whatsoever, Paulino was a broken man—stripped of power and office; his wealth confiscated; sneered at by his former friends; attacked by the press he once controlled and arrested by the secret police he had commanded.

If any moral can be drawn from Paulino's example, it is that not even devoted service saves those who by any chance catch the suspicious eye of "the Big One." People hold their posts as long as Trujillo allows them to stay in office. No place in the pyramid of command is for keeps and no authority except Trujillo's is more than provisional. No wonder the composition of the inner circle has a very fast turnover.

Few men have been in the administration from its inception. Those who helped Trujillo grab power were his first victims. They soon discovered that, contrary to their original hopes, the young soldier would not be a pliant tool of their own political interests. He had his own aims, and in furthering them he maneuvered his former associates into a position of utter helplessness.

As so often happens, the partners quickly fell out over the division of the spoils. Estrella Ureña was one of the first to go, followed by Rafael Vidal, and then Roberto Despradel. It may well be that some of these men were conspiring against Trujillo, but others were not. It seems more probable that they expected in return for their help something Trujillo has never given to anyone—a small measure of recognition, gratitude and appreciation for services rendered. Or perhaps they were dismissed, imprisoned (and some killed like Desiderio Arias) only because Trujillo thought them too powerful or too strong willed to have around him.

Whatever the reasons, they were soon replaced by a group of personal friends of the Dictator, picked from those men who had socially promoted Trujillo during the bygone and unspeakable days when the shortsighted aristocrats were shutting their doors in the would-be Benefactor's face. These men, however, though they lasted longer than the old-style politicians, were eventually cast out. By 1946 there were very few of them still active in government and though some (as it is the case with a few of the 1930 political chieftains) still come and go in government posts they no longer have any active part in the implementation of the main policies of the regime. They have been replaced by trained bureaucrats without roots in the political, economic, social or cultural fabric of the nation; men devoid of personal prestige and lacking any future of their own. Without political significance of their own (although sometimes technically and intellectually competent) the only role these men play is that of complacent, hard-working messenger boys for "the Big One." With a big stake in the regime, these people are the strongest supporters of the *status quo*.

Notwithstanding the elimination from national leadership of most of the prominent political figures of the past, Trujillo's inner maneuvering is by no means over. The present Cabinet Ministers and the rest of the clique recognize that they owe their current positions to the always blessed "generosity and benevolence" of the illustrious Benefactor of the Fatherland. Although there is not the slightest hint of independence within the Government's ranks, the Generalissimo does not lower his guard lest one of his subordinates think that the time is approaching when his own star deserves to shine.

To avoid such a possibility Trujillo follows the ancient rule of "divide and conquer." Knowing that no one is a kingdom by himself, that no one can do anything alone in the realm of political action, he does not allow the formation of dangerous cliques among his collaborators, either civilian or military. He regards all personal ties among his associates as suspicious. Thus, even though individual friendships within the ruling coterie are not formally forbidden or outwardly declared reprehensible, they are nevertheless viewed with the utmost distrust and discouraged as much as possible. As soon as two officials are known to be on friendly terms or if their families visit each other with unusual frequency, the machinery of insidious intrigue is set to work to break the link of intimacy.

Trujillo often personally takes care of planting the seeds of discord whenever the chosen victims are among those in direct contact with him. His favorite method is to tell someone a particularly offensive and unpleasant truth about his own private life or official conduct (usually gathered by the secret police) and to ascribe the source of this information to the closest friend the man has at the moment. Knowing the truth of what Trujillo has said (or highly offended if it is a lie), the intended victim is likely to believe without further investigation that his unfaithful, treacherous friend betrayed him to the Benefactor. The reaction usually is "Did he say *that* about me? Well, now listen to *this* about him." After that the friendship is ruined for good.

In this way political rivalries have been transferred from the public platform to the palace chambers, from the press to the boudoir. Intrigues grow—for no one knows who is holding the dagger that will stab him in the back—and individuals fight constantly among themselves to retain the favors of the tyrant. Hardly anyone is to be trusted and those who feel real friendship for one another soon learn to cover up their feelings. Under the stern eye of "the Big One" Dominican high officials live immersed in an atmosphere of intrigue, duplicity and mutual hatred.

The anxieties to which Dominican officials are subjected are well illustrated by an old custom which has fallen into disuse during the last seven
or eight years. At the outset of the regime, and for many years afterward,
the newspapers, under Trujillo's instructions, used to blow their sirens to
announce the appointment of new cabinet ministers, and many were the high
officials who learned of their sudden demotion by listening to the whistle.
This strange custom gave rise to a series of wisecracks, one of which concerns a Foreign Minister who, in the middle of a conference with a foreign
diplomat, heard *La Nación's* siren and inquired of a subordinate the reason
for the racket. He was politely advised that he better start cleaning up his
desk since his substitute was already on his way down to take over the post.
It is said that the visiting diplomat finished his conversation with the new
appointee. The story may be apocryphal but it lends support to the authentic account of a long-time collaborator of the Generalissimo who, questioned
about his experiences as the holder of a cabinet office, blandly said: "It is
just a period of anguish between two blows of a siren."

Officials must get accustomed to all this. "Discipline is the keynote of the
Dominican Government," wrote an American reporter in an admiring vein
and, perhaps unwittingly, he was pointing out a great truth. The Dominican
civil service of today is a descendant of the military barracks where Trujillo
received his training in the science of government. That the Benefactor is a
man of action, a hard worker, a capable organizer and a stern disciplinarian
is made evident not only by the vast distance he has traveled in his sixty-six
years but by the well-cultivated garden he keeps. It must never be forgotten, however, that the talents of a mule driver should not be confused with
statesmanship. In accordance with Trujillo's unyielding standards, all public
offices start work at 7:30 in the morning and do not close shop until 1:30
P.M. No loafing is permitted among clerks and employees, and in order to
make sure that his instructions are strictly carried out, "the Big One" himself periodically makes unannounced visits to the several departments. His
unexpected appearances have been the occasion for the spectacular undoing
of many a Cabinet Minister caught off base. They earn a yearly salary of
$36,000 which places them among the best paid civil servants in the world.
The high level of salaries is restricted to the top echelons. Rank and file employees live on substandard wages—clerks earn from $60 to $200 a month
and there are still people on the Government's payroll whose earnings are
$30 a month, less the customary ten per cent for the *Partido Dominicano*.
Teachers, as probably everywhere else, are among the poorest of the white
collar workers. Yet, the custom of closing public offices at 1:30 P.M. is a
blessing for many Government employees, because it gives them enough
spare time to take a second job which allows them to make ends meet.
Others take advantage of the opportunity to educate themselves, as University classes are conducted only during the afternoon and night.

To give credit where credit is due, it must be admitted that there is much truth in the contention that the Dominican machinery of government is well-oiled and adjusted, and seemingly capable of a large output of routine work. On the other hand, it is also true that the Dominican civil service has a total lack of initiative and independence. Nothing is ever decided by a Government department without first being referred to the National Palace. It is at "the heights" that even the granting of sick leave to a minor clerk is approved.

The harsh methods employed to keep official servants in line have been successful only to a certain extent. They insure loyalty and conformity, but they breed mediocrities trained for unreflective subservience. Even the "president" is a victim of the system. In spite of the fact that the office is nowadays in the hands of a trusted member of the family, the Generalissimo insists upon taking all decisions by himself. He is the one who first sees all the correspondence and other official documents—even the private letters addressed to brother Héctor. Documents and official decrees are only taken to the President for his signature. There have been cases when Trujillo has made up a decision on an important matter of state at an hour (or in a place) when Héctor was not available. On these occasions the "president" learns of his own decisions along with the rest of Dominicans—by reading the morning papers.

The "president" has his offices in the west wing of the National Palace and a usual sight is that of His Excellency hurriedly going back and forth, like any employee, from his office to the suite of the Generalissimo on the opposite side of the building. The rest of the time Héctor kills his boredom by practicing his favorite pastime of eavesdropping. He spends hours tinkering with a contraption that allows him to listen in on other people's telephone conversations. A nice hobby for $283,550 a year.

It may be worth noting that the Benefactor still meets with his ministers once in a while. Cabinet meetings, however, are long, boring affairs where hardly a thing of importance is ever taken up. "The Big One" sits at the head of a big mahogany table, with the President at his right, and proceeds to take up minor business, presumably to trip his aides into mistakes or uproot minor deficiencies in the administrative procedures. Yet more than one minister has lost his job over an inconsequential *faux pas,* such as not knowing the name of a clerk the Benefactor had just met a few days before in a far-away part of the country.

The Cabinet meetings are also God-sent occasions for Trujillo to humiliate his aides—with the foulest of language—in front of their colleagues. "Good for nothings," *"imbéciles,"* "thieves" and other stronger epithets are freely hurled by the Benefactor at the cornered and harassed courtiers. Devoid of humor and without command of repartee, Trujillo has not left to posterity a single memorable phrase or an anecdote worth recounting. As a rule, following one of these barbed, brutal tongue-lashings, the battered ministers hurry back to their offices to wait for their substitutes. Queer as it may seem, the audience heartily enjoys the show.

Upon demotion from ministerial rank, Trujillo's aides are usually sent to serve a term in Congress. Both the Senate and the Chamber of Deputies are rather like a purgatory, where the further fate of ousted collaborators depends upon their future behavior. There the purged cronies wait for the forthcoming moment of pardon, although they know that they will never be back in positions of trust, no matter how high-sounding the titles of their future offices. Sometimes, Congress is but the threshold of everlasting oblivion—and even jail and death. In line with this policy at least twenty former Cabinet officers occupy seats in this Dominican "Siberia."

Their humiliations are by no means over. It is possible that one day upon his arrival in the Capital the congressman will be notified that his presence is no longer necessary since his "resignation" (which he signed undated the day he took his oath of office) has been submitted and Congress is all set to "elect" a substitute. This is perfectly legal in Trujilloland since Article 16 of the Dominican constitution provides that "When vacancies occur in the Senate or in the Chamber of Deputies, then the body in question will select the replacement from a trio to be presented by the political party to which the person who caused the vacancy belongs." It is always the first of the three proposed substitutes whom Congress automatically elects.

This practice allows the regime to pull fast publicity stunts whenever it deems fit. When a group of four U.S. Congressmen visited the Dominican Republic in April 1957, the Generalissimo impressed them with the "election" of one of the leaders of the colony of Jewish refugees of Sosua, Mr. Adolf Rosenzweig, as the deputy for a district "predominantly Roman Catholic." The Generalissimo also told the visiting members of the U.S. House of Representatives (Earl Chudoff of Pennsylvania, Isidore Dollinger of New York, Samuel N. Friedl of Maryland and Herbert Zelenko of New York, all Democrats) that his country would open its doors to 5,000 Jewish refugees from Egypt. Both things were excellent headline-catchers and were accepted by the guests. Upon returning to the United States, Representative Zelenko and other members of the group were cited as expressing great praise of the Generalissimo. They also judged the "election" of Rosenzweig as proof of "the freedom of opportunity, freedom of worship and absence of any kind of racial or religious discrimination" in the country. Unfortunately, the visiting Congressmen did not consider it worth-while to ask the brand-new deputy, whose taking of oath they witnessed, either how long he had campaigned or by what plurality he had been elected. Nor did they ask Trujillo *when* and *how* he proposed to make good his offer of help to the Egyptian Jews.

By these and other tricks of unsurpassed cynicism, Trujillo has been able to sell the outside world a lot of tripe about the excellence of his regime. There is, for example, the oft-repeated contention that the Dominicans were so badly off before Trujillo that they had lost all faith in the possibility of an independent existence. "Most Dominicans believed," says one of these acccounts, "the country would have to surrender sovereignty, become a kind of protectorate of the United States or League of Nations. The only alternative seemed anarchy. Then came Trujillo, who not only gave his people back their self-respect but has done away with all the country's defects. People are forthright citizens today, honest, hard working and intent only on what is good for the country according to the directives given to them by the Benefactor. Only the pick of the litter work for Trujillo who has done away with opportunism." Cynics, of which there is an abundant crop in the Dominican Republic at present, say that of this propaganda only the last contention is true. After all, they say, opportunism requires at least some ability to stand up and take chances, and this is no longer possible in the Dominican political vineyard.

Unlike their counterparts in other Latin nations, it is officially proclaimed, Dominican public servants are honest and incorruptible. Grafters have been totally eradicated and the highest norms of administration are enforced throughout all levels of Government. Again cynics say that surely there *is* less graft in the country than elsewhere; there is only one grafter. But, either to hide this latter fact or because the real situation has gotten out of hand, the truth is that on this subject the regime seems to have developed a strange case of split-personality. While most of its propagandists beat the drums about administrative cleanliness for all its worth, others, including the local press, paint a dark picture of utter moral degradation among public servants.

Trujillo has asserted that the only function of a free press is to print criticism "against public functionaries who do not complete their duties in an honest manner," and if such standards are applied to the Dominican situation there is no alternative but to believe that here is either the freest press in the world or the most fraudulent government. According to the letters daily printed in the "Foro Público" of *El Caribe,* the men around Trujillo are all crooked and the present Dominican regime is the most corrupt enterprise in the world. Those people who are not thieves, embezzlers, smugglers, liars, drunks or incompetents are either communists or homosexuals. Only the names of the Benefactor and those of his closest relatives are kept out of this systematic process of debasement incessantly carried on by the parrot press. The "you sinners" theme is played over and over again in letters manufactured in the presidency to soil the names of friends and foes alike. That this gruesome ritual goes beyond its supposed purpose of humiliating high government officials is shown by the fact that recently the Benefactor has been taking a very stern view of charges as reported in the "Foro." In November 1957, following an investigation prompted by one such letter to the editor, he decided upon the mass firing of the members of the corps of traffic cops. Then several high officers of the Army and National Police were accused of taking bribes and grafting on a large scale, and on top of that came the merciless downgrading of Major General Rafael Espaillat (retired), who was stripped of his rank and "resigned" as a member of Congress, in punishment for alleged misconduct. The chastisement of Espaillat was a particularly pointed example, since he had been a trusted personal aide of Trujillo for several years, the author of the preface to the official military biography of the Generalisssimo, and the man who initiated the army cult of "the Chief's" personality by naming, during the middle Twenties, the small lot in front of San Francisco de Macoris fortress "Trujillo Square."

Corruption is so widespread within officialdom that it reaches out of the country into the Diplomatic Corps. In recent years the names of several Dominican diplomats have been involved in international incidents which involved shady deals in money, arms, jewelry and other contraband.

César Rubirosa, younger brother of international "lover boy Porfirio," was for years a chargé d'affaires in several European countries. Somehow, while serving in Switzerland, César began to use his diplomatic immmunity to carry gold and other hot merchandise across international boundaries. One day as he toured the Mediterranean, he got careless and the Athens police caught him at an airport with an illicit $60,000. As he was not accredited to Greece his diplomatic passport wasn't much help. Convicted and sentenced by a Greek court to eighteen months in jail and a $250,000 fine, he served the term but was unable to raise the money. He was forced to stay in the country in order to pay the fine with money earned by his own work, and for a few years he was a forced resident of the city of Corinth. The Greeks were only taking off from his yearly salary an amount equivalent to one per cent of his total debt, which was likely to make him a resident of Greece for the rest of his days. Finally, brother Porfirio made up his mind to intercede with his old pal the Benefactor, who in turn did the same thing with the Greek authorities. As a result César's debt was canceled and the dashing *trujillista* diplomat was deported to the Dominican Republic. The story of César Rubirosa was by no means over, however. Early in 1957 he mysteriously showed up in San Juan, Puerto Rico, despite the fact that his known record of undiplomatic activities in Europe made him ineligible for entry into American territory. For weeks he moved freely about town, until one day he slipped away as quietly as he had come into the island. Upon his return to the Dominican Republic, he was restored to the diplomatic service as a protocol officer.

Sergio del Toro's grisly story is another short course in the twisted realities of *trujillista* diplomacy. Del Toro, a young adventurer formerly associated with the Dominican exiles group in the abortive revolutionary attempt of Cayo Confites, helped by dual nationality status (his late father had been

Puerto Rican) had settled down in New York. There, it seems, he met Consul General Felix Bernardino, then engaged in a Soviet-style "come home campaign" among Dominican expatriates living in Manhattan. Through Bernardino's good offices, del Toro patched up his former differences with the Benefactor and as part of a group of former opponents turned collaborators he visited Ciudad Trujillo in 1952. After a much publicized tour of the country the group went back to New York and shortly afterwards several of them received appointments as errand boys for Trujillo, with the diplomatic status of Commercial Attaches. As a member of this chain stationed in El Salvador, del Toro was responsible not to the foreign office but to Bernardino. In the month of July 1956 the Salvadorian authorities announced that they had caught del Toro with an illegal shipment of small arms in his possession.

With the police on his heels, del Toro crossed the border and went into Guatemala. There, despite the fact that according to a United Press dispatch he was using a properly issued and stamped Dominican diplomatic passport, the Guatemalan police arrested del Toro and sent him back to El Salvador. Given the choice of staying in jail in El Salvador or being deported to Santo Domingo, del Toro decided to face the local punishment. "I'd rather be a prisoner in El Salvador than in the Dominican Republic."

In the meantime the Dominican government disclaimed any responsibility for del Toro's activities. Through its chargé d'affaires in San Salvador (the Ambassador was conspicuously absent throughout the whole process) the Dominican government accused del Toro of using a forged passport to cross the border into Guatemalan territory, of having falsified the chargé's signature, and of being a communist agent of the oft mentioned-never seen "Caribbean Legion." How the Legion was powerful enough to infiltrate Trujillo's diplomatic ranks or why "the Chief" was using a man of del Toro's background went unexplained by the Dominican foreign office.

The stories of *trujillista* diplomatic indiscretions could fill a volume in themselves. For instance, before receiving the official agreement from the United States Government to act as Dominican Ambassador to Washington, the current incumbent, Manuel de Moya, delivered, on April 5, 1957, a controversial speech on the "Galíndez-Murphy Affair" before the San Francisco Commonwealth Club, which raised questions about his acceptability to the American Government.

In his speech de Moya declared that those in the United States who blamed the Generalissimo for the disappearance of Galíndez were either communists or communist dupes. He further declared: " 'Operation Galíndez' and 'Operation Murphy' . . . were beautifully timed and executed propaganda offensives. And both times the opposition succeeded in having non-Communist elements carry the ball."

Then, as reported by the *Washington Evening Star,* de Moya "also ran into trouble at the gaming tables of Las Vegas, Nevada, on his way back East after the April 5 speaking engagement. It is reported Mr. de Moya lost a large amount of money at the desert resort and was told to come home by his government." All of this added up to a tempest in a tea pot, however, and Mr. de Moya is happily performing as the *trujillista* envoy in Washington.

No one can tell for sure what standards Trujillo follows in choosing his collaborators, since his government is an heterogeneous composite of men of different extraction, intellectual ability, and methods of performance. The mark of the Generalissimo's skill is that—whatever his ways of recruiting collaborators—he has been able to rally around him men of all calibers—who willingly or unwillingly serve his purposes loyally—and that he seemingly has at hand at all moments the right person for each mission—from the bumping off an inconvenient foe in the heart of Manhattan to the handling of a delicate matter at the U.S. State Department.

"The Big One" has won over quite different sorts of people, who might normally be on different sides of democratically erected fences. Although in private he prefers to consort with "hoods," and among his closest cronies and drinking companions are a curious medley of pimps, thugs, promoters and shady operators—both imported and domestic—Trujillo can also display decent looking people who impress foreign dignitaries with their charm and intellect and smooth out the more irksome matters of state.

The Benefactor, as a rule, is not stingy with these men. During their tenure of favor, before their final and inevitable relegation to obscurity or some worse fate, the close collaborators, especially those with access to the private aspects of Trujillo's life, are rewarded with gifts and business opportunities. Wealth, however, is as precarious a thing as favor itself. Trujillo is a well-recognized "Indian Giver" and even his former mistresses are stripped of money and property when disgrace strikes. A few, however, of the down-graded aides have been allowed to keep their fortunes after they were no longer in the good graces of the Benefactor. "A Dominican high official must know," said one of the group, "that there is another certain thing besides death and taxes—demotion."

After demotion very few people have been given the chance to stage a real comeback. Many people are taken back into the fold after being severely punished and their special capabilities used for the benefit of the regime, but most of them never regain their former privileged positions of trust. Thus, with the passing of time, the circle of accepted representatives of the *trujillista* ideal grows increasingly narrower. The dubious distinction of a place in the inner sanctum at the National Palace is accorded nowadays only to men devoid of moral scruples, ready to carry out with no questions the most absurd commands received by the Generalissimo. Only those who by hook or crook manage to feed his hankering for narcisstic gratification with fulsome praise and abject denial of self-respect are rewarded by the Benefactor with the rank of "Eagle Scouts" in his regime.

VENTURES INTO TOTALITARIANISM

1. RAFAEL LEONIDAS TRUJILLO'S PEN PALS, BOTH WITHIN AND without the country, make increasingly desperate efforts to present their hero as a shining crusader—a sort of modern Archangel—defending at all times Faith and cherished Christian traditions from the relentless assaults of the atheistic communist beasts.

Patently pleased with his truth-squad's anti-Red build up, "the Chief" proclaims, whenever he has an occasion, his exploits as the self-appointed bulwark of anti-communism. He has saved his country and humanity from the communists who, for reasons never clearly explained, have repeatedly chosen, among all nations, "the Big One's" republic as the target for their main attacks in the Western Hemisphere. No one knows why the communists hate Trujillo so much, but if we are to believe "the Chief" and his Madison Avenue experts, the hatred goes to the point where, in order to discredit the kind Benefactor, they have become accustomed to bumping off critics of the Dominican regime living on American soil.

It is with horror that one must record the ease with which Trujillo has managed to make political capital out of the well-justified fear of communism. Exploiting this widespread apprehension, this man—who flouts the constitution of his land and derides his oath of office—has achieved a self-assumed position of so-called leadership within the highly honorable anti-communist crusade. In the name of democracy, Trujillo has acquired a free ticket for trampling upon the liberties and freedoms without which democracy is a sham. And, worst of all, not always is this proclamation of "democratic" leadership looked upon as a spurious by-product of a well-greased propaganda apparatus. This brazen stand—so obviously tainted with cynicism and hypocrisy—has earned the Benefactor a reputation as a "useful" and "friendly" dictator in certain sectors of American officialdom. He is seemingly accepted without reservation by political leaders of high standing, including such distinguished members of the American Congress as the House Majority leader John McCormack (D.-Massachusetts) and the senior ranking Republican of the Senate Foreign Relations Committee, Alexander Wiley, of Wisconsin.

Trujillo's overriding passion for power has upon several occasions brought him into close contact with totalitarianism of both the right or left varieties, both at home and abroad. His ventures into totalitarianism have included deals and alliances with practically every dictatorship of any importance in contemporary history. Aside from his close relations with all Latin American strong-men, from Juan Perón to Marcos Pérez Jimenez, his known flirtations with Mussolini, Hitler, Franco and Stalin are now a part of history.

The Generalissimo's natural inclinations have led him to look for, not always wisely, rapprochements with Old World totalitarians. Yet, anyone who carefully analyzes the intricate maneuvers of this political strategist will discover that he has an uncommon ability to detect the faintest sign of a shift of wind. Whenever the tide of favor turns away from one of his allies he will cut his relations with that man. Whenever reasons of expedience make advisable the severance of dubious connections, this cunning, unfaithful and unscrupulous operator has dropped his fellow travelers without hesitation or remorse.

As a firm believer in only one "ism"—that of Trujilloism—the Benefactor has displayed unusual dexterity in getting rid in due time of each one of the perilous associations upon which he has entered. Sometimes he has nearly lost his equilibrium, but never has he tumbled into disaster. His shrewdness, his subtle hypocrisy, his innate dishonesty, and his unbelievable good fortune have, in each instance, saved him.

Nowadays he plays ball with Washington and bullies the small nations of the Caribbean. This he has found to be a much more satisfactory set-up than his former love affairs with the wolves of Europe. That his heart still beats in totalitarian rhythm is proved, however, by his close and apparently genuine friendships with such men as Francisco Franco. The situation is understandable enough, for no matter how much love he pretends to feel for democracy, he will always be on guard and ill at ease in Washington.

For the Benefactor to deal with Fascists is no novelty. The beginning of his association with foreign brands of totalitarianism may be traced back to the days when he still was an obscure army officer, lacking in social prestige and political standing. In those days he enjoyed a close diplomatic and personal relationship with Mussolini. It was Il Duce who awarded General Trujillo the first foreign medal ever to gleam from his chest. On January 11, 1929, the Consul of His Majesty the King of Italy pinned to General Trujillo's dress uniform the medal of Commander of the Crown of Italy.

This rapport had a curious and perhaps amusing epilogue. After more than six years of cordiality between the Fascist regime and the Trujillo administration, the Benefactor fell victim to a congenital weakness: greed. Due to a "grab" attempted by the Benefactor, a sudden coolness came over the relations between the two countries and there was even some talk of Italian sailors landing on Dominican soil. This "rhubarb" started when the Italian Consul, Amadeo Barletta, became involved in a sordid disagreement with Trujillo over which of them should enjoy the sole rights of selling cigarettes and distributing motor cars in Dominican territory.

To settle the difference, Trujillo promptly threw the Consul in jail and, as is his custom, charged his enemy with a combination of political and common crimes—plotting against the regime and tax evasion. The Italian government strongly protested the action, and when their note met with complete silence, *Il Duce* threatened to send a warship to the island. To avoid such an extreme unpleasantness, the Italian Consul was released and Mussolini mollified, but this bitter incident cooled, if it did not actually kill, the friendship started under such promising auspices a few years before. Nevertheless, Fascist activities were not totally curbed in the Dominican Republic and the Italian regime continued to spread its propaganda, through radio stations and subsidized dailies, until the moment when the United States entered World War II.

Though seemingly a diplomatic defeat, the Barletta incident was presented during the war not as a predatory expedition in the field of business but as a proof of the high democratic principles of the Dominican dictator. In a pamphlet entitled *Nuestra Actitud* (Our Attitude), the Dominican Foreign Minister Manuel Arturo Peña Batlle portrayed "the Chief" as a true democrat who had actually *initiated* the fight against Fascism in the Western Hemisphere.

Trujillo's dealings with Hitler were founded upon a sounder basis. The relationship between the Caribbean's Little Caesar and the Fuehrer progressed with more speed and cordiality than did the Mussolini-Trujillo entente. "The Chief" has always been a convinced admirer of everything Hitler stood for and of Germany's economic and military might. The problem of working out an agreement between the two regimes was an easy matter, and a warm friendship quickly developed between the Dominican Republic and the Third Reich.

After a series of transatlantic overtures, German agents were moved into the Dominican Republic to occupy strategic positions. They worked in the usual guises of scientists, medical research men and trade representatives. In a reciprocal gesture the Benefactor sent a special mission to Germany prepared to offer the fullest cooperation with the Nazis and to establish a barter agreement in the economic field. To the natural discomfort of both parties, news of these secret negotiations leaked out. They were exposed by

La Voz, a Spanish language newspaper in New York City. This paper published an account of an impending agreement between Germany and the Dominican Republic under which Hitler would settle 40,000 able-bodied Nazis along the always sensitive Haitian-Dominican border. At the same time it was reported that Trujillo, in partnership with a syndicate of influential Nazi officials, was interested in a gold washing venture in the northwestern part of the Republic. These deals failed to materialize, due no doubt to the advance publicity they received.

Another more important project was carried through successfully with the establishment of the German-Dominican Institute in the Dominican capital. This organization—staffed entirely by Germans—had as its ostensible purposes the studying of tropical diseases and of making botanical investigations throughout the country. Movements of this team of scientists were conducted in great secrecy and to ensure the success of the operation there was a liberal sprinkling of Gestapo agents among the German personnel. Very few Dominicans set foot inside the headquarters of this so-called Institute. Years later it was established beyond any doubt that the Germans did not devote themselves so much to the study of tropical diseases as to the study of marine plant life and water depths off the Dominican coast. Their main task was to draw up charts of Dominican shore lines and harbors and to establish strategic shelters and fuel depôts for German U-boats.

One measure of the rapport between the Third Reich and the Dominican Republic was that Dominican official circles were seriously considering changing the compulsory study of English in public schools to that of German. Overtures of friendship were continuous and deepening. In Trujillo's message to his Congress on February 27, 1936, he proudly announced that he had been awarded the medal of the Ibero-American Institute of the University of Hamburg. This organization, as became known later, was a front for the espionage activities then conducted under the direction of General Wilhelm von Faupel, Latin-American expert in the Nazi hierarchy.

In 1938, at the summit of this friendly interchange a flotilla of German warships, led by the cruiser *Emden,* visited the Dominican Republic. Its arrival was followed by a series of social and official pleasantries. At the conclusion of this natural interchange of courtesies, the German flotilla made certain surprise appearances at isolated and strategic points along the country's coastline, including the famous Samana Bay. At points prearranged by the "German scientists," Nazi sailors stocked up fuel dumps to be used at a later date by German submarines on combat duty in the Caribbean. Time has made it clear that this apparent "good-will" visit by a part of the Nazi navy made possible the great success of the U-boats that prowled the Caribbean at the beginning of 1942, nearly crippling navigation in those vital sea-lanes.

"The Chief," of course, will swear that he knew nothing about German activities in his country, but it is doubtful that such a vast long-time operation could be carried out without the full knowledge and at least passive compliance of the local authorities.

Upon successful completion of "Operation Emden," the members of the "German-Dominican Institute" were recalled one by one by the German government. They left behind an espionage set-up whose members were "business men" seemingly engaged in legitimate commercial ventures. To keep their contacts with the Dominican upper-crust the Nazis began to use the already established channels of the Spanish totalitarian organization *Falange*. The latter group was operating freely within the Dominican Republic. Due to its large membership within the Spanish colony in the country, as well as for reasons of language, customs and traditions, *Falange* was considered a most appropriate vehicle for the infiltration of Dominican institutions. Through the Spanish group the Nazis got a foothold in the old Trujillo-controlled *Listin Diario*. To handle its totalitarian-fed foreign news department, *Listin* employed a young journalist, Enrique de Marchena, who later rose to such official positions as Foreign Minister and head of the Dominican delegation to the United Nations.

The attitude of the Dominican press best illustrates the complicity of the Trujillo regime with the Nazi-Fascist axis. Even privately owned Dominican papers would never dare to pursue an editorial policy inimical to the thoughts and feelings of the Benefactor. Trujillo's orders, or at least complacency, explain why *Listin* jumped openly on the Spanish nationalists' chariot from the outset, while the Dominican Government maintained diplomatic relations with the Loyalist regime during the Spanish Civil War, not recognizing Franco until its end.

However, if for business reasons (Trujillo was selling huge quantities of cattle and foodstuffs to the Loyalists and the Dominican Legation in Madrid was making millions selling "safe-conducts" to Nationalists), the Dominican government maintained formal diplomatic relations with the Spanish Republic, certain highly placed members of the Trujillo administration made no bones about their totalitarian sympathies. The then President of the Superior Board of the *Partido Dominicano*, Mr. Emilio Morel, wrote a series of pro-Franco articles in *Listin Diario*. As soon as Franco won the war Morel was appointed Dominican Minister to Madrid. Upon his arrival there his first official act was to place a wreath on the tomb of the founder of *Falange*, José Antonio Primo de Rivera, in the Benefactor's name.

The Benefactor himself felt no qualms about fraternizing with Nazis and Nazi sympathizers. Dr. Carl T. Georg, a German physician who had come to the Dominican Republic in the early Twenties and established himself in San Pedro de Macoris in the country's sugar belt, was an habitué of the presidential box at theatrical functions and concerts. Georg was fairly well known in the Dominican Republic both for his philanthropy and his out-spoken preaching of Nazism.

This obvious flirtation with Nazism could not go on for long without catching the eye of American intelligence. Soon Trujillo discovered that all Nazi sympathizers in the Dominican Republic, including himself, were under observation. But the Benefactor knew that as long as there was peace no one could do anything—the Dominican Republic is a sovereign nation and any direct snooping by American officials or intelligence agents into the Generalissimo's intrigues would have been received with loud cries of "intervention," a word with nasty connotations in Latin America.

About the beginning of 1939 word spread throughout the Dominican Republic, where the fascist feelings of the regime were not universally shared, that the activities of those connected with the Nazis, including "the Chief," were being closely watched with a view to action in case war broke out. Taking the hint, Trujillo decided, for the first time, to take a long-postponed vacation in foreign lands. He was not President any more and he could not be blamed officially for the things to which the Americans were objecting.

While the trip was in progress the Benefactor finally met his share of trouble. Upon arrival in United States waters his yacht was thoroughly inspected by federal authorities who found that its powerful wireless set was more suitable for use on a battleship than on a pleasure boat. The set had to be whittled down to the bare necessities of transatlantic travel and "the Chief" had to sail away on the *Ramfis* (formerly the *Camargo* of the Fleishman family) with a considerably less powerful transmitter than he had arrived with. In France, where the Trujillo family was sojourning, the press did not wait long before attacking the Benefactor for his fascist sympathies. Altogether it was not a pleasant period for the Benefactor, and to avoid further inconveniences he decided to alter the rules of the game. Without risking a clean-cut break with the Nazis, he began to use more caution in dealing with the totalitarian powers. For one thing, he stopped altogether further direct deals with the dictatorships. As intermediaries he chose the Spanish Legation in Ciudad Trujillo and the Benefactor's Minister in Madrid, Emilio S. Morel.

The Spanish Legation was entrusted with the delicate mission of transmitting confidential correspondence between Germany and the Dominican Republic. The Spanish diplomatic mission was also employed as a forwarding station for the information service the Axis maintained in the Caribbean. German and Italian diplomats in Ciudad Trujillo were left as mere figureheads, although they continued to entertain the local bigwigs lavishly, particularly on such occasions as the fall of Paris.

Other signs of the impending shift were the new directives secretly passed to the local press. During the period between the beginning of the war in Europe and the Japanese attack on Pearl Harbor, *Listin Diario* and *Diario de Comercio* continued at full blast their job of spreading Nazi propaganda. From the *Listin* newsroom de Marchena would broadcast several times a day the latest news about the German victories and practically nothing else. On the other hand, *La Opinión,* whose owner René de Lepervanche was a French national, took an early pro-Allies stand. Furthermore, from its first issue the new Trujillo-owned daily *La Nación* made clear that its editorial policy and general presentation of news would be favorable to the Franco-British coalition.[1] At the same time, by further adroit maneuvering and sheer power of double talk, it was possible for "the Chief" to escape new complications. He even managed to score a point when upon his personal instructions (a thing he took pains to make clear) the Dominican delegation to the Meeting of Consultation of Ministers of Foreign Affairs, held in Havana in July, 1940, offered dramatically "the land, the sea and the air" of the Dominican Republic for the purpose of hemispheric defense.

It may well be that Trujillo's brand-new democratic pose fooled a lot of people, but not all people. For instance, the influential Puerto Rican newspaper *El Mundo,* in an exposé of Nazi schemes in Latin America, asserted that the "center of the [Nazi] conspiration and of Hitler's plan to conquer America has been the Dominican Republic." In an article printed on August 31, 1941, *El Mundo* pointed out that a thorough investigation had led one of its reporters to feel assured that German fifth column activities had been established in Santo Domingo "formally and definitely for more than four years" and cited as the "center of the conspiration" the German-Dominican Scientific Institute.

Upon the Japanese attack on Pearl Harbor, the Benefactor announced, from the United States which he was visiting, that his country would enter the war immediately at the side of the Americas. He momentarily forgot that he was no longer President, but the *faux pas* proved of no consequence as the Dominican Congress waited in session until a message arrived from Trujillo before deciding upon a proposed declaration of war on the Axis powers. Though the only Dominicans who actually fought in the war were those inducted into the American army, "the Chief" has since bragged of his war-time exploits.

The Dominican entrance into the war had no permanent effect on Trujillo's sympathies with Nazism. A group of his cronies kept proclaiming for all to hear their allegiance to the Nazis. So embarrassing became this attitude that the representatives of the Allied powers felt under obligation

[1] To this day it is still a matter of controversy among well-informed Dominicans as to whether *La Nación's* editorial policy was a deliberate movement on the part of Trujillo or whether it was a matter of simple coincidence due to the selection of Rafael Vidal as its first editor. It seems, however, that Trujillo had been advised by his American brain-trust to launch his own newspaper as a democratic bulwark in order to disprove the accusation of Nazi sympathies. Knowing Vidal's liberal principles, it was natural that Trujillo should bring him back from oblivion.

to impress upon Trujillo the need for putting an end to such indiscretions. As a result, several of the more outspoken officials were put in "moth balls" for the duration, including Major Miguel A. Paulino, the infamous boss of *La 42*. Once the war was over, however, Paulino was restored to his post as head of intelligence and shortly thereafter appeared in the uniform of a lieutenant colonel of the Army. Currently he is a colonel, head of the Ciudad Trujillo garrison.

Yet, if the allied nations could do little aside from sending courteous warnings wrapped up in diplomatic language about the local Nazis, they could do a lot about the foreign agents roaming freely within the country. They knew so well the identity and whereabouts of each one of them that in a matter of a few days a large dragnet had successfully hauled in all the spies (including Trujillo's pal Dr. Georg) and they were sent for internment to United States camps. I still remember our widespread surprise at *La Nación* when meek, innocent-looking, five-foot-tall Mr. Spitta, one of our translators, was sent along with the rest to the United States as a dangerous Nazi agent. For several months he had been with us in the news room without arousing suspicions about his exciting double life.

For the Benefactor it is almost impossible to stay out of trouble for long periods. In June 1942 alert American intelligence agents discovered that the Captain of a Spanish ship had deposited $300,000 in a Ciudad Trujillo bank in old American gold-certificate notes. Reportedly the money was going to be used to meet the cost of a tobacco shipment from the Dominican Republic. The fact, however, that this was a very unusual transaction, since export shipments are usually paid with sight drafts and other commercial papers, led to the suspicion that the money was really intended for some other purpose—perhaps for the payment of Nazi agents in the Americas. Another suspicious little detail was that the serial numbers of the American bills corresponded to those of money known to have been in circulation inside Germany and, therefore, frozen at the beginning of the war.

Naturally enough, American Treasury agents were interested to learn more about this large amount of cash. When the Benefactor stalled, showing a suspicious reluctance to surrender the bankroll, the story was quietly leaked to several newspapers in the Caribbean area. Fearful of unfavorable publicity, the Benefactor thereupon stopped balking. He promptly announced that he was confiscating the $300,000 and delivering it to the American authorities—which he did.

The American writer Allan Chase, in his book *Falange,* reports that until the news broke in the press, "the Big One" had been maneuvering to convert the money into less "hot" currency. According to Chase, the Benefactor "had been attempting to convert the money into Cuban currency." His agent in this transaction had been Sánchez Arcilla, former staff writer of the *Diario de la Marina,* who was serving as Cuba's Minister to Santo Domingo.

This rebuff came on top of many rumors around the Caribbean that Trujillo was allowing the Germans to use the Dominican coastline for refueling their U-boats, which were then playing havoc in West Indian waters. At this point the Caribbean master of deceit came up with a good one in answer to these persistent rumors: he proudly announced that he too had been the victim of Nazi submarines. He had lost his two best ships in the submarine-infested Caribbean Sea. The sinking of the ships was true; but the feeling in the Dominican Republic has long been that both (suspiciously sunk in rapid succession after several months of safe operation) were scuttled to prove "the Chief's" point. The purpose, so the story goes, was double—first, to collect the insurance, and second, to put an end to a situation which was becoming embarrassing. For several weeks a Cuban radio station had been observing that ships from every nation *but* the Dominican Republic had been sunk in the Caribbean. Proclaimed the radio station: "Travel on Trujillo's merchant ships if you want to be safe."

Notwithstanding Trujillo's frantic efforts to stop the rumors about his close ties with the Nazis, the subject once again aroused widespread attention when the late Andrés Requena, then a Dominican diplomat, jumped ship while serving in the Dominican Embassy in Santiago, Chile. Upon his escape, early in 1943, Requena let it be known that he had in his possession plenty of evidence about the Generalissimo's secret dealings with Hitler.

When Requena arrived at Havana a plane was already waiting for him and he was flown at once to the United States. It is understood that Requena surrendered all the evidence in his possession to the proper intelligence authorities, but the long-awaited blast was not forthcoming. Whether the documents taken by Requena from the Santiago Embassy's files were not incriminating enough or, as Trujillo promptly claimed, they were not authentic is something that has never been officially told. The results of the investigation, if any, were not made public and to all intents and purposes the Benefactor emerged from the procedure cleared of all charges.

Whether or not the American authorities believed Trujillo's protestations of innocence is also unexplained. The best guess is that, confronted with the alternatives of taking a strong action against an allied regime in the middle of the war or accepting Trujillo's promise of mending his ways, the United States Government followed the latter course as a matter of expediency. Otherwise they would have had to take strong action inconsistent with avowed policies of non-intervention. For the sake of Western Hemisphere solidarity, so it seems, Trujillo was spared the experience of being exposed as a traitor to the cause he was claiming to espouse.

Trujillo could not rest in peace, however. He could never be sure that other incriminating documents were not going to fall into Allied hands, particularly at the end of the war, whose outcome he did not have to be a prophet to forecast. The fortunes of war had definitely tipped the balance on the United Nations side and he felt it was high time to prepare a convincing alibi "just in case." He needed to be able to produce within a short time a scapegoat he could hang on the scaffold of Nazi collaboration.

This scapegoat was found in the person of Emilio Morel, the man who knew most about Trujillo's dealings with the Nazis. This master stroke was intended to make possible the killing of two birds with one stone—to exonerate the Benefactor from any responsibility springing from the secret dealings that had been conducted on his behalf with the Nazis in Madrid, and to remove the man (Morel) who knew most about the subject.

To begin with, Trujillo spread a story of how his Minister to Spain had dealt secretly, behind his back, with the enemy. Morel was charged with preparing, unbeknown to the Benefactor, a detailed plan for eventual German-Dominican cooperation in the event of a Nazi victory. According to the Trujillo-inspired rumor, Morel had been promised the presidency of the Dominican Republic to ensure his betrayal of his country and political allegiance.

Upon launching this damaging rumor, Trujillo recalled his Minister from Madrid. The diplomat—one of the earliest associates of the Benefactor—knew too well the dark corners of his chief's nature and refused to risk a return to the Dominican Republic. He decided to stay abroad at a safe distance from the Generalissimo's revengeful arm.

Furious over this defection, Trujillo unleashed upon Morel the customary campaign of vilification. He was publicly accused of all sorts of improper acts, among them of having stolen the funds of the Dominican Legation in Madrid. That the charges were coarse fabrications is proved by the fact that Morel was granted asylum in the United States, where he lived until his death in 1958.

Emilio Morel discovered at last how ephemeral is the glory of *trujillismo*. No journalist had basked more in the Dominican literary sunlight than Morel; he was Trujillo's favorite writer and had occupied positions of trust alongside the Generalissimo. Now, alas, he was finding that the Benefactor demands complete and lasting servility from his favorites. After years of favor, he was now branded as a "deserter," "thief," "traitor" and—of all things—"slanderer!"

As a hangover from the days of his admiration for Hitler remains Trujillo's vigorous championship of Franco's Spain and all that Spain represents. Trujillo never misses an opportunity to pay tribute to the Motherland's "spiritual guidance" and he appointed himself, during the days of the United Nations boycott of Spain, as the chief advocate of the Franco regime in the UN.

During the war years Franco and Trujillo rendered each other mutual services and the Spanish Legation in the Dominican capital was allowed not only to transmit orders from Madrid to the Falange groups in the country, but also to act as a clearing-house for highly confidential material sent by the Nazis to Dominican government officials.

To express his sympathy for Franco, the Benefactor chose the United Nations. "The Chief" not only paid less than lip service to the UN recommendation about breaking relations with Spain, but jumped with enthusiasm on the band-wagon of those pleading for Spain's admittance.

When Spain was finally admitted into the United Nations late in 1955, the Dominican press hailed the event as a triumph for the Benefactor.

The Benefactor's bootlicking activities were rewarded in 1954 with an invitation to come to Spain as guest of Generalissimo Franco. Prior to the invitation, Trujillo had bought an ancient Spanish castle which he reconditioned for his official residence during his visit. Madrid, according to *Time,* "dressed itself gaily in honor of the island nation's self-styled Benefactor, with fresh yellow sand in the streets and the red-yellow-red or the blue-white-red of the Spanish and Dominican flags floating from every window."

When Franco and Trujillo exchanged backslapping embraces during the welcoming ceremony at the Principe Pio Station, "an emotional tear rolled down Trujillo's cheek." "The immediate order of business," reported *Time,* "that afternoon was for the two rulers to decorate each other. First, the Benefactor pinned the Order of Trujillo upon Franco, saying 'Generalissimo, this could not rest on a more noble and heroic breast.' Then the Caudillo presented the Grand Collar of Isabel la Católica to Trujillo, saying, 'Generalissimo, in few cases has the decoration I am giving you been so well deserved.' The mutual admiration over, they plunged into the crowded twelve-day program—bullfights, receptions, luncheons, hunting and sightseeing—that the Caudillo had planned for his guest."

A new era in the relations between Spain and the Dominican Republic was inaugurated. On Trujillo's return from the Old World a new flow of Spanish conquerors discovered Hispaniola. These new discoverers were made up, as were the crews of Columbus's ships, of all sorts of people, from poor dispossessed farmers to impoverished noblemen, from illiterate hoodlums to schemers of grandiose and fantastic projects.

Among others, a group of Army officers came to the Dominican Republic to instruct the Benefactor's soldiers and a contingent of policemen were brought in to reinforce the local Secret Police.

2.   NO OTHER INTERNATIONAL RED-BAITER HAS MADE SO
much political hay out of an allegedly uncompromising anti-Communist
stand as has Trujillo. For years his public relations master-minds have
concentrated, particularly for the benefit of the United States, on depict-
ing the Benefactor as the "first anti-communist of the hemisphere." The
Dominican dictator himself has repeatedly asserted that the benefit of his
wise counsel on anti-Red matters has been sought by investigating bodies
in both the executive and legislative branches of the American Government.[2] Yet, the only time that the Communist Party, then known as
Partido Socialista Popular (Popular Socialist Party), ever blossomed legally and freely in the Dominican Republic was during a year-long period
in 1946–47, with the Benefactor's blessing and sponsorship.

Prior to his discovery of anti-communism as a justification for domestic
violation of basic freedom, the Generalissimo had entered upon a series
of deals with the Dominican Reds as well as on flirtations with the Kremlin
itself on the diplomatic level and with the most noted of the international
leaders of what he was to vigorously denounce later as "the communist
conspiracy on the Continent."

The first inkling of Trujillo's unexpected *rapprochement* with the Communists came in the form of his noiseless repeal of all laws punishing
communist activities in the country (in 1936, as a result of the Spanish
Civil War, Trujillo had made Congress pass stringent provisions against
"communists and anarchists"), a move which followed closely Dominican
entrance into World War II. Then the cagey Generalissimo tried to make
the most of the occasion. To the July 1943 conference of the Executive
Committee of the Communist-dominated *Confederación de Trabajadores
de América Latina* (CTAL), headed by the renowned fellow-traveller and
self-styled "independent Marxist" Vicente Lombardo Toledano, Trujillo
sent a former cabinet member, Dr. Wenceslao Medrano, and an official
of the Foreign Ministry, Mr. Alberto Borda, as Dominican delegates.

Despite the fact that the fake Dominican trade unions (then so patently
under Trujillo's thumb that in each province they were presided over by
the local governor) had never been members of CTAL, Medrano and
Borda were not only accepted as legitimate representatives of the oppressed Dominican workers, but were seated in all executive committee

---

[2] During a visit he made to the United States in the summer of 1954, Trujillo made
a statement to the press whereby he made it known that his files on the subject of
communist infiltration in the Western Hemisphere had been placed at the disposal of
a House Subcommittee of Investigation, then presided over by Republican Congress-
man Patrick J. Hillings.

meetings, attended on. that occasion by seventeen delegates, of whom eleven were known communists. A delegate of the so-called *Confederación Dominicana del Trabajo* (CDT) attended the Third Congress of the CTAL in Cali, Colombia, in December 1944. The CDT (later the CTD) remained affiliated with the CTAL until 1948.

Then, for the celebration of the first centennial of the Dominican national independence, in February 1944, it was announced that the Soviet Union was sending a special mission composed of two of its diplomats, Dimitri Zaikin and Victor Ibertrebor. The presence of the Soviet diplomats at this celebration was hailed by Dominican propagandists as a heaven-sent boost for the Generalissimo. This, however, was only part of a vaster political scheme. On March 12, 1945, the Dominican foreign office released a diplomatic note announcing that as a result of "conversations between the Dominican Republic and the Soviet Union" both countries had agreed to establish diplomatic relations. According to the communiqué the talks had taken place in Mexico City between the Dominican Secretary of Foreign Affairs, Lic. Manuel A. Peña Batlle, and the Soviet Chargé d'Affaires, Vasily P. Yakuvoiky.

Without waiting for the Soviet Union to name its diplomatic representative, Trujillo proceeded to appoint Dr. Ricardo Pérez Alfonseca as Minister to Russia. While the new Minister was already on his way to Moscow to take over his post, the Benefactor sent a lengthy message to the Senate, on June 11, 1945, asking for the confirmation of the Pérez Alfonseca appointment. Trujillo wrote:

"The appointment of this distinguished diplomat, who passed the entire war period in Europe as head of our mission to the suffering and heroic city of London, to inaugurate the first Dominican Legation with permanent residence in Moscow, constitutes an act signifying the sincere desire of the Dominican Government to regularize officially and to establish closer relations with the Union of Soviet Socialist Republics, relations that in fact have always existed between the Russian people and the Dominican people, on the basis of mutual respect and cordiality."

After praising the "heroic" Russian resistance during the war, Trujillo recalled the appointment of two Soviet diplomats to the Centennial festivities. Then he added: "As a result of their noble and powerful contribution to the victory of the United Nations, and of the imminent constitution, in the historic Conference of San Francisco, California, of the world organization for the perpetuation of peace, security, justice, and cooperation, the Soviet Union, whose material power has been made evident in defense of a high cause, will always be recognized as one of the great forces for good and progress upon which the democratic world can count."

The Soviet Union never reciprocated the compliment. Soon Trujillo discovered the exasperating difficulty and the aggravating exhaustion of dealing with the Soviet Government. Despite the fact that rightist writers loudly proclaim the Dominican Republic as a pivotal land in the strategic chain of Caribbean islands and, as such, a continuing target of all communist attempts, the Soviet Union did not even bother to open a Consulate. The realization of Russian disinterest in the Benefactor marked the end of this phase of Dominican foreign policy. In 1946 Trujillo recalled Pérez Alfonseca, thus ending what one of his official biographers describes as "ephemeral and lukewarm relations."

In the meantime, Trujillo had no trouble with communism locally. If there was any domestic communist movement it was very tiny and ineffectual, restricted to a few young intellectuals who, out of the frustrations they met in such a narrow society, were seeking salvation in the tenets of Marxism. Apparently their first contact with communist doctrine was through their readings of communist literature which—by a strange quirk of Dominican censorship—could be freely bought at any local bookstore. Many of the romantic Marxists of that epoch (the late thirties)—such as Héctor Inchaustegui, José Angel Saviñon, and Ramón Marrero Aristy— were never militant communists and later turned out to be strong supporters of the Trujillo regime. It seems that their lofty ideology was the result of their financial insecurity, and that as soon as they became affluent their whole outlook on life changed.

There were others who stuck to their Marxist guns and slowly but inexorably achieved a definite political stand. So, when the first Spanish refugees arrived late in 1939, those of them who were avowed communists found in certain intellectual and student circles fertile ground in which to work. As Galíndez points out in his book: "when I arrived in the Dominican Republic in November, 1939, there already were communists and pro-communists. I do not know if there was an organization, properly speaking. The only Dominican who spoke to me in those days in favor of communism, and who argued bitterly with me over various aspects of the Civil War in Spain for which I had attacked the communists, was the then obscure journalist, José Angel Saviñón. This young man was editor of *República*, a publication which appeared in Ciudad Trujillo at the time of the Spanish Civil War, at first favoring the Spanish Republican cause in general but then little by little revealing a pro-communist tendency." The Galíndez appraisal is supported by José Almoina, former private secretary of the Benefactor, who wrote a book entitled *I Was Trujillo's Secretary,* in which he calls Saviñón a "restless and fighting young university student" who had a reputation for "very liberal ideas and was even in sympathy with communism." About Marrero Aristy, author of a sociological novel entitled *Over,* dealing with the life of the exploited sugar workers, Almoina says that this was "an agile and advanced writer of socialist ideology akin to the Communist."

It seems that—in contact with the small but active group of Spanish communists—a group of intellectuals finally established an underground Communist party, whose leaders were Francisco Alberto (Chito) Henriquez and Heriberto Nuñez, the same judge who in 1930 had almost thrown a stumbling-block into Trujillo's path to the Presidency. This group was particularly active in the sugar plantations of the eastern part of the country, where they organized in 1942 a strike, which was put down in a blood bath by the Dominican Army. At the time of this strike the Dominican authorities ordered a roundup of the Spanish communists throughout the country, but they were later released. Some of them had been involved in the preparations for the sugar workers' strike.

For another two years there was no political agitation in the country, except the usual rallies, meetings, lectures, homages and tributes organized by the *Partido Dominicano*. Yet, around 1944, the United Nations democratic propaganda and the climate created by the Allies' successful fight against Nazism and Fascism in Europe and against Japanese imperialism in Asia were being felt in the Dominican Republic. There were long-drawn-out intellectual discussions among young students and professionals of different ideologies, but I myself know there were not yet—although I suspect that the communists were already organized—clearly established underground groups.

At about that time, Pericles Franco Ornes returned to the Dominican Republic from Chile, where he had been studying on a Chilean government fellowship. He was destined to play an important role in the Dominican communist movement as well as in the fight against the Trujillo regime. As in the case of many other communist leaders before him, Franco Ornes was the scion of two middle-class families from Santiago and Puerto Plata. He had left the country for Chile while still a teenager, more interested in learning the Australian-crawl swimming style than in politics. While in Santiago he got in contact with left-wing elements and it seems that shortly after he was converted to all-out Communism.

When Franco returned to the Dominican Republic in 1944, he was already a devout, disciplined communist, ready to start his assigned work among the Dominican university students. He made a lot of headway, if not in actually converting people to Communism at least in creating a strong underground movement of anti-Trujillo youngsters. This fierce and intent young man soon rallied around him quite a large group of young intellectuals and students, a few of whom became dedicated communists. Others were so democratically inclined that, although they did not sever relations with him, they did not join the communist ranks. As a result, the anti-Trujillo underground split into three different groups. The communists rallied under the banners of the *Partido Democratico Revolucionario* (Dominican Democratic Revolutionary Party); a large number of elder intellectuals, professionals and businessmen formed the *Unión Patriotica Revolutionaria* (Patriotic Revolutionary Union); and the non-communist students and young professionals made up the *Juventud Revolucionaria*. The three organizations joined forces in the anti-Trujillo underground fight through an organization known as the *Frente Nacional Democratico* (National Democratic Front). This set-up I know well, for as a member of the Central Committee of the non-communist Revolutionary Youth I was also a member of the Front.

The period between 1945 and 1946 was one of intense underground political activity, although due to the natural ideological differences between the communists and the others the Front was never the cementing force it was intended to be. Sometimes the communists managed to give the impression of being more interested in furthering their own ends than in fighting Trujillo. As almost always happens when alliances are entered upon with them, they tried hard to dominate the Front, producing many a clash and slowing the actual work of organizing an underground.

By the end of 1945 Trujillo had already spotted the work of the Front, and although unsuccessful in his initial attempts to destroy it, he managed to deal a few hard blows to the underground opposition.

One of these opportunities was afforded by the opposition itself. Taking advantage of the presence of a large number of foreign youngsters invited by the Dominican Government to participate in a Trujillo-controlled Youth Congress, the opposition decided to make a tour de force. On the night of May 18, 1945, groups of Revolutionary Youth and a few young communists joined forces to distribute anti-Trujillo pamphlets. In one night the whole city was covered with posters, handbills, and other sorts of literature. Even in the rooms of the Hotel Jaragua propaganda was placed. It was a successful operation, but the Government did not wait long to retaliate.

A round-up of youth leaders and university students was carried out by the police under the command of then Lieutenant Colonel Ludovino Fernández. Some of the leaders, including Chito Henriquez, Pericles Franco Ornes, and others took refuge in foreign embassies, but others were arrested and severely beaten by the police. A Cuban boy, Rafael Fernández, was hospitalized because of injuries received at the hands of the police. On the next day an elderly printer, Ramón Espinal, suspected of printing part of the anti-Government pamphlets, was shot and killed by the police near the Bank of Nova Scotia in the heart of Ciudad Trujillo's business section. The owner of the printing shop, Julio César Martínez Sobá, escaped miraculously, taking refuge in the Embassy of Mexico.

These and other blows had destroyed the Front's effectiveness by the spring of 1946. Until that moment the Patriotic Union had managed to keep its cadre almost intact, but by a curious twist of fate it was to be hit hard where it really hurt. In May 1946, General Federico Fiallo, Chief of Staff of the Army, while questioning the imprisoned communist leader Heriberto Nuñez, asserted that when it came to serving the Benefactor he did not owe allegiance to anyone else, even his own family. Upon hearing this statement, Nuñez got so indignant that without stopping to think about the further consequences of his words he said: "General, if that is so, you had better send right away for your three nephews, doctors Viriato, Antinoe and Gilberto Fiallo, who are the leaders of the Patriotic Union."

Fiallo kept his word, but the arrest of his nephews brought about a chain reaction which totally wrecked the underground movement. All the members of the Front, myself included, went to jail. Trujillo's underground opposition had been almost destroyed.

The lack of an opposition would have been a blessing for Trujillo under normal conditions, but 1946 was not a normal year. The postwar period had brought a political upheaval in the countries surrounding the Dominican Republic. The long suppressed democratic spirit was awakening in the Caribbean zone. In Cuba, Grau San Martin had succeeded Colonel Batista as a result of one of the cleanest elections in the annals of that Caribbean island. In Guatemala, a revolution had put an end to the hated Ubico dictatorship. In Caracas, Provisional President Rómulo Betancourt announced that Venezuela would not recognize Trujillo and his "assassins of liberty." In London, just a few months before, the World Youth Conference had expelled the two Dominican representatives because they did not represent a democratic regime.

The writing was clear on the wall. In order to stay in power Trujillo would have to make concessions, but by a quirk of fate that was precisely the moment his Secret Police had chosen to dispose of the remnants of the underground opposition.

Without waiting further Trujillo released most of his jailed opponents— he did not even bother to file charges against them. Although not a man of much education, the Benefactor can read political predictions very well. He also knows that, as a rule, democratic winds of the sort then blowing subside sooner or later; the weathering of such storms is a matter of endurance, patience and fortitude. He decided to ride with the wind and make temporary concessions.

The internal opposition, however, was too sore to play ball with him. His amnesty went unheeded. So, with an election year approaching fast, "the Chief" turned his eyes toward the exile groups living in Cuba and other countries. He sent an emissary to make contact with the Dominican exiles in Cuba. The person chosen was Ramón Marrero Aristy, who still had a few friends among the leftists in exile.

The non-communist exiles, already preparing the forlorn revolutionary adventure of Cayo Confites, rejected Trujillo's overtures, suspecting that they were a hypocritical face-saving device. Help, however, came from an unexpected group: the communists! During a series of trips to Cuba negotiations were conducted between Marrero and the communists which led to the formation of the *Partido Socialista Popular* (Popular Socialist Party) in the Dominican Republic.

What actually happened during the negotiations is a well-kept secret which neither Trujillo nor the communists have yet let out. It seems, however, that the communists were promised freedom to legally organize their party and a free hand in the reorganization of Dominican trade unions—in exchange for a promise of never attacking Trujillo directly, a thing they refrained from doing at least while Trujillo kept *his* part of the deal. As a mark of the new friendship, Havana's communist paper *Hoy* lashed out at democratic Dominican exiles as "reactionary adventurers." Pointing to previous pacts between Stalinists and Latin American dictators, the democratic exiles said: "First Nicaragua, then Brazil, and now the Dominican Republic. Lombardo Toledano and his Communist friends have become the technicians for the salvaging of Latin American tyrannies."

Dominicans first knew of the new developments when *La Opinión* published on July 1, 1946 a letter from the Central Committee of the Communist Party. *La Nación* immediately replied, expressing surprise that there was such a party in the country. There was a strange lull for more than a month and then, on August 18, *La Nación* published an official decree pardoning several political prisoners, including the known communist leader Freddy Valdez.

On August 27, *La Nación* printed a manifesto of the newly created Partido Socialista Popular (Communist) in which its signers cited the statements made by the Benefactor favoring the formation of political parties and the return of exiles. Then they referred to themselves as Marxist-Leninist-Stalinist and stated their purpose of achieving their objectives "by means of a struggle in accordance with the democratic rights and freedoms as contained in the Constitution now in force." Signers of the document were two labor leaders just arrived from Cuban exile, Mauricio Baez and Ramón Grullon; Freddy Valdez, and a *trujillista* agent already infiltrated in the Central Committee of the PSP, Luis Escoto Gomez.[3] Illustrating the news story was a very poor photograph of the new hierarchy of Dominican communism.

Commenting editorially upon this "communist manifesto," *La Nación* under the headline of "Communism Comes Out into the Light" posed the following question: "What better reply with respect to the existence of a democratic government than the fact itself of the formation of the

[3] Years later Escoto Gomez was an Inspector of the *Partido Dominicano* and an Under Secretary of State of the Interior and Police.

Partido Socialista Popular and the fact that its leaders can express themselves in such terms?" Next day, however, the same daily showed another aspect of the problem. It printed a letter signed by six government employees in which they said that they had considered joining the *Partido Socialista Popular,* but had refrained from this "insane idea" when they saw the photograph of its leaders, "wretched ones . . . with the genuine aspect of troglodytes."

The trap was set. While Trujillo in letters to members of his Cabinet and to Congress was breathing the spirit of moderation, order, peace, co-existence and democracy, his henchmen, particularly Virgilio Alvarez Pina, then President of the *Partido Dominicano,* took an uncompromising attitude, admonishing their followers to "annihilate and crush anyone who tries to deprive them of the political gains obtained under Trujillo's leadership." Thus when the request for registration of the PSP was formally denied, Trujillo himself wrote a letter to his Secretary of the Interior, J. M. Bonetti Burgos, recommending that the Party's registration be accepted. In this letter, *La Nación,* October 16, 1946, Trujillo wrote:

". . . Communism, whose existence in the Republic is now an important fact, has its undoubted origin in the organizations of the Union of Soviet Socialist Republics, and in order to understand its role in guiding political and social activities, it would be well not to forget the self-sacrificing co-operation which the U.S.S.R. gave to the democracies in the recent World War. Its existence among us, furthermore, is a round and eloquent rebuttal to those calumniators who without foundation accuse the Dominican Republic of not being a democratic country. . . ."

The communists promptly expressed their gratitude to the Generalissimo in a letter printed by *La Nación* on October 18. But Alvarez Pina expressed his energetic opposition to his boss's attitude in a letter also printed in the same daily. The stage show was proceeding on schedule with all in the cast performing faithfully their assigned roles. Almost a year was to pass before Trujillo himself shifted to the oratorical style of his followers, but by then the cold war had already started and it was no longer fashionable to speak words of democracy to communists.

In the meantime the communists had kept themselves active. The main emphasis was put on the organization of the trade unions and the preparation of a labor congress to form a new central labor union. To this congress came a group of Lombardo Toledano's leading aides, the Cubans Buenaventura Lopez and Ursinio Rojas, and the Mexicans Fernando Amilpa and Luis Gómez. A sort of "united front" was achieved inside the new *Confederación de Trabajadores Dominicanos* (CTD). The most important executive post, that of Secretary General, was given to a *trujillista,* Julio César Ballester, but the communists assured for themselves most key positions. The post of Organizational Secretary went to Mauricio Baez and that of Cultural and Propaganda Secretary to Ramón Grullón. The opening speech of the congress was delivered by the Benefactor.

From Cuba more communists had arrived. They were Chito Henriquez and Felix Servio Doucoudray. The only leader still absent was Pericles Franco Ornes, the top actor in the Dominican communist vaudeville.

Up to this time the going had been smooth for both sides. Trujillo was having his loyal opposition, and, for that matter, an opposition circumscribed to the communists. The Reds on the other hand were acting freely within the labor movement. Both were seemingly keeping their promises. Yet, in the latter part of October two things were to happen that would destroy the harmony of this cozy scheme.

The first was the sudden appearance on the political stage of a new opposition group named *Juventud Democratica* (Democratic Youth). This organization made up of University students and young professionals (along the lines of the earlier Revolutionary Youth) played an utterly ambiguous role. Although its President, Dr. Virgilio Díaz Grullón, and many of its leaders were not communists, there is no question that its rank and file were heavily infiltrated by the Reds. Furthermore, it soon established a close alliance with the PSP, a fact that in the eyes of suspicious government officials made the organization a Red satellite.

This was the kind of organization the Benefactor could not allow to flourish. He had already had more than his share of trouble with students and nothing was farther from his plans than to go through an open fight with fiery students when an election was soon forthcoming. Moreover, Trujillo firmly believed, as do many people inside and outside his Government, that Democratic Youth was a communist front and, hence, the product of a Red betrayal of the working agreement. Thereupon "the Chief" ordered the heavy guns of his propaganda machine to be trained on the new group. On October 17 there appeared in *La Opinión* a savage assault on Democratic Youth under the headline of "Down with the Mask, Liars."

Whether or not Democratic Youth was communist-dominated or only communist-infiltrated is rather academic. The truth is that from the outset both groups operated jointly in the organization of a number of political rallies which provoked a violent reaction in high official circles. After the appearance of Democratic Youth hostilities broke out in full swing, and for the first time the communists used their small newspaper *El Popular* to launch sharp attacks on Trujillo himself.

The second and perhaps most important event proved to be the showdown. The joint activities of the PSP and JD culminated in the announcement of a big public rally to be held in Colon Square on the night of October 26. Believing that with such a bitter publicity campaign against the two groups already under way, not many people would dare to show up, the authorities granted the license to hold the rally. During the day, however, disquieting reports were received about the preparations and more important still, about the surprising expectation of a big crowd.

The government first tried, through Marrero Aristy, to dissuade the Communists, but to no avail. Then hoodlums, "veterans" and retired members of *La 42* were hurriedly summoned to the offices of Major General (retired) J. Joaquin Cocco Hijo. There they received orders and were armed.

Long before the scheduled hour of the meeting many more people were in Colon Square than Trujillo had ever been able to gather for one of his own rallies. Probably this crowd was not as well dressed as the *trujillista* ones but they made up with ardor what they lacked in sartorial elegance.

Were all these people communists? Hardly. It seems that during the short period of anti-Trujillo propaganda all the dissatisfaction accumulated by the Dominican people in sixteen years of oppression had been channeled into the only organized opposition in existence. People did not actually care about the ideological stand of the PSP and JD leaders as long as they were fighting Trujillo. They had scarcely heard of communism but they knew plenty about Trujillo. They had seen this group of youngsters fighting Trujillo openly, and what they were hearing—stripped of its dialectical-materialism jargon—they could easily understand. Other people went to the meeting out of curiosity.

The faithful and the curious all got their share of clubbing from Trujillo's veterans that night. Shortly before the first speaker ascended the rostrum, strong-arm squads went into action. Wild fights broke out, and as a result the demonstration was disrupted. Then, contrary to the Government's expectations, instead of the supposedly terrorized crowd running for cover a strange thing happened. The feelings of hatred toward the regime seemed to be galvanized by the assault into a grim determination to fight. Instead of everyone going home to lick their wounds in hiding, the whole body of people took to the streets, singing the Dominican National Anthem. The crowd paraded in front of several foreign embassies, including the American, where they showed their injured to the diplomatic representatives as evidence of Trujillo's widely advertised "democratic" procedures.

The demonstration did not turn into riot due to the shrewdness of the Benefactor. Notified of what was going on by his astonished henchmen, Trujillo had the good sense to order his Chief of Police, Colonel Ludovino Fernández, to stand pat. The police were instructed to watch the demonstration without attacking the enraged crowd. They hoped that if the irate populace did not encounter resistance the drive would lose momentum. Trujillo was right. The parade dissolved after much shouting, chanting of patriotic slogans, and hurling of insults at hated Colonel Fernández, who that night passively heard a recounting of his many alleged crimes. The reprisals would come later.

With his knack for turning apparent defeat into triumph, Trujillo tried to profit from his setback. On that same night his faithful minion Manuel de Moya filed a circular telegram to American newspapers volunteering a slanted version of the happenings. As printed by the *Miami Herald* and reprinted by the *New York Times,* de Moya's cable read: "Last night (Saturday) the Communists tried a coup d'etat. They notified the authorities of their intention to hold a meeting. In the early afternoon they distributed knives, machetes and clubs, and at 10 P.M. attacked foreigners and unarmed citizens."

The Dominican Information Center in New York followed suit with a communiqué along the same lines, adding that the Mexican Embassy had been "violated" during the disturbances.

The United States Embassy in Ciudad Trujillo came out for the truth. To the *New York Times* a spokesman for the Embassy confirmed that an "incident" had occurred Saturday night, but it had involved no foreigners or foreign interests and the American embassy had not been "invaded" as Dominican reports had stated. According to the *Times* things happened in the following way: "The incident could more properly be described as a demonstration than as a riot," the spokesman told the Associated Press in New York by telephone. No deaths or injuries were reported and no gun-firing was heard at the embassy.

"The disturbance occurred in Ciudad Trujillo's Colon Park and some reports said that the rioters entered the United States and Mexican Embassies and the Cuban Legation.

"The spokesman said he had received no reports that either the Cuban Legation or the Mexican Embassy had been entered.

"He explained, however, that he understood that a group of demonstrators passed the Mexican and Cuban offices on their way to the United States Embassy. The group 'came to the chancery of the American Embassy,' he added. 'They were admitted into the office section of the embassy by a guard who was on duty. They came to make a report on the incidents of the evening. They were advised to return during office hours the following week.' "

The Dominican Government has stuck to its version despite early definite denials. In a slanderous "White Paper" on communism in the Dominican Republic recently published (whose only claim to distinction is that it brands as a communist everyone who opposes Trujillo), the Minister of the Interior and Police asserts that the members of the PSP rioted against anti-communist Dominicans, leaving a toll of several wounded among both groups. "Various communists, armed with clubs, threw themselves into the attack, beating peaceful citizens who watched the communist meeting from a prudent distance. . . . It was a major disorder of the kind Dominicans have not seen since Trujillo inaugurated his era of peace and work."

The happenings of October 26th gave the government a pretext for clamping down. Trujillo already had proof in his hands that he had granted a modicum of opposition and that only the Communists had taken advantage of the opportunity, since the rest of the citizenry were faithful *trujillistas*. Besides, after the American Embassy reaction to his distorted communiques he was not even sure he was causing any embarrassment to the United States State Department, a motive many suspected then and now to be behind Trujillo's velvet-handed treatment of Communists. *La Nación* on October 29 published an official notice requiring that official permission be obtained eight days in advance of any public meeting. From that time on no more public meetings were held by the two opposition groups.

To stave off any new show of strength by the communists a wave of reprisals was set in motion, although Trujillo did not yet dare to touch the Party's leadership. Rank-and-file members met with economic reprisals, many were thrown in jail on trumped-up charges of common crimes, and a few "got lost." Lists of members of the PSP were passed around among employers with a short phrase from the military authorities—"fire them." The trick always worked.

Through agents infiltrated in the communist hierarchy, Trujillo was kept well posted about each and every movement of the opposition. The printer who published *El Popular* received visits from several government inspectors, who found a host of labor, health and taxation irregularities. That same day the newspaper began to print on a mimeograph machine. Next came the newsboys. Their parents were told that there were regulations against barefooted boys walking the streets either at night or during school hours, which made the parents responsible. The leaders of the PSP had to peddle their own newspaper on Conde Street and other important thoroughfares.

Nine months of this kind of political warfare were to pass before Trujillo took the final step of outlawing the communist party. In the meantime in the pervading terror all progress by the communist movement was stalled. Not that the communists were ever a mass party. In the heyday of its activities the PSP's membership never surpassed 2,000, and not all of those who joined the party were convinced communists. Many *antitrujillistas* joined simply because the communists were the only ones fighting the regime inside the country. The American writer, W. H. Lawrence, in an appraisal of communist strength in Latin America published by the *New York Times* on December 30th, 1946, pointed out accurately:

"Although this nation (the Dominican Republic) is governed by a tight dictatorship, President Rafael Trujillo recently has permitted some open activity by the Partido Socialista Popular or Popular Socialist Party, which is in fact a Communist group with perhaps 2,000 supporters. Its importance lies in the fact, however, that it is the only open rallying point for anti-Trujillo sentiment. Its public rally of Sept. 14 was the first opposition meeting permitted since President Trujillo came to power.

"There are good signs that the Communists have made progress in undermining the Trujillo Administration in the labor unions, which, on the surface at least, are Government controlled."

By the beginning of 1947 a tighter official policy was much in evidence. On January 29, 1947, the President of the Dominican Party, Virgilio Alvarez Pina, told the Attorney General that the communists were ready to intensify their activities due to the announced visit of the Secretary General of the United Nations, Trygve Lie. Alvarez Pina asked prompt intervention by the judicial authorities.

On February 18 Alvarez Pina made another anti-communist pronouncement, blaming the Spanish refugees for the introduction of the "infectious virus of communism." And in March, upon the occasion of the return to the country of Pericles Franco Ornes, the attacks were renewed, not only against the communists but *Democratic Youth* as well. Although it was never reported at the time, the "White Paper" states that the communists were trying to put over at this time a plot to assassinate the Benefactor. The *trujillista* report, probably apocryphal, says that the Reds even chose the "assassin" by lot. The man who "won" the drawing, Ercilio García Bencosme, according to the White Paper, refused to carry out his mission.

Physical attacks on the members of the PSP and JD became commonplace. One of the most abusive assaults was perpetrated on the person of a young lady, a member of *Juventud Democrática*. A prostitute tore the girl's clothes off right on the sidewalks of the Palace of Justice in Ciudad Trujillo. No action was ever taken against the prostitute.

In the following weeks all the members of the PSP and JD who had not been able to get out of the country were arrested. On June 9 Trujillo created the "Commission of Investigation of Un-Dominican Activities," made up of legislators, secret police, and military and government officials. Five days later Congress passed a law banning communist or anarchist groups or others opposed to the "civil, republican, democratic and representative form of government of the Republic."

Writing about the aftermath of this strange political venture Jesús de Galíndez says: "The young men arrested in 1947 remained in prison until early in 1950 when the Commission of Investigation of the Caribbean Situation (of the Organization of American States) arrived in the Dominican Republic. An amnesty law was passed in February, and all were released except Freddy Valdez, who had died in prison, and who was said to have been assassinated. The principal communist leaders went into exile again shortly thereafter."

The destruction of the tiny communist minority—as well as practically every other known opposer of the regime—had been completed. The brief pseudo-democratic interlude was over as well. The question of Trujillo's aims in playing with the communists has since been argued at great length. Many hypotheses have been advanced to explain the queer situation. Unquestionably the Benefactor reaped profits in more than one respect. He emerged with his hold over the country unshaken. He had, moreover, discovered a new and effective battle cry—the "you communist" line so adroitly used in the years that followed.

Furthermore, by playing with the communists and not with a democratic opposition, "the Chief" was keeping up his sleeve a trump card. His American advisers had told him that sooner or later the wartime friendship between Russia and the United States was bound to deteriorate and give way to friction. They knew that there would be a reaction against Communism and by artificially creating and maintaining a Red minority inside the country he would later be in the position of playing the role of savior of his country from the Soviet menace. As his biographer Stanley Walker points out, "some observers say that the Trujillo regime likes to keep a few Communists in hand to be used as pets, stooges, whipping boys, or whatever the occasion demands. The idea makes some sense."

There are many who believe that by allowing communism in the country Trujillo, who was irritated by a United States refusal to sell him arms, was trying to embarrass the State Department. In support of this contention, it is pointed out that Trujillo's favorite theme in those days whenever a visitor expressed concern over the communist growth in the country was: "But, what can I do? It is the State Department that wants democracy and, unfortunately, my only opponents are communists." Further confirmation may be found in the editorials printed about the subject by the controlled press, particularly the one that appeared in *La Nación* on August 27, 1946, to salute the emergence of the communist movement.

In a word, the so-called democratic stand of the Benefactor was pregnant with political blackmail. The rationale was that the political activities of the communists could warn the United States Government that should it try to exert pressure on the Trujillo regime in order to ensure real democracy in the country the result would be the upsurge of a more powerful communist party.

On the other hand, what did the communists stand to gain by playing with Trujillo? By entering into a deal with Trujillo they sought to gain a secure foothold within the Dominican labor movement. They knew that politically they did not have a chance, but when they eventually realized that they were being used by Trujillo to further his own aims they put up a courageous fight—even to sacrificing their leaders and destroying chances of keeping an underground organization inside the country.

It seems that when they agreed to come back to the country they decided to take a calculated risk. They knew that other exiled groups were already planning a military invasion of the Dominican Republic and they wanted to get ahead of them. Had the abortive Cayo Confites attempt triumphed, the new democratic government of the Dominican Republic would have found the communists already entrenched in the labor movement. Yet, when all their calculations along these lines failed to materialize, they dragged down with them in their fall all that was good in the country, ending chances of a democratic solution for years to come.

EXILES IN OPPOSITION

1. As A MAN WHO DESPERATELY WANTS TO BE LOVED, Rafael L. Trujillo does not dare to admit the existence of any opposition to his person. His police periodically make roundups of those suspected of harboring dangerous political ideas and some of these unfortunate souls "get lost," but "the Chief" incessantly strives to convey the impression that everyone in the Dominican Republic (and sometimes even out of the country as well) is blindly loyal to him.

This seemingly absurd craving for affection accounts for some of the baffling traits of the almost incredible Dominican situation. It is behind the stage-managed elections fixed in advance to show the people's overwhelming, unanimous love for the Benefactor. It may be found as well behind Trujillo's intense hatred, expressed through slanderous editorial denouncements and Government-paid pamphlets, against certain foreign publications such as the *New York Times* and *Time* in the United States and *Bohemia,* in Cuba, whose objective and accurate appraisals of the Dominican regime have aroused "the Chief's" disgust. The same psychologically immature driving force is responsible for the strange show of universal accord discerning Dominicans have learned to put up whenever visitors question them concerning their feelings toward the Benefactor.

This climate of well-nigh perfect harmony is responsible as well for the prevailing Dominican atmosphere of apathy and tranquility. This political vacuum is filled with *trujillista* propaganda and the degrading cult of "the Big One's" personality.

The *trujillista* cynicism, double-talk and sheer lack of ethical and moral scruples have had no counterpart in the Western World since the disappearance of Hitler and Mussolini. For instance, when the important facts that there are neither opposition parties nor newspapers are pointed out to Trujillo and his aides, they blandly explain the situation as a result of the existence in the country of some sort of natural harmony. Criticism of the government is lacking not because the regime has stifled it, but because no one has ever thought of any need for objections.

To be fair, however, one should say that not all the alleged support of the regime is a fake. There are a few sincere, dedicated believers in the virtues of the administration, especially among those who have made their wealth and political fortunes under the tight control of the Benefactor and who know that a false step is enough to sink them in the depths from which they emerged. There are others, particularly among the illiterate peasants and workers, who have been swayed by the blaring *trujillista* propaganda conducted through the radio and loudspeakers by trained crews of the *Partido Dominicano*. They believe what they hear.

Then come those who have been carried along by the Trujillo-inspired wave of enthusiasm for building the nation. These people claim, as an excuse for their *trujillismo,* that the Benefactor has given the country generations of material progress in less than three decades. Among these people are those who form the hard core of regression and reaction in the Latin American countries: the propertied class, always fearful of any civic upheaval, made up of the big landowners, the small but powerful, wealthy capitalist sector and the representatives of the foreign interests doing business in the country, who selfishly believe that their investments are better guaranteed by a feudal despot.

These people, even though they suffer in their own flesh the pressure of Trujillo's methods and in private are perhaps the most severe critics of the administration's tax measures and fiscal policies, will never oppose the regime. Trujillo means safety for them. Safety from the strict enforcement of the dead-letter, progressive social legislation already in the statute books; from the emergence of independent, free trade unions; from the long-postponed land reform; from radical political parties or, for that matter, political parties at all; from a critical responsible free press; in a word, from freedom itself. They have come to consider Trujillo as the lesser evil and even if some of them do not like the Benefactor personally he can count upon their full support anyway.

Last but not least among Trujillo's staunch supporters are the bureaucrats, high and low, as well as the professional politicians. Since the Dominican Church is overwhelmingly pro-Trujillo, this has been a great source of support for "the Chief." The clergy, headed by the Archbishops Ricardo Pittini and Octavio Beras, are among the foremost propagandists for the regime. To these we must still add a great number of women to whom Trujillo gave the suffrage and whom the Church leads to the polls.

But as always happens in Latin America, Trujillo remains in power through the support of the military establishment and the chillingly efficient secret police. At present Trujillo appears to command a good measure of loyalty from the well-paid and well-treated military caste. The Armed forces have been raised to a high level of technical efficiency and the officers' class does not seem dissatisfied at all. There is no record of any friction inside the armed forces within the last decade. However, although there does not seem to be any serious military contender for power, Trujillo, who fully understands what personal ambitions can be, keeps a close eye on officers. There is as much fear of reprisals in the military as in the civilian life. The big brass dreads the *Foro Publico* as much as the bureaucrats.

Despite all this, Trujillo's dictatorship has by no means succeeded in removing all threat of opposition. This fact is in evidence in the occasional proclamations of the Generalissimo inviting those who disagree with his policies back into his fold. Gilded with the usual double-talk, of course, this problem has been expounded by Trujillo himself in several opportunities. To one of his official biographers he once said: "In our case there have been enemies who have left here and made attacks from foreign shores. But no matter what they have done, if they want they can be useful. Several times I have stated that all of those who have been away, even if they have tried to discredit their country, may return with the greatest freedom if they are willing to work where they may be useful, so they may really do something for their country. The Government has stood ready to pay their expenses back to the Dominican Republic."

High sounding pronouncements like this one have been made by the dozen throughout the last 27 years by the Benefactor. They do not impress the Dominican people any longer. They have seen Trujillo break his own word so many times that they have learned to take his promises with a grain of salt. This is a marked trait that differentiates Trujillo from the classical Latin American dictators. The *caudillos* obey certain rules and one of their proudest boasts—confirmed by people who have dealt with them—is that they always keep their word. The Caribbean sea, however, is crowded with corpses of credulous persons who believed Trujillo.

Throughout the years of dictatorship there have been a number of plots. From the early thirties, when the students, emulating the example of their colleagues in other Latin American countries, began to plant bombs in the schools and public buildings of Santiago, to the late forties, when the last vestiges of organized underground opposition were finally wiped out ruthlessly, there were so many plots that an enumeration of them would fill pages of this book. Yet, excellently planned as some of these abortive revolutionary attempts may have been, there was always to be found at least one *trujillista* agent infiltrated in the ranks of the conspirators.

At present, there is not an organized underground movement nor are there leaders to direct and encourage such a movement if it existed. Those who could actively take over the task are either exiled, imprisoned or under close surveillance.

There is no way to communicate safely between groups even inside the country—telephone lines, as a routine matter, are tapped; correspondence is either rifled or carefully scrutinized; and movements across provincial borders are thoroughly checked. Participants in any suspicious meeting, if reported by neighborhood informants, are questioned by the Secret Police. To possess a clandestine mimeograph machine is as dangerous as having a machinegun, and punishment for the latter offense is death sentence by the kangaroo courts. Under such conditions it is impossible to circulate political literature and even newspapers and periodicals coming into the country are impounded by the authorities. *Newsweek* once pointed out that "travelers arriving at Ciudad Trujillo are required to submit to a minute inspection of their documents, and all newspapers they bring in are confiscated."

Yet there is the possibility that minuscule revolutionary cells, particularly inside the students and workers groups, are working within the country. There are many people, including government officials and businessmen, who at a grave risk dare to smuggle in and out of the country news and propaganda. Undoubtedly there is a freemasonry of dissatisfaction and an intense longing for a change, even among people high in official circles. This inarticulate mood of hostility, although deep, is too nebulous to be exposed and dispersed by the Secret Police; it is also too amorphous to constitute an imminent danger to the regime. In tribute to the *trujillista* Gestapo it must be said that whenever this sentiment of dissatisfaction tends to materialize in the form of a revolutionary plot, this is promptly detected by the Government sleuths. Literally speaking, all anti-Trujillo plots throughout the years of the Era have died aborning. Yet there is no honest American journalist who visits the Dominican Republic who does not come out with the latest story about an abortive attempt on Trujillo's life. Murray Kempton of the *New York Post* wrote, July, 1956, that "late in May (a group of conspirators) attacked and eliminated a 10-man garrison near Salcedo and thus provided their weapons caché. They then wired and mined with explosives a church at Moca which was to have been dedicated by the Generalissimo in the presence of his entire family on June 9. And they had made provisions to wait in the house across the way for any Trujillo man who tried to escape from the ruins. An informer turned the conspirators in early in June, and the Moca church dedication went off safely as scheduled." Over a year later Milton Bracker of the *New York Times* wrote: "There was a confirmed incident of discontent in the south coast sugar port of San Pedro de Macoris last spring. Agricultural workers defaced public buildings in such a way as to leave no doubt as to their feelings about their Benefactor." He then added that although exiles in New York had charged that this led to reprisals of the most brutal and public sort "a high Trujillo aide, while confirming the incident, insists that what he called 'communist' offenders benefited by due process of law." Knowing Trujillo's "due process of law" it is fair to assume that in this case both the exiles and the *trujillista* aide were right.

It is therefore unlikely that any anti-Trujillo movement of magnitude will develop within the country in the foreseeable future. However, underneath the outward signs of "satisfaction" with the present regime there are the root factors of discontent—a steadily rising cost of living; marked inequalities between the favored few and the impoverished masses; and, for the intellectuals and other members of the upper middle class the general, pervading feeling of political stagnation.

It would be the height of folly to expect the Trujillo empire to collapse of its own weight. Yet, if there is anything that cannot be discounted and that Trujillo ought to fear, it is assassination, not revolution. The current movement against dictators in Latin America has not passed as unnoticed as Trujillo would have wished in Santo Domingo. The Government arrested many people at the time of Fidel Castro's landing in Cuba to start a revolution against President Batista. A story going the rounds speaks volumes on what the people felt.

An old lady boarded a crowded bus. No one offered her a seat. Finally, in exasperation, she said aloud: "Is there no man here who might offer me a seat?" A woman next to her replied: "Do you not know, my dear, there are no men here in Santo Domingo? If you want men, you must go to Cuba to find them."

This embittered self-denying expression of Dominican humor brings one to a more serious question that is always posed by those interested in the Dominican situation. How is it that Dominicans and Cubans are so different in their respective attitudes toward dictatorship?

The question is a complex one. To begin with, I do not believe that Cubans love freedom more than Dominicans. Both are freedom-loving peoples and whenever Cubans have fought for their own liberty there have been Dominicans at their side. The Dominican Máximo Gómez accompanied José Marti, the Cuban liberator, in the invasion that set off the last war for Cuban independence. A Dominican sailor was the captain of the yacht *Gramma* that took Fidel Castro and his small band of heroic and by now legendary band of revolutionists to launch the Sierra Maestra campaign in December 1956. On the other hand, there have been Cubans by the hundred, side by side with the Dominicans, whenever preparations have been made to start a revolution in the Dominican Republic. Fidel Castro himself is a veteran of the ill-fated attempt of Cayo Confites.

Other factors that favor the Cubans account for the difference of attitudes. While Dominicans are a people totally disarmed since the days of the American occupation, Cubans are armed to the teeth. While there is not among the active opponents of the Trujillo regime a single man of wealth (Juan Rodriguez García the only millionaire who ever fought against Trujillo is now a ruined man), there are scores of rich men in the ranks of the anti-Batista forces. While the well patroled coasts of the Dominican Republic are far off from any Continental point of embarkation, the longer, less protected Cuban shoreline is within small boat range of Mexico and the United States. While the Batista dictatorship is not consolidated yet, the Trujillo regime has been sitting tightly on the lid for the last 27 consecutive years.

These are the contributing factors to the difference of attitudes. They explain why while Dominicans look passive, apathetic, uninterested, the Cubans are active, painstaking and very much interested in the sad plight of their country.

2.

IF THE TRUJILLO REGIME IS CONFIDENT OF ITS DOMESTIC strength and does not worry unduly about its internal opponents, it does not take chances with its enemies on foreign soil. It admittedly keeps a watchful eye upon the activities of the Dominican exiles, whose leaders and organizations are at all times under close surveillance by Dominican diplomats and secret police. The Dominican embassies abroad, the *trujillista* press agents, lobbyists and spies do whatever they can to hinder the activities of the emigré groups, particularly those operating in the United States. At the recent federal trial in which John Joseph Frank, Washington attorney and former FBI and Central Intelligence Agency agent, was charged with acting for the Dominican Republic in the United States without registering as a foreign agent, evidence was introduced to prove that Trujillo had paid fees of $20 an hour for the privilege of keeping track of the movements of opponents residing in American territory.

Trujillo's fears are somewhat justified. Dominican exiles afford the only organized—and sometimes articulate—opposition to his strong arm rule. They are the only ones who keep the flame of resistance alive.

An impartial survey of the exile political scene leads, however, to the conclusion that for the time being the Generalissimo does not have much to fear from his loosely organized external opposition. Thus far, the exiles have not been able to make any serious, direct contribution toward the overthrow of the *trujillista* state. Their two known attempts at bringing about the downfall of Trujillo through armed action—the ill fated revolutionary invasions of Cayo Confites and Luperon—failed tragically because of combined adverse factors not always under the revolutionists' control. At present, the exiles do not possess the armed strength to smash their way to power, nor have they found yet a specific political formula for winning power in any other way.

Moreover, the years of undeserved misfortunes, martyrdom and untold sufferings in exile do not seem to have endowed the anti-Trujillo leaders with great political insight.

By a weird twist of fate, exile seems to bring out the worst rather than the best in people. Thus, instead of concentrating on the common purpose of defeating the dictator, many Dominican exiles show a marked inclination to enter into endless arguments with their colleagues, and, for that matter, with all the force they should reserve to combat the Generalissimo.

Unquestionably, a fact bearing heavily upon the whole exile predicament is that although many exiles are men of intelligence and comprehensive vision and are imbued with genuine democratic convictions, an overwhelming feeling of frustration and loss of status increasingly gets hold of them as they immerse themselves deeper in the new and not always friendly environment in which they live. Considering themselves neglected and misunderstood, they become victims of petty squabbles and endless bickering over matters of small consequence. They do not expect the United States nor any other nation to land marines in the Dominican Republic to liberate the country, but they do expect to be treated as people who have made heavy personal sacrifices out of loyalty to democratic ideals. Instead, they hear from American high government officials and legislators constant words of praise for the Dominican dictatorship and they find that—apart from a handful of responsible newspapers as well as democratic organizations and leaders—no one seems to be particularly concerned because democracy is trampled upon in their native land.

The aforementioned problems are aggravated by the fact that not all the exiles are convinced democratic idealists. Some of them fled their country after losing their juicy plums at the time of the downfall of the Vásquez regime. Others are totally unknown within their own country, and being aware of this fact, they seem to be more interested in the passing glory they have mustered for themselves during their years of exile than in looking for permanent solutions to the Dominican tragedy. Still others regard themselves as a sort of a government-in-exile, or at least as the censors of a very exclusive club, with exclusive rights to interfere with and veto any project which is not agreeable to them. These latter people have fought tooth and nail to acquire positions which they will seek to retain on the great day when they return to their homeland riding the victory chariot. They feel offended whenever someone suggests that a new generation which no longer knows them has grown up in the Dominican Republic. Some of these people believe they will return to the year

1931, others to 1937, still others to 1947. Not many seem prepared to go back to the post-Trujillo Dominican Republic.

The point is academic because it will most likely be those who have lived and suffered these many years under the brutal yoke of "the Big One" who will be better equipped to direct the country's political future than the men in Havana, New York City and San Juan, Puerto Rico.

Those who left the country in the early Thirties (the clean ones, the pure who did not play ball with Trujillo) are scornful of all the others who turned to exile later. Those who broke in the middle Thirties feel superior to those who did not break until the days of Cayo Confites. These in turn look down on the later disillusioned exiles. Since everyone who comes out of the Dominican Republic already has the stigma of collaboration, there is a marked tendency among the pseudo-aristocracy of the exile world to reject any newcomer on the ground of his recent connections with the dictatorship. This position is not only devoid of political realism, but it is also self-defeating. These people forget that aside from a few of the leaders of the first generation of refugees—men like Dr. Angel Morales, Dr. Miguel A. Pardo and Dr. Guaroa Velazquez—a large proportion of the exile leadership is made up of former collaborators of the regime.

The customary lofty rejection of the newly arrived serves Trujillo's interests. First, it lends support to the oft-repeated *trujillista* contention that exiledom is a big industry—a monopoly in fact—exploited for the benefit of a few who have made a profitable career out of it.

Second, it transplants to the exile groups the practical *trujillista* strategy of sowing dissension and playing off one political group or individual against another in an endless contention.

Third, since people who make the grave decision to leave behind family, home, former friends and sometimes wealth and social position, to plunge into the uncertainties of exile life at least expect to find a spirit of democratic solidarity on the other side, this habit of according hostile receptions to those who break with Trujillo, cuts down to a minimum the number of defections.

The largest—and probably the most active—colonies of anti-Trujillo Dominicans are centered at present in New York City and San Juan, Puerto Rico. The Puerto Ricans are especially sympathetic hosts to the hundreds of Dominicans and Cubans who have gathered in their island. According to *The Nation,* "the Puerto Ricans, proud of their own democracy, are pleased to have their island serve as a port in the extended dictatorial storms, and the exiles find much popular support here, as well as official protection."

New York City, the most liberal city in the world, lends much support to the refugees of tyrannical regimes. There Dominican exiles find a sympathetic press and a group of fine liberals such as Norman Thomas, the

Socialist leader, Miss Frances Grant, Secretary General of the Inter American Association for Democracy and Freedom, Roger Baldwin, of the American Civil Liberties Union, Louise Crane, publisher of *Iberica,* and others who are always ready to lend their support to a just cause.

Since a recent rapprochement between the regimes of Fulgencio Batista, in Cuba, and Trujillo, the activities of the large colony of Dominican exiles living in Cuba have been severely curtailed. The formerly vocal and quite active groups that had found haven and a sympathetic audience in Cuba are almost silent and their members live in constant fear of the long arm of the Benefactor.

Venezuela, a country that from 1945 to 1948 was under the protection of the left of center regimes of Romulo Betancourt and Romulo Gallegos, a stage for the launching of much anti-Trujillo propaganda, was long closed as a base of operations for Dominican exiles, for reasons much like those prevailing in Cuba. In Caracas and other Venezuelan cities live a group of anti-Trujillo emigres of considerable economic power. Yet, it was understood that few of the Dominicans settled there would risk either their liberty or their comfortable livelihoods to defy the close alliance which for years existed between Pérez Jimenez and Trujillo.

Mexico had been until recently one of the most secure places of refuge for those fleeing from Trujillo's terror. Finally, Trujillo's lethal arm reached into that country and since the frustrated attempt on the life of the exile leader Tancredo Martínez García, terror has been rampant. The Ciudad de Mexico newspaper *La Prensa* recently reported that Dominicans in México are living "in fear that the knife or pistol of a mercenary may end their lives." The same paper asserted that the exiles are "defenseless against the long arm of the Trujillo regime."

In a word, the activities of the Dominican exile colonies in Latin America are at the mercy of prevailing political winds. If the Government of the country where they are established is democratically inclined the exiles prosper and sometimes even get active financial support from their sympathizers. Otherwise they have to shut up and pray for a change before Trujillo gets them.

The activities of the exile organizations are rather deceptive. There are a few groups which may be considered more or less permanent.

The oldest, and one of the most active throughout the years, is the *Partido Revolucionario Dominicano.* Founded in the early Forties this party has its headquarters in Havana. It has branches in Venezuela, Mexico, Puerto Rico and New York City. The PRD main source of strength is to be found in middle class groups, but it also seeks support among the organized workers and peasants. Its political program specifies lucidly a set of principles aimed at the creation of a democratic order in the Dominican Republic. The PRD publishes a periodical *Quisqueya Libre* as well as a monthly bulletin which is edited by its New York section.

Among the central figures of the PRD are Juan Bosch, a vigorous intellectual and fiction writer, who has played a leading role in the shaping of the exile movement; Angel Miolan, a dedicated fighter against the regime since his student days in Santiago and at present the secretary general of the organization; Alexis Liz and Buenaventura Sánchez, two politicians of the pre-Trujillo days. The New York Section, which is registered with the Justice Department as a foreign agent, is under the direction of Nicolas Silfa, a steadfast and articulate *antitrujillista*, who has become one of the pet hatreds of the Benefactor.

The PRD has been particularly active since the disappearance of Jesús de Galíndez; it organizes picket lines, political rallies and memorial meetings. Its leaders were among the first to charge the Trujillo regime as responsible for the kidnapping and murder of the Spanish professor. In their righteous indignation over the political crime they made a mistake when, obviously misled by a *trujillista* agent provocateur, Nicolas Silfa charged publicly that Dr. Galíndez had been thrown alive into one of the furnaces of the Dominican freighter *Fundación*. After the ship had been searched in vain for four hours by the New York police, informed sources suggested that Silfa might have received his information from people interested in sidetracking the investigations.

In 1956, Silfa, Bosch and Miolan traveled to Europe to attend a meeting of the executive committee of the International Confederation of Free Trade Unions. As a result of their pleading, then strongly backed by the organized Cuban workers headed by Senator Eusebio Mujal, the I.C.F.T.U. executive committee adopted a resolution accusing the Trujillo dictatorship of suppressing the free labor movement and calling for consultation with labor regional organizations on a possible boycott of the Dominican Republic. The resolution also accused the Trujillo regime of failure to enact adequate social legislation (it would have been more accurate had it said "failure to enforce"), leniency toward Communism, a monopolist position in many fields of industry, and attempting to interfere in the foreign policies of other countries, particularly Cuba.

The committee asked all its affiliates and international trade secretaries to join a world-wide campaign to protest the "policy of terror, crime and persecution pursued by the Trujillo regime, as well as against its intrigues and its murderous attacks on the foes of the regime."

Batista and Trujillo were then engaged in one of those political feuds that occasionally stir the waters of the Caribbean Sea. As one of Batista's stooges and head of the CTC (Confederation of Cuban Workers), Mujal gave open support to the threatened boycott, which for a time looked as if it had a chance to be enforced. Yet, a few months later, Trujillo's efforts to blackmail Batista into political submission were crowned with success and the latter was received in "The Chief's" fold. Mujal then lost all interest in restoring democratic freedoms for the Dominican workers, and thereupon the boycott idea was promptly forgotten.

Although the PRD is moderate and its activities are marked out by advocacy of a democratic program, minimum social legislation and a temperate attitude toward the Dominican Church, some of its main battles have been against the clergy. In September, 1957, Silfa formally filed a complaint with the Pope against what he called the "political activity" of the Dominican Archbishop Monsignor Ricardo Pittini. The complaint was based, Silfa said, on a statement in which Archbishop Pittini defended the Trujillo regime in terms "exceedingly emphatic" and in "utter disregard of the truth."

Then a Solemn Mass scheduled to be celebrated at St. Patrick's Cathedral on November 9, 1957, for the "health and welfare" of Dominican workers-in-exile and their families, was canceled on the ground that its sponsors were using it for political purposes. The sponsors were the Dominican Democratic Workers in Exile, whose secretary general is Nicolas Silfa, of the PRD.

Silfa insisted that the Mass was in no way a political matter, and had been requested to invoke divine blessing for the health and welfare of Dominican workers. Concerning the cancellation, Rev. Bernard P. Donachie, a member of St. Patrick's Cathedral staff, said that he had entered upon an understanding with Silfa that the Mass would not be used for political purposes. "When it came to my attention that the scheduled Mass was being so used, I felt I had no choice but to cancel it."

In a letter to Cardinal Spellman, Silfa expressed his "shocking disbelief at the action" and denied charges of political intention on his part. He then told Cardinal Spellman that he had been informed that a request for a Mass would have to be made through the offices of the Consul General of the Dominican Republic in New York, and added: "This is quite impossible. To us this is equivalent to asking Catholic Hungarian freedom fighters to place their request with the Communist Hungarian Consul General." To the press Silfa charged that Dominican Republic consular officials had told Father Donachie that the sponsoring group was "Communist." He denied that it was.

There can be no doubt that among the distinct political forces whose voice is now heard in the forum of Dominican opposition one of the most effective is *Vanguardia Revolucionaria Dominicana*. To the degree that it is possible to assess the relative strength of the exile groups, it appears that VRD, though one of the newest and perhaps smallest, is also one of the most influential. Since its founding in 1956 this party has rallied around its banner a representative leadership from professional and intellectual groups—doctors, lawyers, writers, professors and former diplomats. Yet, though it has an essentially burgeois center of gravity it disclaims all pretences of being an "elite party" and does not discourage admission into its ranks of members of the working and peasant classes, who form the hard core of the Dominican population in exile.

Perhaps because its leadership has been better trained and politically more mature than that of the majority of the other exile groups, VRD has often seemed to think more clearly and to act with surer purpose. They have carefully avoided issues which could easily divide the opposition, while maintaining their own clear-cut political identity. There is, however, a perilous tendency to feud with the PRD, which should be avoided.

The top leadership of *Vanguardia* is concentrated in Puerto Rico, though it has a branch in New York City and a representative in Mexico City, in charge of coordinating the publication of the official organ of the Party. Its President is Dr. Miguel A. Pardo, one of the long-time anti-Trujillo fighters, with a clean and honorable record of struggle for the freedom of the Dominican people. A measure of the importance Trujillo gives to VRD is that Dr. Pardo and other leaders of the Party have been subject to a domestic press and radio campaign of smear and vilification, an honor the Benefactor only accords to people with established prestige inside the country, since he is not interested in building up the local reputation of unknown exile leaders.

Secretary General of VRD is Horacio J. Ornes, one of the youngest veterans of the exile movement. Ornes founded the widely-publicized and now dictator-wielded Caribbean Legion when he commanded part of the rebel forces in the Costa Rican civil war launched in 1948 by current President José Figueres to rout the Red-dominated regime then entrenched in the Central American nation. Ornes also participated in the abortive attempt of Cayo Confites, being sentenced in absentia for its participation to thirty years in jail. In June, 1949, he commanded the airborne invasion of Dominican territory known as the attempt of Luperon. Captured with a group of his fellow-invaders, all were sentenced to 30 years at hard labor after a mock public trial. As a result of an amnesty passed by the Trujillo Congress on February 20, 1950, Ornes and his companions were freed and took anew the road to exile. (Recently Trujillo threatened to ask Ornes's extradition for alleged violation of the terms of the amnesty. Ornes challenged Trujillo to start a suit in a free American court.)

The Executive Committee of VRD is made up of three distinguished professionals, Drs. J. Edmundo Taveras and Felix García Carrasco, two prominent physicians established in Puerto Rico with a large practice, and Dr. Ricardo Roques Martinez, who earned his spurs in the underground fight against the Benefactor inside his own police-ridden domain. Roques also acts as head of the New York section of the party. Other leaders of the party are former University professors like Dr. Moises de Soto; young writers like Oscar Torres, solid businessmen like Luis Ortiz Arzeno and labor leaders like Herman Voigt.

Since its inception the strength and prestige of VRD have grown swiftly. One revealing index of the amount of activity of this movement has been the quality and volume of its propaganda. The editorial merit of its publications is conspicuously superior to the average of exile propaganda; more newsworthy, more persuasive and generally better printed and illustrated. The main publicity organ is a magazine called VRD.

VRD was the first exile organization to denounce publicly, in a letter to Senator Wayne Morse (D.-Ore.), the link between the murder of the young American flyer Gerald Lester Murphy, inside the Dominican Republic, and the kidnapping of Professor Jesús de Galíndez.

On August 16, 1957, VRD made public in New York a letter to Attorney General Herbert Brownell, Jr., protesting "the actual intervention of the Trujillo regime in the lawful processes of the judicial institutions of the United States." The letter questioned the legality of a private *trujillista* investigation of the Galíndez affair and demanded the United States notify Generalissimo Trujillo that his "incriminated regime will not be allowed to intervene in the domestic affairs of the United States" and that the Galíndez investigation was the "exclusive competence" of American judicial authorities.

Also with headquarters in Puerto Rico is the *Partido Populista Dominicano,* one of the most active, publicity-wise speaking, of the exiles groups. Leader of this organization that claims a large membership is Francisco Javier Guilliani.

The PPD leads a weekly picket line outside the Dominican Consulate General in San Juan, Puerto Rico, makes broadcasts to the Dominican Republic and conducts a vigorous publicity campaign against Trujillo. In a recent statement to the *Nation* it was stated that the PPD's aim "is not so much to draw people out of the Dominican Republic, but to establish a sympathetic following within it for his party and its stated principles of democratic politics."

The magazine then added: "The Populist Party has never attempted any military attack on Trujillo's regime, and they say that they are planning none. Guilliani has little hope of an uprising within the tight military control that Trujillo has imposed upon his country with the help of U.S. arms aid."

As quoted by the *Nation* Guilliani will just wait till Trujillo dies. "Then we will return, and with the help of our followers inside the country, set up a democratic government and democratic elections before another dictatorship starts."

At present the Communists are perhaps the least active of the groups of

Dominican exiles. Still licking the wounds suffered during their ill-fated "legal" adventure in the Dominican Republic during 1946–1947, the Reds concentrated first in Guatemala and, after the victorious revolution of the late Col. Carlos Castillo Armas, in Mexico. There they edit a monthly organ *Vanguardia* and make occasional pronouncements against Trujillo and American imperialism. They are taking it easy, however. They know they have got to be patient and patience is a commodity they can well afford. First, they know that with their prestige shattered as a result of their past dealings with the Trujillo regime they will have to wait a long time before reasserting themselves in the eyes of the sceptical Dominican people. Second, while the present international balance of power prevails they do not have a chance of taking power in such a strategic country as the Dominican Republic.

As a consequence of an effort to unify the different exile groups a few popular front style organizations emerged a few years back in New York, San Juan, Havana and Mexico. Many democratic exiles raised their eyebrows, suspecting a Communist-inspired movement. Everyone, however, pointed out that the fronts were not dominated by the Communists and no proofs have been presented otherwise.

The Dominican opposition in exile still derives its main source of strength, despite the increasing importance of the political parties, from the prestige of a handful of individual figures who command a great deal of respect both among fellow-emigres and foreign political and intellectual leaders. Among these outstanding exiles are Juan Rodriguez García, Dr. Angel Morales, Dr. Horacio Vicioso, Dr. Guaroa Velazquez, Dr. José Antonio Bonilla Atiles, Dr. Miguel A. Pardo, Juan Bosch and others.

UNMYSTERIOUS MYSTERIES

ON MARCH 12, 1956, ONE OF THE MOST ARTICULATE CRITICS OF the Trujillo regime, the Basque scholar Dr. Jesús de Galíndez, lecturer in Spanish and Government at Columbia University, disappeared from his New York home at 30 Fifth Avenue. From the moment he vanished, Dr. de Galíndez posed for American authorities a riddle surrounded by the cloak-and-dagger aura of international intrigue; a web of murder and lawlessness protected by diplomatic immunity and the complicity of a foreign government which evolved into the most noted *cause celebre* of the present.

Dr. de Galíndez' disappearance did not come as a complete surprise. His friends, and the police, knew that his life was in danger. He had been threatened by anonymous callers.

Jesús de Galíndez, 42, had been a resident of New York City since early 1946. A hard-working, affable, sociable intellectual, de Galíndez had finally achieved a doctorate at Columbia. Born in Madrid, de Galíndez considered himself nevertheless a citizen of the short-lived autonomous Basque republic, abolished by Franco in 1937.

De Galíndez had fought the Spanish Civil War on the loyalist side. He paid the price of defeat in exile, first to France, then, from November 1939 to January 1946, in the Dominican Republic. There he took a teaching job at the School of Diplomatic Law attached to the Dominican Foreign Office (where one of Trujillo's sons, Rafael, Jr., was his pupil). Later he became Legal Adviser to the Labor Department.

While serving in the Labor Department, de Galíndez first incurred Trujillo's wrath. As a secretary of the minimum wage commission, the young lawyer helped to settle during December 1945 and January 1946 a series of labor strikes in the still American-owned sugar industry, in a manner regarded as too favorable to labor. Charged with a pro-labor slant, de Galíndez became a marked man. There is also the possibility, not established clearly, that de Galíndez was involved in some degree in the activities of the democratic underground.

Tipped off by friends, Galíndez decided to leave the Dominican environment; through friends in the United States he got a visa to come to New York City where he settled.

Trujillo's absolute one-man rule became the consuming interest of Galíndez. "In time," recalled Professor Frank Tannenbaum of Columbia University, "de Galíndez came to resemble nothing so much as a walking one-man intelligence bureau. He knew more about Trujillo than anyone else in the whole wide world."

De Galíndez did not forget the Dominican Republic. He became active in three different sectors of Manhattan: among the exiled Spaniards, the large Latin American colony, and the liberal, anti-Communist New York intellectuals. He was also appointed official representative of the Basque Government in exile, whose seat is in Paris.

He was a founder and sometime President of the Ibero-American Poets and Writers Guild. He became a director of the International League for the Rights of Man, a United Nations consultant agency, and a member of the United States Committee of the Inter American Association for Democracy and Freedom. He also acted as a consultant for American law firms on complicated issues of international law. He found time to write a book on Latin American history and many scorching attacks on Trujillo in magazine and newspaper articles and pamphlets published in the United States, Mexico, Cuba, and other Latin American countries.

"He was a scholar well respected by his teaching colleagues and held in warm affection and regard as well by his students," wrote Grayson Kirk, President of Columbia University, to the New York *Times*.

In his book-cluttered, file-bulging apartment, Galíndez patiently assembled all the known facts about Trujillo. Most of the research went toward a 750-page damaging critical analysis of the Dominican dictatorship, entitled *The Era of Trujillo,* which he submitted for his Ph.D. degree. De Galíndez also worked on a scathing novel about the Dominican strongman.

As his doctoral thesis neared completion, Galíndez received numerous threats, which he reported to friends and the FBI. "He was apprehensive," said a fellow professor, "but he didn't let the threats depress him. He didn't look behind his back."

De Galíndez completed his damaging indictment of Trujillo's regime, submitted it to Columbia's history department (he discussed it on February 27, 1957, Dominican Independence Day) and went ahead with plans for publication.

He took a number of precautions. As he slowly worked over the manuscript, writing first in Spanish and then making a literal translation into English for editorial polishing by American friends, he deposited a copy, chapter by chapter, with a friend. When the work was finished he gathered all the copies. He then submitted the English version to the University, but after the thesis had been accepted by Columbia all copies were returned to him for minor corrections. He disappeared before the manuscript could be returned to the University.

Nevertheless, before he vanished he put into the hands of a Chilean friend, Alfonso Naranjo, a complete copy of the Spanish typescript, to take to Chile for safekeeping.

Naranjo hid the manuscript and after de Galíndez' disappearance made arrangements for publication by Editorial del Pacifico of Santiago, Chile. De Galíndez himself put an English copy in the hands of the New York University Press, but did not sign a contract for its publication, an oversight that has prevented, thus far, publishing of the complete thesis.

De Galíndez also reinforced the locks of his apartment. This he did after the mysterious visit to the building of a man later identified as one of the most sinister operatives of the *trujillista* espionage network. This man, whose right name may never be known, is famous in the exile world by his nickname of *El Cojo,* the Lame One.

Jesús Martínez Jara (one of his many names) cut a bizarre figure. A short, thin, leathery, middle-aged man, he walked with a limp and had a cast in one eye. Wherever he went, crime was scheduled. American investigative agencies have collected as many as 75 aliases by which he has been known.

A Spanish Republican refugee himself (although of another vintage), *El Cojo* had been a loyalist stool pigeon during the Spanish Civil War. He went into exile and found refuge in Cuba, Mexico, Colombia, Costa Rica, Jamaica and Puerto Rico. His stay in each was short because of his habit of falling out with the authorities over a variety of accomplishments ranging from counterfeiting of currency to illegal practice of medicine.

Sometime in 1954 he arrived in Port-au-Prince, Haiti, penniless and without a passport. Promptly picked up by the Haitian police, he landed in jail. Shortly afterwards the Haitian authorities also picked up a group of Dominicans fleeing from the *trujillista* furies, who were waiting for the disposal of extradition procedures initiated by the Dominican government. The Trujillo secret police needed an inmate to keep a watchful eye on the refugees; they found their man in *El Cojo.*

Apparently he did a good job, because after the men were set free by a Haitian court, which refused to extradite, *El Cojo* too was freed. After that the Dominican ambassador, Luis Logroño Cohen, personally arranged his release. He was given a safe conduct and sent to Ciudad Trujillo, where he went to work for the secret police of the Benefactor.

El Cojo was assigned the mission of infiltrating exile groups in Mexico, Cuba and Puerto Rico. For a time he was successful, but after the killing in 1955 of the Dominican oppositionist Manuel J. ("Pipi") Hernández, in Havana, the exiles began to suspect him.

In fall 1955, *El Cojo* began to drift toward the American mainland. On November 22, *El Cojo* called on Dr. de Galíndez. The latter was startled when the switchboard operator told him that a stranger wanted to come up to his apartment. The professor asked the operator to hold the stranger and went down to meet him. The visitor introduced himself as Manuel Hernández, merchant seaman from Puerto Rico, and he pressed to see Dr. de Galíndez "privately" about a "confidential matter."

The man spoke with an accent which was not Puerto Rican. Of this interview there is a fairly good record. Andrew St. George, a writer who has researched the de Galíndez case, described the visit in an article for *Argosy* in words that are exactly those de Galíndez used to recount it to the author of this book.

St. George wrote: "He (de Galíndez) rejected the stranger's request for a chat in a 'quiet place' and insisted that he state the purpose of his visit on the spot.

"The man who called himself Hernández spoke reluctantly and mysteriously. He made veiled references to a connection with the Dominican Republic and under the professor's prodding he finally came out with it. He had access to some secret Dominican papers, revealing among other things, the identity of Trujillo's confidential agents in the United States.

"By this time, Dr. Galíndez was thoroughly skeptical. In fact, he scented danger. He told the stranger abruptly that he was not interested in any piece of his proposition and rang for the elevator.

"The odd caller, however, refused to give up. Speaking rapidly, he admitted that Dr. Galíndez had reason for distrusting him; that his name was actually not really Hernández, but Velázquez, and that he had not told the *whole* truth. But the secret documents, said Hernández-Velázquez excitedly—those were real.

"The disturbing scene ended with the arrival of the elevator. Galíndez dismissed the stranger by slamming the door in his face."

De Galíndez also described *El Cojo's* visit in a letter he wrote to Dr. Angel Morales, in San Juan, Puerto Rico. It seems that *El Cojo* went to see Galíndez twice more. Of later visits there is not a clear record.

Then, on Monday, March 12, 1956, at twenty minutes past nine in the evening, Dr. de Galíndez finished his lecture in Columbia's Fayerweather Hall and left with two students, a young man and girl. With them he walked for about two blocks. When the man left he accepted a lift from the girl, who lived on East 57th Street. She volunteered to drop him at the subway entrance, corner of 57th and Eighth Avenue.

The girl recalls that riding downtown, de Galíndez talked of the forthcoming Pan American Day parade on April 19 (the first of its kind in New York City) in whose preparation he was taking a leading part. "He was enthusiastic; neither depressed nor frightened," said the girl.

On this corner de Galíndez left the car, waved to his pupil, and ducked into the downtown subway entrance. No friend has seen de Galíndez, alive or dead, since.

No one knows whether he met with criminal attack before reaching the subway platform, while in the station after leaving the subway, upon reaching home or whether he was lured out later that night by a phone call from someone he trusted. The general belief is that he reached his apartment. The girl student later identified the overcoat found there as the one he had been wearing when she left him at the subway entrance. Moreover, the bed was unmade, although people who knew de Galíndez well asserted that he was a sloppy housekeeper and may not have slept there that night. On the bed the police found the Monday evening papers, but none of Tuesday morning. It may be that an abductor was waiting at the apartment, but the possibility is remote since the police found no sign of a struggle. Even his papers were seemingly in order, though a brown briefcase, which was said to be always full of "confidential" papers, was found open and empty in the apartment.

De Galíndez had many friends in New York and a number called him in the next few days, but almost a week was lost before the police were called in. De Galíndez had only one other class at Columbia that week; his failure to show up was no cause of alarm. Friends who telephoned assumed he was out. Finally, Mr. Tomás Santana, one of the organizers of the Pan American parade, after a few unsuccessful calls, sounded the alarm. Instead of calling the police Santana got in touch with one of the Spanish language newspapers, *El Diario de Nueva York,* and talked with its editor, Stanley Ross.

At last the police were notified by Ross, who before going to the authorities paid a visit to de Galíndez' apartment in the company of a girl named Lydia Miranda. They were assured by the help that they had seen the professor, or thought they had, on Wednesday. The superintendent opened the apartment and they entered, but discovered nothing to alarm them. All the same the police were notified.

At this point a very strange thing happened. Ross failed to print the story promptly in his newspaper, thus losing the scoop of the year. It was the other Spanish daily, *La Prensa,* which broke the news in its Sunday edition. Ross later argued that the police had requested withholding publication until further word from them. *La Prensa* denied there was such a request.

De Galíndez became case #5254 in the files of New York's Missing Persons Bureau.

The police searched de Galíndez' apartment at least forty times. No evidence of violence was ever found, nor anything that could lead to the apprehension of anyone. The police found in one filing cabinet carefully dated cards listing the individuals Galíndez had met over the years, but none of these names provided a clue. In another file they found a note, dated October 4, 1952 (two days after a Dominican exile, Andrés Requena, had been shot to death in a lower Manhattan tenement) addressed "to the police." It said: "In case anything would happen to me, I have serious reasons to believe that my aggressors could be agents from . . ." Police have declined to reveal the remainder but let it be known Galíndez meant the Dominican Republic.

Also detectives found the draft of a will, unsigned and not notarized, directing that in event of his death any assets be used to publish his papers concerning the Dominican Republic, that his other documents be given to the Basque Government in Spain and his body taken back to his native Basque country for burial.

The respected socialist leader Norman Thomas and other leaders of American civic groups pointed the finger of suspicion at the Generalissimo. Dominican officials vehemently denied any responsibility for the disappearance.

An important group of more than a dozen American, Spanish-American and Inter-American organizations immediately appealed to the United States Attorney General Herbert Brownell for an all-out FBI investigation. The highly influential Inter-American Press Association asked President Eisenhower to give personal consideration to the disappearance and to order an investigation by the FBI. The American Foreign Law Association asked for an intensive investigation. So did many individuals.

For the police time was vital; already too much had been lost. A swarm of detectives was thrown into one of the most intensive man hunts in New York police history, while the press made a clamor. Two weeks after the disappearance Manuel G. Graymore, an assistant district attorney for New York City who had been assigned to the case, admitted that all the evidence, scant though it was, pointed to kidnapping and murder by Dominican agents for political reasons. To the *New York Post* Graymore said: "We have conducted a painstaking search for any other possible motive and there is none." Under pressure from the Dominican Information Center and Dominican consular and diplomatic officials, the District Attorney's Office disavowed Graymore a few days later.

From the beginning, the investigation ran into blind alleys. There was the presence of two Dominican ships in New York harbor the night of March 12—the *Fundación* and the *Angelita*. One, the *Angelita,* went to sea the same night, and then executed a curious maneuver. After five hours the ship reversed its course and returned to port. The captain blandly claimed engine trouble. A broken pinion was available as proof. The other sailed for the Dominican Republic a few days later.

"We could not question the captain," Graymore said, "because the ship was on the high seas at the time and beyond our jurisdiction." The ominous implications were that de Galíndez could have been dumped overboard on the *Angelita's* five-hour trip to sea, or smuggled back to the Dominican Republic.

Late in May the mystery of the missing man took a singularly ugly turn. Nicolas Silfa, New York representative of the Dominican Revolutionary Party, said he had learned from the Dominican "underground" that Dr. de Galíndez had been thrown—alive—into the furnace of the Dominican freighter *Fundación,* while the ship was in New York harbor on or about March 13. Dominican officials called this theory "fantastic." There were anti-Trujillo demonstrations in front of the Madison Avenue office of Franklin D. Roosevelt, Jr., then a legal representative of the Dominican government.

Next time the *Fundación* docked in New York the police went aboard, searched the ship and questioned the crew. They found no evidence that a man might have been murdered. The mystery was as deep as ever. It took some time to realize that the Dominican government was very much interested in planting that story and calling attention to the ships in order to sidetrack the investigation.

At the beginning the police discovered what they thought was a "key witness." *El Cojo* had been seen in Miami a few days before Galíndez' disappearance and he was talking freely. To a young Cuban salesman named Orestes Portales y Carrasco, he confided that he was in the United States on a mission from the Benefactor himself. He revealed the nature of the assignment—the job was to hire someone willing to do away with a couple of Trujillo's enemies in New York. One happened to be a teacher named Jesús de Galíndez.

Portales saw a lot of *El Cojo;* every time the man would bring up in conversation the nature of his mission. One day he appeared at the hangout where Cuban and other Latin exiles met and told Portales that the FBI was after him.

According to Portales, the Spaniard made a hurried phone call to the Dominican Consulate. Then he showed a telegram he had received that same day (Portales recalls it was March 1) from Ciudad Trujillo which read: "Leave mission in abeyance. Return immediately."

The last time Portales saw *El Cojo* was when he flung himself into the back seat of a green sedan that had pulled up at the curb in front of the café where they were. It appears that *El Cojo* left Miami the same day, by way of New Orleans and with the help of the Dominican consulates in both places, for the Dominican Republic—and has never been heard of or seen since.

During his last visit to the United States *El Cojo* was seen escorting a petite redhead, whom he introduced as his wife. The girl was not his wife but his mistress, Ana Gloria Viera. No one knows how Miss Viera (who many people say was Puerto Rican and therefore an American citizen) went back to the Dominican Republic. One day, however, in August, 1956, the body of Ana Gloria was found mangled in a wrecked automobile. Since she was alone in the car the presumption is that she was driving when the "accident" occurred. The only trouble, wrote Herbert Matthews in the *New York Times,* was that people who knew her said she had never learned to drive a car.

The conviction grew that *El Cojo's* presence in Miami and all his talk about hiring killers served one purpose—*El Cojo* was a "finger man" all right but this time he had been sent as a decoy. He had been purposely sent south to seek out a "trigger man," while the real master minds of the kidnapping were doing the actual work up north. With his talk and his suspicious movements he would contribute to making a false trail. And so the pieces of the puzzle multiplied, and the file on the paradoxes called the Galíndez case lengthened.

The case provoked so much interest and concern that the subject was brought up at two of President Eisenhower's press conferences. After saying the first time that he knew nothing about the matter, the President on May 9, 1956, replied: "The Attorney General went after the case as quickly as it arose, went into New York City. The F.B.I. is standing by on the first intimation that it has a right to step in. The city police of New York have it in hand. As far as the case stands now, it is a pure case of disappearance and not a case where the F.B.I. has any right to step in."

The Galíndez affair touched off a feud between groups of anti-Trujillo Dominicans in New York and the colony of Dominicans who, through love or fear, remain loyal to the Trujillo regime. Picket lines were set up by the exile groups in front of the Dominican consulate in New York. On the other hand, *trujillistas* threw eggs at the exile demonstrators, picketed newspapers, magazines and even Columbia University, and printed leaflets and pamphlets vilifying de Galíndez and his defenders.

On June 5, 1956, Dr. Jesús de Galíndez received a degree of Doctor of Philosophy in absentia at Columbia. The degree was awarded for work in political science that included writing his *The Era of Trujillo* thesis. Dean Jacques Barzun of the Graduate Faculties cited "the name of our colleague, Jesús de Galíndez, whose unexplained absence for three months we all lament." A spokesman for the university stated that this unprecedented procedure was designed as an "expression of interest and concern."

It was clear that the police authorities were trying to do their best, but hemispheric public opinion was disturbed. Much of the criticism was directed at the State Department, which, many thought, was over friendly with the dictator.

Marquis Childs in a column in the *New York Post* on June 6, 1956, asserted that "in the nearly three months that have elapsed since Dr. Galíndez' disappearance not a single government agency in Washington, whether in the executive or Congressional branch, has made any move to try to discover whether he has, in fact, been the victim of the espionage system of a foreign power operating with complete disregard for American law and the tradition of American haven for refugees from oppression."

On September 12, 1956, Norman Thomas accused the Federal Government of adopting a hands-off policy because "any thorough investigation might distress Generalissimo Rafael L. Trujillo of the Dominican Republic and have repercussions in the United Nations."

Governor Luis Muñoz Marin, of Puerto Rico, also had strong words to say. "Suspicion is very strong and widespread in Latin America that a certain dictatorial government has in fact exercised the right of extra-territorial execution of its opponents within the United States—and with apparent immunity."

Only the Dominican Republic seemed unaffected. Aside from a few newspaper articles charging de Galíndez with all the crimes on the statute books, the case did not seem to exist for the Dominican people. "The great paradox about the Galíndez case in this dictatorial republic is that 'everybody' knows about it and nobody talks about it," wrote Milton Bracker in the *New York Times*.

By the end of the year speculation about the Galíndez affair had faded. So entangled were the threads of conspiracy that they might never have been disengaged except for another disappearance—this time in Ciudad Trujillo. On December 3, 1956, a co-pilot of the Trujillo-owned *Compañía Dominicana de Aviación,* Gerald Lester ("Gerry") Murphy, 23, of Eugene, Oregon, was done to death in the Dominican capital.

This time to the normal political outcry were added some strong voices. Murphy's parents, a determined couple who would not be blackmailed or frightened by Trujillo, and two of the more courageous liberal legislators now in the American Congress—Senator Wayne Morse and Representative Charlos O. Porter, both from Murphy's home state of Oregon. At last the United States State Department joined the chorus to press Dominican authorities for an explanation.

At the beginning no one thought there was any direct link between the disappearance of the young American flyer in the Dominican Republic and the kidnapping of Dr. de Galíndez in the city of New York. Not long afterwards the relation was established by Dominican exiles. In a letter addressed to both Senator Morse and Congressman Porter, *Vanguardia Revolucionaria Dominicana,* whose main listening post is in San Juan, Puerto Rico, called their attention to the fact that Dominicans believed that Murphy was murdered because he knew too much about the disappearance of de Galíndez.

The Dominican authorities promptly produced an explanation of the Murphy disappearance. The explanation, according to *Life,* was "shocking and ingenious but unconvincing."

As in the Barnes case, the Benefactor quickly looked around for a scapegoat willing to assume the blame for the murder of a foreign citizen. For a time he thought he had his man in Octavio Antonio de la Maza, a CDA pilot himself. Had de la Maza gone along with the Generalissimo's scheme, all would have come out dandy. Brought to trial before a not too prying *trujillista* judge, de la Maza would plead guilty to the murder of Murphy and explain that death happened quite accidentally and in self-defense during a drunken cliffside brawl. In his own defense de la Maza would plead he was repelling the homosexual advances of the young flyer.

However, Trujillo made a slight miscalculation. De la Maza, an adventurous, hot-headed man of personal courage, refused to play ball to the extent of incriminating himself with the murder of an American citizen. This was totally unforeseen, since de la Maza had always been a faithful soldier who had done "special services" (which sometimes include murder) for the regime and who, more important, owed a debt of gratitude to the Benefactor for setting him free after the alleged self-defense killing of another man, the notorious Luis Bernardino (Felix's brother), during a drunken fracas in London, where both men were attached to the Dominican embassy as part of its diplomatic personnel.

Confronted with the refusal of de la Maza, Trujillo found himself in need of an alternate story. De la Maza had already been arrested as the author of Murphy's murder, so it was too late to look for another scapegoat. A new story had to be made up hurriedly and sure enough he came out with one good enough to kill, as we shall see, two birds with one stone. The Benefactor, through his aides, announced that Murphy had died in shark-infested waters after a quarrel with de la Maza. The latter after his arrest was so filled with remorse he hanged himself from a shower pipe in his cell, leaving a note addressed to his wife in which he admitted guilt for killing Murphy. De la Maza reportedly used his mosquito netting for the macabre task.

The Generalissimo had the hope that this version would satisfy the never-too-curious American Department of State, which several times before had been placated with formal excuses. He did not count, however, on a few factors beyond his control. For instance, the fact that Murphy had a courageous American fiancée with whom he had talked at great length. This, coupled with the circumstance that the state of Oregon had two representatives who would take no nonsense from a small-time Caribbean dictator, proved to be the unexpected break the police investigators always pray for.

As *Life* put it, "Murphy, just before he disappeared, had done a lot of talking, and some writing, about a curious assignment he had once undertaken. Now, as a result of what he said, it was possible to piece together a theory connecting Galíndez' case, Murphy's disappearance and De la Maza's death. Galíndez had apparently been kidnapped and drugged in a New York subway and hauled in an ambulance to an airport near the city. Hired by the Dominicans, Murphy had been waiting with a plane. Galíndez was placed aboard and Murphy flew him to Montecristi in the Dominican Republic."

U.S. officials were by now suspicious that both de Galíndez and Murphy had been done away with by Trujillo's thugs. The Department of State demanded an explanation.

As a result of a combination of the State Department's published notes to the Dominican Government, the trial of a Trujillo informer and the extraordinary achievements of American journalistic ingenuity, it is now possible to put together, in bits and pieces, the inside story of what happened to de Galíndez and Murphy.

Born in Minot, North Dakota, in July 1933 and brought up in Oregon, Gerry Murphy was a clean-cut American boy with a good record. His parents considered him a sober, honest, conscientious, dutiful son. His former employers had only words of praise. In his childhood days he filled his room with airplane books and models and spent every spare moment studying the art of flying. He soloed at 16, and at 23 had earned a commercial license with instrument, instructor and mechanic ratings. He worked as a flight instructor and aeronautical draftsman.

Trujillo is a master corrupter and he and his hoods know that every man has a price or a weakness or both. Murphy had a great weakness. One thing had been denied him—good eyesight. Because of poor eyesight he had been turned down by the armed services and by the airlines. And the thing he wanted most in life was to fly.

Prompted by his passion for flying, Murphy moved to Florida sometime in 1955. He took a job as draftsman and rented a room on SW 9th Street. What he was making as a draftsman wasn't much and he tried to get a pilot's job with Riddle Airlines. He did not make the grade with Riddle but began flying occasional charter jobs for Tom Guthrie's air taxi service.

About that time Murphy made a couple of new friends. Murphy met the American-educated, aristocratic Colonel Salvador Cobian Parra, then chief of the extremely efficient Dominican security service. It is common knowledge now that Cobian had been sent to Miami by the Benefactor himself to scout for a specific kind of talent. They were, at the time, very much in need of a capable airman willing to do a job for pay. The man had to be either a seasoned operator who would not ask many questions or a naive soul ready to fall for the tempting offers of wealth and welfare in the bountiful realm of "the Chief." Apparently they settled for the latter alternative. Either by design or by accident Gerry Murphy turned out to be their man.

After a few preliminary meetings, Colonel Cobian introduced Murphy to a tall, slender, cold-eyed, feline, amusingly cynical chap who gave his name as Arthur. As Murphy later learned, he had met West Point graduate (class 1943) brigadier general Arturo R. Espaillat, better known to his fellow officers as "the Yellow Cat." As Under Secretary of the Armed Forces, Espaillat was Cobian's boss. It is probable that Murphy met other Dominicans as well as another "fine young man" and former FBI and CIA agent, Washington attorney John Joseph Frank, then employed as a sort of errand boy, bodyguard, security adviser and legal counselor for the Benefactor.

It is almost impossible to ascertain how many times Murphy met with his new, fun-loving, night clubbing, Dominican friends. At this writing Espaillat is the only man still alive who might tell, but it is very doubtful that he will come to the U. S. to talk truthfully.

After meeting Cobian and Espaillat, Murphy made several trips to the Dominican Republic, where the red carpet was rolled out. From the expensive hotel Jaragua, Gerry sent home a post-card: "Not a bad place to stay when the local government is paying the bill."

Sometime during one of these trips Murphy was told about the reasons for the sudden *trujillista* love of him. Was he told the truth and nothing but the truth, or was he given a sugar-coated pill with double-talk? Murphy knew that the mysterious operation he was about to perform involved something beyond simple transportation back to his home-land of a "wealthy invalid." Perhaps he did not know the identity of his "patient" or if he knew it, it did not mean anything to him at the outset. As Andrew St. George put it, "There is the damning evidence of Gerry's behavior in preparing for the fatal flight of March 12: he lied and falsified entries about it not once but a dozen times."

In early March, 1956, Murphy told friends in Miami he had a good charter proposition and was going to take it. He then reached a close friend, Air Force Sergeant Harold L. French, an airplane mechanic, then on 30-day leave. He asked his friend to wait for him in Washington since he would need his help for a job.

On March 4, Gerry picked up French at the Washington National Airport. The next day they went by train to Elizabeth, N. J., and took a cab to Linden, where they registered at the Rahway Tourist Motel, remaining until March 11.

Shortly after noon on March 6, French and Murphy went to the Linden airport, where Murphy introduced French to a man named Kane. (At the subsequent trial of John J. Frank, French identified the defendant as the man introduced to him as "Kane".) He also met two unidentified Dominican citizens, whose names he later forgot. However, at the Frank trial in which he was a witness for the prosecution French did identify the other two men by pictures introduced in evidence by Justice Department Attorney William C. Hundley. (Earlier in the trial the men in the pictures had been identified by the author of this book as Maj. Gen. Arturo R. Espaillat and Felix W. Bernardino, both former Dominican consul generals in New York City.) Apparently Espaillat and Bernardino were there to oversee the operation.

"We made arrangements to lease an aircraft, which we subsequently did," French said. "It was a surplus model military plane, a twin-engine Beech aircraft." After giving the plane's number as N68100, French identified a photo of it.

They rented the plane from an aircraft sales and rental company called Trade-Ayer, owned by Anthony J. Ming. When closing the operation Murphy said he wanted the plane to take some businessmen on air junkets. Later one of the officers of the charter company recalled that pilot Murphy paid $800 cash. When he got his receipt, Murphy requested it be made to the man who had supplied the money—a man named John Kane.

After renting the plane French helped Murphy to add extra fuel tanks in the forward end of the passenger cabin to increase the range from 800-900 miles to 1,400 miles. Murphy asked Sergeant French to be his co-pilot, but the latter refused.

Two days later, on March 8, French and Murphy met "Kane" in the lobby of Pennsylvania Station in Manhattan. Murphy sent French away while he had a private conversation with Frank. They were also in constant telephonic communication. At the Frank trial the prosecution produced toll slips for March 4, 6, 7 to prove Frank had conversed with Murphy.

On March 9 Gerry made a test flight and took off for Newark the following day, landing at 5:50 P.M. From there Murphy hopped over to Staten Island in the late afternoon of March 10. While there, the extra tanks were installed in the cabin. An airport worker who asked where the plane was going received a flat reply: "Azores."

On March 12 at 9:44 A.M. Murphy took off from Newark Airport, after listing his destination as Miami. Instead of flying south, he detoured and flew east, bringing his plane down at Zahn's Airport at Amityville, L. I., at exactly 10:30 A.M. He announced his departure time as a half hour later but did not leave. French saw Murphy there again shortly after noon. He helped Gerry to load the plane with blankets, a pistol, "sundry small hand tools" and "survival equipment."

There Murphy waited all day and far into the night until an ambulance arrived. (That night de Galíndez disappeared.) A stretcher case was transferred from the ambulance to Murphy's waiting plane. There were only two witnesses to the arrival of the ambulance: Murphy and the night watchman, Anthony Frevele. After the "patient" was put on board a heavy-shouldered, felt-hatted figure climbed into the plane after Murphy. At least one other person boarded the plane, perhaps two. One of them is known to have been Murphy's co-pilot Octavio Antonio de la Maza. The night watchman told his relief watchman and later his daughter that he had seen an ambulance come up and a man who "could not move a muscle" put into a wheel chair and carried into the plane. The airport manager, Edwin Lyons, also vouched for the fact that the watchman told that story.[1]

The next episode is a hitherto unexplained mystery. Murphy and N68100 were next seen early on the morning of March 13 at Miami's Tamiami Airport. Murphy landed there ostensibly to refuel. Airport attendants told him that it was too early—the gas pumps were not open. So he took off for Lantana Airport near West Palm Beach. The oddity of the maneuver lay in the fact, according to reporter Fred J. Cook, that it wasn't necessary. "Arrangements had been made days in advance, by a mysterious telephone call from New York, for Murphy to refuel at Lantana early on the morning of March 13."

In Lantana Murphy's plane was refueled by a mechanic named Donald Jackson, who a few months later told his story anonymously in a C.B.S. broadcast. He also talked with the authorities. "The important thing was," wrote Herbert Matthews in the *New York Times,* "that in order to fill the additional gas tanks which had been installed inside the passenger's part of the plane he had to take his hose into the Beechcraft. He said he saw an unconscious or lifeless body on a stretcher in the plane and noted a 'peculiar stench' which he thought was indicative of a drug."

When the case of John J. Frank was ready to be brought to trial the Government subpoenaed Jackson to appear in court and take the stand on November 12, 1957, the day the trial was to begin. "However," writes

[1] Frevele's testimony would have been of the greatest importance for a definite clarification of the case. Unfortunately he died of a coronary thrombosis in September, 1956, although, according to Rep. Porter, he was "57 years old and had a history of good health." Since what they may say is considered hearsay, and therefore inadmissible as court room evidence, neither the other watchman nor Frevele's daughter could testify at a trial. Moreover, Frevele's daughter has already changed her original testimony. In an affidavit for the group of Trujillo-paid investigators headed by the noted attorney Morris Ernst she now asserts that the "stretcher case" incident did not occur until long after March 12, 1956.

Matthews, "it had to be postponed until Nov. 18 and he was so notified. On Nov. 12, Jackson left in a private plane with his father for a two-day trip to Texas. The plane crashed and they were both killed. There were no witnesses. Could there have been any foul play? The F.B.I. has no jurisdiction to investigate such cases which are the concern of the states." [2]

At Lantana Murphy paid cash for $95 worth of gas (thus avoiding signing the gas slip) and gave a $15 tip. Then with his strange cargo on board he took off, destination unknown.

After its investigation, *Life* asserted that Gerry took off for Montecristi airport on the Dominican northwestern coast. Representative Charles O. Porter has repeatedly stated the same belief.

On the other hand, Dominican government sources assert that "it would be very hard to prove" that the plane went to their country. From General Espaillat himself came a seemingly convincing denial of this angle of the story. In a letter to *Life,* Espaillat, who had already assumed office as Dominican Consul General in New York [3] stated that "we checked to see if a plane had filed its flight plan at any airfield from which it could take off from the United States for the Dominican Republic. No such flight plan was filed."

Espaillat also pointed out that "since the U.S. is protected by an airtight radar screen and also an alert fighter-plane command, it would be impossible for an unidentified plane to have spirited Galíndez from an American airport." *Life* did some checking of its own. It found out that "private planes flying from Florida do not have to file. The U.S. checks very few outbound aircraft from Florida."

At the Frank trial something resembling concrete evidence came up. While Sergeant French was at Linden with Murphy, the latter made a map in the sergeant's presence drawing a line on it from New York to Miami to end of the journey—the Dominican Republic.

It is almost impossible to give any account of what occurred upon arrival of Murphy's plane in Trujillo-dominated territory.

Frances R. Grant, Secretary General of the Inter-American Association for Democracy and Freedom, in a press conference held in September 1957 said she had received new details on the case from exile sources. Miss Grant reported that her information was that Dr. de Galíndez had been "lured

---

[2] It has been established that the Jacksons were accompanied by a friend on the fateful plane trip. The man also died in the crash.

[3] The appointment of Espaillat to fulfill a diplomatic assignment in the United States right in the wake of the Galíndez disappearance is considered one of the most daring maneuvers of the Trujillo regime. It was apparently thought that the presence of the General right at the center of the storm would either sidetrack the police investigation or would erase any suspicions that might have fallen on the new Consul. It also served a practical purpose: Espaillat could keep a watchful eye on those parties involved in the kidnapping who had stayed out of Dominican jurisdiction.

from his home, drugged and taken by automobile to an airport" where Gerald L. Murphy was waiting.

Upon arrival at Montecristi, said Miss Grant, Dr. de Galíndez was transferred to another plane piloted by de la Maza. From another source I have learned that the transfer was thought necessary in order not to take the Beechcraft to Ciudad Trujillo airport where its presence might be noted by too many people, including members of the American embassy.

Miss Grant asserted that de Galíndez was later taken to the *Hacienda Fundación,* Trujillo's ranch in San Cristobal. There, so the story goes, Trujillo himself is said to have struck the first blow in Dr. Galíndez' face and then to have turned the Basque over to military men who finished the job. There is no direct evidence to support this version, but every time an account of what occurred to de Galíndez is smuggled out, it coincides with it.

The trip down to the Dominican Republic was the end of a phase of young Murphy's life and the beginning of another. Two weeks later he returned the plane. At Guthrie's he told a number of stories. He said he had flown a "wealthy invalid" from New York to Tampa. He recounted how he had had extra tanks installed for the flight. And, still more significant, he was suddenly affluent. "He was so broke when he went to work for me," said Guthrie to *Life,* "that he had sold his car for money to eat." Now he bought and paid cash for a 1956 Dodge convertible, explaining that his father had sold property which he had not.

The next month Murphy told Guthrie that one of his charter plane acquaintances had fixed him up with a job as a pilot for the *Compañía Dominicana de Aviación,* in Ciudad Trujillo. "When Gerry reported to CDA, in Ciudad Trujillo," reported *Life,* "George Burrie, then general manager, refused him a captaincy because he was short on experience. His status was settled by Dictator Trujillo, who ordered that Gerry be hired as co-pilot." After that Murphy bragged to friends that he could have "anything I want down there." As a co-pilot for the Dominican airline his salary was $350 a month, but to friends he confided he was making $800 a month plus "overtime." In addition to his Dodge, which he kept in Miami, Gerry bought a British Ford car in Ciudad Trujillo. He kept apartments in both Miami and the Dominican capital.

Shortly afterwards he met pretty, petite brunette Celia (Sally) Caire, of Wichita, Kans., a Pan American World Airways stewardess. In September they were engaged and made plans to be married January 10, 1957. To Celia, Gerry made a number of interesting confidences. Once she queried him about his heavy spending in Miami night spots just after they became engaged. "He told me he was working part-time for Trujillo and got extra pay for that. He did little favors for them when they needed him."

Miss Caire said later that Murphy told her of a few of these "little favors." In one case, she asserted, her fiancé had flown $30,000 to Havana to "finance a revolution." He told her he received $1,000. She said also that Murphy had flown to Havana a few weeks later in November, 1956, aboard the plane she was serving as a stewardess. His purpose, according to her, was to photograph an airfield to be used in the future for landing a C-46. On still another mission for the Trujillo forces, Murphy had told her of going to Mexico City and locating a man. "He told me he knew the seriousness of what he was doing," she said. "I warned him he could lose his citizenship if they found out what he was doing, but he assured me he wouldn't have anything to do with homicide."

Andrew St. George rooted out a number of interesting facts. In an article in the October 1957 issue of *Real,* St. George wrote: "Gerry traveled to Havana, Cuba, with a suitcase containing $30,000, a few charges of a secret plastic explosive called hexite (kneaded inside some large hard rolls), and a set of glass time fuses resembling oven thermometers. He delivered these goodies to a fellow pilot, trusted Trujillo contact and underground revolutionary leader: 31-year old Calixto Sánchez White, secretary general of the Air Worker's Union in Cuba."

Some ten days later, Colonel Antonio Blanco Rico, chief of the SIM, the Cuban military intelligence, was murdered. One of the people pinpointed by the Cuban police as having made arrangements for the killing was Murphy's contact Calixto Sánchez.

There was also a plot to bomb the Cuban Presidential Palace in order to kill General Fulgencio Batista, with whom Trujillo had a running feud at the time. Murphy balked. It seems his refusal to carry through the assignment had something to do with his eventual death. Later Trujillo himself changed his mind about Batista and formed an alliance with the Cuban strong man; by then Murphy was dead. Calixto Sánchez lived to see the peace treaty but a few months later was killed supposedly leading a revolutionary attempt against Batista.

It seems that after Miss Caire learned the true nature of Murphy's employment she kept a steady pressure upon him, begging him to get out of the Dominican Republic and look for work in the United States. It might be that the sudden death of his first Dominican friend, Colonel Cobian, brought him to his senses. Upon hearing the news, Murphy said: "My God! They've killed my protector." In November he notified Sally he was resigning his CDA's job. On November 17 he wrote home that his stay on the island had "served its purpose" and he was coming back to the United States.

Murphy, according to his fiancee, returned to the Dominican Republic on December 2, despite her protests. He went back to sell his possessions and speak to Trujillo about a business venture. He was trying to sell the Benefactor a plan for using laminated identification cards to be carried by all Dominican citizens. He hoped to sell them to Trujillo for 40 cents and "the Chief" would resell them to the Government for $1.

On December 3, he placed an ad in *El Caribe* offering his car and furniture for sale. That afternoon he saw Miss Caire at the airport, during the stop-over of her flight at Ciudad Trujillo, and told her he had a 5 P.M. date at the dictator's palace. She begged him to get out but he wouldn't listen. Miss Caire was afraid because she knew Murphy had blabbed about his participation in the de Galíndez affair to several friends. According to her, Murphy had been restricted twice to Ciudad Trujillo because American authorities were investigating the disappearance.

Next morning, Dec. 4, the Dominican police found Gerry's Ford abandoned on a cliff near the city's slaughterhouse. The Dominican police reportedly searched the city and dragged the bay but found no trace of Murphy. "Since slaughterhouse offal is dumped in the bay, the water swarms with sharks," commented *Life*.

Murphy was an American citizen and U.S. Ambassador William T. Pheiffer could not close his eyes at his disappearance. The American Embassy, however, waited until the 6th and then requested the Dominican police to make a search for Murphy. The Embassy informed the Department of State by telegram of Murphy's disappearance, and this information was transmitted, Dec. 7, to his parents at Eugene, Oregon.

The same day the Embassy also sent to the Department of State information concerning Murphy's activities in the Dominican Republic. Upon the basis of this information, the Office of Security of the department entered the case and communicated the information to the Department of Justice and other United States investigative agencies.

On December 10 Dominican police gave the Embassy a first report dated two days before. It stated that Murphy's car had been found early on December 4, abandoned off the highway near the sea. Presuming it to have been stolen, the police had sent a notice to Murphy's address requesting that the car be picked up. When it was established that Murphy had not returned home by Dec. 6, the car was towed to police headquarters and an intensive search began, the police report stated.

On Dec. 11, according to the State Department, based on information received from the U.S. Embassy in Ciudad Trujillo, security officers of the department interviewed Murphy's fiancee, Sally Caire, in Miami. On Dec. 15 American Ambassador William T. Pheiffer told Secretary of State Without Portfolio Manuel de Moya, Attorney General Francisco Elpidio Beras and Chief of Police Col. Antonio Hart Dottin that the United States took a "very serious view" of the case. He was assured that "the most detailed investigation possible" would be carried out by Dominican authorities.

On the afternoon of December 17, U.S. Consul Harry Lofton notified Attorney General Beras that, under instructions from Ambassador William T. Pheiffer, he was passing on "the information that bad blood existed between Murphy and Octavio de la Maza of CDA, and de la Maza should be investigated."

De la Maza was arrested, interrogated and according to a *trujillista* mouthpiece "detained when he was totally unable to account for his movements during the evening of Murphy's disappearance." Where and how Ambassador Pheiffer obtained this piece of information has never been revealed.

Ever since the fact that de la Maza's arrest was prompted by information supplied by the American embassy has been adroitly used by the *trujillista* propaganda. The Generalissimo told an American correspondent he did not understand all the fuss over de la Maza's being framed, since the pilot had been arrested "at the request of the American embassy."

Now, after the American diplomatic representative, unwittingly, had served so well their purposes, the Dominican police "confirmed," with the help of the chief pilot of CDA, Ernest Charles Haeger, as well as de la Maza's relatives, that the two fliers were bitter enemies. Furthermore, as the Attorney General put it in a press statement for foreign consumption exclusively, the U.S. Chargé d'Affaires in Ciudad Trujillo "was present when these persons were interrogated and (when they) reiterated bad blood existed between Murphy and de la Maza."

Prior to his detention de la Maza appeared to have had an inkling of things to come. Either he had been already approached with a proposal to play the part of scapegoat Trujillo had assigned him, or his participation in the de Galíndez kidnapping made him uncomfortable now that his partners in crime were being killed or had been warned by a friend. He seemingly knew he was slated to play a role for which he did not want to be cast. People who saw him in those days say he was restless and looked worried. He was well aware that it was impossible for him to escape Trujillo and, therefore, there was nothing much he could do. The flyer sought at least to place his aging father outside the reach of the Benefactor's strong arm. On December 6 he showed up at the American embassy and applied for U.S. visas for both his father and sister, giving as a reason his father needed medical treatment. The visas were granted and his relatives made the trip but later returned to the Dominican Republic.

In a statement to the *New York Times,* Miss Frances R. Grant said that on the occasion of his visit to the embassy de la Maza had furnished information to American diplomatic officers concerning the Galíndez-Murphy case. The State Department, however, denied this. It reported that de la Maza did not supply information on de Galíndez or Murphy's disappearances.

On December 17 Attorney General Beras was at the American embassy discussing the case, when Murphy's father and Miss Caire called at the Ambassador's office. They had come to Ciudad Trujillo, they said, to find out whatever they could. There they talked to the Attorney General and later were informed of all developments in the case to date by Embassy officers. They also saw several Dominican high officials, who told them nothing. Instead they were interrogated persistently about what Gerry might have told them of his activities.

A war of nerves was launched the moment the couple set foot on Dominican soil, which was to be continued throughout their stay. They found themselves shadowed by plain clothesmen. While they packed Gerry's belongings they were interrupted by mysterious callers who would say nothing. Nevertheless they managed to keep their minds open. One thing they noticed was that Murphy's briefcase was missing. It had contained, as Miss Caire knew, his insurance policy, bank stubs and statements and other personal records. Prior to their arrival police had barred all access to the apartment. A report of the police search and sealing of Murphy's apartment was later provided by Dominican authorities to the American embassy.

After four days the American embassy advised Mr. Murphy and Miss Caire to leave the country for their safety's sake. When she spoke on the CBS radio program about the case, Miss Caire said that American Ambassador Pheiffer gave them a Marine guard and told them to get out fast because "this man," meaning Trujillo, "is capable of anything." Following the CBS broadcast Pheiffer, no longer ambassador, denied saying this.

Even after they got back to Miami, U.S. officials warned Sally not to stay there because the town was "full of Dominicans." Rep. Porter later cited Miss Caire as saying that she had been forced to quit her stewardess job because PAA officials said it would be too dangerous for her to continue because of possible repercussions of the case. She told Edward R. Murrow, over the CBS network, how she always looked in all directions before crossing any of her home town streets in the state of Kansas.

On December 20 the American Embassy sent a note to the Dominican Ministry of Foreign Affairs expressing its concern over the still-unresolved disappearance of Murphy. On December 31 the Embassy was told that inquiries "are taking place with the rapidity and zeal required" and that, when complete, a copy of the police report would be furnished.

It was up to the Dominicans to produce a solution. Apparently all the delay had been occasioned because the police had not lost all hopes of convincing de la Maza he should cooperate by taking publicly the blame for the crime when brought to trial. De la Maza remained adamant in his refusal. Finally they despaired of obtaining de la Maza's cooperation and took the only road open to them under the circumstances.

At noon on January 7, 1957, the American Chargé d'Affaires, Richard Stephens, was informed by the Dominican Attorney General that de la Maza had hanged himself with a piece of mosquito netting tied around a shower pipe in his jail cell, at around 4 o'clock that morning. The Chargé was shown what the Dominican authorities claimed was de la Maza's suicide note and given a typewritten copy.

Addressed to de la Maza's wife, the note claimed the Dominican pilot had made no confession of any kind to the Dominican police and that he was taking "this fatal decision because something very grave happened which only you should know."

The note said that a few nights before "an old companion of mine from the company," Murphy, had invited him to have some drinks in a place beside the sea. While there, Murphy had made homosexual advances to de la Maza. The Dominican flyer rejected Murphy's advances and during the ensuing struggle Murphy fell into the sea and could not be saved. "For this reason remorse is killing me and that is why I am putting an end to my life."

In addition to the inevitable charge of homosexuality, the note contained other instances of the Benefactor's personal style of vilification of fallen adversaries. It said that "he (Murphy) began to reproach me and insult me telling me that we Dominicans were uneducated brutes and that the personnel of the Dominican airlines were no good. You know that this American left there because he was a rumor monger and a traitor . . ."

De la Maza's body was transported for burial to his home town of Moca, more than one hundred miles north of Ciudad Trujillo. There went two members of the personnel of the American Embassy who, probably without the knowledge of the police, were allowed to look at the flyer's body. A few months later a U.S. Senate Foreign Relations Committee Report cited the two officers as having seen what "looked like a wound" on de la Maza's left side, a little above the hip.

This fact, coupled with a number of absurdities in the note, deepened the suspicions of the Embassy officers. A few questions needed clarification. For instance, nothing in Murphy's record was found to substantiate de la Maza's charges of homosexuality. Moreover, it seemed absurd for de la Maza, after denying everything to the police, to commit suicide and leave the confession of something he considered so grave that only his wife should know in a place where he knew Dominican authorities would be the first to find it.

Openly skeptical, Stephens visited, on January 8, the cell where de la Maza allegedly had hanged himself. What happened there outraged the local authorities to such an extent that the Attorney General filed a formal complaint that was channeled to the American State Department. Reported Beras: "He (Mr. Stephens) assumed an offensive attitude that could not but hurt my sensitivity. I did not then protest, in order to avoid being blamed for breaking the cooperation—extreme cooperation—in which we have conducted the investigations . . . Several times the chargé d'affaires with his own hands exerted pressure on the arm of the shower in which the body of de la Maza was found . . . presumably to prove the resistance to the weight of a normal man. This was not all. Mr. Stephens took the noose of cloth with which de la Maza had hanged himself and after pulling strongly on it

. . . he put it round his neck. All of which no doubt implied a suspicion of the veracity and seriousness of the Dominican authorities."

On that same day the Dominican people were fed the first of the only two stories ever printed by the local press on the Murphy case. It was a terse Attorney General's communiqué giving an account of de la Maza's suicide and repeating all that had been told privately to the American embassy.

On January 16 a serious development took effect. Stephens called on the Minister of Foreign Affairs to deliver a note recalling the Dominican note of December 31 which promised a copy of the Dominican police report then under preparation. He also asked for the "fullest possible" report from the Dominican authorities on Murphy's activities in the Dominican Republic which might shed light on a motive for his disappearance.

Still more important, the note stated that the United States Government could not, on the basis of information available, accept the Dominican Government's position that Murphy's disappearance was solved by de la Maza's confession.

Repercussions were being heard for the first time in Congress, where Trujillo had always been careful to cultivate friends. In cooperation with Senator Morse, Representative Porter started an investigation of his own.

After reading the Dominican explanation of Murphy's death Porter had become convinced that it was "intentionally false" and that the Dominican Government "was responsible for Gerry's disappearance." To express these opinions, he chose the occasion of his maiden speech on the floor of the House of Representatives on February 28.

Porter put a few blunt questions of his own. "I have seen a photostat of the note," he said. "It is patently absurd. . . . In order to hang himself from the shower fixture, de la Maza had to keep his knees flexed to keep his feet from touching the floor . . . I believe that the State Department and the FBI are no more convinced than I am of the veracity of the Dominican tale."

Porter analyzed what he called the "stark contradictions" that leap out from de la Maza's alleged suicide note. Noting that de la Maza wrote that he had accepted an invitation to have some drinks with Murphy by the seaside and confronting this supposed admission of friendship (people who hate each other do not get drunk together) with the earlier statement about the existence of a bitter enmity between the two flyers, Porter asked: "If there had been bad blood between de la Maza and Murphy, would the two have gone off on a joyride on Murphy's last day on the island?"

Porter then pointed out that "it seems absurd for de la Maza, after denying everything to the police, to commit suicide and leave for his wife alone a confession which the police would necessarily be the first to find."

As to remorse as a motive for suicide, Porter asserted that "is nothing short of ridiculous." He then recalled that several years before, while military attaché in London, de la Maza shot to death a fellow Dominican, the *trujillista* stooge Luis Bernardino. "Saved from British justice by diplomatic immunity, he escaped punishment at home on the grounds of self-defense. It was never noted that he was remorseful over the murder."

Then Porter who had talked with the author of this book a few days earlier went on to quote me as telling him that "suicide for remorse" is one of the favorite methods employed by Dominican police for eliminating prisoners. He stated that "from what I have been able to learn of Dominican jails, prisoners on admission are stripped of all their possessions. Where would de la Maza have gotten hold of pencil and paper? Witnesses who have been inside of Dominican prisons also ridicule the idea of mosquito netting in Dominican prison cells."

Porter revealed that he had received evidence that the Dominican regime employs an expert state forger, one Alonso Alonso. "His value to Trujillo is clearly shown by his effrontery," wrote Porter on another occasion. "He (Alonso) once had the colossal nerve to forge the signature of Trujillo's wife on a bank check, and the only punishment he received was a slight reprimand!"

Porter's speech got more criticism than praise on the House floor.

Only a single Representative, Edward A. Garmatz (D., Md.), echoed the call for Congressional action to insure an investigation. Mr. Garmatz inferred that establishment of the facts would serve "to put asleep the seemingly fantastic stories which of late have been abroad."

At one point Porter was chided by Representative James G. Fulton (R., Pa.), for having criticized "so many people" without first giving each "the courtesy of an advance notice." Then he attacked the freshman from Oregon for criticizing a "friendly" neighbor.

Fulton's statement prompted an angry comment by the usually restrained *New York Times:* "Just because one of the worst dictatorships in Latin America is pro-United States does not make it any the less of a tyranny. It should not be the part of the State Department or of Congressmen to curry favor with dictators just because they are 'friendly'."

From all quarters doubt was being expressed about Trujillo's version of the murder of Murphy. *Life* with its circulation of nearly six million had contributed a great deal to awaken public interest.

The State Department was moving faster now. On Feb. 21 the Dominican Ambassador to Washington was informed that the Department did not consider the Murphy case closed. The Department's position was then set forth in a note delivered in Ciudad Trujillo to the Dominican Government on March 16.

The chilly note from the State Department "urgently" asked the Dominican Government to reopen the case of Gerald Murphy.

Among other things the note stated that de la Maza's "suicide note" was, according to the State Department's own handwriting analysis, a forgery.

(The Dominican Government had already supplied the American authorities an analysis of the note prepared by the Spanish "expert," Manuel Ferrandis Torres, of the University of Madrid, attesting, on the basis of comparison with purported specimens of de la Maza's handwriting, that the suicide note was genuine.)

According to the note, the examination of documents and other evidence revealed "a contradiction between the report of the Dominican Attorney General which states that Murphy's 'political influence' in the Dominican Republic was the 'object of investigation without anything serious being produced to justify it,' and other available information. Our investigations indicated that Murphy was well acquainted with high Dominican officials, among them the late Col. Salvador Cobian and Brig. Gen. Arturo R. Espaillat."

With respect to Murphy's income the note said: "It would also appear that Murphy's income while in the Dominican Republic must not have been limited to the $350 per month salary which the Dominican Attorney General states he earned as a copilot for the Dominican Aviation Co. (CDA). Our investigations have confirmed the statements made by several American CDA pilots to the Dominican authorities that Murphy, in the words of one of them, 'had more money than the rest of us' and that he owned two cars, one in Miami and one in Ciudad Trujillo."

The State Department note was received by the influential *Washington Post* as a "half-step in the right direction by ending its silence on the strange goings-on in the Dominican Republic."

In the meantime the Dominican authorities had been doing some spade work of their own and thrown a great deal more of mud. In the second and last mention of the Murphy murder in the Dominican press, the Attorney General announced officially, through another communiqué, that on February 6 in the city of Moca had been performed the autopsy of de la Maza's body. The necropsy had been performed, said the communiqué printed by *El Caribe* and *La Nación* on February 8, on order of the judicial investigator "with the purpose of finally clarifying the circumstances in which the suicide took place."

The autopsy, stated the Attorney General, had been directed by a Peruvian physician, Dr. J. R. Ravens, a Dominican government employee, in the presence of a large array of witnesses. One of these overseers, according to Beras, was Dr. William A. Morgan, prominent American physician and long-time friend of the Benefactor.

The Attorney General further admitted that it had taken the step to establish whether the speculations on the case in foreign lands as well as in "foreign circles of our own country were well founded." The communiqué promised to make public the result of the autopsy as soon as received by the Attorney General. It was never published.

In February the results of an investigation conducted in the Dominican Republic in behalf of Rep. Porter were made public. The investigator had been Robert D. Abrahams, a lawyer and long-time honorary vice-consul in Philadelphia for the regime of Generalissimo Trujillo.

Abrahams came back from a short trip to the Dominican Republic absolutely convinced Murphy was slain by de la Maza. On receiving Abrahams' findings, however, Porter insisted the former "has no convincing proof that Gerald Murphy is dead or that de la Maza killed him."

In support of his conviction Abrahams cited the evidence of the findings of the Dominican judge who inquired into the Murphy case, plus what he called de la Maza's past record.

Abrahams recalled the slaying of Luis Bernardino and said that in 1953, while de la Maza had been air attaché at the London Embassy, he had battled three policemen who arrested him for drunken driving.

"Everything points to the fact that de la Maza murdered Murphy," Abrahams said. Then he pointed out that the American Embassy itself had said there was bad blood between the two flyers. He said Murphy had refused to fly with de la Maza and had submitted photographs he had taken to show de la Maza "was improperly running his plane." The photo-taking incident has been recounted by Dominican sources in different ways, however. Trujillo's private lawyer, and Dominican Government's Director of Mining, Juan Arce Medina, in an "open letter" to *Life* after rejecting an allegation that Murphy and de la Maza were friends asserted that "CDA executives tried to keep them apart. But on one of their few trips together Murphy photographed nearby mountain peaks and trees to show the low altitude of the aircraft over dangerous terrain. He then turned the pictures over to the operations manager as proof that de la Maza was a reckless, irresponsible pilot."

Arce Medina went on to assert that de la Maza did not kill Bernardino in a "gun battle," as *Life* had reported. "Is that the clearest way you can say de la Maza shot to death a fellow Dominican for the very same type of provocation that Murphy gave him? De la Maza believed that the victim, Bernardino, had informed their superiors of a drunken brawl de la Maza had with the London police. His reaction to Murphy's photo-snapping can be imagined. Unfortunately, Murphy did not stay away from him." A theory that not only destroyed the basis of the alleged self-defense acquittal of de la Maza when brought to trial for Bernardino's killing, but also suggests an element of premeditation which makes de la Maza appear as an unrepentant hardened criminal and runs counter to the earlier versions of the Murphy murder.

Notwithstanding that Porter was not convinced by Abrahams' arguments regarding de la Maza's guilt, the parents of Murphy, upon counsel of the Philadelphia lawyer, acceded to filing a civil law suit in the Dominican courts against the so-called de la Maza estate. First papers were served late in

February. Lawyers for the plaintiffs were Mr. Abrahams himself and a trustworthy high official, Hernán Cruz Ayala, who as president of the Central Electoral Board is the caretaker, every five years, of the unanimous *trujillista* poll returns. Strangely enough, the lawyer who represented the defendants in this suit was the author of the anti-de la Maza "open letter" to *Life,* Mr. Juan Arce Medina.

Civil courts move their dockets exceedingly slow in the Dominican Republic. Yet, in a matter of a month the Murphy family had been awarded a $50,000 indemnity. To dispel any idea that this was part of any cozy arrangement, Abrahams made clear that the money had been paid by Antonio de la Maza, on behalf of his dead brother and the latter's widow, as directed by the court.

When advised of the rapid court decision (in violation of all rules of Dominican civil procedure) the puzzled father of Gerry Murphy said he had authorized the filing of the suit at the suggestion of Mr. Abrahams, but added that he was not sure about accepting the money.

Rep. Charles O. Porter said: "In my opinion, the money paid in settlement of the claim against the de la Maza estate actually came from the Dominican Government."

Murphy and his wife solved their dilemma by acceptance of the check of $35,000 sent to them by Mr. Abrahams (representing the indemnity less lawyer's fees), but for a special use. The money would be put into a trust administered by the Murphys, their pastor, and Representative Porter. It was announced that it was to be used to finance further investigation into the death of Gerry Murphy. The *Washington Post* commented in an editorial entitled "Buying Silence?" that the shabby travesty of justice added "the ugly implication of a bribe to an already unsavory picture." Murphy's parents have never accepted, notwithstanding the law suit against de la Maza's estate, the Dominican Republic's official explanations.

The Dominican Government replied to the United States note of March 16 in three successive notes. March 29 it stated that further investigation had confirmed its previous view that Murphy had no more than "ordinary and casual contact" with Dominican officials.

On April 4 the Dominican Government stated that additional investigations had led its Attorney General to conclude that Murphy did not have large sums of money during his stay in the Dominican Republic nor did his income exceed his salary as a CDA copilot.

On April 13 the Dominican Government asserted that it continued to regard valid the findings of the Spanish handwriting expert that the suicide note attributed to de la Maza was actually written by him. For the Dominican Republic to accept as conclusive in this matter an opinion to the contrary by agencies of a foreign power would be equivalent to abdicating its sovereign rights as a state!

By the Spring of 1957 American investigative agencies had made so much progress that the Justice Department put the whole affair in the hands of a Federal Grand Jury, which since then has been developing material furnished by the FBI, the American Embassy in Ciudad Trujillo and the New York Police. The grand jury is still investigating intermittently and will not be discharged finally until June 1958.

A large array of witnesses have testified in front of this grand jury during the months it has been conducting hearings in Washington. Rep. Charles Porter appeared voluntarily at the request of the U.S. Department of Justice. He suggested to the jury that it draw up an indictment against Generalissimo Trujillo. However, observers presumed that Porter used the proposal for indictment only as a means of bringing his points against the Dominican dictatorship sharply before the jury.

One of the first acts of the Grand Jury was to hand down an indictment charging John J. Frank, alias John Kane, with four violations of the Foreign Agents Registration Act. Two counts charged that Frank had taken payments since May 1954 from the Trujillo regime for collecting information. The other counts charged Frank with spending or paying out money for the Dominican Republic in Washington and New York. Frank was immediately arrested and later released on $10,000 bail.

Things were moving faster now, with the focus of attention shifting from the Justice Department to the State Department. On May 29 the State Department announced that it had sufficient evidence to indicate a link between the disappearance of Dr. Jesús de Galíndez and the missing Gerry Murphy. It revealed that on May 2 the Dominican Ambassador in Washington had been informed that as a result of an investigation into Murphy's activities in the United States prior to his disappearance, which still was incomplete, "sufficient evidence has now been uncovered to indicate that Mr. Murphy may have been connected with the disappearance of Dr. Jesús de Galíndez in New York City on or about March 12, 1956, acting on behalf of or in association with certain Dominican and American nationals."

The Dominican Ambassador was further informed that the name of Arturo R. Espaillat had repeatedly cropped up in the official American investigation. In view of official Dominican statements of willingness to cooperate in solving Murphy's disappearance, as well as similar personal assertions by General Espaillat, the United States note declared that it appeared "desirable and appropriate" that the general's diplomatic immunity be waived by the Dominican government "in order that he should be amenable to the usual and lawful procedures in matters of investigation and trial" in the United States.

When the note was delivered General Espaillat had already been recalled from his post of Consul General in New York. On May 4, two days later, he left the country. Since no reply had yet been received from the Dominican Government there was nothing the American authorities could do to stop him from going back home. One of the biggest fish had escaped the net. Upon return to Santo Domingo Espaillat was promoted to the rank of major general and appointed Secretary of State without Portfolio. When a new espionage set-up was established under the name of Ministry of National Security, the major general was its first head. Recently however he was transferred to the rather obscure post of Inspector of the Navy. Some Dominicans believe that one of these days he will meet with an accident.

The *New York Times* hailed the announcement of the May 2 note as a positive step toward the solution of "one of the most sensational cases in the recent history of the Western Hemisphere."

The Generalissimo chose not to state his case before the American justice. For a while he did not deign to answer either the May 2 note or two reminders that followed. When he finally got around to answer, it was to refuse the request to waive Espaillat's diplomatic immunity. The Dominican reply to the State Department petition was that it would be "improper" for a man of Espaillat's high station in life to face a judicial process in the United States.

In the middle of November, Frank was brought to trial in Washington before Federal District Judge James R. Kirkland and a jury of nine women and three men. On Monday, December 9, the jury convicted him of acting illegally as an agent of Generalissimo Rafael Leonidas Trujillo and of the Dominican Republic's government. Ten days later Judge Kirkland sentenced Frank to eight months to two years on each of the four counts of the indictment. The court stipulated that sentences were to run concurrently.

The evidence presented during the trial threw much light upon the Galíndez case, while bringing out the links between Frank and Murphy as well as Frank and Trujillo. It was proved that one of the acts Frank had performed as an agent for Trujillo was part of the arrangements involved in the airplane kidnapping of Galíndez.

The testimony, however, fell short of solving the Galíndez mystery, but this was due to the fact that its scope was limited and the prosecution could not go farther than proving a violation on the defendant's part of the Foreign Agents Registration Act. The Justice Department Lawyers— William Hundley, who was the chief trial counsel, Plato C. Cacheris and John F. Lally—aided by some good work by the FBI, did a notable job unravelling the thick web of *trujillista* intrigue.

Evidence introduced during the trial proved that Frank had been working for Trujillo since 1954, first as a bodyguard when the dictator visited Spain in 1954 and again when he went to Kansas City in 1955; then as an errand boy, security and legal counselor as well as investigator. Once a Dominican diplomatic passport was issued in his name.

One of the witnesses revealed that early in 1955 Trujillo commissioned Frank to investigate a reported assassination plot. Among the supposed plotters under surveillance was Jesús de Galíndez. For this job Frank hired a number of informers and billed Trujillo at $20 an hour for his own services; but failed to uncover any plot. The star witness was Murphy's friend Air Force Sergeant Harold L. French.

Frank's trial lasted 15 days and, according to *Time,* "seemed painstakingly fair." The defendant got considerable help from his friends in the Dominican Republic. Trujillo sent two "voluntary" witnesses to take the stand for him. One was the "open letter" writer, Attorney Juan Arce Medina.

After being sentenced Frank was allowed to remain free under his original $10,000 bond, pending an appeal. His attorney Edward L. Carey had asked for a suspended sentence, saying his client had been "stigmatized as long as he lives." On the other hand, Prosecutor William H. Hundley urged a "stiff sentence." He described the defendant as perhaps the only person within the court's jurisdiction "who could help us solve the disappearance" of de Galíndez and Murphy. Instead, Hundley said, Frank "remained silent" and "thwarted" the grand jury and the F.B.I. "Unless the court deals severely with him we will never be able to solve crimes of this kind."

Before imposing sentence, Judge Kirkland noted that he had received several letters on behalf of Frank. He described the defendant as "a typical ambitious young American" who had waited on tables to help pay his way through college, and had served "very honorably" in the F.B.I. and the Central Intelligence Agency.

The conviction of Frank, according to the *Washington Post,* dealt a "stunning blow to the dictatorship of Generalissimo Rafael Trujillo."

Aside from a few solid facts brought out while Frank was nailed as an unregistered foreign agent, the evidence in the Galíndez-Murphy twin mystery, however overwhelming and impressive, remains circumstantial. Still more ominous is the fact that everyone of importance connected with this case (with the exception of Frank, Bernardino and Espaillat) is dead. Those alive do not want or are not allowed to talk.

Although international public opinion has already rendered its verdict of guilty as charged regarding Trujillo, the duty of taking the twin mysteries to the American tribunals still rests on the shoulders of the U.S. law enforcing agencies.

They are by no means resting the case. No sooner had Frank been sentenced than the grand jury that indicted him was called back to session. Subpoenaed to testify was a New York private detective named Horace W. Schmahl. He fought unsuccessfully to get his subpoena quashed. Before Federal District Judge Luther W. Youngdal he insisted, on December

18, 1957, that the grand jury doesn't want to hear from him as a witness but as "a potential defendant" in kidnapping and murder charges.

In the meantime Galíndez' book has been printed in Spanish by the publishing house Editorial del Pacifico, of Santiago, Chile. *The Era of Trujillo,* by what has been called a "disquieting and possible fatal irony," has attracted far greater attention than would ordinarily accrue to such a study. The kidnapping of its author has given its point much more impact.

There is a long way still to go before the mystery is solved, if solved it ever is.